KU-709-506

Zeev Sternhell

with Mario Sznajder and Maia Asheri

THE BIRTH OF FASCIST IDEOLOGY

FROM CULTURAL REBELLION TO POLITICAL REVOLUTION

Translated by David Maisel

UNIVERSITY OF WOLVERHAMPTON
LIBRARY

Acc No. 2136226   CLASS 14

CONTROL 0691032890   320.
533

DATE -7. JUL 1998   SITE WV   STE

PRINCETON UNIVERSITY PRESS   PRINCETON, NEW JERSEY

Copyright © 1994 by Princeton University Press

Translated from Zeev Sternhell, with Mario Sznajder and Maia Asheri,
Naissance de l'idéologie fasciste. Copyright © 1989
Librairie Arthème Fayard, Paris

Published by Princeton University Press, 41 William Street,
Princeton, New Jersey 08540
In the United Kingdom: Princeton University Press, Chichester,
West Sussex
All Rights Reserved

Library of Congress Cataloging-in-Publication Data

Sternhell, Zeev.
[Naissance de l'idéologie fasciste. English]
The birth of fascist ideology : from cultural rebellion to
political revolution / Zeev Sternhell, with Mario Sznajder and
Maia Asheri : translated by David Maisel.
p.   cm.
Includes bibliographical references and index.
ISBN 0-691-03289-0
ISBN 0-691-04486-4 (pbk.)
1. Fascism—Europe—History.   I. Sznajder, Mario.
II. Asheri, Maia.   III. Title.
D726.5.S7413   1994
320.5′33′094—dc20   93-17629   CIP

This book has been composed in Bitstream Caledonia

Princeton University Press books are printed
on acid-free paper and meet the guidelines for
permanence and durability of the Committee
on Production Guidelines for Book Longevity
of the Council on Library Resources

Third printing, and first paperback printing, 1995

Printed in the United States of America

3   5   7   9   10   8   6   4

THE BIRTH OF FASCIST IDEOLOGY

WP 2136226 2

To the memory of Jacob L. Talmon

Contents

Acknowledgments

THIS WORK is an expanded and improved version of a book published in France in 1989 and represents the results of an inquiry begun several years ago. It is also some time since several Ph.D. students in the history and political science departments of the Hebrew University in Jerusalem, whose work I had the privilege of supervising, began to interest themselves in the growth of Fascist ideology. In so doing, some of these young scholars came to investigate certain paths I had indicated in previous works. This applied particularly to the process of transition of the Left toward fascism.

Some of these studies have now come to fruition. Two of them have been incorporated into this book, to which each brings its own contribution. Chapters 3 and 4 are by Mario Sznajder, a specialist in Italian revolutionary syndicalism. Only a concern for presentation and a desire to offer the reader an integrated text caused me to revise their structure. Most of the material that enabled me to write Chapter 5 was provided by Maia Asheri, who has completed a study of early Italian fascism. Thus, many of the qualities this work may possess can be ascribed to my collaborators, but since the intellectual responsibility for the book and its general conception is mine, I am prepared to take the blame for its weaknesses.

As in all such cases in the last eighteen years, this book has benefited from the assistance of Georges Bensimhon. Whether it is a matter of essential problems or of the French language, Georges Benshimon has allowed no omission, no obscurity to pass him by. My gratitude toward this friend far exceeds anything I am able to express in these few lines.

The initial idea for this book took shape in my mind in 1983–1984, when I was a member of the Institute for Advanced Study in Princeton, New Jersey. The book progressed at Columbia University, where I spent profitable months in the summer of 1986, and two years later, thanks to an invitation from the French government, I enjoyed an especially rewarding period of work in Paris. The main part of the work, however, was carried out in 1986–1987 at the Institute for Advanced Studies at the Hebrew University of Jerusalem. My acknowledgments are due to its director, Menachem Yaari, and to the whole administrative staff headed by Shabtai Gairon and Bilha Gus. The invitation to pass a year in this center of research relieved me of my teaching responsibilities and allowed me to devote myself entirely to the preparation of this book. Our seminar of multidisciplinary research, in which Amatzia Baram, Sana Hassan, Menachem Friedman, George Mosse, Emmanuel Sivan, Michael Walzer, and Jay Winter in particular took part, was a source of great enrichment for me. As an assistant to this group, Anat

Banine could not be faulted. Most of the reading and writing for the English edition of this book was done during the year 1991–1992, which I was happy to spend at the Woodrow Wilson International Center for Scholars in Washington, D.C. I want to thank the center's director, Charles Blitzer, and the director of fellowships, Ann Sheffield, for providing me with the opportunity to work in an outstanding intellectual environment and make the best use of my time.

Special thanks are due to the staffs of the following libraries: the National and University Library in Jerusalem, the Bibliothèque Nationale in Paris, the Italian National Libraries and Archives in Rome, the libraries of the universities of Columbia and Princeton, and the Library of Congress.

I am grateful to the S. A. Schonbrunn Foundation and the Leonard Davis Institute for International Relations at the Hebrew University for the financial assistance I received in most stages of my work on this book.

My final thanks go to David Maisel for an excellent translation, to Lauren M. Osborne, Editor, History and Classics, for her good advice along the way, and to Dalia Geffen for her skills and devotion in editing the manuscript.

—Jerusalem, Fall 1992

THE BIRTH OF FASCIST IDEOLOGY

Fascism as an Alternative Political Culture

THIS BOOK is based on two assumptions. The first is that fascism, before it became a political force, was a cultural phenomenon. The growth of fascism would not have been possible without the revolt against the Enlightenment and the French Revolution which swept across Europe at the end of the nineteenth century and the beginning of the twentieth. Everywhere in Europe, the cultural revolt preceded the political; the rise of the Fascist movements and the Fascist seizure of power in Italy became possible only because of the conjunction of the accumulated influence of that cultural and intellectual revolution with the political, social, and psychological conditions that came into being at the end of the First World War. In that sense, fascism was only an extreme manifestation of a much broader and more comprehensive phenomenon.

The second assumption, which follows from the first, is that in the development of fascism, its conceptual framework played a role of special importance. There can be no doubt that the crystallization of ideology preceded the buildup of political power and laid the groundwork for political action. Fascism was not, in Benedetto Croce's famous expression, a "parenthesis" in contemporary history. It was not, as he thought, the result of an "infection," of a period of "decline in the consciousness of liberty" following the First World War.[1] It was not the product of some kind of "Machiavellian" renaissance to which twentieth-century Europe fell victim. Contrary to what Friedrich Meinecke and Gerhard Ritter have sought to convince the generation after the Second World War, fascism was an integral part of the history of European culture.[2]

Similarly, fascism was not a sort of shadow cast by Marxism, as claimed by Ernst Nolte, whose brilliant and well-known book continues the work of Meinecke and Ritter. One should also not exaggerate the "anti" quality of fascism; fascism was not only a form of antiliberalism (to use the expression of Juan Linz, the writer of a remarkable study). Nor was fascism a "variety of Marxism," as claimed by A. James Gregor, a normally perspicacious scholar and the author of major works.[3] Moreover, fascism cannot be reduced, as the classical Marxist interpretation would have it, to a simple antiproletarian reaction that took place at a stage of declining capitalism.[4] Between these two extremes is an abundance of interpretations. With regard to the scholarly publications of the last twenty years, the reader should refer to the work of Karl Dietrich Bracher, Emilio Gentile, A. James Gregor, Roger Griffin, Pierre Milza, George L. Mosse, Stanley G. Payne, Fritz Stern, Domenico Settembrini, Jacob Leib Talmon, and Pier Giorgio Zunino.[5]

In *Interpretations of Fascism*, the highly respected doyen of Italian scholars, Renzo De Felice, has given us a survey of different interpretations deserving of mention. He has also given us his own interpretation, based on a dual typology of countries and forms of regime. De Felice emphasizes the importance of regional characteristics, especially in the case of Italy.[6]

The present study is conceived quite differently. First, fascism is regarded as an independent cultural and political phenomenon that was not less intellectually self-sufficient than socialism or liberalism. Second, the book is devoted to a discussion of ideology and assumes that the intellectual content of fascism had the same importance in the growth and development of the movement as it had in liberalism or later in Marxism. The ideology is described in this book as a product of the interaction of culture and politics, reflecting the inner relationship between the adoption of intellectual positions and the shift to action. Then, we seek to demonstrate that the conceptual framework of fascism, created long before August 1914, was nonconformist, avant-garde, and revolutionary in character. Due to this intellectual content, fascism became a political force capable of assailing the existing order and competing effectively with Marxism not only for the support of elites and minority groups but also for the allegiance of the masses.

In this book, we focus on the formative period of fascism. We analyze the development of the thinking of the movement and of the intellectual structures it created within the context of the Franco-Italian cultural complex. The France of integral nationalism, of the revolutionary Right, was the real birthplace of fascism. We have already demonstrated this elsewhere, so it does not have to be dealt with here.[7] Moreover, France was the birthplace of Sorelian revolutionary revisionism, the second elementary component of fascism. Originating in France, it was in Italy that revolutionary syndicalism developed into an intellectual, social, and political force. In the summer of 1914, the Italian revolutionary revisionists, in alliance with the nationalists and futurists, found the adherents, the situation, and the leader who enabled them to transform the long intellectual incubation dating from the beginning of the century into a historical force.

Before proceeding any farther, we have to insist on another element of the definition we are proposing. Fascism can in no way be identified with Nazism. Undoubtedly the two ideologies, the two movements, and the two regimes had common characteristics. They often ran parallel to one another or overlapped, but they differed on one fundamental point: the criterion of German national socialism was biological determinism. The basis of Nazism was racism in its most extreme sense, and the fight against the Jews, against "inferior" races, played a more preponderant role in it than the struggle against communism. Marxists could be converted to national socialism, as indeed quite a number of them were; similarly, national socialism could sign treaties with Communists, exchange ambassadors, and coexist with them, if only temporarily. Nothing like this, however, applied to the Jews. Where they were concerned, the only possible "arrangement" with them was their destruction.

Certainly, racism was not limited to Germany. At the end of the nineteenth century, biological determinism developed in a country like France too; but if it was a factor in the development of the revolutionary Right, racism in its French variant never became the whole purpose of an ideology, a movement, and a regime.

In fact, racial determinism was not present in all the varieties of fascism. If Robert Brasillach professed an anti-Semitism very close to that of Nazism, George Valois's "Faisceau" had none at all; and if some Italian Fascists were violently anti-Semitic, in Italy there were innumerable Fascist Jews. Their percentage in the movement was much higher than in the population as a whole. As we know, racial laws were promulgated in Italy only in 1938, and during the Second World War the Jews felt much less in danger in Nice or Haute-Savoie, areas under Italian occupation, than in Marseilles, which was under the control of the Vichy government.

Racism was thus not a necessary condition for the existence of fascism; on the contrary, it was a factor in Fascist eclecticism. For this reason, a general theory that seeks to combine fascism and Nazism will always come up against this essential aspect of the problem. In fact, such a theory is not possible. Undoubtedly there are similarities, particularly with regard to the "totalitarian" character of the two regimes, but their differences are no less significant. Karl Bracher perceived the singular importance of these differences, which Ernst Nolte (this was his chief weakness) completely ignored.[8]

Having clarified this question, let us now return to our definition of fascism. If the Fascist ideology cannot be described as a simple response to Marxism, its origins, on the other hand, were the direct result of a very specific revision of Marxism. It was a *revision* of Marxism and not a *variety* of Marxism or a *consequence* of Marxism. One of the aims of this book is to study this antimaterialistic and antirationalistic revision of Marxism. It is absolutely necessary to insist on this essential aspect of the definition of fascism, for one can scarcely understand the emergence of the fundamental concepts of fascism and of the Fascist philosophy and mythology if one does not recognize, at the same time, that it arose from an originally Marxist revolt against materialism. It was the French and Italian Sorelians, the theoreticians of revolutionary syndicalism, who made this new and original revision of Marxism, and precisely this was their contribution to the birth of the Fascist ideology.

In this respect, the rise of fascism was one of the aspects of the intellectual, scientific, and technological revolution that overtook the European continent at the turn of the twentieth century. This revolution changed the prevailing way of life to a degree hitherto unknown, transforming the intellectual climate as well as social realities. All of a sudden, one saw the inadequacy of the social and economic laws Marx propounded. Confronted with problems that the previous generation had not even envisaged, the new generation proposed totally unexpected solutions.

Consequently, anyone who regards fascism as no more than a byproduct of the First World War, a mere bourgeois defensive reaction to the postwar crisis, is unable to understand this major phenomenon of our century. A phenomenon of civilization, fascism represents a rejection of the political culture prevailing at the beginning of the century. In the fascism of the interwar period, in Mussolini's regime as in all other western European Fascist movements, there was not a single major idea that had not gradually come to fruition in the quarter of a century preceding August 1914.

Although an ideal prototype of a disruptive ideology, fascism cannot be defined only in negative terms. Undoubtedly, fascism rejected the prevailing systems: liberalism and Marxism, positivism and democracy. This is always the case; a new ideology and an emerging political movement begin by opposing the systems of thought and political forces already in place. Before offering its own vision of the world, Marxism began by opposing liberalism, which a century earlier had risen up against absolutism. The same was true of fascism, which conflicted with liberalism and Marxism before it was able to provide all the elements of an alternate political, moral, and intellectual system.

In the form that it emerged at the turn of the century and developed in the 1920s and 1930s, the Fascist ideology represented a synthesis of organic nationalism with the antimaterialist revision of Marxism. It expressed a revolutionary aspiration based on a rejection of individualism, whether liberal or Marxist, and it created the elements of a new and original political culture.

This political culture, communal, anti-individualistic, and antirationalistic, represented at first a rejection of the heritage of the Enlightenment and the French Revolution, and later the creation of a comprehensive alternative, an intellectual, moral, and political framework that alone could ensure the perpetuity of a human collectivity in which all strata and all classes of society would be perfectly integrated. Fascism wished to rectify the most disastrous consequences of the modernization of the European continent and to provide a solution to the atomization of society, its fragmentation into antagonistic groups, and the alienation of the individual in a free market economy. Fascism rebelled against the dehumanization that modernization had introduced into human relationships, but it was also very eager to retain the benefits of progress and never advocated a return to a hypothetical golden age. Fascism rebelled against modernity inasmuch as modernity was identified with the rationalism, optimism, and humanism of the eighteenth century, but it was not a reactionary or an antirevolutionary movement in the Maurrassian sense of the term. Fascism presented itself as a revolution of another kind, a revolution that sought to destroy the existing political order and to uproot its theoretical and moral foundations but that at the same time wished to preserve all the achievements of modern technology. It was to take place within the framework of the industrial society, fully exploiting the power that was in it. The Fascist revolution sought to change the nature of the relationships between the individual and the collectivity without destroying the impetus of economic activity—the profit motive, or its foundation—private property, or its necessary framework—the market economy. This was one aspect of the novelty of fascism; the Fascist revolution was supported by an economy determined by the laws of the market.

When the Fascist regime in Italy practiced a corporatism based on a liberal economy, when the Fascist movement, long before it came to power, declared through Mussolini that the revolution would relieve the state of its economic functions, this was not mere opportunism. On the contrary; Mussolini was only repeating the lessons of political economy taught throughout the first decade of the century by the intellectuals of revolutionary syndicalism.

This point requires special emphasis. If fascism wished to reap all the benefits of the modern age, to exploit all the technological achievements of capitalism, if it never questioned the idea that market forces and private property were part of the natural order of things, it had a horror of the so-called bourgeois, or, as Nietzsche called them, modern values: universalism, individualism, progress, natural rights, and equality. Thus, fascism adopted the economic aspect of liberalism but completely denied its philosophical principles and the intellectual and moral heritage of modernity. Similarly, it was not the practice of Marxism that was questioned—certainly not where the role of violence in history is concerned—but the rational, Hegelian content of Marxism, its determinism. Its disapproval was directed not at the element of revolt, but at historical materialism.

In its essence, Fascist thought was a rejection of the value known in the culture of the time as materialism. For fascism, liberalism, which at the end of the nineteenth century developed into liberal democracy, and Marxism, one ramification of which was democratic socialism, represented one and the same materialistic evil. In the sense in which it was understood at the end of the nineteenth century, antimaterialism meant the rejection of the rationalistic, individualistic, and utilitarian heritage of the seventeenth and eighteenth centuries. In terms of political philosophy, antimaterialism meant a total rejection of the vision of man and society developed from

Hobbes to Kant, from the English revolutions of the seventeenth century to the American and French revolutions. In terms of political practice, antimaterialism meant a rejection of the principles applied for the first time at the end of the eighteenth century and carried out on a far larger scale a hundred years later by the liberal democratic regimes of western Europe. It was thus a general attack on the political culture dominant at the end of the nineteenth and the beginning of the twentieth century, on its philosophical foundations, its principles, and their application. It was not only the theory of natural rights and the primacy of the individual that were questioned, but all the institutional structures of liberal democracy. However, antimaterialism was not just a negation of liberalism, whether in the form found in the "social contract" school of thought or in the one represented by English utilitarianism, which from the beginning implied the democratization of political life and the reform of society. To an equal degree, toward 1900 antimaterialism also represented a rejection of the main postulates of Marxist economics and an attack on the rationalistic foundations of Marx's thought. It was the revolutionary syndicalists, those dissidents and nonconformists of the Left, who by means of their criticism of Marxist determinism created the first elements of the Fascist synthesis in the first decade of our century.

Thus, antimaterialism, a direct assault on liberalism and Marxism, at the beginning of this century represented a third revolutionary option between the two great systems that dominated the political life of the period and that, over and above all their differences, nevertheless remained the heirs of the eighteenth century. Fascism was antimaterialism in its clearest form. But if it was opposed to liberalism and Marxism, it took from liberalism a respect for the power and vitality of the mechanisms of the market economy, and from Marxism a conviction that violence was the motive force of history, which was governed solely by the laws of war.

If, in its philosophical essence, fascism represented a rejection of the rationalistic and individualistic principles that constituted the foundation of Marxism as well as of liberalism, where political ideology and political movements were concerned it represented a synthesis of an organic, tribal nationalism with the revision of Marxism that Georges Sorel and the Sorelians of France and Italy proposed at the turn of the century.

These were the two great supporting pillars of the Fascist edifice, which, taken as a whole, represented a coherent, logical, and well-structured totality. Let there be no doubt about it: fascism's intellectual baggage enabled it to travel alone, and its theoretical content was neither less homogeneous nor more heterogenous than that of liberalism or socialism. Nor were the incoherences and contradictions greater in number or more profound than those which had existed in liberal or socialist thought for a hundred years. The opportunism of the various Fascist parties and movements, including that of the Mussolini regime, hardly differed from the way in which socialist parties struggling to gain power, or that had already gained power, compromised on principles. Thus, when the process of the fascistization of the state was completed, an ever-increasing number of militants called for a return to the roots and assailed dubious compromises with the bourgeois, clerical, or royalist Right—complaints that recalled the lamentations of the no less numerous "purists" of European socialism when confronted with the harsh realities of practical politics.

Certainly, fascism did not derive from a single source as socialism derived from Marx, but neither did liberalism have a Marx, and one can hardly say that in the first half of the twentieth century it attained a higher intellectual level than fascism. Moreover, even in Marx's lifetime Marxism was already split up into tendencies, groups, and sects, and a few years later, after Engels passed away, who could still claim to represent the authoritative interpretation of Marxism? Who was recognized as worthy of the title "defender of the faith"? Who, around 1910, could say he was a Marxist? The same sort of question may be asked with regard to fascism, and the absence of a common source comparable with that of Marxism need not necessarily be taken as a sign of incoherence.

The first of the two essential components of fascism to appear on the political scene of the end of the nineteenth century was tribal nationalism, based on a social Darwinism and, often, a biological determinism. In France, this type of nationalism was found in its clearest form in the work of Maurice Barrès, Édouard Drumont, Charles Maurras, and the representatives of Action française.[9] In Italy, Enrico Corradini demonstrated, in a truly fascinating manner, the evolution of Italian nationalism from the time, still close, of the struggle for independence. From the end of the nineteenth century, the new nationalism truly expressed the revolt against the spirit of the French Revolution. The gulf that divided Corradini from Mazzini, or Barrès, Drumont, and Maurras from Michelet, reveals the distance between Jacobin nationalism and that of *la Terre et les Morts*, the Land and the Dead. This formula of Barrès was in fact only the French counterpart of the German formula *Blut und Boden* (Blood and Soil), and it showed that the old theory, consecrated by the French Revolution, that society was made up of a collection of individuals, had been replaced by the theory of the organic unity of the nation. In this respect, the system of thought developed in France by the generation of the 1890s was scarcely different from the one that grew up in the same period on the other side of the Rhine. The nationalist fervor of the French writers of the time was in no way inferior to that of their contemporary Heinrich von Treitschke, the celebrated theoretician of German nationalism at the end of the nineteenth century. Drumont and Wilhelm Marr, Jules Guérin, the marquis de Morès, Adolf Stöcker and the Austrian Georg von Schönerer, Georges Vacher de Lapouge and Otto Ammon, Paul Déroulède and Ernst Hasse, the head of the Pan-German League, were as alike as peas in a pod.

We are here in the presence of a general European phenomenon. For this new nationalism—which was situated at the opposite pole from the one that, from the French Revolution to the Commune of Paris, had attempted a synthesis of the "religion of the fatherland" with the religion of humanity— the nation was an organism comparable to a sentient being. This "total" nationalism claimed to be a system of ethics, with criteria of behavior dictated by the entire national body, independently of the will of the individual. By definition, this new nationalism denied the validity of any absolute and universal moral norms: truth, justice, and law existed only in order to serve the needs of the collectivity. The idea of society as something isolated and shut in, a violent antirationalism, and a belief in the supremacy of the subconscious over the forces of reason amounted to a truly tribal concept of the nation.

Here one can feel the full weight of the influence of social Darwinism, even among the Maurrassians who did not, as readily as Barrès, compare animal instinct with human reason, to the detriment of the latter. The idea that the depths of the irrational and the instinctive have to be separated from the factitiousness of rationality was widespread among the members of that generation.

This cult of deep and mysterious forces that are the fabric of human existence entailed as a necessary and natural consequence the appearance of a virulent anti-intellectualism. For this school of thought, the fight against intellectuals and against the rationalism from which they drew their nourishment was a measure of public safety. There were a great many nationalists at the turn of the century who, like those of the interwar generation, constantly attacked the critical spirit and its products, opposing them to instinct, intuitive and irrational sentiment, emotion and enthusiasm—those deep impulses which determine human behavior and which constitute the reality and truth of things as well as their beauty. Rationalism, they claimed, belongs to the "deracinated"; it blunts sensitivity, it deadens instinct and can only destroy the motive forces of national activity. Barrès believed that only the emotional content of a situation had any real value; for him, the process of what is known as thought took place on the level of the unconscious. He concluded from this that to attack the unconscious was to divest the national organism of its substance. Consequently, in order to ensure the welfare of the nation, one had to turn to the people and exalt the primitive force, vigor, and vitality that emanated from the people, uncontaminated by the rationalist and individualist virus. For the revolutionary Right of 1890 as for that of 1930, the incomparable merit of popular opinion was its unreflecting spontaneity, springing from the depths of the unconscious. At the turn of the century as on the eve of the Second World War, these were the new criteria of political behavior.

Since the masses were truly the nation, and since the primary aim of politics was to ensure the nation's integrity and power, nationalism could not accept that the social question should remain unsolved. Barrès, the major theoretician of this "Latin nationalism," which was even more genuine than "Latin Marxism," was one of the first people to understand that a "national" movement can exist only if it ensures the integration of the most disadvantaged strata of society. At the same time, he understood that a "national" movement cannot be Marxist, liberal, proletarian, or bourgeois. Marxism and liberalism, he claimed, could never be anything other than movements of a civil war; a class war and a war of all against all in an individualistic society were merely two aspects of the same evil. As a result of this way of thinking at the end of the nineteenth century there appeared in France a new synthesis, the first form of fascism. Barrès was one of the first thinkers in Europe to employ the term "national socialism."[10]

The idea of national socialism quickly spread throughout Europe. It was a response to a problem of civilization created in the second half of the nineteenth century by the rise of the proletariat and the industrial revolution. Very soon, more or less everywhere, theoreticians claimed that the social question could be solved by means other than an unbridled capitalism or a socialism of class struggle. A solution based on the idea that the survival of the nation demanded peace between the proletariat and the body of society as a whole was put forward in France at the turn of the century by Barrès, and in Italy in the first decade of the twentieth century by Enrico Corradini.

Like Barrès, who had preceded him by some twenty years, Corradini sought to revive what he called the fundamental pact of family solidarity among all classes of Italian society. In 1910 he used the term "national socialism" and fixed the aims of this socialist and national movement. First, he said, the Italians had to be made to understand that their country was materially and morally a proletarian country. Then they had to be taught the necessity of international war, in the same way as socialism taught workers the principles of class warfare. Finally, one had to make peace between the proletariat and the nation.[11] After the First World War, during the rise of the Fascist movement, Corradini summed up in a concise formula the concept he had developed for years, since the foundation of the Nationalist Association in 1910: "Because nationalism is by definition national in politics, it cannot fail to be national in the domain of economics, as the two things are interconnected."[12] In his way, the theoretician of Italian nationalism borrowed the idea of class struggle from Marxism and transposed it onto a higher level, that of war between national groups. The principle remained the same: violence is the motive force of history.

Essentially, the principles of Italian nationalism were hardly different from those developed in France some twenty years earlier. Corradini's only original contribution was the idea of the "proletarian nation," intended to prepare the Italians for the struggle for existence, in other words, war. The state of war, he said, was the natural state of relations between nations in all periods; discipline, authority, social solidarity, the sense of duty and sacrifice, and heroic values were all conditions necessary for the survival of the country. Anything that made for unity was positive: a strong government, the individual always at the service of society, and the social classes united in a single effort for the sake of national greatness. Similarly, anything that constituted a factor of diversity was to be eliminated. The philosophy of the Enlightenment and the theory of the rights of people, internationalism, and pacifism, like bourgeois or proletarian class egoism, were to be destroyed. The same applied to democracy: democracy was nothing other than the expression of the class interests of the bourgeoisie. As for Marxist socialism, it divested the body of the nation of its substance in order to serve the class interests of the proletariat. And finally there was reformist socialism, which, under the pretext of improving the lot of the proletariat, entered into an alliance with bourgeois democracy. This alliance of the politicians, said Corradini, was the greatest lie of contemporary democracy. To liberal democracy, "business" democracy, Corradini opposed a form of democracy that was an "ethnarchy"; to "business" politics and a plutocracy, to "class parasitism," he opposed a regime of order and authority based on natural hierarchies. This regime was to be a regime of producers, a regime of class collaboration, responsible for the well-being of all.[13]

The second main component of fascism, which, together with antiliberal and antibourgeois nationalism, made up the Fascist ideology, was the antimaterialist revision of Marxism. This revolt, which involved both the nonconformist extreme Left and the nationalist Right, allowed the association of a new kind of socialism with radical nationalism.

At the beginning of the twentieth century, the socialism of western Europe (including, of course, Germany to the west of the Elbe) had to confront two phenomena of major importance. It was obvious, first, that the great prophecies of Marxism had not been realized. Nobody at that time could claim that social polarization and pauperization—two sine qua non preconditions for the future revolution—had truly come to pass. On the contrary. Already, in the last third of the nineteenth century, the standard of living of the working class had risen and its purchasing power increased, and if social differences always remained the same, the conditions of life of the lower classes had improved considerably. This evolution resulted in an economic and political situation without precedent in Europe. One should also mention the great technological and scientific revolution of the end of the nineteenth and the beginning of the twentieth century which affected the forms of production and consumption, changed the rhythm of life, and offered new perspectives of progress and well-being. The technological revolution undoubtedly ensured the triumph of the bourgeoisie, but it nevertheless deeply affected the relationship of classes. Half a century after the *Communist Manifesto*, a quarter of a century after the commune of 1871, one was a long way, in western Europe, from the industrial hell of Manchester or the "Bloody Week" of Paris.

Social relationships became less brutal, for it was in the interests of everyone to avoid confrontations that could turn into pitched battles. Since the end of the Franco-Prussian War, the international situation had also stabilized, and the continent enjoyed a calm hitherto unknown. All these factors, to which one should add a demographic upsurge made possible by the improved conditions of life, led, at the end of the nineteenth century, to a period of unprecedented expansion and prosperity. This new prosperity, which seemed to last, created an environment in which political and economic phenomena were very different from those which Marx had been able to observe. Socialist thought consequently had to confront a series of new problems that were hard to explain in terms of orthodox Marxist analysis. With this new situation began the celebrated "crisis of Marxism."

To the economic changes were added two other transformations, which also lessened the relevance of traditional Marxist analysis: the democratization of political life and the growth of national consciousness among the masses. Liberalism was a political system invented by an elite in order to govern a society in which political participation was limited. The adaptation of the representative system to universal suffrage, the adaptation of liberalism to democracy and the masses, did not take place without major jolts. It was with tremendous difficulty that liberalism, adopting the principle of political equality, developed into liberal democracy. This was one of the main aspects of the crises of the turn of the century as of those of the interwar period.

The new urban masses created by industrial concentration thus gained access, if only partly, to the decision-making mechanisms. In a regime of universal suffrage, one cannot constantly govern against the interests of the majority. Marxism had not foreseen a situation in which the proletariat, organized in syndicates, socialist parties, and local pressure groups would one day come to the conclusion that bourgeois democracy could also serve its own interests. Universal suffrage—even where, as in Germany at the beginning of the century, it was not accompanied by political liberty—showed itself to be a true force of integration. To this one should add a continuous economic expansion and the undeniable social progress to which it led. The founding fathers of socialism had not foreseen the eight-hour working day, the weekly day of rest, or social insurance, any more than they had dreamed of free and compulsory education.

It appeared, moreover, that the democratization of political life, like social progress, did not necessarily favor socialism. On the contrary, the modernization of the European continent and the political participation and mobilization of the masses led to a growth of national consciousness among those masses. Very soon, it appeared that compulsory education, the spread of literacy in the countryside, and the working class's slow but continuous acquisition of culture encouraged not the class consciousness of the proletariat, but rather an increased consciousness of national identity. The creation of new strata of wage earners and the development of new tertiary activities proved that modernization, contrary to all expectations, worked against socialism. The famous process of polarization failed to take place, and, in the political field, the national movement in France, Italy, and Germany reaped the benefits of this development. The nationalist, populist, and revolutionary movement gained the most from the intellectual revolution of the end of the nineteenth century. After all, neither social Darwinism, nor antipositivism, nor the new social sciences like psychology and sociology (which, with Pareto, Simmel, Durkheim, and Max Weber represented the response of the European university establishment to Marxism) were favorable to socialism. This new reality and the new intellectual climate that developed within it led to the revision of Marxism.

This revision of Marxist theory (really a reinterpretation of the ideological corpus associated with Marx's thought and its adaptation to the new realities) took place following the great debate on Marxism, whose first protagonists were Engel's two associates, Eduard Bernstein and Karl Kautsky. Bernstein's attack, Kautsky's reply, the participation of all the major figures in international socialism, and the sheer importance of the controversy, which lasted for years, gave the celebrated *Bernstein debatte* an exceptional significance.

It should be pointed out that Kautsky, who had collaborated closely with Bernstein between 1880 and 1895, never intended to separate socialism from democracy. If Bernstein, who for a long time had been under the influence of the Fabians, seemed ready to come to terms with a constitutional monarchy, Kautsky envisaged the establishment of a radical republican regime.[14] There was no disagreement between them, however, with regard to the necessity to work, by means strictly compatible with universal suffrage and the law of the majority, for the democratization of the German state and society. For Kautsky, the "revolution" meant that the accession to power of the Socialist party would necessarily be accompanied by a total change in class structure, with everything else being left to democracy.[15]

Kautsky, it should be remembered, was the principal author of the "Erfurt Program" of 1891, adopted immediately after the expiration of Bismarck's antisocialist laws. The Erfurt Congress consecrated both the "Marxification" of the German Socialist party and its entry into the political life of the empire. Thus this document reflected from the beginning a fundamental ambiguity that soon became a prime example of the difficulties western Marxism faced. This ambivalence stemmed from an apparent contradiction between the revolutionary, very "class-struggle" character of the theoretical part of the program and the purely democratic and "reformist" character of its practical, political part. In 1892 Kautsky wrote a document of 260 pages, *Das Erfurter Programm*, in which he expressed his thinking and which immediately became a classic of socialist literature. This exposition contributed greatly to making its author the official theoretician of the party. A few years later, when the great debate on Marxism began, this document became the chief target of the revisionists.

Thus, the German Social Democratic party was endowed with a revolutionary doctrine at the very moment when it committed itself to the path of democracy and no longer even dreamed of violence or revolution. If Bebel and Liebknecht, the two leaders of the party, ever had any revolutionary inclinations, nothing remained of them at the moment the party became Marxist. To many foreign socialists, this contradiction looked increasingly like a dubious opportunism, especially as the German party was regarded as the truest repository of the thought of Marx and Engels. Had not Engels remained until his death in 1895 in continuous contact with Kautsky?

This gulf between theory and practice can be explained by the situation that existed in Germany, where doctrinal intransigence was a characteristic of all political parties. Prevented by the political structures of the empire from assuming real responsibilities, all German parties were free to exhibit their doctrinal purity. The *Erfurter Programm* was written not only to satisfy Engels, but also in order to demonstrate the specific intellectual content of Marxism. At the same time, the Socialist party was fighting for the democratization of political life in Germany. It believed in the virtues of democracy and in the possibility of attaining the objectives of socialism by democratic means.[16]

It soon became obvious, however, that the revolutionary ideology could not stand up to the demands of political life, and the contradiction between the theory of class struggle and the tacit acceptance of the existing order finally became insupportable. From this long debate, most of which took place between 1895 and 1905, practically the whole of western European socialism emerged bearing the label "revisionist." Revisionism, moreover, began not in 1899 with the publication of Bernstein's critique of Marxism, but five years earlier, at the Frankfurt Congress, with the controversy over the sections of the *Erfurter Programm* dealing with the problem of the peasants, and following the revolt of the Bavarian socialists against what they saw as the excessively Marxist character of the program.[17] This intellectual debate divided the whole socialist movement of western Europe into two schools of thought of very unequal importance. These two trends, which differed completely with regard to the content of reformism and its ultimate objectives, were in agreement with regard to method: they sought to harmonize the theory with the practice and to alter the theory, and also, wherever necessary, to alter the practice.

These two schools of thought were not comparable from the point of view of their immediate importance. One of them encompassed nearly all of western European socialism; we are referring to the "reformist" type of revisionism—a revisionism that was liberal and democratic in the accepted sense of these terms. In the form it assumed in the writings of Bernstein, Turati, and Jaurès and in the political behavior of the socialist parties of Germany, Italy, and France—where the unification of the Socialist party in 1905 resulted in a reformist party very similar to the German Social Democrats—this revisionism accepted both the legitimacy of liberal and democratic values and the rules of liberal democracy. One had, in fact, not only a compromise with the existing order but an acceptance of its principles. At the beginning of the century, the great majority of western European socialists had resigned themselves to the perpetuity of the capitalist regime and of bourgeois society.

There remained a minority that also recognized the failure of classical Marxist predictions but that nevertheless rejected ideological and political compromise with the established order. This minority, which retained its revolutionary characteristics, very correctly laid claim to the title "revolutionary revisionists."[18] Indeed, by about 1905, these revisionists were the only socialists to remain revolutionary in western Europe. They sought to revise Marxist doctrine in the opposite direction from that of Bernsteinian revisionism. They claimed that instead of watering down Marxism by interpreting it in democratic terms, they were returning to the roots of Marxism in order to make it once again what it should never have ceased to be: a mechanism of war against bourgeois democracy. The revolutionary revisionists sought to reexamine the original doctrine in order to place it once more at the service of the revolution. They felt that it was a betrayal of the proletariat to regard it as an aggregate of electors or as the backbone of a political mass movement that relied on numbers in order to take over the government and reform society. The proletariat was and had to be the agent of the revolution.

Here one was dealing with questions relating to the particular situation that existed in western Europe. In Austria-Hungary, in Poland, divided into three, in Russia, and also in Prussia, the problems were different. Here, too, Karl Kautsky played a major role. His synthesis of orthodox Marxism and democratic socialism inspired the revolutionaries of central and eastern Europe. A whole generation was reared on the writings of Kautsky, who, together with Plekhanov, was the spiritual father of Russian Marxism. The function of the revolution in Kautsky was to bring a full and complete de-

mocracy, not the "dictatorship of the proletariat." The great difference between Kautsky and Bernstein was the importance that Kautsky gave, in this
transition to democracy, to the mechanism of class struggle, which, in turn,
reflected the workings of the capitalist economy as described by Marx.[19]

But if Kautsky was attacked by the Bernsteinian revisionists who rejected
his interpretation of economics as a whole and his conception of class struggle in particular, he also came under fire from a faction of the Left led by
Rosa Luxemburg, who objected to his "fatalism." These leftists maintained
that Kautsky's deterministic theories had the effect of confirming the party
in its traditional wait-and-see attitude.

Most of the radicals of central and eastern Europe belonged to a younger
generation than the Marxist "old brigade" of Kautsky, Mehring, Victor
Adler, Axelrod, and Plekhanov. Rosa Luxemburg, Otto Bauer, Rudolf Hilferding, Martov, Radek, Trotsky, and Lenin shared a conviction that eastern
Europe, and perhaps all of Europe, was on the eve of a tremendous earth-
quake. The problems that confronted this East European generation of
1905, which were totally different from those which existed in France or
Italy, lie outside the scope of this book, but conditions in eastern Europe
explain why these nonconformists remained firmly attached to their Marxist
roots, while quite a number of "Latin" dissidents, after having attempted a
correction of Marxism, turned away from it—some of them to such a degree
as to found another revolutionary movement, fascism.

Indeed, these East Europeans, unlike the nonconformists in France and
Italy, never deviated from the final objective: the destruction of capitalism
by the proletariat. For them, the revolution never had any other purpose
than to put an end, above all, to capitalist exploitation and the system of the
market economy. The instrument and the beneficiary of this revolution always remained the proletariat. These people may have differed considerably
among themselves about the revolutionary tactics to adopt or the role of the
party, the state, or the dictatorship of the proletariat, but they never lost
sight of the real objective. This factor united the Austro-Hungarian school,
with Karl Renner, Rudolf Hilferding, Otto Bauer, Friedrich Adler, and Max
Adler, the German-Polish group gathered around Rosa Luxemburg and Karl
Liebknecht—which also included Parvus (pseudonym of Alexander Israel
Helphand) and Karl Radek—the group of Mensheviks to which Trotsky in
fact belonged, and the Bolsheviks, including Lenin. All these people were to
have very different destinies and to give birth to contrary schools of thought
and political currents, and terrible rivalries were to develop among them;
yet they all remained faithful to the rationalist, materialist, and Hegelian
content of Marxism. The conceptual framework created by Kautsky under
the watchful eye of Engels always remained the common denominator. This
factor also distinguished the central European innovators from the Sorelian
ones. That was the reason why the former group always, each in its own way,

remained true to the essence of Marxism while the latter group embarked on a revision of Marxism that voided the system of its original content.

Within these limits, however, Marxism showed itself to be sufficiently flexible to enable Max Adler to discover in Marx a quasi-Kantian sociologist, or to inspire Otto Bauer's works on the question of nationalities and the problems of imperialism, or those of Rudolf Hilferding on finance capitalism.[20] All three of them made contributions of high quality and of major importance to Marxism. If the works of Max Adler represent, above all, an intellectual tour de force, those of Hilferding and Bauer opened up new avenues not only for Marxist thought, but also for the political actions of the socialist parties in the Austrian empire, then on the point of disintegrating. The Leninist conception of imperialism was in fact a simplification of Bauer's and Hilferding's theoretical ideas.[21]

The first edition of Rudolf Hilferding's *Finance Capital* appeared in Vienna in 1910 and had immediate success. A dry, austere, and technical work, *Finance Capital* was recognized at once as one of the few original contributions to Marxism that, relating to new developments, took Marxist theory a stage farther. The major figures in socialism immediately hailed Hilferding's work: Jaurès praised it in the Chamber of Deputies, and in 1916 Lenin was inspired by it to write *Imperialism, the Supreme Stage of Capitalism*. Between these two dates, the book was translated into seven languages.[22] The works of Luxemburg, Parvus, Radek, and Trotsky were also, despite enormous theoretical difficulties, firmly rooted in Marxism—a Marxism relatively close to orthodoxy. Luxemburg made a major contribution to Marxist theory concerning capitalism in underdeveloped countries; her description of the accumulation of capital in a "closed" system and of capitalist expansion in nonindustrialized countries remains important for an understanding of the question of economic growth. At the same time, Luxemburg maintained that capitalist expansion undermined its own foundations, so that the ultimate collapse of the system as a whole could be regarded as a historical certainty. Here one finds most of the analytical weaknesses of her work, which derive essentially from her need to prove the inevitability of the fall of capitalism on the basis of premises elaborated by Marx.[23] But if Luxemburg and Hilferding could arrive at opposite conclusions from the same statistics, they nevertheless remained true to Marxist methods and tools of analysis.

This clearly explains the great difference between the French and Italian nonconformists and those of central and eastern Europe. While the Austrians, Poles, and Russians (most if not all of whom sprung from the Jewish intelligentsia) made impossible efforts to stick to Marx's economic theories, to the deterministic character of his system, to the idea of historical necessity, and to the materialistic basis of the Marxist view of history and spoke of a "permanent" international revolution, in France and Italy there began an antimaterialist revision of Marxism based on a violent criticism of Marxist economics. Whereas Kautsky, the prophet of orthodoxy, became in fact the architect of the change of orthodox Marxism into democratic socialism, in France and Italy a ferocious struggle was waged against democracy itself.

Moreover, these internationalist and revolutionary Jewish intellectuals— Luxemburg, Hilferding, Parvus, Radek, Trotsky, Otto Bauer, Max Adler, and many others—functioned in an environment poisoned by national and religious hatreds. All of them detested the tribal nationalism that flourished throughout Europe, both in the underdeveloped countries of the east and in the great industrial centers of the west. These people never bowed down before national collectivity and its soil, religious piety, traditions, popular culture, cemeteries, myths, prides, and animosities. Consequently, these political thinkers and leaders were immunized against collaboration with conservatives and nationalists.

The first signs of the great onslaught on Marxism appeared with the publication in 1894 of the third volume of *Das Kapital*. The attack was initiated by the Austrian economist Eugen von Böhm-Bawerk, who in 1896 wrote *Zum Abschluss des Marxschen Systems*. Immediately translated into Russian and English, the work was a great success, both in Europe and in the United States. Thrice minister of finance and a professor of political economy at the University of Vienna, Böhm-Bawerk was one of the most respected and influential economists of the period. His critique of the Marxist theories of value and surplus value represented a kind of official reply to Marx by professional economists.[24] Universally acclaimed by the anti-Marxist camp, Böhm-Bawerk's work also inspired the criticism of Marxism within the socialist camp. Vilfredo Pareto and Benedetto Croce, for instance, moved in the same direction. Pareto's criticism appeared in two stages: first his introduction to *Karl Marx: Le Capital, extraits faits par M. Paul Lafargue*, which was published in 1897, and then his two large chapters in *Les Systèmes socialistes* (1902–1903).

It is interesting to observe how close Pareto's critique of Marxism was to Sorel. Pareto launched a general attack on socialism, Marxist economics, and the theory of surplus value. His attack on the descriptive part of *Das Kapital* was based on a critique of the Marxist method and its "sophisms," but he concentrated mainly on a criticism of the theory of surplus value.[25] Pareto, who knew Böhm-Bawerk and recognized the value of his work, made a strong defense of free enterprise, without "exonerating or even excusing the abuses that exist in our societies"—abuses that resulted from the state's intervention in the economy. Since any restriction of economic freedom is wrong, wrote Pareto, the intervention of the state in the economy has to be strictly limited.[26] Pareto returned to these ideas in his celebrated work *Les Systèmes socialistes*. Here the attack on Marxist economics and the theory of surplus value was accompanied by a criticism of the materialist theory of history and a conviction that "from the scientific point of view, the sociological part of Marx's work is far superior to the economic part."[27] All these ideas without exception could also be found in Sorel, whom Pareto praised for opposing "the sweet and sickly socialism and democratic humanitarianism that are gaining so much ground these days."[28] Sorel, however, was considered by others—Croce, for instance—as "an eminent French Marxist,"[29] which was clearly not the case with Pareto.

At the same period, Croce also made a critique of Marxist economics, stressing the same elements as Pareto. From 1896 on he criticized the weaknesses of the theory of surplus value.[30] Sorel came to the same conclusions as the two Italian thinkers, who had a great influence on him and his school. Thus we see that in Vienna, where at that time one could be only Marxist or anti-Marxist, revisionism did not take root, despite the debate Böhm-Bawerk initiated, while in France and Italy, the special breeding ground of revolutionary syndicalism, the situation was quite different. There one could launch an attack on the economic principles of Marxism while invoking the authority of Marx, whom one saw solely as a sociologist of violence. There one could appeal to Marx against the eighteenth century and its rationalism, against Descartes, intellectualism, and positivism.

For in France and Italy, around 1905—the year that, for Europe to the east of the Elbe, heralded the coming revolution—the question was whether Marxism still provided the key to universal history, if it had a correct vision of social and economic realities, and if, in the final analysis, Marxism, as stated in the ninth thesis on Feuerbach, was still able to explain the world and to transform it. When asked in a country like France, where the industrial proletariat seemed to have reached the peak of its numerical strength but did not hold the strategic position it had in Russia, these questions produced a number of original answers.

The rupture began with the critique of Marxist economics. It was here that revolutionary revisionism and its progenitor, Georges Sorel, started off. Sorel, to be sure, could scarcely claim to be a serious rival to Rosa Luxemburg or Rudolf Hilferding. His *Introduction à l'économie moderne* (Introduction to modern economics) or his collection of selected writings, translated into Italian and published under the title *Insegnamenti sociali dell'economia contemporanea*, can hardly stand a comparison with *The Accumulation of Capital* or *Finance Capital*. In the same way, the Viennese intellectual milieu at the beginning of the century was infinitely superior, where socialist thought was concerned, to the one frequented by Georges Sorel in the Latin Quarter. The importance of a work, however, cannot be judged solely on an absolute plane; one should also take into account its influence and its political function. Sorel's writings represented the conceptual space in which the theoreticians of revolutionary syndicalism evolved.

At the start of his career as a Marxist theoretician, Sorel attacked the theory of value and came to the conclusion that Marxist economics were

quite superflous for anyone who regarded Marxism as it ought to be regarded: a weapon of war against bourgeois democracy. This was an idea that
Parvus, one of the first promoters, if not the inventor, of the theory of "permanent revolution," would never have thought of. Similarly, despite their
fierce opposition to the methods of social democracy, such an idea would
never have occurred to Lenin, Luxemburg, or Antonio Labriola. (Antonio
Labriola is the father of Italian Marxism, while Arturo Labriola founded the
Italian Revolutionary Syndicalism.)

Some people today claim that Antonio Labriola, the chief Marxist theore-
tician of the period in western Europe, was the representative of a "Latin"
Marxism, at the opposite pole from the German and Polish "economism."
Sorel, according to this view, was another "pioneer of the nondogmatic
Marxism of our period," a prophet of the ideology of self-management, who
can be regarded as the equal of Antonio Labriola, Rosa Luxemburg, and
Benedetto Croce.[31] However, if Antonio Labriola was the first person to
interpret historical materialism as a "philosophy of praxis"—the Italian version of the philosophical aspect of Marxism—based on noneconomic factors,
he never thought of offering the labor movement a completely new system
of economics.[32] There was a great difference between the act of singling out
the noneconomic aspects of Marx's work and that of declaring the whole
economic aspect of Marxism obsolete and proclaiming the perpetual validity
of capitalism. Antonio Labriola understood this very well and in 1898, after
an initial period of infatuation, broke off his relations with Sorel. "What am
I to do?" he asked in his preface to the French edition of *Socialism and
Philosophy*. "Do I have to write an *anti*-Sorel after having written a *pro*-
Sorel?" Labriola felt the need to apologize to his readers for this passing
wave of enthusiasm. "I could not imagine in 1897," he wrote, "that he would
become so soon, in 1898, the herald of a *war of secession*."[33] Antonio Labriola made no mistake about the significance of Sorel's position.

As for Luxemburg, her ideas on the general strike may recall those of
Sorel. She too was primarily interested in the moral content of action. Peter
Nettl has shown, however, that for Sorel the general strike was the specific
fulfillment of a general concept of action, whereas Luxemburg considered it
a tactic dictated by the situation of the moment. Similarly, violence, for her,
was never the object of a cult, as with Sorel. She, like him, could have the
greatest contempt for the neutrality of the social sciences; she, like him,
wanted to influence ways of thinking and to change the world,[34] but she
never sought to give the proletariat the gift of a theory of moral and spiritual
revolution that would fail to touch the bases of capitalism.

Much the same applied to that other nonconformist, Otto Bauer. One
need only glance at his pamphlet *The March toward Socialism* in order to
see the deep gulf between the Sorelian revision of Marxism and not only
orthodoxy, but everything that constituted the basis of European socialism.
This series of articles, which summarized the plan of action of Austrian so-

cialism, envisioned the socialization not only of heavy industry, banks, and
large-scale private property, but also of agriculture, land for building, and
private homes.[35] This is precisely what Sorel rejected, quite simply because
he refused to touch private property and because he believed neither in
equality nor in social justice—values that, for him and his school, would
never be anything other than the whinings of Rousseauist anarchists or
Jaurèsian socialists with sickly souls.

For Sorel did not simply single out certain aspects of Marx's thought in
order to develop them in a more specific manner, as Max Adler and Antonio
Labriola did, nor, like Luxemburg, did he intend to create a complement to
Marx's economic writings. No. He regarded Marxism as a whole, including
Marx's own works and the codification of Marxism by Engels, Kautsky, and
Bernstein as a kind of receptacle that could be voided of its original contents
and filled with another substance. This principle applied not only to the
means but also to the end of revolutionary action.

The Sorelians always stuck to the idea that all progress depended solely
on a market economy, and that consequently any interference in the mechanisms of the liberal economy or any legislation that interfered with the free
play of social or economic forces constituted a lethal danger to socialism.
Sorel unhesitatingly identified Marxist economics with Manchesterian economics; both, he believed, possessed the same foundations and the same
principles. Only these principles, he claimed, would ensure social polarization and the development of an all-out class struggle—violent, open, loyal,
without mercy or compromise. This concept was by no means untrue to
Marx's original idea that capitalism itself creates the forces that will destroy
it, but the great difference between the Sorelians and all the other socialists
was that with the Sorelians, from the very beginning, capitalism as such was
never questioned. They had nothing to put in place of capitalism and they
did not conceive of a postcapitalist era. This was where, from the appearance
of Sorel's *Introduction à l'économie moderne* onward, they parted company
with all other European socialists, including all the western European reformist theoreticians who, resigning themselves to the existence of capitalism, nevertheless remained true to the idea that a society based on the collectivization of property would always be better than a society that made
private property its fulcrum.

The fact that the socialization of property is no longer in fashion in socialist parties, intellectual cafés, and the editorial rooms of leftist reviews is
quite irrelevant. At the beginning of the century, there could be no socialism
without the socialization of property, and there could be no socialist revolution without the elimination of the capitalist economy. The Sorelians were
the first revolutionaries of leftist origin to refuse to question private property, individual profit, or the market economy.

"A class liberalism! That's what syndicalism is!" exclaimed Arturo Labriola, the founder of Italian Sorelianism, in 1905. "It combats legal privi-

leges for the other classes and for itself, and it is only from the struggle and free play of organized economic forces that it expects the emergence of new historical formations and the great hopes of a humanity pacified in work."[36]

This indeed was the crux of the problem. Since the Marxist prophecies showed no sign of coming to pass in the foreseeable future, and since the capitalist economy, on the contrary, was in excellent shape, it was difficult to conclude, like Kautsky, that socialism was an economic necessity. Capitalism, in short, did not seem to carry in itself the seeds of its own destruction. It followed in the dissident's view, that in order to destroy bourgeois society one first had to develop the factors favorable to class struggle; and then, still more important, one had to introduce to Marxism new elements that would *artificially* produce the effect of division, of permanent violence, of insidious warfare not produced by capitalism—a capitalism that was far more dynamic and efficacious than Marx had thought or than most of his disciples had wanted to believe, a capitalism that had shown itself capable of adapting to all conditions of production. Moreover, even when a conflict did arise, the bourgeoisie and the socialist parties that spoke in the name of the proletariat, because they operated in a liberal democratic regime and could function only according to the logic of the system, hastened to reach a compromise that would satisfy the immediate needs of the proletariat. In this way, any combativeness that existed in the working masses was neutralized. According to the Sorelians, this produced a fundamental incompatibility between socialism and democracy which necessitated the immediate destruction of the existing system.

In this situation, the dissidents came to the conclusion that the revolution could take place only if three conditions were met simultaneously. These three elements, or rather, these three series of elements, taken together and as a single whole, constituted revolutionary syndicalism. It was the totality that counted, and this totality finally developed into national syndicalism and then into fascism. As we said at the beginning of the introduction, this evolution, which took place during the first twenty years of this century, forms the subject of this book.

The first of the three elements that ensured the development of Fascist thought was the idea that the revolutionary dynamic was dependent on the market economy, which was regarded as representing the universal laws of economic activity.

The second element was the introduction of new and very special types of catalysts into Marxism. Intended to create a cleavage, these in fact totally changed the content, significance, and character of the system. Since the economic mechanisms had failed to produce a catastrophe, one had to have recourse to social myths, and since the material cleavage did not take place, one had to create a psychological and moral cleavage. This attempt at modernizing and improving Marxism left nothing behind except the terminology, especially the concept of class struggle, and it also radically altered the meaning of the fundamental concepts of socialism. Indeed, in the period of *Réflexions sur la violence*, the label no longer indicated the nature of the product; the notion of class struggle now represented an ideology in which vitalism, intuition, pessimism and activism, the cult of energy, heroism, and proletarian violence—sources of morality and virtue—had replaced Marxist rationalism. In addition, violence, from being an impersonal technical tool, became a source of morality and greatness, a barrier to the decline of the West into ruinous degeneracy.

Marxism was a system of ideas still deeply rooted in the philosophy of the eighteenth century. Sorelian revisionism replaced the rationalist, Hegelian foundations of Marxism with Le Bon's new vision of human nature, with the anti-Cartesianism of Bergson, with the Nietzschean cult of revolt, and with Pareto's most recent discoveries in political sociology. The Sorelian, voluntarist, vitalist, and antimaterialist form of socialism used Bergsonism as an instrument against scientism and did not hesitate to attack reason. It was a philosophy of action based on intuition, the cult of energy and *élan vital*.

This was the very original solution Sorel proposed for overcoming and superseding the crisis of Marxism. Since the free play of economic forces was unable to start up the revolutionary process, psychology had to compensate for the deficiency of economics. One had to summon the deep forces of the unconscious and of intuition and to mobilize these sources of energy that formed the greatness of ancient Greece, of early Christianity, and of the armies of Napoleon. One needed myths—myths being "systems of images" that can neither be split up into their component parts nor refuted. Proletarian violence was a myth that aimed to produce a continuous state of tension leading to breakdown and catastrophe, an insidious state of war, and a daily moral struggle against the established order. In this way, Sorel sought to rectify Marx by introducing irrational elements into Marxism. Myths and violence were key elements in Sorel. They were not expedients but permanent values, as well as being means of mass mobilization suited to the needs of modern politics. There was thus a progressive shift in the main emphasis of Marxist doctrine: psychology replaced economics as the motive force of revolutionary activity.

The third principle of revolutionary revisionism was the destruction of the liberal democratic regime and its intellectual norms and moral values. Since recent history had shown that democracy was simply a swamp in which socialism had become bogged down, the labor movement had to be freed from the dominance of the socialist parties, and all connection between the workers' syndicates and socialist political institutions had to be severed. In short, one had to destroy the democratic system as a whole.

Such were the principles of the revolutionary revisionism that in two major stages was transformed into fascism. In the first stage, the Sorelians, metamorphosing Marxism, constructed a new revolutionary ideology. The second stage proved much more difficult. They now had to deal with a wholly unexpected problem: at the end of the first decade of the twentieth century it became clear that not only the socialist parties but also the workers, including the minority organized in syndicates, were quite unwilling to engage in battle. In the first stage, Sorel still believed that a proletarian elite, organized in syndicates in fighting units, would carry the burden of the revolution. It soon became apparent, however, that the proletariat had absolutely no intention of fulfilling its role as the standard-bearer of the revolution. This realization gave rise to a need to find someone else to play this role, and in about 1910 the Sorelians decided to confer this task on the entire nation. The nation was to be enlisted in the struggle against democratic and rationalist decadence. Thus, a new way progressively opened out between the two total conceptions of man and society that are liberalism and Marxism. This new revolutionary path reflected the various forms of the revolt against liberalism and socialism but was also close to developments in liberalism and socialism. The Sorelians shared with the democratic reformists the conviction that capitalism, far from containing the seeds of its own destruction, encouraged technological progress and seemed unlikely to sink in the foreseeable future into a catastrophic crisis. Both agreed that capitalism was a factor of social progress and well-being. The reformists, however, while accepting the fact of capitalism, did not abandon the final objective of the socialization of property. The same could not be said of the Sorelians, who, for their part, recognized the laws of capitalist economics as having a permanent value. Moreover, to the reformists, liberal democracy was all of a piece. An acceptance of the capitalist economy necessitated an acceptance of all aspects of political liberalism. Against this, the revolutionary syndicalists expressed a fierce hatred for democracy and its spiritual heritage and wished to obstruct and finally destroy its institutional mechanisms.

Sorelianism, at that time, represented a revolutionary aspiration relying exclusively on an elite of the industrial proletariat entrenched in its autonomous strongholds. It was convinced that this proletarian elite, organized in fighting units in its syndicates, was and remained the sole agent of change. In this, revolutionary syndicalism differed profoundly from Leninism. Formulated in a highly industrialized country, this doctrine ignored the peasantry. Moreover, Sorel could not conceive of placing the responsibility for changing the world in the hands of a team of professionals. Nothing was less congenial to him than the idea of a group of Blanquist technicians assailing not only the regime but also all the achievements of capitalism. Moreover, it should be remembered that the Bolshevik Revolution was in the final analysis a revolution on behalf of the proletariat, and that it was made in its name. The revolution of the Sorelians, by contrast, developed into a national revolution. Only at the end of his life, when all his works had been written and he looked at the world around him with a deep sense of despair, did Sorel publish in September 1919 his famous epilogue to the fourth edition of *Réflexions sur la violence*. His hatred for the bourgeoisie and for democracy was so great that he even greeted with shouts of joy the revolution taking place in Russia, which was a rebellion led by professional revolutionaries such as he had disdained all his life. At the same time, he did not disown the use that the Fascists made of his name.

There was a time at the beginning of this century when the Sorelian revolution seemed to be coming to pass. The *Réflexions* provided an ideological foundation for the new labor militancy that had appeared in France and Italy, and that, when strikes were taking place, could be interpreted as both a revolt against the bourgeois state and a rebellion against the existing socialist parties. Indeed, the syndicalist ideology was a good reflection of the dialectical relationship that always exists between thought and action. Even if this ideology developed out of the syndical organizations and immediately provided an ideological justification for the existing labor activism, it nevertheless soon gained an autonomous existence. In the beginning, the Sorelian theory did little more than to reflect the actions of the syndicates as they developed in France in the final years of the nineteenth century. Once it became an independent system of thought, however, this theory preceded action, which it sought to lead and utilize in order to shape reality. In Italy, revolutionary revisionist theory preceded syndical actions; in France, it followed them at first and preceded them later on. At the end of the first decade of the twentieth century, France and Italy were at the same point. In both cases, the theory provided a complete conceptual framework for the revolution, but the revolution failed to come.

It was at the point when the syndicalist theory was some way ahead of the reality of the labor movement, when the revolutionary ideology was no longer a reflection of the reformist practices of the proletarian organizations, that the ideological crisis developed which permitted the fusion, both in France and Italy, of the Sorelians and the nationalists. Indeed, very soon, the limitations of proletarian action became evident, whether it was a matter of the capacity of the syndicates to undermine the bourgeois state or of their will to go farther than fighting for the immediate well-being of the workers. The proletariat of the great industrial centers of western Europe corresponded to the portrait Le Bon had painted of it: it too was only a crowd, and a crowd is conservative. In Germany to the west of the Elbe, in France, and in Italy, where frequent, violent strikes seemed to herald the rise of a new militancy, it became evident that this proletariat of universal suffrage, of the eight-hour working day, of compulsory education, and of military service was no longer the proletariat of the Commune of Paris, nor that of the struggle against the antisocialist laws of Bismarck. This proletariat was no longer, and would never again be, an agent of the antibourgeois revolution. One had therefore either to follow it into its retirement or to find an alternate revolutionary force capable of destroying liberal democracy and rescuing the world from decadence.

The main reason for the facility with which revolutionary revisionism was able to change its concept of the nature of the generator of the revolution was that this movement lacked the safety valves possessed by the variants of Marxism opposed to democratic reformism. Democracy for one school, permanent revolution or a faith in the logic of Marxist economics for another, or a belief in the "avant-garde" party of the revolution for a third were positions that allowed one to adhere to the fundamental principles of Marxism while postponing the revolution indefinitely, or to work for the revolution in the expectation of a conflagration that, in view of the international situation at the beginning of the century, was a quasi-certainty. The adherents of revolutionary syndicalism lacked a perspective of this kind. This was why their solution to the dilemma that preoccupied them was of a different nature: the ineffective proletariat would be replaced by the great rising force of the modern world, born of modernization, wars of independence, and cultural integration—that is, the nation. The nation with all its classes joined together in the great fight against bourgeois and democratic decadence. This process was completed before the war, and without being in any way connected with it.

The adherents of this form of socialism needed the proletariat only as long as they believed it capable of fulfilling its role as the agent of revolution. Listen to Lagardelle, writing in the summer of 1912:

> The labor movement interests us only to the degree that it is the bearer of a new culture. If the proletariat trails along in demagogy or egoism, it no longer has any attraction for those who seek the means by which the world is transformed.[37]

That is why so many Sorelians, like many other people of the Left both before and after the war, slid into fascism. When these leftists of all shapes and colors came to the conclusion that the working class had definitely beaten a retreat, they did not follow it into this attitude. Their socialism remained revolutionary when that of the proletariat had ceased to be so. Having to choose between the proletariat and revolution, they chose revolution; having to choose between a proletarian but moderate socialism and a nonproletarian but revolutionary and national socialism, they opted for the nonproletarian revolution, the national revolution.

Thus, it was quite natural that a synthesis would arise between this new socialism, which discovered the nation as a revolutionary agent, and the nationalist movement, which also rebelled against the old world of conservatives, against the aristocrats and the bourgeois, and against social injustices and which believed that the nation would never be complete until it had integrated the proletariat. A socialism for the whole collectivity and a nation-

alism that, severed from conservatism, proclaimed itself as being by definition the messenger of unity and unanimity thus came together to form an
unprecedented weapon of war against the bourgeois order and liberal democracy.

That was the nature of the synthesis that produced fascism. The Sorelians
contributed the idea of a revolution that must eradicate the liberal democratic regime and its moral and intellectual norms without destroying all the
structures of the capitalist economy. To the world of traders and hair split-
ters they opposed another, all heroism and virility, where pessimism and
puritanism were made into a virtue—a world in which the sense of duty and
sacrifice was glorified. The new society would be dominated by a powerful
avant-garde made up of an aristocracy of producers joined to a youth avid for
action. Here we come upon the great discovery Sorel made: the masses need
myths in order to go forward. It is sentiments, images, and symbols that hurl
individuals into action, not reasonings. It was likewise from Sorel in particular and the Sorelians in general that fascism borrowed something else: the
idea that violence gave rise to the sublime. Fitted out in this way, revolutionary action could now overcome all the resistances of the material world.

To this combination of revolutionary revisionism and integral nationalism
was added, in about 1910, a third element: futurism. This total synthesis
infused fascism, giving it its character of a movement of rebellion and revolt:
of cultural revolt, and afterward, political revolt. One can hardly exaggerate
the significance of the avant-gardist element in the original fascism, the importance of the revolutionary aesthetic it contained. To this combination of
revolutionary syndicalism and radical nationalism that was coming to fruition in the first decade of the century, Marinetti, with the publication of the
Futurist Manifesto in 1909, brought the enthusiastic support of cultural
avant-gardism.

> 1. We intend to sing the love of danger, the habit of energy, and fearlessness. 2.
> Courage, audacity, and revolt will be essential elements of our poetry. 3. Up to
> now, literature has exalted a pensive immobility, ecstasy, and sleep. We intend
> to exalt aggressive action, a feverish insomnia, the racer's stride, the mortal
> leap, the punch and the slap. 4. We say that the world's magnificence has been
> enriched by a new beauty: the beauty of speed. A racing car whose hood is
> adorned with great pipes, like serpents of explosive breath—a roaring car that
> seems to ride on grapeshot—is more beautiful than the Victory of Samothrace.
> 5. We want to hymn the man at the wheel, who hurls the lance of his spirit
> across the Earth, along the circle of its orbit. 6. The poet must spend himself
> with ardor, splendor, and generosity, to swell the enthusiastic fervor of the
> primordial elements. 7. Except in struggle, there is no more beauty. No work
> without an aggressive character can be a masterpiece. Poetry must be con-
> ceived as a violent attack on unknown forces, to reduce and prostrate them

before man. 8. We stand on the last promontory of the centuries! . . . Why
should we look back, when what we want is to break down the mysterious doors
of the Impossible? Time and Space died yesterday. We already live in the
absolute, because we have created eternal, omnipotent speed. 9. We will glorify
war—the world's only hygiene—militarism, patriotism, the destructive gesture
of freedom bringers, beautiful ideas worth dying for, and scorn for woman. 10.
We will destroy the museums, libraries, academies of every kind, will fight
moralism, feminism, every opportunistic or utilitarian cowardice. 11. We will
sing of great crowds excited by work, by pleasure, and by riot; we will sing of
the multicolored, polyphonic tides of revolution in the modern capitals; we will
sing of the vibrant nightly fervor of arsenals and shipyards blazing with violent
electric moons; greedy railway stations that devour smoke-plumed serpents;
factories hung on clouds by the crooked lines of their smoke; bridges that stride
the rivers like giant gymnasts, flashing in the sun with a glitter of knives; adven-
turous steamers that sniff the horizon; deep-chested locomotives whose wheels
paw the tracks like hooves of enormous steel horses bridled by tubing; and the
sleek flight of planes whose propellers chatter in the wind like banners and
seem to cheer like an enthusiastic crowd.

Standing on the summit of the world, we once more send a challenge to the
stars![38]

With his sense of theater, Marinetti knew that in order to strike the imagination of his contemporaries, this cry of rebellion had to come out of Paris.
The mecca of arts and letters, an unequaled cultural center, Paris was also a
major center of Italian culture where the most famous Italian writer of his
period, the nationalist hero of the immediate postwar era, Gabriele D'Annunzio, lived and worked. Moreover, Marinetti and D'Annunzio often wrote
in French and participated in the intellectual life of the French capital.[39]

The manifesto of February 1909 was followed by a whole series of declarations of principles applying to various artistic domains such as music, paint-
ing, and architecture. There was even a futurist science and a futurist cui-
sine. And Marinetti's influence was more or less—and more, rather than
less—felt in most of these areas. The Fascist synthesis meant that aesthetics
became an integral part of politics and economics.[40]

The Fascist style, striking in its aggressivity, well expressed the new ethical and aesthetic values. The style expressed its content; it was not simply a
means of mobilizing the masses but represented a new scale of values, a new
vision of culture. All the futurists had the cult of energy, of dynamism and
power, of the machine and speed, of instinct and intuition, of movement,
willpower, and youth. They professed an absolute contempt for the old bourgeois world and praised the necessity and beauty of violence.[41]

Was it not natural that these rebels recognize the Sorelians as their veritable twins, especially as this "poetry of heroism" involved a cult of direct

action and war? And finally (this, from the point of view of its historical function, was most important), it was violently nationalistic. According to Giovanni Lista, the profoundest political convictions of Marinetti, to take only him, can be summed up in the two ideas of violence and fatherland, or of war and nationhood. His anticlericalism and anarchic individualism, meant to bring about the total liberation of man, were adopted within this framework. "Revolutionary patriotism" was the criterion of his political futurism, a nationalistic and bellicose ideology to which he remained true to the end of his days.[42]

In his espousal of an antitraditionalistic and antibourgeois nationalism, which, together with anarchic individualism, formed a single religion of violence as the generator of the future, Marinetti found himself in 1910 in the same camp as the Sorelians and the nationalists. This encounter of nonconformist and avant-gardist revolutionary forces took place several years before the war and had no connection with it.

Futurism, an artistic avant-garde par excellence, which had a profound influence long before 1914, was at this period the first intellectual current to give a political formulation to an aesthetic conception. Italian futurism and the British vorticism of Ezra Pound and Wyndham Lewis, close to futurism, are good illustrations of the cultural aspect of fascism. One can explain the attractiveness that this school of thought had, throughout the first half of our century, for large segments of the European intelligentsia when one understands that they found in it an expression of their own nonconformism and their own revolt against bourgeois decadence, and that in addition to proposing a conception of the relationships between the individual and society, this ideology represented a new ideal of the beautiful and the admirable.

This was the true common denominator of the revolutionary revisionists, the nationalists, and the futurists: their hatred of the dominant culture and their desire to replace it with a total alternative. The Sorelians, who had opened up a new revolutionary path and provided the initial idea, gave the nationalists the social basis and the forces that enabled the idea of protest to be translated into a political movement. Futurism brought to this fusion artistic flair, the spirit of youth and boisterousness, and the magic of cultural nonconformism.

Sorelians, nationalists, and futurists could no longer fail to encounter one another. Their hatred for the dominant culture placed them on the front line against bourgeois democracy. The proletariat having proved defective, nationalism provided the critical mass that could transform a system of ideas into a political force. This was a realization of the hope of the revolutionary syndicalist Robert Michels, who called for a "grandiose union" of the revolutionary idea with the great revolutionary force of the hour. Michels had hoped that the proletariat would fulfill this role. When that failed to happen, he too fell back on the nation. Toward the end of the first decade of the century, revolutionary syndicalism contributed the idea and the nationalist movement provided the troops.

But this was not all. Nationalism also brought to the original fascism the cult of a strong authority. Of course, the theoreticians of revolutionary syndicalism never attacked authority as such; these advocates of labor autonomy were not anarchists. A syndicate is a fighting unit, not a club. Nevertheless, they did not have the cult of political authority, so important to the nationalists. In this respect, the war played a vital role in the crystallization of the Fascist ideology, not only because it offered proof of the mobilizing capacities of nationalism but also because it revealed the tremendous power of the modern state. The state was seen as the emanation of national unity, and its power depended on the spiritual unanimity of the masses. But, at the same time, the state was the guardian of this unity, which it developed, using every possible means of strengthening it. The war demonstrated the greatness of the individual's capacity for sacrifice, the superficiality of the idea of internationalism, and the facility with which all strata of society could be mobilized in the service of collectivity. The war showed the importance of unity of command, of authority, of leadership, of moral mobilization, of the education of the masses, and of propaganda as an instrument of power. It showed, above all, the ease with which democratic liberties could be suspended and a quasi-dictatorship accepted. From the Fascist point of view, the war largely proved the validity of the ideas of Sorel, Michels, Pareto, and Le Bon: the masses move forward under the impulsion of myths, images, and feelings. They wish to obey, and democracy is merely a delusion. For the founders of fascism, the Great War was a laboratory where the ideas they had put forward throughout the first decade of the century were entirely vindicated.

With regard to political theory, the fascist synthesis was already clearly expressed around 1910–1912 in publications like *La lupa* in Italy and the *Cahiers du Cercle Proudhon* in France. After the first manifestations of the Fascist synthesis in France, the war was needed in order that a situation should exist in Italy that would enable this movement of ideas to be transformed into a political force.

Indeed, for reasons related to a semipermanent crisis that prevailed in Italian society at the beginning of the century, this synthesis flourished in Italy and became a political force. Sorel was regarded as a patriarch, an authority, and a continual inspiration. It was the pure Sorelians, the proponents of an ethical, vitalist, and voluntarist revisionism, the advocates of creative and moral violence, who formed the real ideological core of fascism and provided it with its initial conceptual framework. The first biography of Sorel, by Agostino Lanzillo, appeared in Italy in 1910. It was again among the youth in the Italian universities that his theories, mingled with scientific data, took root.

At the end of 1902, Arturo Labriola began the publication of a weekly, *Avanguardia socialista*, which soon became the center of activity for Italian revolutionary syndicalism. Labriola was at that time the spokesman of the extreme Left of the socialist movement, which was opposed to the reformist policies of Turati. He adopted Sorel's theory of proletarian violence, whose champion in the *Avanguardia socialista* was Sergio Panunzio. Panunzio was the major theoretician of fascism in the 1920s: only Giovanni Gentile outshone him, later on. In 1905 Enrico Leone and Paolo Mantica founded a syndicalist review, *Il divenire sociale*. They were followed by one of the major future ideologists of fascism, Angelo Oliviero Olivetti, who in 1906 published in Lugano another revolutionary syndicalist journal, *Pagine libere*; this was already nationalist in its orientation and heralded the approaching convergence between nationalists and syndicalists. This encounter seemed natural—just as it appeared inevitable in France—after the expulsion of the revolutionary syndicalists from the Italian Socialist party in 1908. It took place around the journal *La lupa*, founded in October 1910. Despite its ephemeral character, this review was a particularly important milestone in the process of the intellectual incubation of fascism, for it brought together for the first time the nationalists grouped around Enrico Corradini and the theoreticians of revolutionary syndicalism: Paolo Orano, Arturo Labriola, Lanzillo, Olivetti, and Michels, who had come from Germany. Other syndicalists chose an even shorter route and joined Corradini's Nationalist Association.

In Italy the synthesis of nationalism with revolutionary syndicalism was based on the same principles as in France: on one hand, a rejection of democracy, Marxism, liberalism, the so-called bourgeois values, the eighteenth-century heritage, internationalism, and pacifism; on the other hand a cult of heroism, vitalism, and violence. Robert Michels, one of the outstanding figures of revolutionary syndicalism, an Italianized German and one of the foremost theoreticians of fascism until his death in 1936, said that in order to shatter the conservatism of the masses, a vitalist and voluntarist ethic was needed, and an elite able to lead the masses into combat. Michels is known not only for his contribution to Fascist ideology, but also for his pioneering work *Political Parties*, which even today is a classic of political science. Together with Pareto and Mosca, he brought to fascism the support of the new social sciences.

After the encounter between the Sorelian revisionists and the nationalists, the national-socialist synthesis developed quickly. The major revolutionary syndicalist intellectuals were strongly in favor of the Libyan War of 1911, and from August 1914 on all the revolutionary syndicalists threw themselves enthusiastically into the campaign in favor of Italy's intervention in the European war, which had just broken out. Like the Leninists, the revolutionary syndicalists considered the war an event that could change the face of the continent, a truly revolutionary war. The war, they believed, created an environment in which the great human and social virtues—violence, heroism, altruism, solidarity between the classes—could be expressed. The war established the conditions for a moral and spiritual renewal. In the hour of battle, there was no place for talk of natural rights, justice, and equality, for all that humanistic lachrimosity that had characterized liberal democracy and democratic socialism.

During the war years and in the months that followed the armistice of November 1918, revolutionary syndicalism developed into national syndicalism. This new type of syndicalism was, as Sergio Panunzio said in 1921, no longer a revolutionary, negative, partial labor syndicalism but a syndicalism reuniting all social classes. At the beginning of the 1920s, national syndicalism already embodied the essence of the Fascist ideology, and the transition to corporatism took place smoothly.

Not all Italian revolutionary syndicalists became Fascists, but most syndicalist leaders were among the founders of the Fascist movement. Many even held key posts in the regime founded by the most famous fellow traveler of revolutionary syndicalism, Benito Mussolini. In 1909 Mussolini declared that he had become a syndicalist during the general strike of 1904, but in fact, at the time of his exile in Switzerland between 1902 and 1904, his connections with the revolutionary syndicalists were well established. Before 1905, he collaborated in the *Avanguardia socialista*, read Sorel and Pareto, and was decisively influenced by theoreticians and leaders of revolutionary syndicalism such as Olivetti, Panunzio, Alceste de Ambris, and Filippo Corridoni. Mussolini soon became one of the best-known leaders of Italian socialism. A charismatic personality, at once an intellectual and an outstanding leader, he quickly rose in importance. From being a provincial socialist leader, he became the head of the revolutionary Left of the Socialist party and the editor of *Avanti!* At that period, in the European socialist parties, the task of editor was reserved for a dominant personality, for one of the leading figures, if not for the head of the party himself. Jaurès, Blum, Vanderwelde, Bernstein, Kautsky, Plekhanov, and Lenin were all editors. During this period, Mussolini often crossed swords with heretics who preferred to leave the party or who were dismissed, especially in connection with the political decisions of the organization. A chapter of this work is devoted to Mussolini, his political activities, and his ideas. It is nevertheless necessary to point out at this stage that his opposition to the revolutionary syndicalists concerned only political tactics, not major ideological options. From the beginning of his association, Mussolini in effect subscribed to the fundamental principles of revolutionary syndicalism.

In 1913 the socialist leader rejoined the people who had shaped his thinking. When he seemed to have reached the peak of his ascension within the party, Mussolini did something unexpected: he began to publish a journal with the symbolic name *Utopia*, opening its pages to the dissidents that the party had excluded from its ranks a few years earlier. This was a quite calculated step that reflected the deep intellectual crisis through which the socialist leader was passing at that time. At the end of his soul-searching and under the pressure of the dramatic events of the summer of 1914, Mussolini put an end to the ambiguity that for two years had characterized his relationship with the leadership of the party he was supposed to guide at the time of the European war. The leader of the socialist Left quit the party and joined the revolutionary syndicalists, who were already organized in aggressive and vociferous pressure groups and demanded Italy's participation in the Anglo-French alliance. The ideological crisis Mussolini passed through had begun long before the war and had no connection with it, but the war brought it to a head. Like all European socialists, Mussolini had to cease wavering. A heroic socialism extolling vitalistic values had always captured the heart of this young man who had fought democratic socialism from his first day of political activity. Twelve years after he had started in the wake of Arturo Labriola, Mussolini found practically all the revolutionary syndicalists in the interventionist movement. But the war also added something else: the mobilizing power of nationalism. When the armistice arrived, Mussolinian fascism was almost complete. In any case, he had already incorporated the ideas of revolutionary syndicalism.

Many years later, he correctly wrote, speaking of his formation and his intellectual debt:

> Reformism, revolutionarism, centrism—these are terms the very memory of which is forgotten, but in the great river of fascism you will find currents that go back to the Sorels, to the Péguys, to the Lagardelles of the *Mouvement socialiste*, and to that group of Italian syndicalists who, thanks to Olivetti's *Pagine Libere*, Orano's *La Lupa*, and Enrico Leone's *Il Divenire sociale*, between 1904 and 1914 introduced a new note into socialist circles emasculated and chloroformed by the Giolittian fornication.[43]

The presence of Péguy in this list may at first seem surprising. Some will see it as an additional reason to doubt the credibility of this well-known text. In reality, the opposite is true: Mussolini has reconstructed with exactitude the atmosphere of his militant youth. The mention of Péguy does not reveal any apologetic tendency on the part of the Duce; on the contrary, it draws attention to one of fascism's sources of inspiration: the revolt of intellectuals from the Left who, with the failure of democratic socialism, discovered a source of strength and hope in nationalism. This is the memory that Mussolini had of Péguy, a former Dreyfusard whose venomous attacks on Jaurès, the living symbol of the democratic republic and reformist socialism, have seldom been surpassed.

There is thus nothing surprising in the fact that the Duce remembered Péguy's invectives as one of the factors that influenced his own thinking, for who condemned more vigorously than Péguy—and Sorel—a socialism steeped in parliamentary decadence? Who more forcefully deplored the degeneration of the Dreyfusard "mystique" into socialist and liberal-democratic politics? Who more than he lambasted Jaurès, the ally par excellence of the Italian reformists, the sworn enemies of the fiery young revolutionary from Forlì? Péguy called Jaurès that "dishonest man," that "traitor in essence," that "drum major of capitulation."[44] At any rate, twenty years later, that is what Mussolini remembered of Péguy: not the defender of Dreyfus, the committed and forceful enemy of anti-Semitism, but the detractor of reformist socialism in particular and the policy of compromise in general. In their ferocious hatred of liberal and democratic socialism, which had now become an integral part of the established order, the editor of *Avanti!* and the author of *Notre Jeunesse* turned out to be natural allies. Their mutual discovery of the nation pushed the Italian socialist even farther toward the French Catholic writer. Moreover, for Mussolini, this exceptional figure, who met a fate that the proponents of heroism could only regard as heroic (Péguy was killed in the war), was the object of an interest bordering on admiration.

Undoubtedly, Mussolini's dictatorship would have horrified Péguy and Sorel, but this assertion does not allow us to question the authenticity of Mussolini's contribution to the *Italian Encyclopedia*. Written in 1932, this article was no more an a posteriori reconstruction than it was an attempt to confer some intellectual respectability on fascism. In fact, it gives a good account of the realities at the beginning of the century. Innumerable texts of that period, both by Mussolini and by other militant socialists who were among the founders of fascism, prove this beyond a shadow of a doubt.

CHAPTER ONE

Georges Sorel and the Antimaterialist Revision of Marxism

THE FOUNDATIONS OF THE "CORRECTION" OF MARXISM

"I have reason to believe that the doctrines of *Réflexions sur la violence* are ripening in the shade. The sycophants of democracy would surely not so frequently declare them to be perverse if they were powerless."[1] This is how Sorel, in 1910, ended his major essay "Mes Raisons du syndicalisme" (My reasons for syndicalism), which definitely terminated his career as a socialist theoretician. Unlike claims in the hagiographies and apologies that have abounded recently, Sorel never sought to disguise the meaning and purpose of his thought.[2] He drew attention to the place where his main intellectual contribution was to be found: *Réflexions sur la violence*, "a book," he wrote, "that has a place of paramount importance in my work." Sorel considered this work to be so important that he admitted, in the prefatory note to the *Avenir socialiste des syndicats* (Socialist future of the syndicates), that he had thought for a long time "that it was inappropriate to put into circulation a little work whose main ideas might seem more than once not to harmonize easily with the main ideas" of the *Réflexions*.[3]

The *Réflexions*, together with *Les Illusions du progrès* and *La Décomposition du marxisme*, constitute a relatively well-structured whole that occupies a central position in Georges Sorel's work. The importance of *Matériaux d'une théorie du prolétariat* lies chiefly in the ideological panorama offered by this collection of essays, prefaces, and introductions dating from 1897 to 1914. Here one should also mention *Le Procès de Socrate*—a work that well illustrates the main preoccupations of Sorelian thought—*Introduction à l'économie moderne*, and the *Insegnamenti sociali della economia contemporanea*. In these last two works, Sorel dealt with subjects of which, by and large, he had an uncertain grasp, but which no socialist theoretician could afford to overlook. In these books, as in his other works on economics, he helped to lay the foundations of a theory of revolution based on private property. However, these writings by no means revolutionized the Marxist thinking of the period. For that, one had to await the appearance of *Réflexions*.

It is thus necessary to distinguish between Sorel's original offering, his real intellectual contribution to the movement of ideas at the beginning of the century, and whatever is secondary. We should also remember that Sorel had his limitations and he knew them. He did not claim to be a Bergson or a Nietzsche. If he could immediately grasp the significance of a philosophical system and was capable of assimilating it quickly and making use of it, he was incapable of producing philosophical thought. He did not have the encyclopedic mind of Renan or the formation of Rudolf Hilferding or Max Adler; he did not have Taine's power of synthesis, he was not a writer of quality like Barrès, and by and large he disliked the spirit of Maurras's system, which was the mainstay of l'Action française. Sorel did not even trouble to work up his major writings. Thus, they all bear the imprint of what they originally were before being put into a volume: review articles hastily thrown into the ideological battle.

In Sorel, the expression of an extraordinary talent exists side by side with the most blatant crudities. Sorel believed that the Jews of eastern Europe ritually murdered Christian children. His political analyses and criticisms of parliamentary democracy scarcely rose above the level of invective; compared with those of his contemporary, the revolutionary syndicalist Robert Michels, his were laughable. Neither a metaphysician, nor a sociologist, nor a historian, nor even a writer of literature, but a philosophe in the eighteenth-century sense of the term, Sorel was fascinated, from the time of his earliest writings, by the role of myths in the history of civilizations, and he elaborated, in the course of a long process of intellectual fermentation and political involvement, an idea of real genius: the theory that heroic myths and violence were creative of morality and virtue. Grafted onto the Marxist view of history, this idea modified Marxism to such an extent that it immediately transformed it into a neutral weapon of war that could be used against the bourgeois order not only by the proletariat but by society as a whole.

It should also be pointed out that Sorel never sought to create a homogeneous ideological corpus, nor did he try to conceal what he called his "variations." Honest as he was, he never attempted to cover up the various stages of his development or, as he said, "the multiplicity of opinions I have successively adopted."[4] Indeed, he had no reason to do so. Despite appearances, his intellectual progress was perfectly coherent and followed a strict political logic.

From his *Procès de Socrate* to his famous appeal "Pour Lénine," Sorel hardly changed where the main issue was concerned: he always had a holy horror of bourgeois society and its intellectual, moral, and political values; of Cartesian rationalism, optimism, utilitarianism, positivism, and intellectualism; the theory of natural rights and all the values inherited from the civilization of the Enlightenment and generally associated, at the turn of the twentieth century, with liberal democracy. Socrates, Descartes and Voltaire, Rousseau and Comte, the "great ancestors" of the time of the French Revolution and their successors, headed by Jaurès—this, according to Sorel, was the intellectual path that inexorably led to decadence. History, for Sorel, was finally not so much a chronicle of class warfare as an endless struggle against decadence. Opposite the forces of degeneration, one always found the agents of resistance: Anytus, representing the heroic society, confronted Socrates and the Sophists, those intellectuals of the Athenian democracy and first corrupters of martial values. In the seventeenth and eighteenth centuries, Pascal opposed Descartes and Voltaire, but religious feeling was no longer able to stem the rising tide of materialism or to prevent the collapse that followed. Fortunately, Nietzsche, Bergson, and William James heralded a movement of renewal capable of repairing the damage caused by Rousseau and Diderot, Condorcet and Auguste Comte.

Maurras and Lenin fulfilled the same function: both provided Sorel, each in his own way and at different times, with weapons with which to fight bourgeois democracy. At one time it was Maurras who was praised, because the "Action française seeks to persuade the educated youth that the democratic idea is in retreat; if he [Maurras] achieves his aim, he will take his place among the men who deserve to be called *masters of the hour*."[5] A few years later, Lenin was declared to be in the forefront of the battle against the accursed "plutocratic democracies." Sorel proclaimed him "the greatest theoretician socialism has had since Marx."[6]

From a purely analytical point of view, Sorel's work can easily be reduced to certain main lines of thought, which deserve our attention. Similarly, his accumulated writings, impressive in quantity if one considers the number of pages, in fact amount to a smaller volume. The breakdown gives us some twenty books and pamphlets, several dozen important pieces in journals, and hundreds of minor articles and book reviews. In reality, most of his books were created on the basis of already published articles or were simply collections of articles. Almost all his work was studded with repetitions and reiterations. The same themes recur ad nauseam, on many occasions transcribed word for word from one book to another.

The undeniable originality of Sorel's thought lies in the fact that it was a living reservoir that served as a receptacle and then as an agent of dissemination for all the ambiguities and difficulties of a period of gestation, the period that saw the elaboration of the new syntheses of the twentieth century: fascism, for instance, which is no easier to classify than the thought of Sorel. Sorel's work attracts yet disconcerts; it captivated a large segment of a whole generation of Europeans by its unexpected, nonconformist, and contentious character. The same could be said of fascism, in which many people found a heroic and dynamic quality at the opposite extreme from bourgeois decadence.

At the beginning of this "long march" one finds Marxism. In 1893 Sorel, a retired engineer, an autodidact who had read and reflected a great deal and already published two large volumes and a few articles, stated in a well-known letter to the editor of the *Revue philosophique* that he had discovered in "modern socialism . . . a true economic science." As a good disciple of Marx, he asked for the "theorems" of socialism to be applied, for "that which is rational and proved ought to become real." He demanded, moreover, "that public authorities should act in conformity with the rules of a rational state," in accordance with the idea, deeply rooted in France, that the "rational principles of all societies" should "be reflected in legislation." Furthermore, if Sorel regretted that socialism had been "exploited by the Jacobins," he recognized that "the Jacobins were the only ones to come to its aid. Without them, moreover, would any legislative concessions have been obtained?" True to this way of thinking that advocated a constant exercise of political pressure, he boldly stated: "All changes must come about through force. It is true that this cannot be used in as brutal a manner as at the time of the Revolution."[7] The pages of the *Revue philosophique de la France et de l'Étranger* thus reveal to us a new adherent to the cause, ready to operate through the traditional channels.

This initial impression is confirmed by another position he adopted the following year. In the Marxist journal *L'Ère nouvelle*, Sorel declared that Marx's theory was "the greatest innovation in philosophy for centuries; it was the starting point of a fruitful transformation in our form of speculation. All our ideas must concentrate around the new principles of scientific socialism."[8] Also in *L'Ère nouvelle* he published at this period two long essays in which he spoke disparagingly of the "idealistic bric-a-brac" that the Marxists were reproached with neglecting.[9] In Marx, Sorel not only found a way of "discerning true from false science," but discovered an "exact, absolute science of economic relationships." "The transformation effected by K. Marx," he wrote, "had the consequence of setting . . . philosophy on its feet. For a long time, it had been made to walk on its head." Thus, one was finally able "to study the relationships of science and the economic environment and finally uncover the social principles so long neglected, by means of which it is possible to gain a rational knowledge of man."[10] At the end of his ideological journey, in 1910, after having carried out the deepest and most radical revision of Marxism of the beginning of the century, Sorel wrote to his Italian disciples, already working on the ideological synthesis that was to bring them to fascism, that at that time he had been "full of rationalistic prejudices."[11]

Indeed, these texts, which followed Sorel's discovery of Marx, reveal, in the words of Édouard Berth, an "orthodox Marxist Sorel."[12] And yet, at the same time as he involved himself in doctrine, his Marxism changed. Four years later, Sorel wrote his preface to the French translation of Antonio Labriola's *Essays on the Materialist Conception of History*. Labriola had discovered Sorel through the journal *Le Devenir social*. On 25 April 1895, he wrote to him a famous letter, which Benedetto Croce would one day see as the beginning of theoretical Marxism in Italy.[13] Sorel, in turn, introduced Antonio Labriola to France. The Italian professor's Marxism had strong Hegelian qualities,[14] which seems to have been particularly acceptable to the French at that period. Antonio Labriola sought and found in Marxism much more than he was offered by the very strict and limited orthodoxy represented by certain aspects of the interpretation of Marxism that Kautsky or, in France, Paul Lafargue gave. Sorel at that time felt himself close to Labriola, whose Marxism was far more sophisticated than the Guesdist, "vulgar," and "positivist" version that explained history solely through economic factors.

Sorel's introduction to Antonio Labriola's work was a vigorous defense of historical materialism and of Marxism in general, and a defense of Marx against his detractors, the most vehement of whom at that period were the so-called French socialists. Their leader at that time was Rouanet, editor of *La Revue socialiste*; Sorel took it upon himself to refute an essay by Rouanet published in 1887 and entitled "Marx's Economic Materialism and French Socialism." He tried to "show how false and futile are the *great objections* that are made against Marxism."[15] The future writer of *Réflexions sur la violence* was at that time so concerned with the preservation of Marxist purity that he opposed Jaurès's attempted synthesis of Marxist materialism with a certain form of idealism. At the same time, however, Sorel insisted that the vulgar materialism, the simplistic determinism, and the celebrated "fatalism" of which Marx was so readily accused were in fact completely alien to him. Sorel insisted on the importance that the "great socialist philosopher" gave to both the "human turn of mind" and to morality: "Is not the development of *class consciousness* the crux of the social question in Marx's eyes?" But, he wrote, "to bring morality down to earth, to rid it of all fantasy, is not to ignore it. On the contrary, it is to treat it with the respect due to the works of reason." That, he suggested, was why there were "so many moral judgments in *Das Kapital*."[16]

If Sorel took up Marxism with such enthusiasm and stuck to it so faithfully, it was precisely because he perceived in it a moral content that was very important to him. It was true that socialism considered "*economic preformation* to be the condition for any change."[17] That was its strength and its originality, and it was precisely in this that it differed from the utopism of Fourier or Cabet,[18] but "that is no reason," wrote Sorel, "to consider it amoral."[19] Later he insisted on "the ethical character of the class struggle" and on the fact that, according to Marx, "the full development of a class" involves "a union of intelligence and heart."[20]

In the last years of the century, Sorel, driven by his interest in the ethical aspect of Marxism, drew close to the liberal revisionist current of the type represented by Bernstein. He approved of the return to Kant that was seen to be taking place in Germany. He said that in the largest and most important socialist party, the one that had always set the tone for the Socialist International, some people had become aware that at the present time there was "a serious deficiency in socialist ethics"—namely, the belief that "the environment had an automatic effect."[21] Sorel deplored the vulgarization of Marxism that was especially prevalent among the French Marxists, and he condemned their Blanquist tendencies.[22] He could not accept the idea that the human being in society acts solely in consequence of the necessities of production, as Paul Lafargue claimed, for instance: "It is in the economic milieu, and only there," wrote Lafargue, "that the philosophical historian must look for the first causes of evolutions and social revolutions."[23] For Sorel this absolute dependence on the means of production was by no means self-evident. He did not believe that "religion and morality are to such a degree dependent on capitalist production and on the corresponding conditions of appropriation."[24]

If Sorel displayed much optimism with regard to the future of socialism, it was because he was convinced that "nearly all the Marxists strongly regret the exaggeration with which, for a long time, the beauties of materialism had been lauded."[25] Finally, he concluded his argument by recalling that "originally, socialism was a *philosophical doctrine*."[26] On this point, he was categorical: "Socialism is a moral question, inasmuch as it provides the world with a new way of judging all human acts, or—to use Nietzsche's famous expression—with a total revaluation of things."[27]

Precisely the importance that he gave to moral considerations in social life made Sorel involve himself enthusiastically in the Dreyfus Affair. In supporting the Dreyfusard camp, he was convinced that he was faithfully following Marx's teaching. "The International urges one to protest and to assert the rights of Justice and Morality," he wrote. For that reason when "the efforts of the proletariat have proved fruitless," the proletariat "gives its support to that element of the bourgeoisie that defends democratic institutions." Sorel was aware that when that happened, "the struggle took on a paradoxical character and seemed to contradict the very principle of class warfare,"[28] but he nevertheless believed that "a temporary coalition for a specific, non-economic purpose between members of groups that the theoreticians of Marxism would regard as implacably hostile is not fatally injurious to the independence of socialist thinking."[29] The position the proletariat adopted is not arrived at merely through a theoretical analysis but represents a genuine popular reaction, for "when the people have been touched by the social spirit, they do not hesitate; they do not listen to the theoreticians. Without entering into any bargaining, they walk side by side with the bourgeois." Sorel pointed out that in the Dreyfus Affair the most authentically proletarian elements adopted that position most enthusiastically; the left-wing followers of Jean Allemane were the first to throw themselves into battle for "the defense of Truth, Justice, and Morality. This is proof that in proletarian circles the ethical idea has not lost its importance."[30] The political conclusion that Sorel drew from this analysis was that "socialism, in France, is becoming more and more *a labor movement within a democracy.*" This position was the most extreme he ever adopted, and it survived neither the consequences of the Affair nor the realities of the social conflicts at the beginning of the century. At this point, Sorel began to evolve an argument that he developed a great deal subsequently, although in a selective manner. He tried to dissociate Marx from Engels and took up the defense of Marx, not only against those Marxists who failed to take into consideration the evolution of his thought from the *Communist Manifesto* onward,[31] but also against Engels. This demonstrated a relatively profound knowledge of Marxism in relation to the French socialist milieu, whose doctrinal ignorance at that period was surprising.[32]

However, the main Sorelian contribution to Marxism was not the adoption of this position, which in fact was fairly common in the international milieu of the 1890s, but a revision and correction of the system intended to improve and complete it. Sorel conceived of the system elaborated by Marx as incomplete. Marx, he wrote, "seems to have feared more than anything else leaving a philosophical system that was too closed and rigid . . . ; he did not attempt to finish any theory," including that of value and surplus value. Accordingly Sorel called on Marx's disciples to undertake a "work of completion." This process lasted for ten years, and its results formed the heart of the Sorelian opus. Sorel was the first of those disciples who devoted themselves to an attempt to fill the gaps and reinforce the vulnerable points in order to "complete the work of their master."[33] This great enterprise of completion, wrote Sorel, would of course be carried out "by Marxist methods."[34] The question was first to know "what the metaphysical basis of this doctrine was," and then one would have to consider the fact that Marx "brought into operation a large number of psychological principles that were not generally expressed in a scientific form."[35]

The critique of Marxist economics was the real starting point of Sorelian revisionism and the criterion of all of revolutionary revisionism. As a good Marxist, Sorel made a considerable effort to understand his master's economic conceptions. In 1897 he set out to study "the Marxist theory of value," and he immediately discovered a "major deficiency"—that to treat this theory as something universal was an error. He agreed with Pareto that one cannot treat "economic problems, as provided by experience, in a strictly scientific manner."[36] Three years later, in the midst of the Bernstein debate, whose main lines he summarized for the benefit of the French public, the future author of *La Décomposition du marxisme* very clearly questioned the main principle of Marxist economics. "The Marxist theory of value," he wrote, "no longer has any scientific usefulness and . . . gives rise to a great many misunderstandings."[37]

We should also draw attention to another point, which does not seem to have been sufficiently noticed. Although Sorel rejected the theories of value and surplus value, he also rejected the idea of the socialization of property. In an article in *La Revue socialiste* published in March 1901, he praised rural cooperation and then came to the conclusion that "socialization could not be accepted by the peasants if it were not given a new form. . . . One must therefore necessarily revise the doctrine." Sorel attacked the subject by going straight to the point. "For a very long time," he wrote, "the schools of socialism failed to pay attention to the great differences that exist between the *socialization of production* and *the socialization of commerce*." Consequently, "this revision should apply . . . first of all to the classic formula, *the socialization of production and commerce*." As a good Marxist, which he still wished to be, Sorel could not permit himself simply to deny one of the main principles of Marxism. He was unable to say that the social and economic reality, the evolution of capitalism, and the existence of an enormous mass of peasants who were resistant to Marxist socialism caused him to abandon the idea of socialization. No, Sorel—as was usual among Marxists, and in accordance with the aim he had set for himself—proceeded to improve and rectify the system. Consequently he sought first to dissociate Marx from Engels, and to support Marx against Engels, in order later to be able to dissociate the idea of the socialization of commerce from that of the socialization of property. Marx, wrote Sorel, would not have formulated the obvious truism "the socialization of production and commerce" without a reason, since the socialization of property necessarily implied that of commerce. Marx must therefore have "meant to say something other than what Engels makes him say." One must suppose that "he recognized that there were two distinct questions where his friend saw only one." But if Sorel rendered homage to Marx's intelligence, he also honored Marx's pet aversion. He expressed satisfaction at what he saw as a return to Proudhon, which he believed he also detected in Bernstein: "There is a new spirit in socialism . . . which corresponds to a doubt concerning the necessity of combining in an indissoluble manner the socialization of production and that of commerce— and of carrying out the revolution all at once."[38]

In his *Insegnamenti*, Sorel was still more explicit. He specifically distanced himself from the position Jules Guesde took at the congress of the Socialist International held in Paris in September 1900. There Guesde made the declaration, which became famous, that "the liberation of labor is subordinate to the question of expropriation, to the question of the transformation of capitalist property into Communist or social collective property." Sorel thought that "all this is obscure," and that the socialists, headed by Jaurès, persisted in making these problems even more incomprehensible. Once again, Sorel referred to Proudhon and the distinction between property and the economic sphere.[39] This distinction had already appeared in *Introduc-*

tion à l'économie moderne, a work to which he referred in *Insegnamenti* in a chapter entitled, precisely, "Socialization in the Economic Sphere." Sorel not only took up the classic Proudhonian positions ("the negation of property is a matter for weak minds"), but dissociated himself from Engels's famous preface of 1895 to *La Lutte des classes en France, 1848–1850*. In this preface, Engels insisted that the appropriation of the means of production was the characteristic that distinguished the form of socialism he called "modern" (by which he meant Marxist) from other varieties. The extension of this formula to the appropriation of the channels of commerce was for Engels a necessary consequence of this fundamental proposition. Sorel declared himself in total disagreement with Engels's conclusion.[40] In reality, he was opposed to a fundamental principle of Marxism and one of its major distinguishing features.

Thus, the first stage of Sorel's revision of Marxism naturally took the form of a revision of Marxist economics. It seems that at the time he wrote his work on economics, he was seeking to remove all possible doubt. "*To reform in a bourgeois society is to affirm private property*," he wrote. "This whole book thus presupposes that private property is an unquestionable fact."[41] Farther on, he reaffirmed his attachment to Proudhon's economic conceptions, and there too, as in the case of Marx, he wanted to complete Proudhon's work: "It is one of Proudhon's chief claims to fame to have determined, better than anyone had done hitherto, the domain of property and that of the economic sphere. I do not, however, believe he exhausted the question. . . . I am taking it up, and I will show how the socialization of the milieu can give rise to a great number of reforms that do not harm property."[42]

This conception of private property was in keeping with the analysis of capitalism that Sorel made in a long study published by *La Revue socialiste* in 1902. The aim of this study was to distinguish those elements in social and economic evolution which were prescribed and determined and those which were not: "In Marx, there are two radically distinct laws of historical development: the proletariat *can* be actuated with a free movement, of such a liberty that it moves toward the absolute ruin of the social edifice, while capitalism is subject to a movement of absolute fatality."[43]

Now, this idea of "capitalist fatality" was one of the main features of Sorelian thought, but it is to be understood in a special sense. According to Sorel, nothing could replace the modernizing capacity of capitalism; no historical force could fashion the future or create a new society in place of capitalism. It is capitalism that causes economic progress and can consequently lay the foundations of a future society.[44] For Sorel, "capitalist *fatality* has all the appearance of a physical phenomenon. *A combination of many chance factors produces the fatality of the movement*: if one examines an isolated fact, it is not possible to assign it any cause and it is really a chance phenomenon, but the whole is so well determined that if anyone seeks to oppose the movement, he will inevitably be broken."[45]

What, then, is the mechanism that gives "this movement . . . the necessary character of natural movements"? Sorel's answer is significant: it is "the action of free competition, raised to the highest degree." Thus, the future depends on the free play of the market economy. Sorel asserted the impotence of the state before the force of "economic movement"; here he used arguments employed by Engels in his polemic against Dühring, and he paid tribute to the positive elements in the thought of Lassalle, who described "the rigidity of capitalist society—that system of *conjectures* which ends by setting up an iron chain between all things." Sorel did not fail to note that Engels's conception in this matter was close to that of "the most classical economists." Farther on, he summed up his thinking as follows: "The more deeply one examines the actual conditions on which Marxist economics is based, the more one finds that it resembles Manchesterian economics. We have already seen that it presupposes a complete judicial independence of employers and workers, the fatality of the capitalist movement, and the indifference or impotence of the state. These are the three great principles of classical economics."[46]

There is, in fact, a difference, but "only with regard to the distinction made by Marxism between the fatality of the movements of capitalism as such and the liberty of the labor movement."[47] This liberty, wrote Sorel, quoting Marx, consisted in the "conscious participation" of the workers "in the historical evolution." This "conscious participation is very easy wherever, capitalism being highly developed, there is an absolute separation between the *head* and the *arms* of industry, so that workers can move freely without ever having to feel a solidarity between their class and the capitalist class."[48]

Hence the conclusion "that touches the very principles of the doctrine":[49] the free play of economic forces gives rise to labor emancipation. The market economy creates the conditions for the appearance and development of class consciousness in the proletariat. Only economic liberalism permits the mechanism of class struggle to be set in motion. Everything that encourages the organization of the proletariat, its unity, and its discipline, everything that makes it into a fighting force, is positive, but everything that weakens it works against socialism. A policy that hinders the free play of economic forces is deplorable; economic protectionism, cooperative enterprises, the participation of workers in management, and the various forms of participation in government all distort this essential mechanism of socialism.[50]

Sorelians and "liberists" (free marketeers) were in complete agreement on the most extreme principles of economic liberalism. The term "liberism" was employed in Italy by all the supporters of economic liberalism who strongly opposed both the political and philosophical content of liberalism and the Giolittian establishment. These people advocated an extreme economic liberalism but loathed any kind of intellectual infrastructure associated with the theory of natural rights or the principles of the French Revolution. It was therefore not surprising that the *Insegnamenti* appeared with a preface in which its author, Vittorio Racca, describing himself as an "impenitent liberist," wrote that he undersigned "Sorel's splendid volume with both hands."[51] Both sides rejected any social legislation, any protectionist measures, anything that could inhibit energies, neutralize the will to power, or interfere with free competition, that merciless struggle for life and victory. These elements of social Darwinism and primitive Nietzscheanism, common to the most extreme liberals and the revolutionary revisionists, clearly precluded any compromise with either political democracy or social democracy. This liberalism, a simplified and adapted form of social Darwinism, was supposed to express the laws of life and to represent the absolute necessity of progress. It was violently opposed to the theory of natural rights and the teachings of English utilitarianism. It was by definition the very negation of democracy.

This liberalism was also in close agreement, in this domain, with Marxism as described by Sorel and his disciples. Since Marxism was reduced to class struggle, it had a strong need for a Darwinian economy and could only be opposed to anything that distorted natural social antagonisms. This was why Sorelian Marxism necessarily resulted in a negation of liberal democracy and democratic socialism. Indeed, said the Sorelians, one can always speak of socialism in the sense of 1848, one can go back to pre-Marxist socialism, but one cannot practice both Marxism and democracy, the most powerful possible obstacle to social polarization and the normal development of social conflict. On this question, Sorel scarcely changed his opinion. In *La Décomposition du marxisme*, an important text, complementary to the *Réflexions*, in which Sorel summarized his thought at the International Symposium of Revolutionary Syndicalists in Paris in 1907, he returned to the ideas he had expressed in 1902. He stated that Marxism was close to the school "of *political* economics called Manchesterian . . . , which divides society into two classes between which there is no connection," and that "democracy can work effectively to prevent the progress of socialism."[52] If one wishes to be true to Marxism, one must therefore go back to the main principle: the promotion of class struggle.

Here we must stress this fundamental aspect of Sorelian thought: the revolutionary struggle depends on a market economy; it is determined by the most absolute economic liberalism. In practice, economic liberalism is a sine qua non of the coming revolution. But, at the same time, Sorel advocated the destruction of *political* liberalism, whose disappearance he regarded as a necessary precondition. Thus, this revision of Marxism proposed a new conception of the revolution, which the Italian revolutionary syndicalists developed in turn and which became an essential element of early Italian fascism.

Sorel was aware of the great complexity of the problems he was trying to explain. "We know that things do not happen as simply as Marx supposed in 1847," he wrote. Not only did capitalism not develop as quickly as was supposed, but also "the labor movement was oversimplified by Marx." Here Sorel broached the great question that was to preoccupy him throughout the first decade of the century: "We have to admit that, at the present time, we do not yet know everything that ought to be done in order to bring the proletariat to effectiveness." One thing, however, was clear: "Socialism is . . . the organization of revolt, and a syndicate with a revolutionary orientation is the thing that is most specifically socialist."[53] Sorel henceforth remained true to this conception of struggle against bourgeois society. When he was forced to submit to the evidence and to resign himself to abandoning a proletariat more and more dominated by trade unionism and social democracy, he went off in search of another agent of revolution.

The great intellectual debate that shook European socialism, and to which Sorel desperately sought an outcome, was dominated by what he called the "decadence"[54] or the "decomposition" of Marxism. This last expression formed the title of the famous pamphlet in which Sorel analyzed the phenomenon then most commonly known as the "crisis" of Marxism.

This text belonged to a period when Sorel was at the end of the process of the revision of Marxism, even if in reality, as we have said, the Sorelian view of the intellectual problems faced by Marxism had not changed a great deal since 1900. In his opinion, the primary cause of this crisis of Marxism was the "immobility in which Kautsky claimed he was preserving it."[55] Thus, in a major article published in 1900 in which he analyzed the significance of Bernsteinian revisionism, Sorel attacked Kautsky for making Marxism look "like something very old."[56] He also showed much respect for the intellectual effort Bernstein made and for the courage he demonstrated in pointing out the weaknesses of Marxism: the theory of value, of course, but also "*historical necessity*" and, finally, Marxist dialectics. After glancing at the conceptions of Benedetto Croce, Enrico Ferri, Antonio Labriola, and Jean Jaurès, he finally got to Kautsky. "We are promised *science*," he wrote, "but we are offered only words: we are not given any new means of acting in the world."[57] This was Sorel's principal charge against him: Kautsky's triumph would mean "the definite ruination of Marxism." That is why he resolutely supported Bernstein. Bernstein, to be sure, had not created a new philosophy, but "his aim was not so ambitious. He wanted only to make us think for ourselves while preserving the core of Marxism."[58] That was precisely the aim which Sorel assigned to "the *new school* . . . Marxist, syndicalist, and revolutionary."[59] In the first decade of this century, the journal *Le Mouvement socialiste* was the center of this effort of renewal, but what was sup-

posed to be a renaissance of Marxism led finally either to the Cercle
Proudhon or to Georges Valois's Faisceau and later to the Charte du Travail
(Charter of Work) of the Vichy government.

Sorel, however, took only the revisionist method from Bernstein: the
means but not the content. In supporting Bernstein against Kautsky and
Liebknecht in 1900, Sorel was merely drawing attention to the innovative
role of the German social-democratic theoretician, for the revisionism the
French theoretician initiated was in fact at the opposite pole from Bernstein's. This revolutionary, antirationalist, and mythical revisionism was
based on what Sorel believed to be a stratum of Marxist thought that nobody
had suspected before him, on a "Marxism of Marx"—an original contribution to socialism expressing the genius of the author of *Das Kapital*, and
completely different from the borrowing whose source was found in the "old
socialist tendencies."[60] If this essential part of Marxism had long been con-
cealed, it was because "there were not yet any major labor organizations that
corresponded to it," and if Bernstein did not recognize it, it was because he
had a good knowledge of only England and Germany.[61] Now that a new
labor movement had come into being (he was speaking, of course, of the
organized proletariat in France), Marxism had to be looked at in a completely new way. In the light of this renaissance of the revolutionary idea
and action in France, associated in his mind with Fernand Pelloutier, who
strongly advocated the principle of the separation of the classes and stipulated the necessity of abandoning any hope of political renewal, Sorel stated
that "Marxism could not be transformed as Bernstein thought." It could not
be transformed into a mere political theory, nor into a political party like the
others, nor into an electoral machine disputing the labor constituency with
other political organizations. In making it into a tool to prepare the proletariat for rebellion, the new school gave Marxism life, and in proceeding in a
quite different manner from Bernstein, it had succeeded in uncovering the
very essence of Marxism.

The following is Sorel's description of the contribution of the new school
to the renaissance of Marxism: "It finally rejected all formulas that came
either from utopism or from Blanquism, and thus purged traditional Marxism of all that was not specifically Marxist, and it sought to preserve only that
which, in its opinion, was the core of the doctrine, that which assured Marx's
prestige." The element that precisely represented "the value of the work"
was its "symbolic parts, formerly regarded as of doubtful value." Bergson
was mentioned here as teaching "that movement is expressed primarily in
images, that mythical formulas are the clothing of a philosopher's fundamental thought, and that metaphysics cannot use the language appropriate for
science."[62]

This text is one of the keys to the Sorelian approach; class struggle and the
final catastrophe, those two main principles of Sorel's interpretation of

Marxism, are explained in terms of sentiments, myths, and images. The socialists were invited to consider the history of the church in order to find
hope and consolation. The role of the revolutionary syndicates "that saved
socialism" was compared to that of the religious orders in the rejuvenation
of the old Catholic edifice.[63]

At the same time, Sorel maintained that "the present crisis of Marxism"
could not be explained solely in terms of the debates between the theoreticians—whether the debate surrounded Bernsteinian revisionism or concerned the Dreyfus Affair; it was also caused by "changes that have taken
place in social conditions."[64] This conclusion reinforced his tendency to consider Marxism as a weapon that would break the resistance of the world of
matter.

It is true that, as Maximilien Rubel has demonstrated, Sorel read the writings of Marx known in his time in a way that was often approximative and
selective; he probably did not have a sound knowledge of the first book of
Das Kapital. Moreover, his knowledge of German was far from being sufficient to allow him to study the original texts. Leszek Kolakowski has claimed
that Sorel often manipulated Marx in an arbitrary manner, as in the definition he gave of the concept of class.[65] Indeed, anyone who has taken the
trouble to study Marx knows that the following definition of *class*, given by
Sorel in his *Matériaux*, does not correspond to Marx's ideas: "A fully developed class is, according to Marx, a collectivity of families united by traditions, interests, and political opinions, which has reached such a degree of
solidarity that one can ascribe to it a personality and regard it as a being that
reasons and acts in accordance with its reasons."[66]

For Sorel, however, a deep knowledge of Marxist philosophy and economics was never really necessary in order to understand the value of Marxism as a weapon of combat. "The theory of surplus value is useless" for the
purpose of waging "a ceaseless war" between the bourgeoisie and the proletariat, he wrote in 1909.[67] In *Saggi*, he had already questioned the feasibility
of turning socialism into a science.[68]

There was a clear reason for this attitude: at the beginning of the century,
Sorel saw that science did not activate the masses. People do not sacrifice
themselves for surplus value! This was why he sought to minimize the scientific aspect of Marxism. What was the use of the herculean efforts of Rudolf
Hilferding, Max Adler, and, on a different level but in the same direction,
Trotsky and Lenin? Will one start a revolution if one persuades the workers
that Marxism is a science? Will one succeed in destroying democratic and
liberal socialism and take away its proletarian followers?

For Sorel, the answer to these questions was obvious. Thus, he initiated
a vast campaign against the rationalistic and scientific illusion. In the work
entitled *Les Illusions du progrès*, which accompanied his *Réflexions*, Sorel
stated not only that "there is both charlatanism and puerility in speaking of

a *historical determinism*,"[69] but that history is of "an inextricable complexity," which "the Marxist method (when correctly understood)" has the great advantage of preserving. Unlike the superficial Cartesianism, Marxism, wrote Sorel, has "a respect for this fundamental mystery which a frivolous science evades."[70] History, like economics,[71] belongs to the domain of mystery. The aim of socialism is not to solve this mystery but to transform the world by means of the extraordinary dynamism Marxism provided. "The experience of the Marxist theory of value," wrote Sorel, "shows us how important obscurity can be to give strength to a doctrine."[72] Rousseau and Hegel, who preferred shadow to light, he wrote, testified to this in their own way.[73]

This, he believed, was why the essence of Marxism lay in the symbolic and apocalyptic content of the system. The idea of the general strike was a translation into concrete terms of the Marxist apocalypse, and the sole real historical function of Marxism was to act as an instrument of war. If Marxism were to be given back its youth, one would first have to save the proletariat from those "oratorical, philanthropic, and demagogic forms of socialism that Jaurès was trying to revive," he observed in *Mes Raisons du syndicalisme*, a work that marked the final stage of his hopes for a syndicalist renewal. "Marxism," he wrote, "should be subjected to a revision that would ensure the preservation of anything fruitful it had brought to the study of societies, to the art of understanding the transformations of history, and to the conception of the revolutionary mission of the proletariat." In the last pages of this essay, a sort of ideological testament, which was published in Italy in 1910 by his pupils who had just brought about the union of revolutionary syndicalism and the nationalist movement, he explained what he was trying to achieve. While Bernsteinian revisionism wished to harmonize the theory with the practice of the socialist parties that had now become part of liberal democracy, Sorel wanted to carry out "the real revision of Marxism," which would be to create a theory of revolutionary action, of "direct action," "a doctrine of the labor movement that would be perfectly adapted to the form of labor struggle" advocated by revolutionary syndicalism.[74]

Sorel gave a definition of this central core of Marxism in one of his major articles, which appeared in *Le Mouvement socialiste* and which he later incorporated in *Matériaux d'une théorie du prolétariat* and published at the beginning of his study *L'Avenir socialiste des syndicats* under the title *Préface de 1905*. "Class struggle is the alpha and omega of socialism," he wrote. After twelve years of activity as a socialist theoretician, after having participated vigorously in the *Bernstein debatte*, after having been one of the first to be involved in Dreyfusism, Sorel came to the conclusion that it was class struggle that represented "what was really true in Marxism, what was powerfully original, superior to all formulas." What mattered was class struggle and not Marxist economics or Marx's historical conceptions, class struggle and not the theory of surplus value or the concepts of alienation or of the dictatorship of the proletariat. Sorel gave the idea of class struggle a precise, coherent, and practical significance. He said that contrary to the opinion of the "orthodox" Marxists, it was not a "sociological concept used by scholars," but the "ideological aspect of a social war waged by the proletariat against the heads of industry as a whole." In this combat, "the syndicate is the instrument of the social war,"[75] and revolutionary syndicalism fulfills the essence of Marxism. Thus, Sorel believed, socialism ceased to be a theory, a pious wish, and became once more what Marx had always intended it to be: a weapon of war against the established order.

The first steps toward this approach were taken in 1897, in the essay "L'Avenir socialiste des syndicats." Directly attacking the methods of the socialist parties, Sorel claimed that according to the materialist conception of history, the definitive struggle for power was not a struggle to conquer the positions of the bourgeois in order to rig oneself out in their garments, but a struggle to divest the bourgeois political organism of any life and to transpose anything useful it may contain into a proletarian political organism created in accordance with the development of the proletariat.[76]

The proletariat, wrote Sorel, can emancipate itself only if it remains a "wholly labor" phenomenon, if it excludes intellectuals, if it refuses to imitate the bourgeoisie,[77] and if, drawing on its "feelings of energy and responsibility,"[78] it relinquishes the democratic heritage. Relinquishing the democratic heritage means first rejecting individualism, liberalism, and certain reforms, such as the celebrated "right to work," introduced by the French Revolution. The emancipation of the proletariat thus passes through a restructuring of society according to principles opposite to those of liberal democracy. Syndicalism believed that "the workers as a whole constitute a body," and that the syndicates were "social authorities" that "take the worker out of the control of the shopkeeper, that great elector of bourgeois democracy." In this way, a "new organization" comes into being, "independent of all bourgeois organizations," which can set up workers' cooperatives and encourage their growth, and which can create, in place of *government by the citizens as a whole*, which has never been anything other than a fiction," and in place of a *"chaotic majority"* and a "purely ideal and utopian equality," a *"just and real organized equality."* In this way a "proletarian spirit" also comes into being. In this way, finally, autonomous workers' organizations are set up which run counter to the classical political organizations— that is, parties, pressure groups, and all the channels of transmission of bourgeois democracy.[79]

In order to preserve this labor autonomy, one had at all costs to prevent the reappearance of a coalition similar to the one that made the Dreyfus Affair possible. In Sorel's opinion, this alliance of the proletariat with the bourgeoisie represented an ideal model of a kind of "political revolution" that is fatal for the proletariat, for the factor that destroys the mechanism of the conflict is democracy, which "mixes" the elements separated by economics. Nevertheless, Sorel was well aware that class antagonisms were never automatically or necessarily produced by capitalism. Capitalism does not *inevitably* produce class struggle; a capitalist "inevitability" exists only in the domain of economics, production, and technology. If capitalism develops as the result of a certain necessity, if the capitalists all have to try and improve their equipment, to find new outlets, to reduce their manufacturing costs, "nothing obliges the workers to unite and to organize themselves."[80] For this reason, capitalism can neither automatically cause social polarization and class antagonisms nor give rise to a combative way of thinking and a spirit of sacrifice. Class struggle materializes only where there is a desire, continually fostered, to destroy the existing order. The mechanisms of the capitalist system are able to give rise to economic progress, create ever-increasing wealth, and raise the standard of living. These mechanisms are a necessary but not sufficient precondition for nurturing a class consciousness. The capitalist system does not by its nature produce a revolutionary state of mind, and it is not by itself capable of creating the conviction that the bourgeois order deserves to be overtaken not only by a "material catastrophe," but also by a "moral catastrophe."[81]

Sorel was aware of the enormous changes that had taken place in the condition of the workers. He believed that political democracy, universal suffrage, social legislation, public education, and freedom of the press worked against the esprit de corps of the industrial workers. At the same time, one saw corporations regain a position of honor and an increasing intervention by both employers and the state in the affairs of the workers. "All this tends to mix together all that socialism had sought to separate and that Marx thought he had totally distinguished," wrote Sorel. Even if he thought these developments too recent or as yet of too little importance to have had "an effect on the present crisis of Marxism,"[82] Sorel nevertheless felt he had perceived a new phenomenon whose importance could only increase in the future, and which Marx could not have known about. True to his objectives of 1897, Sorel thus decided to correct and complete Marxism. In 1914, when very little remained of his Marxist beliefs, he recalled in his foreword to *Matériaux* the days when he had hoped "to be able one day, using the facts revealed in recent inquiries, to complete the brief guidelines that Marx and Engels had provided on the development of the working class."[83] Ten years earlier, Sorel would never have dared to couple the expression "brief guidelines" with the name of Marx, even if, already at that period, he felt that "these last years" had been sufficiently "rich in unexpected facts" to "invalidate those syntheses which seemed to be the best founded."[84]

In fact, Sorelian revisionism was deeply rooted in the social realities of his time and his immediate environment. It was not a mere intellectual exercise;

Sorel set about cultivating the mythical and apocalyptic aspect of Marxism against the background of the great strikes and the upsurge of syndicalism of the first years of the century. Strikes and violence were not metaphors. In the France of 1906, one of every sixteen industrial workers was a striker; they amounted, in all, to hundreds of thousands. Those who were in solidarity with the striking workers were more numerous still. The longer the strikes lasted, the bigger their effect. According to Madeleine Rebérioux, in 1902 strikes lasted an average of 22 days, more than three times the average thirty years earlier. In 1904 there were 1,026 strikes, about twice as many as in 1903; 271,097 workers stopped work, representing nearly four million lost working days. The movement peaked in 1906 with 438,000 strikers—a record that was not broken until the war—and 1,039 strikes of an average length of nineteen days. Some of these strikes caused terrible hardship; at the industrial complex of Forges d'Hennebont, between April and August 1906, 1,800 workers sustained themselves with crabs fished at low tide and a little bread, and at the end of the strike, a striking worker's family lived on 750 grams of bread a week. Soldiers began to shoot; at Longwy in September 1905, at Raon-l'Étape in July 1907, and in the Lens Basin after the catastrophe of Courrières blood flowed after the cavalry came on the scene. Social tensions reached their climax on 1 May 1906. For the first time, a labor movement on a national scale had been systematically organized; new possibilities seemed to open up. Some leaders of the Confédération Générale du Travail (CGT) thought a general strike was taking shape in the strike movement that followed the cessation of work on 1 May 1906. The building, furnishing, and printing trades as well as automobile and metro workers were affected.[85]

The year 1906 was also when *Réflexions sur la violence* and *Les Illusions du progrès* were published. Revolutionary syndicalism was a reflection of this epic period of strike action, and it built its theory around it. It hoped to see the emergence of a heroic proletariat, ready for every sacrifice and conscious of its mission. Sorel was sufficiently clear-sighted, however, to be aware of the other side of the picture: it was not the fate of civilization that preoccupied the striking workers but their living and working conditions. Their demands centered on the eight-hour working day and not the end of bourgeois culture.

Moreover, on 13 July 1906, a law was passed making obligatory a twenty-four-hour weekly day of rest. Economic growth went side by side with legislation improving the workers' conditions (for instance, the law for the protection of women's wages in July 1907 and the law on the retirement of industrial and agricultural workers in April 1910). If the first of May frightened the propertied classes, if the combativeness of the workers was impressive, French capitalism—the same was true in Italy and Germany—found the means to confront the challenge and to meet social demands.[86]

Clemenceau's policy of rupture with the workers organized in syndicates was not enough to cause a general revolt. Even the first of May 1906 did not mobilize the working class as a whole, nor even the entire CGT.

Here one saw the full ambiguity of a situation that was by no means limited to France. The strike actions of the Italian working class were larger in scope and had a greater effect than those in France. In the opinion of Rosa Luxemburg, the Russian Revolution of 1905 had originated in a general strike. Paradoxically, this very ardor and militancy demonstrated the limits of the phenomenon, for it was the German, French, and Italian socialist parties—all reformist—that clearly gained ground. Sorel knew that the social agitation of the CGT could not conceal the gains of the Section Française de l'Internationale Ouvrière (SFIO, French Socialists), and in the final analysis Jaurès's party (the SFIO) reaped the benefit. Between the time of the foundation of the party—representing a victory for the moderates— and July 1914, membership increased from 44,000 to 90,000. In 1906 the SFIO had 900,000 votes, in 1910 1 million, and in 1914 1,400,000, sending 57, 76, and finally 101 representatives to the Chamber of Deputies. In Provence and Languedoc, the Socialist party had overtaken the radicals. Here, then, was a party that was not a mass party nor a workers' party, nor, even less, a revolutionary party, which in the space of two normal legislatures showed itself to be a large parliamentary formation backed by a large number of electors.[87] In Germany, the situation was similar: the Socialist party, as everyone knows, was at that period the largest political party in the empire.

This was the situation to which the revolutionaries had to find a response. On the one hand, there was an undeniable upsurge of labor militancy and bloody confrontations with the bourgeois state, and on the other hand an almost continuous economic growth that made it possible, through reforms that deeply modified the living conditions of the working class, to diminish considerably its revolutionary ardor. This conjunction of circumstances revealed the true significance of the Sorelian theory of myths: it was intended to develop the class consciousness of the proletariat, to encourage its combativeness, to structure a labor elite properly organized in syndicates, and to create a deep psychological gulf between this avant-garde and the ruling bourgeoisie. This psychological gulf had to be deepened day by day through a constant rejection of social reforms; thus social polarization would be accomplished through willpower, and the atmosphere of a crisis of capitalism, which because of economic growth had failed to develop, would become a reality.

Here one can clearly see the social intention of the theory of myths. Since capitalism did not bring society to the final stage of its maturation, since it did not seem that in the immediate future the bourgeois order would collapse of its own accord, since labor violence based on material demands did not raise the proletariat to the level of a historical force able to give rise to a new civilization, and since it became obvious every day that the material interests of the proletariat, and not only of the socialist politicians, disposed it to compromise with the bourgeoisie, new factors had to be introduced into social relationships. A total moral revolt would replace the struggle for better conditions, the psychological method would replace the traditional mechanistic approach, and irrationalism would replace the classical Marxist content of socialism. Since it appeared that the masses could not be activated by reason, since socialism persisted in representing, as the old Guesdist tradition maintained, the "party of the stomach," and since capitalism did not collapse and social polarization did not happen, one had artificially to create a process of rebellion of a new type, suitably adapted to the new social conditions. This was the function of the theory of myths that lay at the heart of the antimaterialist revision of Marxism.

ANTIRATIONALISM AND ACTIVISM: THE SOCIAL MYTHS

Sorel showed an awareness of the new possibilities of a mythical interpretation of Marxism as early as his "Préface pour Colajanni," written at the end of 1899. That means that at the height of his social-democratic period, when he seemed to conceive of socialism as an element of modern democracy, he was already laying the foundations for a revision of Marxism of a new kind, which later contributed to a new type of revolutionary ideology.

The starting point of Sorel's thinking on the symbolic and mythical aspect of Marxism was the idea of class. Seeing that an absolute "class" did not exist, and despite the fact that Marx himself, who often confused logical constructions and phenomena, was not always aware of it, Sorel maintained that "the Marxist theory of classes is an abstraction." This amounted to saying it was an intellectual construction or a methodological necessity. Indeed, wrote Sorel, "the *dichotomous division* of society," which is regarded as being characteristic of Marxism, the opposition of "the have-nots to those who have," does not exist in reality. It is obvious, he wrote, not only that "the middle class does not disappear" and its social importance does not diminish, but also that the idea of class can hardly be applied to the petit bourgeoisie. Sorel believed that the middle class was a diversified entity within which existed a great mobility. For socialism, this "excessive complexity of the social structure" represented an insurmountable obstacle as long as one confined oneself to sociological analyses and accepted the unwieldiness of sociology; but things were quite different when one regarded this famous "dichotomous division" not as the expression of a social reality, but as a methodical necessity. Marx alone, wrote Sorel, was responsible "for the obscurity of his doctrine of class struggle," because "he found it very difficult to separate in his thinking what was properly *scientific* from what was properly educative." Sorel believed that the value of the Marxist theory of class struggle could be compared to "that of an artistic image intended to make us assimilate an idea." It was in this way that the socialist militants had to understand the *"revolutionary idea"* if they were to render it comprehensible to the masses. Sorel's meaning was that the "dichotomous division" was really an "abstraction" that enabled social conflicts to be placed within a theoretical framework, and that it had a mobilizing and ideological value inasmuch as it allowed social conflicts to be organized in accordance with an entirely coherent view of history.[88]

In this light—and bearing in mind that "to concern oneself with social science is one thing and to mold consciousness is another"—Sorel examined the next-to-last chapter of *Das Kapital*, which he held to be the true conclusion of Marx's masterwork. On one hand, he considered that all the hypotheses underlying the conception of the future in Marx, which hardly corresponded to the economic realities of 1867, were of little interest if taken literally. On the other hand, if one took the trouble to interpret "this *apocalyptic text* . . . as a product of the spirit, as an image created for the purpose of molding consciousness, it . . . is a good illustration of the principle on which Marx believed he should base the rules of the socialist action of the proletariat." As Sorel said, the "Préface pour Colajanni" had a position of the greatest importance in the development of his thought. "I believe it was here," he wrote, "that for the first time I indicated the doctrine of myth that I developed in *Réflexions sur la violence*."[89]

Indeed, from that moment on Sorel initiated the process that he believed would complete Marxism. This process continued with *Introduction à l'économie moderne*, in which he attacked one of the leaders of Italian socialism, Enrico Ferri, whom he saw as one of those "retarded people who believe in the sovereign power of science" and who thought that socialism could be demonstrated "as one demonstrates the laws of the equilibrium of fluids." Here Sorel joined battle with positivistic sociology, for which he substituted a pragmatic and relativistic sociology that was justified and could be justified only by its practical utility.[90]

He wished to base this new sociology on the critique of traditional philosophy by Bergsonian philosophy. Reflecting Bergson's question "whether the time had not come to abandon the old Greek method created for geometrical purposes in order to attempt to find reality, motivation, and content," Sorel declared that "knowledge obtained through concepts . . . is as ill-adapted to social facts as could be." He also went a stage farther, drawing, this time, upon the theories of Vico, whom he called "that great Neapolitan," and whom he regarded as one of the chief authorities "for the Marxist. In history," he wrote, "there is first of all . . . a popular wisdom that feels things and expresses them poetically before reflective thought succeeds in understanding them theoretically."[91] This wisdom, he claimed, is in fact an intuition of real social movement that enables it to be grasped before it has run its course and before discursive thought can retrace its development.[92]

Thus, in the opinion of Sorel, not the scientific method but "a theory of social myths" would enable the existing difficulties of socialism to be overcome. He believed that myths had played a considerable role in human thought, which the history of philosophy had not yet understood precisely. In this connection, Sorel referred characteristically to the Platonic myths,[93] which he had already discussed in *Le Procès de Socrate*.[94] A myth, he believed, is a symbol whose function is to transpose relationships of ideas into relationships of facts, which are their image. Paul Kahn said that a myth comes into being whenever symbols assume a narrative and dramatic form and consequently involve characters and action.[95]

Sorel ascribed to his theory of myths a comparable function. This theory, however, was delineated roughly in *Introduction à l'économie moderne*; it was fully developed only in *Réflexions*, which he began to write in 1905 and published in *Le Mouvement socialiste* in the first half of 1906. He thus sought to give Marxism an entirely new significance. Sorel thought he had penetrated "Marx's underlying thought"; he believed he had discovered "the hidden mechanism of the doctrine," whose existence the "official Marxists" led by Kautsky ("too alien to any philosophical reflection") were incapable of even suspecting.[96] Strangely, Sorel launched an attack at this stage on Émile Vandervelde, the rising star of Belgian socialism and one of the best-known spokesmen of democratic revisionism. Sorel defended against him a number of classical Marxist dogmas that democratic socialism at the beginning of the century regarded as obsolete. Whether he took his inspiration from Bernstein or he simply drew conclusions from the social and economic reality, Vandervelde considered three fundamental elements of Marxist thought to be outmoded: the iron law of wages, identified as that of ever-increasing pauperization, the law of capitalist concentration, and the law of correlation between economic and political power.[97] Other socialist theoreticians rejected a far larger proportion of the Marxist heritage. Why did a revisionist like Sorel so strongly defend those aspects of Marxism which he himself had attacked in the socioeconomic studies before *Introduction à l'économie moderne*?

The answer was related to the place that the theory of myths now held in his thinking: Sorel was becoming increasingly aware of the power of myth and of the role it can play as a catalyst for social action. He believed that the salient question was no longer whether the Marxist analysis of capitalism was scientifically correct, whether it simply reflected the economic realities of a certain period, or whether it provided a universally valid explanation—questions that preoccupied social democrats like Ferri, Turati, and Jaurès, orthodox Marxists like Kautsky, and people of Antonio Labriola's ideological orientation. No, that was not the question at all. Because he believed that these debates were beside the main point—the revolutionary action of the proletariat—he decided to initiate the veritable metamorphosis that he was to bring about in Marxism. This metamorphosis became fully possible only when Sorel had liberated himself from his old "rationalistic prejudices," like those, for instance, which he still at that period expressed in an article entitled "The Social Value of Art."[98] The rationalistic conception of aesthetics underlying that article of 1901 would have been unthinkable a few years later. The idea of a permanent struggle against the bourgeoisie required an antirationalistic revision of Marxism. Before this found its full expression in *Réflexions sur la violence* and *La Décomposition du marxisme*, a first sketch of it was given in the last pages of *Introduction à l'économie moderne*.

If Sorel refused to abandon these celebrated "dogmas" of Marxist thought, held by the great majority of European socialists to have lost their scientific validity on account of the direction that the evolution of capitalism took, it was because he had understood that there was no relationship between the truth of a doctrine and its operational value as a weapon of combat. If the most questionable elements of Marxist thought were suddenly so important to Sorel (he said they contained "something essential to the life and progress of socialism"), it was solely because of their apocalyptic character. "It is probable," he wrote, "that Marx already presented the catastrophic conception only as a myth that very clearly illustrated the class struggle and the social revolution." What mattered was that "the *contested theories*" were "necessitated by modern revolutionary action." Sorel claimed that these theories, "which the scholars of socialism no longer accept, but which the militants consider as axioms beyond all question," ought to be "treated as myths."[99] In this connection, Sorel insisted that "Marx was much more felicitous in his expositions of the revolutionary movement than in his perceptions of earlier episodes." According to Sorel, Marxism was thus above all a philosophy of revolutionary action. Sorel also quoted Bernstein, who "a few years ago advised the socialists to concern themselves with the *movement* and not with the *end* to which the revolution will perhaps conduce."[100] At the same time, he wrote, "I wonder if it is possible to give an intelligible explanation of the passage from principles to action without employing myths."[101] The theory of myths thus became the true underpinning of Sorelian thought and the mainspring of the revision of Marxism by the "new school." Launched by people who hoped that "socialism would renew the world,"[102] the Sorelian revision of Marxism was created to provide a theoretical framework for the labor revolt that smoldered at the beginning of the century, and for the purpose of saving an entire civilization from decadence.

For the Platonic conception dominant in *Le Procès de Socrate*, the theory of myths replaced the Bergsonian conception outlined in *Introduction à l'économie moderne* and fully developed in *Réflexions sur la violence*. Sorel used myth as a real operational tool, as a means of generating action, and he conferred on it an absolute value. He then took myth out of the sphere of the intellect and placed it in that of affectivity and activity. Thus, the Sorelian myth possessed two characteristic dimensions: on one hand, it was a new type of thought, and on the other hand it aimed to give rise to a new type of political action. Mythical thought, Sorel believed, was opposed to reflective and discursive thought; it was a religious way of thinking that rebelled against the rationalistic. This type of thought had an immediate function: to mobilize the masses and to change the world. Sorelian myth had an incomparable power of evocation and incitement to action; it was regarded as an inexhaustible source of regeneration, moral improvement, and heroism.[103] Myth was thought and action; it was a creator of legend, and it enabled the individual to live that legend instead of living out history. It enabled one to pass beyond a detestable present, armed with a faith that nothing could destroy. That is why myths and rationality were opposed in Sorel. Because of this opposition he regarded myth as a social force. By galvanizing the masses, it permitted the social and economic reality of the beginning of the century to be surmounted.

Here, precisely, was where the originality of the Sorelian revision of Marxism lay. This way of thinking refused to bow to reality; it sought to be true to the revolutionary impulse of Marxism even if that meant abandoning its intellectual content. Thus, in relation to every variety of Marxism, Sorel appeared to be an absolute rebel. The theory of myths permitted the obstacles of the material world to be overcome and enabled the proletariat to fulfill its historic role. Hence, thanks to this irrational element of myth, a social polarization was effected. Class struggle, which the mechanisms of capitalism were unable to bring about, now became a historical force. The social reality that Sorel had analyzed and found to be terribly complex was suddenly of a luminous simplicity. The great question of human motivation was likewise suddenly simplified. Myth thus appeared to be an instrument of an extraordinary efficacy and possessed, moreover, the advantage of being totally immune to any failure. And finally, it defied classical rational analysis, thus rendering its active potential almost infinite.

Sorelian myths were "systems of images," that is, constructions that enabled "people who participate in great social movements" to conceive "their next action as images of battle ensuring the triumph of their cause." As "outstanding examples of myths," Sorel mentioned "those which were invented by primitive Christianity, by the Reformation, by the French Revolution"; in a similar manner and to the same degree, he wrote, "the general strike of the syndicalists and Marx's catastrophic revolution are myths." Sorel was perfectly aware of the importance of the invention of this irrationalistic interpretation of Marxism. "In employing the term *myth*," he wrote, "I believed I had made a lucky find, because in this way I avoided any discussion with people who wish to submit the general strike to a detailed criticism and raise objections to its practical possibility." The potential of this "theory of myths" lay in the fact that it not only eluded "any control by intellectualistic philosophy" but gave an intelligibility to historical phenomena, psychological reflexes, and modes of behavior "that intellectualistic philosophy cannot explain." Sorel claimed that "intellectualistic philosophy"—that is, traditional philosophy—revealed its impotence whenever it had to explain the propensity to self-sacrifice of the soldiers of the Napoleonic armies, Roman virtue, or the Greeks' love of glory. What could rationalism do with "the myth of the Church Militant?" he asked. Sorel concluded that "intellectualistic philosophy truly suffers from a radical incompetence with regard to the explanation of the great historical movements."[104]

Sorel did not examine the content of myths. He never even defined the term *myth*. He focused on myths' social function; his myths were "social myths" that had to be regarded "as means of influencing the present."[105] "I wished to show that one should not seek to analyze such systems of images by breaking them up into their component parts, that they have to be accepted in their totality as historical forces, and that one should above all avoid comparing accomplished facts with the representations that had been accepted before the action."[106]

The Sorelian "social myth" was "a picture" whose true dimensions could be grasped only "when the masses are stirred up." It "could not be broken up into parts that could be interpreted as historical descriptions," and it offered the immense advantage of being "safe from all refutation."[107] Sorel returned to this idea several times: "It is thus of little importance whether myths contain details that do in fact form part of future history. They are not astrological almanacs; it can even happen that nothing that is in them comes to pass, as was the case with the catastrophe expected by the early Christians."[108]

In a passage of great importance, where he again insisted on the impotence of rational analysis with respect to the new conception of human behavior he had put forward, Sorel summarized his thought as follows:

> Myths must be regarded as means of influencing the present. Any discussion about relating them concretely to the course of history is senseless. *It is only the myth as a whole that matters*: its parts are of interest only insofar as they set off the idea contained in its construction. There is therefore little use in speculating about the incidents that can happen in the course of the social struggle or about the crucial conflicts that can bring victory to the proletariat. Even if the revolutionaries would be entirely mistaken in fantasizing about the idea of the general strike, this idea could be a factor of the utmost importance in the process of preparing the revolution if it embodies in a perfect manner all the aspirations of socialism and if it gives revolutionary thought as a whole a precision and exactitude that other ways of thinking could not have provided.

To appreciate the significance of the idea of the general strike, one must thus abandon all the forms of discussion that are usual among politicians, sociologists, and people who lay claim to practical knowledge. One can concede to one's adversaries all they are trying to prove without in any way diminishing the value of the thesis they believe they are refuting. It is of little importance if the general strike is only a partial reality or only a product of the popular imagination. The whole question is whether the general strike contains all that the socialist doctrine expects of the revolutionary proletariat.[109]

Sorel claimed that although there had seldom been "any myths entirely devoid of an utopian admixture," the "present-day revolutionary myths" were "almost devoid of it. They enable one to understand the activities, sentiments, and ideas of the popular masses entering a decisive struggle." The general strike was a myth of this kind. "The element that makes the general strike so important," he wrote, is its "value as a motive force." The idea of the general strike demonstrated once again that one "can talk endlessly about rebellion without ever giving rise to a revolutionary movement if there are no myths accepted by the masses." However, from the moment one "introduces the myth of the general strike, which amounts to an absolute revolution," everything becomes easy, clear, and well defined. First, socialism regains the sense it had for Marx, who also saw it as having the function of a revolutionary apprenticeship for the proletariat. It ceases to be "a doctrine entirely expressed in words" which can easily be deflected toward the middle of the road—that is, toward democratic socialism. Since "the myth of the general strike became popular and was soundly entrenched in people's minds,"[110] a new, young, and vigorous force rose up "in the face of that noisy, talkative, and mendacious kind of socialism that is exploited by the ambitious of every sort, amuses a few wags, and is admired by the decadent."[111]

Sorel's great ambition, as we saw, was, "instead of commentating" the texts of Marx, as "his wretched disciples had done for so long," "to complete his doctrine." For this purpose, he had recourse to Bergson; "by using the insights we owe to Bergsonian philosophy" he hoped to "deepen the theory of myths," which he made the center of his revision of Marxism. From Bergson, Sorel learned that "to act freely is to regain possession of oneself; it is to replace oneself in pure duration." "We enjoy this liberty," wrote Sorel, "above all when we make an effort to create within us a new man with the purpose of transcending the historical frameworks that confine us."[112] This idea is of absolute importance for an understanding of Sorel's thought; according to his conception, the individual formed in the syndicates was a producer and a warrior, nurtured on heroic values, like the early Christians, the Roman legionnaires, the soldiers of the revolutionary wars, and the disciples of Mazzini. He was a combatant avid for glory, full of abnegation, and ever ready for sacrifice, like the soldiers of Napoleon. Sustained by myths, these men did not expect concrete and immediate results; they abhorred the useful and were enamored of the sublime. They were the only people able to dominate history.

From Bergson, Sorel learned that "movement is the essence of the affective life. It is thus in terms of movement that one should speak of the creative consciousness." And farther on he wrote: "When we act, that means we have created an entirely artificial world placed in front of the present and formed out of movements that depend on us. In this way our liberty becomes entirely intelligible." The operational conclusion that Sorel drew from this was that "these artificial worlds generally disappear from our minds without leaving a trace, but when the masses are aroused there is a phenomenon that can be described as a social myth."[113]

Where the correction and completion of Marxism were concerned, Bergson's teachings were very convenient, for they enabled the rationalistic content of Marxism to be replaced by "revolutionary myths." It was no longer a question of economic or sociological laws or of historical or political analysis. Myths, wrote Sorel, "are not a description of things, but expressions of will,"[114] and "groups of images that can evoke as a totality through intuition alone, before any reasoned analysis, the mass of sentiments that correspond to the various manifestations of the war waged by socialism against modern society."[115] Later, the same formula was repeated word for word, although in an abbreviated form, to describe the general strike in terms of myth.[116] Again, the myth was described as "identical with the convictions of a group," convictions of which it was "the expression in the language of movement,"[117] and it presented itself "to the spirit with the insistence of instincts in all circumstances of life."[118] It was thus logical that it permitted an "intuition of socialism that language was unable to provide with perfect clarity."[119] Sorel was aware of the analogy between "revolutionary socialism" thus conceived and religion. He knew that anything that claimed to be above science and beyond criticism was comparable to religion. Here Sorel once again had recourse to what he called the "new psychology": Bergson, he wrote, "taught us that religion was not alone in occupying the depths of the consciousness. The revolutionary myths have a place there to the same degree." By a suitable employment of this method, Sorel hoped to make possible the "apprenticeship, preparation, and reconstruction of the individual in view of a gigantic operation."[120]

Bergsonian philosophy not only had the function of completing Marxism, but also replaced what was essential in Marxism, and while retaining the vocabulary and the revolutionary objective of Marxism, it radically altered its content. It was no accident that Sorel extolled the virtues of Bergsonian thought precisely in those places where he deplored Marx's "numerous and sometimes enormous" errors. In Sorel's view, Bergsonian thought, while divesting it of its rationalist content, restored all the dynamism of Marxism, held, as it was, in the stranglehold of a Kautsky-type orthodoxy, or, even worse, mired in the idle prattle of reformism. Under the influence of Bergsonian anti-Cartesianism, Marxism, in Sorel's eyes, became once again what it ought never to have stopped being: an ideology of action inspiring a proletarian movement devoted to the destruction of the existing order. Sorel believed that revolutionary syndicalism represented the fullest practical application of Bergson's thought. "In concentrating all of socialism in the general strike," he wrote, the revolutionary syndicalists were applying a method that "has all the advantages that total consciousness possesses over analysis in Bergson's doctrine." Moreover, he added, "Movement, in Bergsonian philosophy, is regarded as an indivisible whole—which brings us precisely to the catastrophic conception of socialism."[121]

Thanks to Bergson, revolutionary syndicalism succeeded in liberating itself from "official" Marxism. Taking its inspiration from Bergson, it yielded to the facts and went back to the roots. Only in this way, wrote Sorel, does one achieve "what Bergson calls an *integral experience*." Sorel was convinced that through Bergsonian spiritualism it was possible to break free from the shackles of social-democratic scholasticism and from Marx's heavy yet flimsy German-manufactured explanations, and, by following "exactly the contemporary transformations of the proletarian idea," to "perfect Marxism."[122] Bergson enabled socialism to liberate itself from the "vain and false science" that supposed "that everything can be ascribed to a mathematical law."[123] Sorel called this "petty science," which was opposed by philosophy and which he associated with positivism. Positivism, he said, had threatened to kill philosophy, but philosophy "is not dead and has had a splendid reawakening thanks to Bergson." Metaphysics had regained its "rights by showing people the illusion of so-called scientific solutions and by taking the spirit back to the mysterious region that *petty science abhors*." Positivism ("petty science"), which with Comte had succeeded in creating a caricature of Catholicism, was disparaged, he wrote, even in cultivated circles that now mocked "the rationalism formerly in fashion at the university." In this connection Sorel mentioned Pascal, who had protested "against those who consider obscurity an objection to Catholicism," and firmly supported him as the figure who, like Brunetière at the turn of the century, was in his opinion the most anti-Cartesian philosopher of his time.[124]

Sorel thought that precisely this mysterious and obscure aspect of a system of thought or of a social phenomenon constituted its greatness. It enabled one to avoid having to take one's stand "on utilitarian grounds," and it allowed one to have, for instance, a total faith in the general strike "even while knowing it is a myth."[125] The obscurity of socialism did not prevent it

from being easy to represent the proletarian movement in a complete, exact, and compelling way by means of the great construction that the proletarian soul conceived in the course of social conflicts and that is called the general strike.

One should always remember that the perfection of this form of representation would immediately disappear if one sought to split the general strike into an accumulation of historical details. *It must be regarded as an undivided whole; and the passage from capitalism to socialism must be conceived as a catastrophe whose process defies description.*[126]

Sorel believed that by evolving within this mythical and irrational sphere socialism would succeed in overcoming the "crisis of Marxism" that *"petty science"* had "greatly contributed to creating."[127] The "characteristic of infinity" of the myth of the general strike at one and the same time gave socialism "such a high moral value and inspired so great a loyalty,"[128] and gave it that absolute confidence in the future which constitutes the greatness of true revolutionary movements, for ever since it had become a work of preparation, ever since it had been nurtured by the myth of the general strike, "a failure," he wrote, "could not prove anything against socialism."[129] Ever since it had expressed itself in the myth of the general strike, socialism had ceased to be a mere model or an intellectual construction or abstraction.

This, according to Sorel, was precisely the great difference between myth and utopia: a utopia is only an intellectual construction that can be analyzed and discussed and that can be refuted. A utopia directs people toward reforms, while "our present myths lead people to prepare themselves for a battle to destroy what exists."[130] They also enable one "to explore with profit the whole vast domain of Marxism."[131] What therefore remained of Marxism after it had been voided of its hedonistic and materialistic substance to the benefit of the mythical, voluntarist, vitalist, and quasi-metaphysical content proposed by Sorel was its function as an instrument of revolution. From being a heavy, ossified, and powerless machine, Marxism, revised, improved, and completed by Sorel, had now become an impressive mobilizing force.

The heroic episode of the strikes thus found its ideological justification. The myth of the general strike, wrote Sorel, had given rise to a "rich and sublime socialist ideology,"[132] an ideology of struggle that made "the fundamental principles of Marxism" intelligible for the first time. Indeed, this new significance of a Marxism voided of its rationalist content and transformed by Bergsonism permitted the ideas of class and of class struggle to be given back their original function. The strike, wrote Sorel, gave reality to the "dichotomous thesis" of a society "split into two fundamentally antagonistic groups." Owing to the strike, society was "clearly divided into two camps, and only two, upon a battlefield." The myth of the general strike gave strikes a completely new significance. Because of it, each particular conflict had the character of an "incident" in a general "social war," and every local strike, however insignificant in itself, created "the prospect of a total catastrophe." The idea of the general strike ensured that "socialism always remains young" and "the split is never in danger of disappearing."[133]

The myth of the general strike, the mobilizing myth par excellence, had another great advantage. Sorel had learned from Le Bon that the "crowd" is essentially conservative. Sorel had great respect for Le Bon, whom he regarded as "one of the most original scientists of our time," and was one of the first people to acclaim his work. Sorel understood the importance of the psychological factor in the process of integrating working-class elements into the bourgeois order: "Self-love, even more than money, is the great motive force in the transition from revolt to the bourgeoisie." But this did not apply only in rare or exceptional cases; "the psychology of the laboring masses was so easily adaptable to the capitalist order that social peace" could easily be bought by the bourgeoisie. To arrest the process of the integration of the proletariat into the bourgeois order, to tear the producers out of the grip of the intellectuals, and to "make the socialist idea more heroic"—these were the functions of the concept of the general strike, and it was in this way that this concept, according to Sorel, reflected Marx's true thinking.[134]

The intellectual, emotional, and psychological motive force of a reformed and heroic Marxism, the theory of myths found its concrete expression in proletarian violence. Here we are not using naive metaphors, but we are speaking of immediate political solutions for the purpose of altering a blocked situation. Since Marxist expectations had not been fulfilled, and since the proletariat had not been "united and organized by the sheer mechanism of production"[135] and did not find itself face-to-face with a vigorous capitalist class that was "frankly and loyally reactionary,"[136] since, in short, the revolution did not and would not take place on its own, the defective deterministic mechanism had to be replaced with a will to revolution. The theory of myths thus became the motive force of the revolution, and violence became its instrument. The use of the theory of myths and the advocacy of violence made Marx accessible: "Marx wished to tell us that the whole preparation of the proletariat depended solely on the organization of a stubborn, growing, and passionate resistance to the existing order of things."[137] This preparation was made through "the *direct and revolutionary method.*"[138]

But, after all, Marx had not foreseen the new situation that had arisen. He had not been able to imagine a bourgeoisie that would avoid a fight, agree to reduce its power, and be willing to purchase social tranquillity at any price. Nor had he predicted that capitalism, which would modernize the world with unprecedented speed, would fail to accomplish its social purpose and to create a united, organized proletariat, conscious of its power and mission. Marx could not foresee that modernization would have results that from the technological point of view were extraordinary but from the social, moral, and political points of view were disastrous. He was able to anticipate neither the bourgeois decadence nor the proletarian decadence. He could not conceive that the socialist parties, those proletarian parties once conscious of their mission, would become instruments of class collaboration and would concoct democratic socialism. Marx could not imagine that in order to save the proletariat and, at the same time, civilization as well, it would be necessary to create everything artificially: class consciousness, will to struggle, social polarization. He could not picture a situation in which, in order to prevent civilization from sinking into decadence, one had to restore the appetites of the bourgeoisie and the ardor of the proletariat. He could not foresee a state of affairs in which the official syndical organization became "a variety of politics, a means of getting on in the world," any more than he could conceive of a situation in which "the republican government and the philanthropists took it into their heads to exterminate socialism by developing social legislation and reducing employers' resistance to strikes."[139] In that case, "should one believe the Marxist conception is dead? Not at all, for proletarian violence comes on the scene just at the moment when social tranquillity tries to calm the conflicts. Proletarian violence encloses the employers in their role of producers and restores the structure of the classes just as the latter had seemed to mix together in a democratic quagmire." Sorel added that "the more the bourgeoisie will be ardently capitalist and the more the proletariat will be full of a fighting spirit and confident of its revolutionary force, the more will movement be assured." This was especially the case because he considered this division of classes to be "the basis of all socialism." This is what created "the idea of a catastrophic revolution" and would finally enable "socialism to fulfill its historical role."[140]

In a key passage of his *Réflexions*, Sorel described the role of violence as follows:

> This violence forces capitalism to preoccupy itself entirely with its material role and restores to it the bellicose qualities that it formerly possessed. A growing and solidly organized working class can force the capitalist class to remain vigorous in industrial combat. If, in the face of a bourgeoisie that is wealthy and eager for conquest, a united and revolutionary proletariat rises up, capitalist society will attain its historical perfection.
>
> Thus, proletarian violence has become a central factor of Marxism. We should add, once again, that it would have the effect, if properly employed, of suppressing parliamentary socialism, which would no longer be considered the master of the working class and the guardian of order.[141]

However—and this is an essential element in his thought—violence in Sorel is not solely an instrument; it constitutes a value in itself inasmuch as it "serves the primary interests of civilization." It "thus appears as something very beautiful and very heroic," for "not only can proletarian violence ensure the future revolution, but it seems to be the only means by which the European nations, deadened by humanism, can regain their former energy." By means of proletarian violence the world will be saved from barbarism, and the revolutionaries will enter into history like the defenders of Thermopylae, who "helped maintain the light in the ancient world."[142]

Undoubtedly, the barbarism in question is found in bourgeois decadence and in the rejection of heroic and martial values. War, precisely, was for Sorel the source of morality par excellence: "Lofty moral convictions . . . do not depend on reasoning or on the training of the individual will; they depend on a state of war in which men agree to participate, and which is expressed in precise myths." The religious struggles and the revolutionary wars, the fight against the devil or for liberty, the sacrifices of the early Christians or the Protestant sects, the struggle of the liberals against the ancien régime or of the German socialists persecuted by Bismarck, are many illustrations of one and the same truth, namely, that only people who live in a state of permanent tension are able to attain the "sublime." The idea of the sublime is mentioned fourteen times in the eleven pages of the *Réflexions* where Sorel deals with this question! This expression is synonymous with the epic and the heroic, with sacrifice, abnegation, and altruism. Morals can exist only when people lead the hard life of the combatant and when the sense of duty is paramount. It is totally incompatible with utilitarianism, materialism, egoism, and probabilism. That is why, wherever one has the idea of the general strike, wherever the struggle is fiercest, wherever blows are exchanged, the "consequences are far-reaching and can give rise to the sublime."[143]

Just as there are two types of general strike—the proletarian and the political—and two socialisms—proletarian socialism and the socialism of the politicians—so, according to Sorel, there are two different kinds of war: the heroic kind celebrated by poets which inspires the noblest and purest sentiments and the war whose object is to divide the adversary's spoils and to "allow politicians to satisfy their ambitions." The syndicalist general strike is related to an ancient tradition: "The proletariat organizes itself for battle . . . subordinating all social considerations to that of combat. It has a very clear sentiment of the glory attached to its historic role and of the heroism of its militant attitude; it aspires to the crucial test in which it will give the full measure of its value."[144]

For Sorel, certainly, proletarian violence did not necessarily require a great show of brutality, apart from that which is inherent in acts of war. Sorel, who never had much respect for the French Revolution and the "great ancestors," hated Jacobinism. If, on one hand, he was careful to distinguish proletarian violence—the violence of soldiers avid for honor and glory, a "neutral" violence, if one may say so, devoid of hatred or ferocity—from the bourgeois use of force, which represented a kind of state terrorism,[145] he took pains, on the other hand, to distinguish proletarian violence from revolutionary terror. He considered Danton and Robespierre as despicable as Jaurès, whom he regarded as "capable of all ferocities against the vanquished." In his opinion, Jaurès, who in his *Histoire socialiste de la Révolution française* "mixed a philosophy sometimes worthy of M. Pantalon with the politics of a purveyor of guillotines," was the prototype of the bloodthirsty democratic politician, as were the "terrorists" of 1793. Political customs hardly change, and Robespierre, through the legitimate function of the parliamentary institutions of that period, was put to death on the day he no longer enjoyed a majority in the National Convention. As against this, Sorel declared that proletarian violence "has no connection with these penalties," and there is no need "for blood to be shed in torrents."[146]

Ferocity and brutality, according to Sorel, were characteristic of Jacobin and bourgeois democracy; they were natural to a government of intellectuals, just as the cult of the state (which, in Sorelian thought, was merely an aspect of bourgeois power) was shared by all politicians, whether socialist, liberal, or conservative. Sorel hated political authoritarianism, of whatever kind; the bourgeois state and the dictatorship of the proletariat were in his opinion very much alike. Like Bernstein, he thought that the dictatorship of the proletariat would only divide society into "masters and enslaved" and could only result in bringing the proletariat under the orders of a small group of politicians. Consequently, Sorel wanted the suppression of the state, which, at the same time, would mean the end of the reign of intellectuals, heads of political parties, and parliaments. In order to eliminate the pernicious effects of democratic socialism and to counter the "elite of politicians" who wanted to use the state in order to rule over the proletariat and enslave it, revolutionary syndicalism wished to create a workshop of freemen. Against this "prudent socialism" which could conceive of no other solution than to "change masters" in favor of the "mass of producers," Sorel appealed to the spirit of rebellion of these same producers who were the only people able to save civilization from the abyss into which bourgeois decadence was drawing it. Thanks to proletarian violence, he wrote, "the modern world possesses the primum mobile that can ensure the morality of the producers."[147]

In his celebrated article "Apologie de la violence," published in *Le Matin* on 18 May 1908, Sorel gave a summary of his thought. Thus, according to this article, a strike was a phenomenon of war, and social revolution was an extension of this war of which each major strike was an episode. The social war, "calling forth the honor that develops so naturally in every organized army," gave "revolutionary syndicalism a great civilizing value," just as formerly war "gave the ancient republics the ideas that are the ornament of modern culture." Similarly, the revolutionary syndicalists, for whom socialism boiled down to "the idea, the expectation, the preparation of the general strike," in undertaking this "grave, fearful, and sublime work . . . raise themselves above our frivolous society and make themselves worthy of teaching the world new paths."[148]

Sorel maintained that in order to save morality and ensure its permanent survival, one had to "change its motivations," one had to summon up the forces of enthusiasm, sacrifice, asceticism, love of glory, and altruism. One had to arouse violence, destroy utilitarianism, materialism, liberalism, and democracy (corrupt and corrupting by nature), and suppress the base and servile parliamentary socialism.[149] In other words, one must destroy all ideologies based on the idea that the well-being of the individual is the purpose of any social organization. One must liberate oneself from positivism as from the banal and complacent optimism of materialists of every kind.

Pessimism is another key element for understanding Sorelian thought. That too was a fundamental aspect of the revision of Marxism. The *Réflexions*, Sorel insisted, were based on pessimism, "a doctrine without which nothing very lofty is achieved in the world." If "Greek philosophy did not have great moral results, it was because it was generally highly optimistic. Socrates was, sometimes to an almost intolerable degree."[150] In *Réflexions*, Sorel returned to what he had already said in his first work, *Le Procès de Socrate*, in order to condemn optimism once more. In *Les Illusions du progrès,* he continued at length to develop his case against Cartesian rationalism and the philosophy of the Enlightenment.

In these themes we can see the true continuity of Sorelian thought. Sorel searched a great deal, but he never changed his fundamental concepts. Antirationalism and pessimism, the cult of heroic ages and values, and a horror of the Enlightenment were basic to his thinking from *Le Procès de Socrate* to his introduction to *Matériaux d'une théorie du prolétariat*. In *Le Procès de Socrate*, he distinguished between two types of ethics: a warrior ethics and an intellectual ethics. The warrior stood for the heroic values of the ancient city, the intellectual for the decadence of the Enlightenment. "In the new Athens . . . ," wrote Sorel, "the ancient civilization, religious and heroic," was destroyed by the Sophists.[151] The prototype of the dialectical, reasoning Sophist, corrupter of morals and manners, was Socrates.[152] All the innovators were condemned with him; the decadence began with the contempt with which the new philosophers regarded Homer, symbol of ancient society.[153] Then came the emancipation of women, "the new social organization based on the fictive family," and the democracy of Pericles.[154] The horror Sorel felt for the open society of the fifth century, the "electoral regime" where "capabilities were overlooked for the benefit of politicians and the déclassés," was exceeded only by his abhorrence of the idea of a "government of scholars."[155] The result of the philosophers' actions, according to Sorel, would be that "there would no longer be any soldiers or sailors, but only skeptical and witty shopkeepers." Ancient society, "based on military discipline, the preparation for war," was ruined by "these famous dialecticians," and that is why Athens descended "to the level of the Italian republics."[156] The intellectuals had taken over from the protagonists of the closed society, who, for their part, "thought that one could form heroic generations only by the old method of nurturing youth on heroic poems."[157] Sorel concluded by describing the cardinal sin of the intellectuals: "The great weakness of the Socratic schools was their optimism. One cannot rouse the masses by singing the praises of order, harmony, and the rationality of existing things."[158]

In contrast to the moral and intellectual corruption disseminated by the Socratics, ancient civilization was sustained by Homeric myths, and as long as these myths survived and the spirit of the heroes of Marathon prevailed, ancient Greece was strong, because brave and disciplined. Here for the first time Sorel expressed the idea, which he never abandoned, that a civilization based on myths is always superior to a rationalistic and materialistic civilization. Socrates and the Sophists were thus guilty before the tribunal of history, and the condemnation to death of Socrates, that carrier of the germs of decadence, must be regarded as a measure of public safety. The obsession with decadence and the hatred of the bourgeois values and spirit were throughout his intellectual career the two great permanent features of Sorel's thought. The theoretician of proletarian violence came to Marxism precisely because, from the beginning of his development, he was preoccupied with the problem of discovering the factors that cause the end of a civilization and those which, on the contrary, permit a regeneration and a new departure. He also came, however, because he believed he had found in Marxism the most extraordinary weapon of war against bourgeois society ever invented. Sorel was concerned with the problem of decadence from his first book; in *La Ruine du monde antique*, he castigated the bourgeois spirit because it was hostile "to the ancient conception of the heroic society." He thought that the same principle applied in all modern countries; if "the military spirit grows weaker and the bourgeois spirit becomes predominant, the social idea grows weaker also."[159] The disintegration of the modern world can be averted only if "the worker in heavy industry replaces the warrior of the heroic society, and machines replace weapons."[160]

Because he was a moralist whose thinking was haunted by the specter of decadence, Sorel regarded politics first as an ethics. For this reason, he reproached Socrates for having "confused morality, law, and knowledge" and consequently for representing "only probabilism in morals, the arbitrary in politics."[161] This was Sorel's main accusation against Socrates: "That whole philosophy leaves us without moral certitude. The good is assessed according to a probabilistic scale of values."[162] That is why Sorel thought that Socrates' accusers were by no means wrong in claiming that he threatened society and corrupted youth: his ethics "were detestable" and socially destructive.[163] Indeed, all of Sorel's work was marked by a search for moral certitude, a way of achieving "moral reform."[164]

Sorel's follower Édouard Berth was quite right in claiming in his article on Sorel in *Clarté* on the occasion of Sorel's death that Sorel's main concern was "to discover if any force existed that could save the modern world from a ruination similar to that which overtook the ancient world."[165] Sorel thought it natural for human nature to slide toward decadence.[166] This drift toward catastrophe therefore had to be stopped; society had to be saved from death and regenerated. If individuals are to resist passions and temptations, to preserve and develop a sense of duty and honor, they need to find something outside themselves that escapes the corrupting influence of modern life. It was to the search for this all-important element that Sorel devoted his entire existence, and that is why his ideas varied so much, without his ever concealing his own variations.

As a study of Athenian society and thought in the time of Socrates, *Le Procès de Socrate* is of only slight interest. One finds, for instance, the statement that "the *Symposium* and the *Republic*" are "two books that dishonor the Greek genius."[167] But the main point of the work lies elsewhere. Throughout the book, Sorel's intention is to draw a parallel between Socratic times and the eighteenth and nineteenth centuries. According to him, Socrates, Descartes, Voltaire, Rousseau, the Jacobins, and the politicians of the end of the nineteenth century belonged to the same lineage.[168] Socrates and the Sophists destroyed Homeric morality; that of the modern world was undermined and then destroyed by the eighteenth century, Jacobinism, positivism, democracy, the money grubbers, and the intellectuals. Sorel was on the side of Anytus. He too opposed the pleasure-seeking bourgeoisie who corrupted the age and practiced the cult of success. He wanted an austere society and a revival of pessimistic values basic to Christian morality.

ANTI-CARTESIANISM AND PESSIMISM

For Sorel, deeply influenced by Eduard von Hartmann,[169] pessimism represented the spearhead of the great struggle against decadence. Pessimism had three aspects. First, it was "far more a metaphysics of morals than a theory of the world"; it was "the conception of a path toward deliverance." Second, it was an awareness of objective obstacles "to the satisfaction of our imaginations." Third—and this was its substance—it was the expression of "a profound conviction of our natural weakness."[170] Only a civilization steeped in pessimism could achieve greatness, for it embodied the great historical forces and the great human virtues: heroism, sacrifice, and asceticism. Pessimism gave birth to the idea of apocalypse and originated the idea of myth. In early Christianity, wrote Sorel, "we find a pessimism that is wholly developed and fully armed." The consciousness of "belonging to a sacred army . . . produced many heroic actions, created a courageous propaganda, and gave rise to serious moral progress." Greek pessimism, steeped in heroism, was the product of "poor, warlike mountain tribes," while the optimism of the philosophers came into being among rich, commercial urban populations "that could regard the world as a huge emporium full of

excellent things with which to satisfy their cupidity." Sorel pointed out that
oriental asceticism is often considered a remarkable manifestation of pessimism, while sixteenth-century Calvinism "offers us a spectacle that is perhaps even more instructive"; the dogmas of sin and predestination "correspond to the two primary aspects of pessimism: the wretchedness of the
human race and social determinism."[171]

Optimism, wrote Sorel, contains all "the illusions of a commonplace philosophy." Beguiled by the successes of material civilizations, the optimist is
of the opinion that universal happiness is going to come automatically to
everyone. Sorel, like Hartmann, believed that the contemporary masters of
the world were propelled into an optimistic mode of thought by economic
forces. Materialistic, egoistic, and superficial, the optimist in politics is "an
unstable and even dangerous person because he is unaware of the great
difficulties presented by his projects." If, by some misfortune, that person is
in a position of great power, "the optimist can lead a country to the worst
catastrophes." Instead of explaining "the evolution of things by historical
necessity, he is liable to do away with people whose ill will seems to him
dangerous to the general happiness." Moreover, "the optimist passes with a
remarkable facility from revolutionary anger to the most ridiculous social
pacifism."[172] This has been seen as a portrait of the Jacobin or the social
democrat, Robespierre or Jaurès—all "partisans of natural rights," all fanati-
cal proponents of rationalism.[173]

The series of articles entitled *Les Illusions du progrès*, which had been
published in the journal *Le Mouvement socialiste* from August to December
1906 before being collected into a volume, continued the condemnation of
rationalism begun in *Réflexions*. Here Sorel went into the history of ideas; he
claimed to approach the subject as a "Marxist historian."[174] In what did this
Marxist attitude consist? Sorel quoted a passage of the *Communist Manifesto*
containing the famous sentence "The dominant ideas [*herrschenden Ideen*]
of a period have always been those of the dominant class." Thus, since "the
theory of progress was conceived as a dogma at the period when the bourgeoisie was the rising class," anyone employing the Marxist method must
"investigate how it [the theory of progress] depends on the conditions in
which one observes the formation, ascension, and triumph of the bourgeoisie."[175] The conception that the dominant class produced the dominant idea
of its period and the principle of class struggle were the essence of Sorelian
Marxism in 1906. It was a Marxism perceived as a method, a working tool,
and a weapon of combat, a Marxism whose rationalistic core was completely
rejected. Sorelian revisionism wanted to preserve Marxism, but by divesting
it of its postulates and its rationalistic philosophy. One could easily apply to
Sorel the explanation that he himself gave to another major change in the
intellectual history of Europe: "The Voltairean spirit disappeared," he
wrote, "when a literary revolution made the tools used by Voltaire ridicu-

lous. One could find few more remarkable examples of the influence of matter over thought."[176] And indeed, when Bergson and Nietzsche, Hartmann, Le Bon, and William James rendered the Marxist equipment obsolete, Sorel went off in search of a new weapon of combat.

The rejection of rationalism was the keystone of Sorelian revisionism, but Sorel did not confine himself to a criticism of positivist vulgarization, which at the beginning of the century was after all fairly commonplace. He chose a more difficult path and decided to attack the core of rationalism: Cartesianism. Undoubtedly, his criticism was often puerile. Thus, he used a second-rate writer like Brunetière as a support against Descartes.[177] But this hardly mattered; Spengler did much the same thing. By and large, what mattered was not the scientific value of the work but its impact and significance.

Sorel said that from the point of view of historical materialism, Cartesianism was a remarkable example of "the adoption of an ideology by a class that found in it the formulas that could express its own inclinations." This "garrulous rationalism" attacked religion; it was "resolutely optimistic"—which could not fail to please a society that wanted to enjoy itself freely—and it "reduced ethics to a rule of expediency that demanded a respect for established customs." This meant that "there was no Cartesian morality," and consequently everything to do with Cartesianism was no more than "literature conducive to nothing useful or certain." Descartes "never seemed to have been preoccupied with the meaning of life"—something suitable to people "who aspired to be liberated from the Christian yoke." Cartesianism was ideal for a society in which morals were slackened and in which superficiality, levity, scientific vulgarization, and "good sense" were dominant; it was an appropriate philosophy "for frequenters of salons." No one typified Cartesianism better than Fontenelle, that clever, mediocre, and influential vulgarizer. That society in which the fear of sin, the respect for chastity, and pessimism were disappearing, where women's morals were dissolute to say the least, and where Christianity had faded away to the point of vanishing, that society which wanted to have a good time and enjoy itself, needed to justify its behavior; it was thus only natural that the end of the seventeenth century should enthrone Descartes. French philosophy was henceforth distinguished by those "very special rationalist characteristics that make it agreeable to people of society."[178]

Cartesianism was also held to be the origin of the idea of "infinite progress."[179] Sorel wrote: "Pogress will always be an essential element in the great current that extends to modern democracy, because the doctrine of progress allows one, in full tranquillity, to enjoy the wealth of today without being concerned about the difficulties of tomorrow. It pleased the old society of idle aristocrats; it will always please the politicians whom democracy brings to power and who, threatened with an impending fall, want to use all the advantages that the state provides in order to profit their friends." Cartesian philosophy, according to Sorel, thus laid the foundations on which modern democracy was built. This democracy was a regime imbued with a science that had the pretension of inventing nature, in the manner of Descartes, and that had nothing in common "with the deep investigation of problems characteristic of true science based on prosaic reality."[180] In *Réflexions*, Sorel, we may remember, called this petty science. This "*bourgeois science*,"[181] he wrote, was all that rationalism could produce. This petty science gave people an unbounded confidence that through the use of reason they could resolve all the difficulties of daily life after having resolved all those which existed in cosmology. For that reason, wrote Sorel, if nowadays "one dares to protest against the illusion of rationalism, one is immediately considered an enemy of democracy."[182]

Sorel now turned to the eighteenth century and launched an attack on Condorcet, who completed the work of Turgot. Condorcet, he wrote, was an apologist for the vulgarization of knowledge, which was to favor democracy, and he approved "the change from literature to journalism, from science to the rationalism of the salons or discursive assemblies, from original investigation to declamation." This light-headed century, whose ideology was that of a bunch of clerks, gave itself up to "an orgy of abstractions." The greatest of these abstractions—Maurras called them "vapors"—was the contractual ideology, based on a conception of the individual as an atom of society and an abstract citizen. Locke's theory of natural rights was explained as being a perception of society as a simple commercial corporation. This rational, utilitarian, and optimistic doctrine passed into the teachings of the physiocrats, while the *Contrat social* "exalted the role of reason identified with the general will."[183]

Frivolous and superficial, the eighteenth century heralded the reign of men of letters, molders of opinion; it bequeathed to contemporary democracy "a secular, patriotic, and bourgeois catechism" that consecrated "the domination of charlatans." In order to describe the spirit of modern democracy, Sorel already invoked the authority of Léon Daudet, who called it a "philosophy of quasi-illiterates." Sorel, however, was not even sure whether democracy, which was based on a vulgarization of the vulgarization of the eighteenth century, merited that description. For that reason it was necessary first to cut the people off from the literature of the age of Voltaire and to liberate the proletariat from the hold of intellectuals infected by the culture of the Enlightenment. Next, one had to lay the foundations of a culture based on work and the experience of the workshop ("the feelings of affection that every truly qualified worker has for the forces of production confided to him") and on high-quality production regarded as an anticipation of art. The worker's relationship to the machine, the sense of sublimity engendered by the war of the proletariat against its masters, and the feeling of grandeur to be felt in revolutionary syndicalism could "serve as the basis of a culture that bourgeois culture could only envy." Based on a pure morality and a classical culture, the producers' civilization could escape democratic mediocrity and prevent the world from sinking into decadence.[184]

Socialism, furthermore, was to be something other than the moral and material corruption of democratic reformism. At the end of *Les Illusions*, Sorel recalled the wish he had expressed in 1899 that "socialism be transformed into a philosophy of morals. This change would infuse grandeur into a movement that lacked it at that time to more or less the same extent as democracy itself." For Sorel, the answer to the problem thus stated had been outlined in *Réflexions*, for only a revision of Marxism (the Sorelian revision, naturally!) could make socialism adopt a path in keeping with "the laws of greatness and decadence."[185]

Moralistic, spiritualistic, and antirationalistic, this revised, corrected, and truly transformed socialism invoked the authority of Pascal and Bergson ("between whom," wrote Sorel, "there was more than one similarity to be established")[186] against its mortal enemies, the intellectual progenitors of all evils, Socrates and Descartes. Sorel was fascinated by Pascal, just as he was dazzled by Bergsonian spiritualism. Pascal opposed atheism and was enthusiastic about miracles; he was thus held to be the perfect antithesis of Descartes, who cleared "the way for the Encyclopedists in reducing God to very little."[187] At a single stroke, which he hoped was definitive, Sorel rejected the core of the intellectual heritage of the seventeenth and eighteenth centuries: Descartes, Locke, and Rousseau; rationalism, optimism, the theory of progress, the theory of natural rights, and the conception of society as a collection of individuals. Sorel detested the atomistic conception of the individual that had prevailed since the time of Hobbes and Locke. He held it responsible for liberalism, democracy, and denatured socialism. At the same time, consistent with himself, he deplored the secularization of French life, a process, he said, that would never have taken place without a slackening of manners and the disappearance of morality.

Sorel, it should be pointed out, abandoned socialism around 1909, but his revolutionary appetite remained as strong as ever. Activism was the natural and necessary consequence of the theory of myths. Practice, for him, preceded theory, and only action really counted. The effectiveness of an act was much more important to him than its intrinsic qualities; neither Kantianism, nor the stoics, nor Proudhon, he said, seemed to have had much influence. In order for someone to throw himself or herself into action, "the conviction" has to "dominate the entire consciousness and to operate before the calculations of reflection have time to come into play."[188] That was why Sorel rejected any intellectual structure, which he called a utopia and to which he opposed the power of the mobilizing myth.

Unlike a myth, a utopia, wrote Sorel, may be broken up into its component parts; it permits one to have an idea of the future and to speculate about that future.[189] The rationalists—that is, the utopians—those "worshippers of vain and false science,"[190] deaden their capacity for action by refusing to submit to the forces of instinct and imagination. Bearers of abstractions, manufacturers of systems, optimists because they are rationalists, from So-crates to the niggling parliamentary socialists, the intellectuals have always corrupted everything: the Greek city undermined by Socratism, the austere classical culture steeped in faith, asceticism and pessimism destroyed by triumphant Cartesianism, the proletariat led astray by glib speakers and so-cial climbers from the universities. The new proletarian barbarism, bearer of sublimity, altruism, and socialism, had to be defended at all costs against the intellectual corruption of the "*civilized* socialism of our official doctors."[191] These same "doctors of *petty science* . . . ," wrote Sorel, "loudly declare that they will allow in their thinking only ideas that are clear and distinct. This, in fact, is an inadequate rule for action, for we do nothing great without highly colored and sharply drawn images that absorb all our attention."[192]

It should be pointed out that this was an attack not on bourgeois intellec-tuals (who were suspect to labor militants more or less everywhere in Eu-rope), but on rationalism, intellectualism, and positivism, and in fact on the scientific method itself where it was applied outside the limited area of the exact sciences.

If the proletariat was incapable of fulfilling its revolutionary role, this did not mean that the revolution had to be abandoned and the world delivered up to intellectualist and bourgeois decadence. With Sorel, one had a new kind of revolutionary impulse, based on a new form of rejection—the rejec-tion of a civilization that was undoubtedly bourgeois, but also rationalistic, deeply optimistic, and secular. The entire humanistic tradition was called in question, that is, the idea of the perfectibility of the individual and the unity of the human race. Of this rationalistic and fundamentally materialistic sys-tem whose utilitarian and instrumentalist concepts he detested, Sorel re-tained only the idea of class struggle and that of the catastrophic polarization that can be created by the power of the myth of the general strike. The ink expended on *Réflexions*, *Illusions*, and *La Décomposition du marxisme* had no sooner dried than the concept of class disintegrated, and all that re-mained of the Sorelian revision of Marxism was a horror of bourgeois, ration-alist, and secular civilization and an unshakable determination to destroy it.

Antirationalism was the real key to Sorelian thought in the first decade of the century. It was consequently natural that it should be the main theme of the foreword to his collection of essays gathered under the title *Matériaux d'une théorie du prolétariat*, in which, on the eve of the Great War, he sum-marized his position.

In this foreword, after having recalled his condemnation in *Les Illusions* of the "intellectualists of the eighteenth century" who had so praised both natural rights and "the ideas of progress, of regeneration and creation, of universal reason," Sorel once again attacked the rationalists who went astray "in historical scientism." Against the rationalism that "contaminates our symbols," that eliminates "as far as possible the psychological forces it encounters on its path" and dispatches us into utopia, Sorel invoked the pragmatism of William James. After his revision of Marxism, even Hegel was not acceptable to Sorel. Hegelian rationalism was replaced by James's pragmatism. Hegel, that "philosopher who managed to pass himself off as profound," was consigned to historical oblivion at the same time as "the founder of scientific socialism," who had been guilty of hoping "that the journals of social democracy would provide the proletarians with a teaching that would ensure the triumph of rationalism in a hyper-Hellenic world."[193] The Sorelian revision of Marxism now rejected not only the orthodox (Kautsky, Guesde, and Lafargue) and the reformists (Jaurès, Turati, and Enrico Ferri), but also Antonio Labriola.[194] The rejection of a whole culture steeped in rationalism, and the wish to see it disappear, made Sorel repudiate both Marx and Engels—naturally—and the Marxists of his own generation. Édouard Berth was right to see in *Réflexions* a clear sign of the end of Sorelian Marxism. In his conclusion to *Les Méfaits des intellectuels*, written in 1913 and symbolically entitled "The Victory of Pascal," Berth wrote: "In his *Réflexions sur la violence*, Sorel sought precisely to rescue the syndicalist philosophy from that insipid optimism, and his letter to Daniel Halevy, which is its preface, demonstrates the full historical value of pessimism. In this, syndicalism clearly separated itself from orthodox Marxism and even from Marxism as such, which still operated entirely on the plane of an optimistic and scientistic conception of life, that is to say, on a bourgeois plane, on an eighteenth-century plane."[195]

Sorel was perfectly aware of the evolution of his thought. On the eve of the war, when he was preparing the publication of *Matériaux*, he reminded the reader that in 1910 the Italian translation of his long article "Mes Raisons du syndicalisme" had been preceded by a short note announcing that the writer was now abandoning "socialist literature." The reasons that led him to this decision, he wrote in 1914, "have lost none of their cogency since then." At that time Sorel adopted as his own Croce's famous aphorism that "socialism is dead." But if socialism was dead, it was not only because of the intellectual process that Sorel described as the "decomposition of Marxism," but also for a far more serious reason. If the "magnificent epic" that Marx had dreamed up turned out to be only a mirage, if "the revolution foretold by Marx was chimerical," it was because the "heroic proletariat, creator of a new system of values, called upon to found, in a very short time, a civilization of producers on the ruins of capitalist society," did not exist anywhere and probably never would.[196] This proletariat, which Sorel still described in *Réflexions* as being in the process of organizing itself "for battle by separating itself completely from the other parts of the nation . . . , by subordinating all social considerations to that of the struggle," this pure and upright, pessimistic and ascetic proletariat that was supposed to regard itself as "the great motive force of history,"[197] showed itself to be as much corrupted by utilitarianism as the bourgeoisie. If the German workers "enrolled in the forces of democracy," it was because "the common man does not participate in a new enterprise unless seduced by the mirage of enormous benefits that seem almost certain and that are anticipated as coming to pass in a short time."[198]

For Sorel, this was undoubtedly the turning point. Ever since he wrote *L'Avenir socialiste des syndicats*, all his socialism was based on the principle that the "new school" had not invented anything, as there was nothing to invent; the producers in their workshops created socialism, and the role of the intellectuals—who had to place themselves at the service of the proletariat—was only to provide the theory of the labor revolt. And now the discovery of a proletariat so similar to the bourgeoisie in its motives, preoccupations, ideas, and behavior dealt a death blow to Sorelian socialism.

Finally, someone who persisted in rejecting the existing order had no choice but to turn toward the true revolutionary force that emerged at the beginning of the century. The Sorelians shared with nationalism a horror of bourgeois democracy, the eighteenth century, the secular spirit, and the French Revolution but also a respect for classical tradition and culture. Sorel's vigorous campaign against the philosophy of the Enlightenment explains his attractiveness for the Maurrassians; this was the common ground between the revolutionaries, who had come from a Marxism divested of its materialistic and rationalistic essence, and the integral nationalists, promoters of a nationalism likewise divested of its materialistic and rationalistic essence—that is, its liberalism, its individualism, and its conception of society as an aggregate of individuals. Antimaterialism was undoubtedly the common denominator and meeting point of the two nonconformist currents of the period.

THE JUNCTION OF SORELIANISM AND NATIONALISM

Sorel came round to integral nationalism during the summer of 1909. In April of that year, after having read the second edition of *Enquête sur la monarchie*, he had already expressed his admiration for Charles Maurras, the founder of l'Action française.[199] Three months later, on 10 July, he published in Enrico Leone's *Divenire sociale*, the leading journal of Italian revolutionary syndicalism, a rousing tribute to Maurrassism, which *L'Action française* reprinted on 22 August under the title "Antiparliamentary Socialists." This article announced a meeting "at the summit" of integral nationalism and the Sorelian version of revolutionary syndicalism—a meeting, but not a real operational synthesis, which was to be achieved by the younger generation of French and Italian Sorelians.

The short introduction *L'Action française* gave to Sorel's article shows the significance of the support of the intellectual leader of revolutionary syndicalism for the Maurrassians. Never had Sorel been praised so effusively; never anywhere, except in the circle of his convinced disciples, had he received so many expressions of admiration. The fact that "the brilliant and profound theoretician of antidemocratic socialism, the already much admired author of *Réflexions sur la violence* and *La Révolution dreyfusienne*," had in fact done no more than produce a flat and stale little article in which he reiterated his oft-repeated attacks against liberal democracy in *La Révolution dreyfusienne* hardly mattered. What mattered was his conviction that "the Dreyfusian revolution has singularly impaired France's moral forces." "A vigorous protest," he wrote, "had to be made against this spirit of decadence: no other group except Action française was able to fulfill a role requiring both literacy and faith. The friends of Maurras form an audacious avant-garde engaged in a fight to the finish against the boors who have corrupted everything they have touched in our country. The merit of these young people will appear great in history, for we may hope that due to them the reign of stupidity will come to an end some day near at hand."[200]

The Maurrassians honored him with a shower of praise; in one place they spoke of Sorel's "incomparable power of analysis" and saw him as "the most profound critic of modernist ideas";[201] in another he was hailed as "the most penetrating and powerful of the French sociologists." And why all this? Because, together with Barrès and "our master Édouard Drumont," he had acclaimed the "new and profound manifestation of French patriotism represented by Péguy's *Le Mystère de la charité de Jeanne d'Arc*," that "magnificent work," as he wrote in *L'Action française* of 14 April 1910, which "will perhaps count as one of the masterpieces of our literature." Thanks to that work, he wrote, it would be possible to put an end to "lies" and "Gambettist cock-and-bull stories," and to "the Dreyfusard revolution," which "would have been impossible if patriotism had not been made ridiculous by the mountebanks of opportunism." Patriotism, he wrote, could not exist without its Christian essence; the nationalist revival was closely connected with the upsurge of Catholicism. Any writer who wished "to speak worthily of the fatherland," had to evoke the "Christian supernatural." So "strongly Catholic an affirmation" was symptomatic of a situation in which "all the boors feel that the political power they enjoy today is threatened," for in imbibing this text "the reader constantly finds himself face to face with the eternal soul of France." For Sorel, Péguy's Catholic patriotism added an extra dimension to the great antirationalist crusade: "Patriotism is thus presented in a manner that will by no means suit the rationalists. . . . Art triumphs here over false science satisfied with appearances, and it attains reality."[202]

Sorel did not suddenly become a nationalist in the vulgar sense of the term; he did not adhere to a crude and chauvinistic patriotism. He did not bow down before Barrès, who had now become a simple conservative politician, rich and covered with honors. A tirade by Déroulède left him unmoved. He did not suddenly develop a royalist soul. Sorel was not Jules Lemaître. He was not drawn by the rationalist and positivistic aspects of the Maurrassian system either; nor was he attracted by the authoritarian and disagreeable personality of the founder of L'Action française. Sorel himself, a sour old man who was generally regarded as a turncoat and who had fallen out with everyone he had to do with since his entry into political life, was by no means easy to get along with. His "variations," whose internal coherence is apparent to the historian, finally made him appear an eccentric, unstable, and baffling figure to his contemporaries. Croce was affectionately disposed toward him, but Antonio Labriola in 1898, Jaurès and Bernstein in 1906, and Lagardelle in 1910 regarded him as an unpredictable character, always liable to take off in a totally unexpected direction.

In reality, his positions, concluding a process of intellectual development lasting several years, were of an extreme consistency. Sorel acted not on a sudden flight of fancy but in consequence of his affinity with certain essential aspects of L'Action française. In advocating violence and in exhorting the proletariat to a fight to the finish against the bourgeois order, liberal democracy, the eighteenth century, and the French Revolution, in praising the virtues of Christian pessimism, was he not at the same time asking the revolutionary worker "to recognize the principle of historical heredity"? He insisted, in connection with the Napoleonic regime, on the "enormous role of conservation in the greatest revolutions."[203] It is obvious that such ideas could not fail to please the Maurrassians. At this stage, Sorel's thought looked like a French variant of the "conservative revolution" that flourished above all in Germany, where it was the local variant of fascism. This school gained celebrity through the work of Oswald Spengler, Arthur Moeller van den Bruck, Paul de Lagarde, Julius Langbehn, and Ernst Jünger.[204] A conservative revolutionary—that was Sorel in 1912.

If Sorel was drawn to the Maurrassian movement, it was because he needed to find a new source of revolutionary energy. It was not the royalism that attracted him, but the "ardent youth that enrolled in L'Action française."[205] It was despite its royalism, not because of it, that Sorel approached this movement. The Action française of that period, one should recall, differed enormously from the movement of patronesses, landed proprietors, and naval officers who dominated it in the 1920s. Indeed, the Camelots du Roi, the students of L'Action française, still set the tone in the Latin Quarter in the interwar period, but the movement no longer claimed to have a popular base or to fuse the "national" element with the "social." That, however, was the ambition of Maurrassism at the beginning of the century.

Pierre Drieu La Rochelle was right to speak in 1934 of the "popular zest of the fascism" of Action française before 1914,[206] and Pierre Andreu, who had a good knowledge of Sorel, was equally correct to entitle his 1936 article on Sorel and the rapprochement between the syndicalist theoretician and the nationalists "Fascisme 1913."[207] "If I was drawn by l'Action française," wrote Drieu, "it was to the degree that it was connected through the Cercle Proudhon to the upsurge of the syndicalist revolution."[208]

Once again, it is worthwhile to turn to Pierre Andreu—the Pierre Andreu of the 1930s—who understood Sorel particularly well: "Of Marxism," he wrote, "Sorel retained only class warfare. This warfare was for him the essence and hope of socialism. He did not oppose socialism to capitalism; he opposed the proletariat to the bourgeoisie, seeing it as a heroic war. Sorel attacked the bourgeoisie much more than the capitalist system of production. He violently criticized all socialist systems; he did not criticize capitalism."[209]

At the same period, another observer, Thierry Maulnier, who was no less involved and no less perceptive, observed that contrary to all appearances Sorel never really changed. Hostile to democracy, he turned toward Maurras or toward Lenin according to circumstances. In Lenin, Maulnier wrote, Sorel saw "the retaliation of the man, the leader, the creator, against democratic vulgarity, the retaliation of proletarian *violence* against the socialist betrayal."[210]

In the years preceding the cataclysm of August 1914, the Action française was the only real movement of opposition. On the Left, the process of integration into the republican consensus was considerably accelerated. The revolutionary syndicalism of which Sorel was the theoretician failed to get off the ground, and the masses of workers took the path of democratic socialism. Even Gustave Hervé, symbol of opposition to the democratic republic, abandoned an extreme antipatriotism well before the time of mobilization. Toward 1912, he, the publisher of *La Guerre sociale*, like Lagardelle, who continued to publish *Le Mouvement socialiste*, made his peace with the established order. The only current that still struggled against the established order, of which democratic socialism was also a part, was the Maurrassian movement, the only one not only to oppose the regime, its institutions and practices, but also to deny its spiritual foundations. The Action française proclaimed the absolute incompatibility of nationalism with the republican regime, seeking the total destruction of the latter, and made it its objective to gain control of the forces capable of defeating liberal and democratic ideas. The Action française wanted to form a "Brigade de fer" (Iron Brigade) that would vanquish liberal democracy, just as in ancient times "the Macedonian phalanx overcame the democratic mob of the peoples of Asia."[211] This was an objective, a way of thinking and a language that could not fail to appeal to Sorel. All in all, the young militants of the Action française with their vigorous, violent leaders, engaged in a daily combat against the despised and hated bourgeois republic, were not only Sorel's natural allies but his only possible ones. For him as for the Maurrassians, the legitimacy of democracy was spurious, contrary to nature, and the very embodiment of evil.

This encounter of people who voluntarily placed themselves outside the democratic system was greatly facilitated by the efforts of the Action française, from the first years of its existence, in labor circles in general and among revolutionary syndicalists in particular. Maurras and his followers knew that there was nothing to be done with the SFIO and its various segments. On one hand, French socialism had now reached the point of no return on the path of democratization, and in this it had done no more than follow the same process as the other socialist movements of western Europe. On the other hand, the Dreyfus Affair had proved to be a factor of integration. The Action française thus turned toward Sorel, the author of *La Révolution dreyfusienne*, a violent criticism of the famous Affair and a vigorously stated attempt to undo its consequences.[212] Sorel now became a symbol and a hope. In nationalist circles in those years,[213] Sorel's contribution opened new possibilities to the forces of revolt in their struggle against the republican consensus.

Indeed, from the beginning, the Maurrassian movement had followed developments in the nonconformist Left with a sustained interest. This novel socialism, based on a profound revision of Marxism—a socialism that questioned neither private property nor profit nor the liberal economy as a whole, but only liberal democracy and its philosophical foundations—aroused much sympathy in the Action française. From 1900 onward, Maurras began to prepare the way for an opening toward the nonconformist Left. "A *pure* socialist system would be devoid of any element of democratism," he wrote.[214] While Maurras undoubtedly attacked Marxist egalitarianism and internationalism, he at the same time declared that "*a socialism liberated from the democratic and cosmopolitan element* fits nationalism as a well-made glove fits a beautiful hand."[215] Jacques Bainville, Jean Rivain, and Georges Valois carefully scrutinized all manifestations of revolt against liberal democracy, universal suffrage, the eighteenth century, and the heritage of the French Revolution, every political action and above all every idea that gave grounds for hope of an impending rupture between the proletariat and the Republic. The appearance of these "antidemocrats of the extreme Left," these "antidemocratic socialists."[216] was appreciated in these circles at its true value, and the youthful Action française regarded it as beyond price.

The Maurrassians were among the first to recognize the full significance of Sorel's work. Jean Rivain did not await the "downfall of the brutes" in order to hail the work of the "most listened to" among "the collaborators of *Le Mouvement socialiste*, the organ of revolutionary syndicalism," the writer of works "of the very first order." This nationalist author did not even take the trouble to analyze *Réflexions*, so self-evident did the conclusions of this book seem to him. His understanding of Sorel's intellectual development and his knowledge of his work were sufficiently precise to cause him to linger over *L'Avenir socialiste des syndicats* and *Introduction à l'économie moderne*. Rivain pointed out, for instance, the elitist character of Sorel's ideas on corporations and cooperatives.[217] Indeed, Sorel thought that if the cooperatives "succeeded, it was because they eliminated the inefficient and had among them a group of people capable of managing affairs in the capacity of employers. They were real associations of small entrepreneurs." In a footnote, Sorel added: "The Greek philosophers would no doubt have called them aristocracies."[218] Rivain understood very well that Sorelian socialism implied the disappearance of neither the capitalist economy nor private property. But this conception demanded elites, and it had a violently anti-democratic and anti-Rousseauist character. It is unnecessary to go into the details of his analysis, which was intelligent, well argued, and supported by long quotations. Rivain perfectly understood the Sorelian view of democracy and the revolutionary tradition. On the "revolutionary philosophy," he wrote, Sorel made "a declaration of principle that could have been taken from *L'Action française* and that we could have signed."[219]

On 7 December 1911, Georges Valois, who was then responsible for contacts with the nonconformist Left, declared at the Fourth Congress of the Action française: "It was not a mere accident if our friends encountered the militants of syndicalism. The nationalist movement and the syndicalist movement, alien to one another though they may seem, because of their present positions and orientations, have more than one common objective."[220] Valois here was only repeating earlier observations. Already in 1908, Jean Rivain had quoted him as saying that the common objective of the syndicalists and the Action française was "the destruction of the republican and democratic regime."[221] Undoubtedly, this merciless criticism of the democratic political culture, its philosophical foundations, and its principles and practices was the meeting point of Sorel and of the Action française. Sorel was attracted by the craving for grandeur, power, and violence that he sensed among the young Maurrassians. He applauded their absolute rejection of the existing moral and political order.

In 1910 Sorel saw Valois a great deal, and it was he who got Édouard Berth and Valois together.[222] At that time the idea of the national-socialist journal *La Cité française* came to fruition. Because of petty personal rivalries, this journal never saw the light of day, but the prospectus that in July 1910 announced its forthcoming appearance well expressed the significance of the enterprise. It was signed by Sorel. "This journal is addressed to people of sense who have been revolted by the stupid pride of democracy, by humanitarian nonsense, and by fashions from abroad, who wish to work to restore to the French spirit its independence and who are determined, in order to achieve that goal, to follow the noble paths opened by the masters of national thought."[223] These ideas were developed in the "Déclaration" of *La Cité française*:

> The founders of *La Cité française* represent various forms of general opinion, but they totally agree on the following point: if one wishes to solve in a manner favorable to civilization the questions that are posed in the modern world, it is absolutely necessary to destroy the democratic institutions. Contemporary experience teaches that democracy is the greatest social danger for all classes of society, and especially the working class. Democracy mixes the classes in order to permit a few groups of politicians, associated with financiers or dominated by them, to exploit the producers.
>
> One must therefore organize society outside the sphere of democratic ideas; one must organize the classes outside democracy, despite democracy, and against it. One must arouse the consciousness of themselves that the classes must possess and that is at present stifled by democratic ideas. One must awaken the virtues proper to each class, in the absence of which none can accomplish its historical mission. . . .
>
> For this struggle we ask, of all those who recognize its necessity, an enthusiastic cooperation and the most absolute devotion.
>
> *Édouard Berth, Georges Sorel, Jean Variot, Pierre Gilbert, Georges Valois.*[224]

Six months after the failure of *La Cité française*, *L'Indépendance* appeared, taking up the objectives of the abortive project of Sorel and Valois. If the *Cité française* never got off the ground because of Georges Valois's animosity toward Jean Variot, and if, out of fidelity to the latter, Sorel decided to obstruct this first joint enterprise of the revolutionary syndicalists and nationalists, he was entirely free to run *L'Indépendance* as he pleased.

The review appeared from March 1911 to July 1913; forty-eight issues came out in all—one every two weeks. Throughout its existence, the journal searched in vain for the proper formula, the correct format, the editorial staff suitable for its founder, assisted mainly by the Tharaud brothers and Jean Variot. In October 1912, Barrès, Bourget, and Francis Jammes joined the editorial staff, but this modification was not sufficient to give bite, color, or even character to the review. Berth and Valois took no part in it, and although it declared that it considered "workers' demands as legitimate as national demands,"[225] *L'Indépendance* did not succeed in distinguishing itself from the weekly *L'Action française*.

One found the same themes there: nationalism, anti-Semitism, the defense of culture, classicism, the Greco-Roman heritage, and the struggle against the university and secular education. *L'Indépendance* waged long campaigns against Gambetta and the national defense (the Republic, it claimed, was the creation of Bismarck) and paid a rousing tribute to the royalist revolt in the south of France.[226] Despite the collaboration of Pareto, Le Bon, and Claudel, it did not succeed in establishing its own identity and failed to supply the needs for which it had been set up. In the period of *L'Indépendance*, Sorel became a mere representative of the Action française and a tool of Maurras. Already in 1910 he had espoused the mediocre quarrels of the Action française and vigorously defended the Maurrassian movement against the conservative Right, which, like all dissidents and revolutionaries, he detested.[227]

L'Indépendance covered the same ground; despite the declaration of good intent in the statement of policy of the new review—"*L'Indépendance* will not be the instrument of any political party or literary movement"[228]—one has the impression of reading a mere supplement to *L'Action française*, but one that was far less well produced, trenchant, and sophisticated than the original. That is hardly surprising. Did not Sorel say in 1912 that "the defense of French culture is today in the hands of Charles Maurras"?[229]

Sorel was at that time so much under the spell of Maurras that he turned his review into an organ of anti-Semitism in no way inferior to Édouard Drumont's old *La Libre Parole* or Jules Guérin's *L'Antijuif*. We know that for the Action française anti-Semitism was a methodical necessity, a real historical requirement. "Everything seems impossible or terribly difficult," wrote Maurras in March 1911, "without the providential appearance of anti-Semitism. It enables everything to be arranged, smoothed over, and simplified. If one were not an anti-Semite through patriotism, one would become one through a simple sense of opportunity."[230] Sorel supported this opinion and threw himself into a long and violent anti-Semitic campaign. He signed a long article in praise of Urbain Gohier, the most celebrated living anti-Semite, whom he encouraged to continue "maintaining that the French must defend their state, their customs, and their ideas against the Jewish invaders who want to dominate everything."[231] In "Aux temps dreyfusiens," he made all kinds of threats against the Jews and held them responsible for the decadence of France.[232] The issues of 1 and 15 May and of 1 June 1912 contained the three parts of a voluminous essay entitled "Some Jewish Pretensions." Here one learned that the Jews, and particularly their intellectuals and writers, sought to conquer France and were "opposed to the spiritual heritage of the society into which they were admitted through the hazards of migration."[233] The issue of 1 July 1913 contained "Jewish Words on the French," a communication claiming to have been addressed to the review by a certain Isaac Blümchen. The aim of this text was to show to the French the nature of the evil that threatened them, apparently revealed by a Jew. The "Notes de la quinzaine" and the "Échos" of the issues of April 1912 and February and April 1913 were similar.

Nor was this all. In all of western Europe between the end of the Dreyfus Affair and the beginnings of Nazism, *L'Indépendance* was one of the few publications that still dared to brandish against the Jews the accusation of ritual murder. It did so more than once, as if it were an undisputed historical fact,[234] quite in keeping with the frequent allusions to the stigmata of Saint Francis and the blood of Saint Janvier which occur in Sorel's letters to Croce, a correspondence in which he proliferated observations on miracles and anti-Jewish remarks. This was no doubt one aspect of his attraction for the irrational. Anti-Semitism was one of the elements in the junction with integral nationalism. In Sorel's letters to Mario Missiroli, anti-Semitic remarks became obsessive;[235] they proliferated in his correspondence with Berth and Lagardelle. At the same time, like many self-respecting anti-Semites, Sorel expressed friendship for particular Jews, admiration for a "good Jew" like Bergson, or a certain fascination for ancient Judea, or an enthusiasm for modern Zionism.[236]

Sorel's anti-Semitism was not a consequence of his subservience to Maurras; a genuine community of ideas existed. Moreover, his easy and rapid integration into the Maurrassian political current, although a passing phenomenon—not much more so than his Dreyfusard phase or his phase of Leninist sympathies—demonstrated his faith in the capacity of nationalism to create a rupture. While the proletarian elites, corrupted by all the evils and vices of the bourgeoisie, exhibited their moral bankruptcy, nationalism, sure of its future, was steadily on the rise. Everyone agreed about this, from the extreme Left to the extreme Right. "We are witnessing a revival of nationalism. It is overflowing at the brim," wrote Francis de Pressensé in April 1911.[237] Two years later, at the sixth congress of the Action française, Valois stated categorically: "Today it is nationalism that carries the forces of reason and sentiment that will henceforth be responsible for social transformations." This "ascension of nationalism," he said, had the result that "one sees national values replacing socialist values in the public mind."[238] Valois and Berth both felt that a new sensibility was coming into being, that dissident circles were preoccupied with new needs. *L'Indépendance* of the old Sorel, who with *Réflexions* and *Les Illusions* seemed to have said his last word, was a total failure. Apart from his adherence to nationalism, it was years since Sorel had expressed a new idea. Berth and Valois, whom Sorel had encouraged to work together at the time of the preparations for launching *La Cité française*, now decided to continue this mutual collaboration. On 16 December 1911 there was an initial meeting of the Cercle Proudhon, and the first *Cahier* of the Cercle appeared in January of the following year.

The "Déclaration" of the Cercle, published at the beginning of this first *Cahier*, reiterated not only the ideas, but also the formulas—sometimes word for word—that had been used in the preparatory texts for the appearance of the abortive *Cité française*. The prospectus announcing the appearance of *La Cité française* had concluded with an invocation of the authority of Proudhon, "the only great socialist writer to have appeared in France."[239] In all respects—with regard to its content, spirit, and formulation—the new review undertook to take up the stillborn project of *La Cité française* at the point where Sorel had been obliged to abandon it. The first two paragraphs of the "Déclaration" at the beginning of number 1 of the *Cahiers* set the tone:

> The founders—republicans, federalists, integral nationalists, and syndical-ists—having resolved the political problem or dismissed it from their minds, are all enthusiastically in favor of an organization of French society in accordance with principles taken from the French tradition which they find in Proudhon's works and in the contemporary syndicalist movement, and they are all com-pletely in agreement on the following points:
>
> Democracy is the greatest error of the past century. If one wishes to live, if one wishes to work, if one wishes in social life to possess the greatest human guarantees for production and culture, if one wishes to preserve and increase the moral, intellectual, and material capital of civilization, it is absolutely neces-sary to destroy democratic institutions.[240]

Why did Sorel not participate personally in the launching of these *Ca-hiers*, which were identical in intention to *La Cité française*? They were, after all, exactly in his line of thought. Indeed, he had some doubts about the Maurrassians' sincerity with respect to Proudhon, and at a certain moment he advised Berth not to have anything to do "with an affair that cannot yield good results."[241] Nevertheless, as Pierre Andreu noted in his introduction to Sorel's unpublished letters to Berth, after these first guarded reactions, Sorel "seems to have been won over by the antidemocratic fervor of the Cercle."[242] This being the case, why the reserve?

The only answer that seems convincing has to do with Sorel's character rather than his ideas. He was not made for teamwork, and he had probably lost the taste for journalistic adventures with their inevitable quarrels and rivalries of personality such as those which had accompanied the attempted launching of *La Cité française*. The founders, it should be said, did every-thing to make their allegiance plain: the Cercle placed itself under the aegis of Proudhon and Sorel. Moreover, the contemporary thought that inspired the Cercle was undoubtedly Sorel's. The content of the *Cahiers* fully attests to this. If the first of the *Cahiers* (January–February 1912) was devoted to Proudhon, the second (March–April) was divided between Proudhon and Sorel (Gilbert Maire contributed an article entitled "The Philosophy of Georges Sorel"), the third, a double issue (*Cahiers* 3–4 [May–August 1912]), was devoted to a "Homage to Georges Sorel." This *Cahier* contained, nota-bly, "Sorel's Work and the Cercle Proudhon," an interesting article by Henri Lagrange, one of the most promising young Maurrassians, who died in the First World War.[243]

Even more significant, Sorel never repudiated the syndicalist-nationalist synthesis of the Cercle Proudhon. The Cercle, we should note, never pub-lished an homage to Maurras, only to Sorel, and invoked the authority of

Maurras less than that of Sorel. Maurras, for his part, published a little article in the *Cahiers*,[244] Sorel only a short letter.[245] If these two authority figures kept their distance from an affair directed by the younger generation,
one can have no doubt about the presence of their shadows. Nevertheless
that of Sorel definitely seems to be the most easily discernible.

It should be remembered that Maurras had his own publications, just like
Sorel, who, when the *Cahiers* were started, continued publishing of
L'Indépendance. The initiative for the Cercle fell to the radical elements,
those who were searching for a new political path and set off on the adventure with all the enthusiasm of youth.

Consequently, even if the Cercle was not Sorel's creation, he never denied it his patronage, his name, or his reputation; he never questioned its
right to be inspired by his work and to draw the appropriate conclusions. He
who was so quick to excommunicate, to criticize, to protest, he who was so
touchy (he broke with Péguy over a trifle), never said a word against the
ideas propagated by the *Cahiers*. Although the entire Left—including the
staff of *Le Mouvement socialiste*, which violently attacked the "split"[246]—
regarded him as a traitor, Sorel never produced an article or a word in print
that gave one to understand that the socialist-national synthesis had been
elaborated against his will or even independently of him. There was nothing
to prevent him from doing so; he edited his own review, he continued to
write—a great deal—and yet he kept his silence. At a time when the Italian
and to a lesser degree the French press were flooded with commentaries on
the subject, which caused a great stir, this silence could be interpreted only
as assent. Did not Sorel, after *L'Indépendance* had ceased to appear, propose
his work to Berth as a source of material? "I suggest that you read the chapter I wrote on the organization of democracy. It contains, I think, quite a few
important ideas. If Rivière cannot use it for the volume *Matériaux pour une
théorie du prolétariat*, I should like it to appear in the *Cahiers du Cercle
Proudhon*."[247]

It was not therefore for intellectual or political reasons that the name of
Sorel did not appear in the editorial committee of the *Cahiers*. The real
reason was that the "grouser of Boulogne-sur-Mer" (*sic*), as one of his most
celebrated Italian disciples, Angelo O. Olivetti, described him,[248] was not
suited to collective enterprises. The authoritarian, often mean side of his
personality, his inability to collaborate for any length of time with anyone
who did not efface himself before him, had already been apparent twelve
years earlier, when *Le Mouvement socialiste* was at its beginnings. Instead of
playing the role of the sage of revolutionary socialism, as his age or even his
intellectual stature required, Sorel never ceased to display a caustic bit-
terness, to show his claws whenever Lagardelle failed to follow his advice to
the letter, and to launch malicious attacks and make offensive remarks every
time something or somebody displeased him.[249] At the moment when Berth

and Valois were beginning a new adventure, Sorel, after many lost battles, was an old man disinclined to get back into harness in the editorial room.

However, in order to demonstrate his solidarity with the socialist-national synthesis, to show which side he was on, he wrote a warm preface to Édouard Berth's *Les Méfaits des intellectuels*. This leaves no doubt on the matter. Written in January 1914, this important text makes it clear that the writer of the preface was in perfect agreement with the author concerning the contents of the book. One should remember that the purpose of the book was precisely to crown the work of the Cercle Proudhon by systematizing it. This was Berth's description of this synthesis, which did not elicit the slightest reservation from Sorel:

> From the fraternal alliance of Dionysius and Apollo emerged the immortal Greek tragedy. . . . Similarly, L'Action française—which, with Maurras, is a new incarnation of the Apollonian spirit—through its collaboration with syndicalism—which, with Sorel, represents the Dionysian spirit—will be able to give birth to a new *grand siècle*, one of those *historical achievements* which afterward for a long time leave the world dazzled and fascinated.[250]

Such was the historical significance of Sorelianism. Its true dimensions began to appear only at the moment of passing of the old nineteenth-century world in the summer of 1914. In January of that year, Sorel already quoted William James to the effect that "on the stage, only heroism has the great roles."[251] Like his Italian disciples, who lived in expectancy of that event, Sorel too awaited the revolution of the war. For a long time, the long European peace had seemed to him not only "a cause of moral and intellectual weakness," but also a cause of "economic weakness, the spirit of enterprise having become less virile." He added: "There is no doubt that this situation will not last indefinitely: very little is needed to arouse a warlike sentiment in France, and such an arousal would cause an upheaval in all of Europe. A great war would have the effect of eliminating the factors that today encourage a taste for moderation and a desire for social tranquillity."[252]

Sorel said the same elsewhere. He looked forward to "a great foreign war that would bring to power men who have the will to govern, or a great extension of proletarian violence that would make the bourgeois recognize the revolutionary reality and give them a distaste for the humanitarian platitudes with which Jaurès beguiles them."[253]

And yet, when war broke out—the war he had awaited so much—Sorel judged it very harshly. He realized very quickly that liberal democracy was not on the point of giving way.

Yet Sorel was not a political man; he had neither the instincts of a Mussolini nor the reflexes of the other Italian syndicalist theoreticians and leaders—Michels, Panunzio, Orano, Olivetti, De Ambris, Bianchi, and that extraordinary leader of men, Corridoni. He did not seize the opportunities provided by the European war. Sorel, we should remember, had little knowledge of the outside world. Old and exhausted, he judged things as they seemed from Ambérieu-en-Bugey, where in September 1914 he wrote Berth a despairing letter, expressing his anguish and his contempt for everything and everyone. For the Union sacrée, first of all, that coalition which put together Albert de Mun and Maurras with Hervé, Vaillant, and Jules Guesde, was in his opinion motivated not "by the necessity of defending the basic possessions of the nation," but by a "hatred for the notions of discipline that Prussia had retained"; for the pope, next, who "was going to make peace with the authors of separation," and finally for Maurras, who "never," he wrote, "had a serious idea of what the social forces in a monarchical country should be."[254]

Sorel soon sensed the coming victory of the wretched coalition that, he wrote, would "finish off everything serious, grand, and *Roman* that is still in Europe."[255] And yet, the first successes of the new revolutionary, antimaterialistic, anti-Marxist, and antiliberal wave were not far away. They were confirmed almost as soon as Sorel died. The nascent Fascist ideology derived its initial basic content from the syndicalist-nationalist synthesis. This synthesis would not have been possible without the original contribution of Sorel, Sorel who had preached hatred for the heritage of the eighteenth century, for Voltaire and Rousseau, for the French Revolution, for rationalism and optimism, for liberal democracy and bourgeois society; Sorel who had advocated a total rejection of democratic egalitarianism, of majority rule, of humanitarianism and pacifism; Sorel who had sought respect for the right of elites to lead the flocks of the society of the masses and demanded veneration for classical culture and a strong faith in the power of tradition and heredity; Sorel who regarded Catholicism as a source of discipline and hence as a fundamental component of the civilization to be defended every day against the forces of destruction; and Sorel whose aim had been to restore to European civilization the grandeur of the Christian, pessimistic, and heroic ages.

And yet (this was an important element in the Sorelian synthesis that underlay fascism), what mattered in Catholicism was its social virtues—discipline, chastity, pessimism—and not its faith. Like all the rebels of the beginning of the century, like Barrès and Maurras, Sorel was interested not in Christian metaphysics but in Christianity as the nucleus of an order that could ensure the future of civilization.

The fate of civilization and not that of the proletariat or the nation preoccupied Sorel. The proletarian community or the national community was never anything other in his eyes than an instrument of the great change he hoped for. For that reason this revolution never touched the foundations of capitalist economy. Sorel's anticapitalism was limited strictly to the political, intellectual, and moral aspects of the liberal and bourgeois system; he never tried to question the foundations, principles, and competitive mechanisms of the capitalist economy. The Sorelian revolution sought to eradicate the theory of natural rights, abolish the rights of man, and uproot the utilitarian and materialistic foundations of the democratic political culture; it never touched private property. When the idea of the proletariat began to replace that of the producer, the Sorelians progressively elaborated their master's revolutionary theory and laid the foundations of a revolutionary capitalism— a capitalism of producers, hostile to the plutocracy and high finance, the stock exchange, the middlemen, and the money grubbers. This revolutionary theory was strongly attached to the market economy, to competition, and to the nonintervention of the state in economic activity.

A new vision of political ideals thus came into existence, one that sought to mobilize the masses by means of myths. It supported the idea of violence, creative of virtue. It envisaged a moral, intellectual, and political revolution. It required a spiritualistic revolution with an intense pessimism and a fundamental antirationalism.

At the moment of putting the final touch on his activities, when he wrote the preface to the book of the disciple who was to continue his work, Sorel showed that he was well aware of the nature of the forces that had been set in motion:

> I am convinced that, in fifteen or twenty years' time, a new generation rid, thanks to Bergsonism, of the phantoms created by the intellectualist philosophers since Descartes, will listen only to people able to explain the theory of evil. . . . It has happened several times that I have looked into the abyss, but without daring to enter. There was a moment when I considered commentating a few texts by Pascal at the end of *Les Illusions du progrès*, but I thought it wiser not to broach a subject so odious to our contemporaries. I believe, however, that I can recognize from a few indications that the era which will assign the metaphysics of evil its proper place is already beginning to emerge.[256]

CHAPTER TWO

Revolutionary Revisionism in France

THE "NEW SCHOOL"

In August 1904, with number 139, the first series of *Le Mouvement socialiste* came to an end. Six years after the appearance of its first issue on 15 January 1899, Hubert Lagardelle's review became a kind of official organ of Sorelianism. Hitherto it had been a high-class journal, but, in comparison with the great German reviews, it did not have any special character of its own in the world of socialism. Throughout its early years, *Le Mouvement socialiste* had published the classic material of the period: many texts by Marx, several contributions from Jaurès, and numerous articles by foreign theoreticians— Kautsky, Bernstein, Luxemburg, the Webbs, Antonio Labriola, and Vandervelde. The *Bernstein debatte* was given the place it deserved there, and calls for socialist unity in France, the Dreyfus Affair, and the Millerand case also had their place.

The conversion of the review to Sorelianism began with the first major articles by Édouard Berth in January and November 1903.[1] Some thirty years younger than Sorel, Berth was the closest friend and most faithful disciple of the latter, for whom he had a boundless admiration. Sorel returned these feelings; after his wife, Berth was the person he loved most deeply. Berth lived in the shadow of Sorel and existed only through his quasi-filial relationship with him, and his works, which were not without value, were really a reflection of the work of Sorel. In the Parisian milieu as in revolutionary syndicalist circles in France and Italy, Berth never was and never became anything other than Sorel's spokesman (later he became the guardian of his memory). This was so throughout their joint careers and thus undoubtedly at the time of the meeting of the French revolutionary revisionists with the Maurrassian nationalists. Even Pierre Andreu had to recognize that if Berth went farther than Sorel in seeking a rapprochement with the Action française, one was perfectly justified in thinking that youthful enthusiasm impelled him to take to an extreme conclusion ideas that Sorel had helped to develop but that age and prudence prevented him from stating more clearly.[2]

Berth discovered Sorel when he came upon a series of articles in *L'Ère nouvelle* entitled "L'ancienne et la nouvelle métaphysique." He was at that time preparing for graduate studies at the Sorbonne.[3] In 1898 he abandoned his studies and, an enthusiastic Dreyfusard, threw himself into the political battle. At that time he professed a run-of-the-mill socialism, which he expressed in a very unexceptional work, *Dialogues socialistes*, which appeared in 1901. Much later, when the war swept away the socialist-national synthesis of the Cercle Proudhon, Berth returned to the Left and was active in the young Communist party, and particularly in the review *Clarté*. On Sorel's death, he published a panegyric of the master and crossed swords with Agostino Lanzillo, Sorel's first biographer. In an article in *Gerarchia*, the doctrinal review of Italian fascism edited by Mussolini, Lanzillo—who on Berth's own admission was a fervent Sorelian—had attempted to reclaim the heritage of *Réflexions*: "Perhaps fascism may have the good fortune to fulfill a mission that is the implicit aspiration of the whole oeuvre of the master of syndicalism: to tear away the proletariat from the domination of the Socialist party, to reconstitute it on the basis of spiritual liberty, and to animate it with the breath of creative violence. This would be the true revolution that would mold the forms of the Italy of tomorrow."[4]

Finally, in 1925, Berth, disappointed with bolshevism, ceased his collaboration in *Clarté* and returned to Sorelian syndicalism. In 1932 he gathered together in a volume his articles published between 1926 and 1929, including an essay on Lenin—"Du *Capital* aux *Réflexions sur la violence*"—which had appeared in *Clarté* in 1924. This was Édouard Berth's last book. Subsequently, and throughout the interwar period, Berth acted as "guardian of the faith." He defended Sorel's work and memory with a fierce devotion that never diminished. When *La Critique sociale*, Boris Souvarine's little review, accused Sorel in 1931 of "a complete lack of understanding" of Marxist economics, concluding that he "had nothing in common with socialism,"[5] Berth proudly replied that "*Réflexions sur la violence* remains, after *Justice* and *The Capital*, the most brilliant work that the modern labor movement has so far inspired."[6] And in 1935, when he took it upon himself to gather in a volume—*D'Aristote à Marx*—the series of articles ("L'ancienne et la nouvelle métaphysique") that forty years earlier had introduced him to Sorel's ideas, Berth paid a final tribute to his master.

At the moment when he published this last Sorelian profession of faith, Berth also took up the defense of Georges Valois, with whom he had taken the initiative of creating the Cercle Proudhon and who in 1925 had founded the Faisceau, the first Fascist movement outside Italy. Meanwhile, Valois had made his own "return to the roots." He had now become one of the most perspicacious critics of both fascism, in its Mussolinian form and its French variants, and Stalinism. Valois's review, *Le Nouvel Âge*, established itself, from its appearance in 1934, as a "leftist" journal with a tendency to see signs everywhere of a giant capitalist "plot." Nevertheless it was often clear-sighted. In 1935 Georges Valois's request to join the SFIO, sponsored by Marceau Pivert, was accepted by the forty-fifth section of the party but rejected by the Conseil fédéral de la Seine.[7] The Comité antifasciste et de vigilance (Anti-Fascist and Vigilance Committee), founded by Paul Rivet, also rejected his candidacy. On 5 March 1935, *Le Nouvel Âge* printed a long article by Édouard Berth on the "Valois case," which *La Révolution prolétarienne* had rejected. This article replied to a diatribe against Valois by a veteran of *Le Mouvement socialiste*, Robert Louzon, whom Berth reminded that, thirty years earlier, he had written a long anti-Semitic article that had caused a great stir.[8] Everyone can make mistakes, Berth was in effect saying; the Cercle Proudhon, the product of an "extraordinary, unprecedented historical situation," had also been a mistake. Berth insisted that however great and bewildering Valois's changes of position may have been, "his sole objective, pursued obstinately and with passion, was never anything other than the emancipation of the working class."[9]

Undoubtedly, in taking up Valois's defense, Berth was trying to explain and justify his own past and that of Sorel to a Left that rejected this most recent attempt to cross traditional boundaries and resolutely opposed the socialist Déat and his "néos," Doriot, Barbé, and their fellow Communists who were sliding into fascism, as well as Bergery and Jouvenel, renegades of the moderate Left. Here once again one has a fusion of the "national" and the "social," and the language, content, and objectives were identical to those of the old Sorelian synthesis of the Cercle Proudhon.

Hubert Lagardelle, the founder of *Le Mouvement socialiste*, was born, like Berth, in 1875. While Berth never went farther than his B.A. degree and never became more than a minor functionary, a treasurer of several Paris hospitals, Lagardelle was a doctor of law and an advocate at the Court of Appeal in Paris. Of the two, however, Berth was the more profound and the more given to theoretical reflection. Close as he was to Sorel and the Italian theoreticians, whom he often translated into French, Berth formulated doctrine. Lagardelle was a publicist, a columnist, the fast-reacting editor of a journal, and not a thinker. He traveled and lectured in Brussels, Constantinople, Milan, Vienna, and the capitals of eastern Europe. He knew German (having studied in Berlin), but he did not participate in the great theoretical debates of the period and did not follow as closely as Berth (who also knew the language of Marx, Engels, Kautsky, Bernstein, and Luxemburg) the details of the theoretical debates in Germany. But he was a party man, in touch with the events of the moment, and took an active part in the internal struggles of French socialism. A convinced Guesdist, a member of the Parti Ouvrier Français (POF) at the age of twenty-one, and an admirer of Kautsky, Lagardelle opposed the Saint-Mandé program of 1896. A Dreyfusard like Berth and Sorel, around 1900–1902 he fought against Millerandism and nationalism and on behalf of socialist unity.[10]

Lagardelle was first acquainted with Sorel probably through the journal *Le Devenir social*.[11] The two men had a relationship that never reached the

level of intensity of the relationship between Sorel and Berth but was sufficiently close for Sorel at the period of their honeymoon to place Lagardelle
and his favorite disciple on an equal footing.[12] Sorel and Berth's collaboration in *Le Mouvement socialiste* ceased at the end of 1908 in the case of the
former and at the beginning of 1909 in the case of the latter, that is, at the
moment when the socialist-national synthesis began to mature.

It was during and after his stay in Berlin that Lagardelle was converted to
Sorelianism. Sorel succeeded in convincing the young Guesdist of the need
of revising Marxism and of rescuing it from the ideological rigidity that characterized French orthodoxy. When *Le Mouvement socialiste* became a
weekly in 1902, Lagardelle was already a convinced Sorelian, at least where
the political and moral aspects of revolutionary syndicalist theory were concerned.[13] Unlike Berth, he was uninterested in the great questions of civilization that preoccupied Sorel, and he felt more at home on the platforms of
political meetings than in philosophical discussions. In his political activities, Lagardelle resembled the Italian revolutionary syndicalists who attempted to conquer the Socialist party from within. Although he did not
have the same ambitions as the Italians, he attacked Guesde, Vaillant, and
Jaurès; at the Socialist party congresses at Nancy in 1907 and at Toulouse in
1908, he vigorously defended syndicalist ideas. Thus a division of labor arose
between Berth the theoretician and Lagardelle the activist, spokesman of
the "new school" to the party authorities. His impressive speech of 14 May
1907 at the Socialist congress at Nancy was a real political manifesto of revolutionary syndicalism and a warm defense of the positions the CGT upheld
before the Socialist party at the congress at Amiens in 1906.[14] This perfor-
mance was repeated the following year at the congress at Toulouse, where
Lagardelle confronted Jaurès.[15] In that same year, on 3 April, an international conference was held in Paris under the chairmanship of Victor Griffuelhes, at which figures such as Robert Michels, Hubert Lagardelle, Arturo
Labriola, and Boris Kritchewski were present.[16]

In 1906–1907 the "new school" saw its activities crowned with success.
Strictly speaking, this meant the activities of Sorel, Berth, and Lagardelle.
Sorel was undoubtedly its leader and its inspiration. Armed with *Réflexions*
and with *Illusions*, which had just appeared, fighting in the party with Lagardelle, and supportive of the immense activity of Michels, Arturo Labriola,
Panunzio, Orano, Dinale, and the other theoreticians of Italian revolutionary syndicalism, the "new school" saw many of its ideas adopted by the
congress at Amiens. The celebrated Charter of Amiens proclaimed in particular the revolutionary aspirations of French syndicalism and its decision to
remain outside party politics.

At the same time, however, the limits of the possibilities available to European revolutionary syndicalism also began to become apparent. First, the
congress of the German social democrats at Mannheim and that of the Ital-

ian Socialist party in Rome were defeats for the revolutionaries, with the result that Robert Michels proclaimed the collapse of German socialism[17] and Paolo Orano declared that "the enemy of Italian syndicalism . . . is the Socialist party."[18] In France, too, the situation deteriorated, and after a short time very little remained of the euphoria of the congress at Amiens. It became apparent that the SFIO, like the other socialist parties, would not have its policies dictated to it. To attack Jaurès, Guesde, and Vaillant from the platform of a congress was one thing; to convince the majority of the party was another. Neither the SFIO nor the vast majority of French workers was ready to follow Lagardelle when he demanded recognition of the "revolutionary value of the syndicalist movement."[19] The CGT was far more interested in the eight-hour working day and other social reforms on the agenda than in the revolution.

At that point Sorel and Berth, who persisted in their revolutionary tendencies, separated from Lagardelle. In 1910 Sorel definitely abandoned Marxism and prepared to launch *La Cité française*.[20] At the same period, the Italian Sorelians left the Socialist party to join Corradini and founded *La lupa*, whose first issue appeared in October 1910. The announcement of the coming together of the syndicalists and nationalists in France aroused enthusiasm in Italian revolutionary-syndicalist circles; Lanzillo, in his apologetic biography of Sorel, Orano in *La lupa*, and the review *Pagine libere*, which in its December 1910 issue spoke of the "Sorel phenomenon," showed a proper appreciation of the significance of the socialist-national synthesis coming into being in France.[21]

It was Sorel who introduced Berth to Valois,[22] whom he no doubt knew from the period when the young anarchist was working for *L'Humanité nouvelle*, to which one owed the publication of "L'Avenir socialiste des syndicats," the essay that marked the beginning of Sorel as the theoretician of revolutionary syndicalism. In 1912 Sorel was present at the foundation of the Cercle Proudhon by people thirty years his juniors (Valois, born in 1878, was just three years younger than Berth), who admired him, showered him with praise, and constantly acknowledged his inspiration without occasioning the slightest reservation on his part.

Lagardelle returned to his original positions. If Sorel and Berth, through hatred of a basely materialistic civilization and on account of their absolute refusal to come to terms with the democratic and liberal order, joined the Maurrassian nationalists, Lagardelle claimed to have rejected only "the abuses of a principle, and not the principle itself," and to have never "condemned, through a radical negation, the principle of representation."[23] This "return to the roots" was made without the examination of conscience one might have expected after such a sudden turnabout. Lagardelle simply informs us in four pages that the "astounding fact" of the socialist-national synthesis of the Cercle Proudhon forced him to define his views on democracy. Earlier we were told that *Le Mouvement socialiste* had made an abortive attempt to fuse with *La Revue socialiste*. Lagardelle seemed to have greatly regretted this failure; in his opinion, the "new problems" that had arisen required a complete union of all socialist forces. *Le Mouvement socialiste*, he added, had never failed in its task, and revolutionary syndicalism was never "a new school, but an always revisable and ever-rejuvenated movement of ideas."[24] That was all—not a very adequate explanation of this intellectual odyssey.

It is interesting to note that the departure of Sorel and Berth from *Le Mouvement socialiste* did not result in the immediate exit of the Italians. While Berth's last contribution—an article for Proudhon's centenary—dated from January 1909, Orano, Olivetti, Panunzio, and Arturo Labriola continued to write for the journal throughout that year.[25] Orano and Olivetti left at the end of 1909 (although the latter gave an interview in March 1910), but Panunzio, Labriola, Leone, Tullio Masotti, and Michels continued to figure in the synopsis for the year 1910.[26] In February 1911, when the publication of *La Cité française* was announced, Lagardelle attacked not only "the projected agreement between Sorel and the neomonarchists," but also the two reviews of the young Italian national-socialism, *La lupa* and *Pagine libere*.[27] The break with the editors of *La lupa* and *Pagine libere*, however, did not prevent Arturo Labriola, Sergio Panunzio, and Robert Michels from continuing to send contributions to Lagardelle. Labriola's last article dated from January 1912, and Panunzio's from July 1913. Even Michels saw fit to reply to Lagardelle, who had criticized his ideas on the oligarchic tendencies of syndicates.[28]

If the rupture with the founders of Italian revolutionary syndicalism did not take place all at once, the character of the review nevertheless changed completely, and the reader, who was now served up J.-B. Séverac, Gaston Lévy, and Francis de Pressensé, was bound to notice that Sorelian socialism was dead and buried. The journal lost its true raison d'être: in its last issue, dated May–June 1914, *Le Mouvement socialiste* offered unpublished letters by Marx and Engels, an article by Lagardelle on the personal relationship between Marx and Bakunin, and contributions from C. Bouglé and Daniel Halévy—two writers who could hardly be regarded as dangerous agitators. One found, finally—something quite extraordinary in a publication that for years had hurled insults and abuse at parliamentary democracy—a long article by J.-B. Séverac in praise of the "electoral successes of the Socialist party."[29]

During the war and in the immediate postwar period, Lagardelle did not engage in any activity worthy of interest. Retired to Toulouse, he preoccupied himself with problems of regionalism. In 1926 he joined the Toulouse branch of George Valois's Faisceau.[30] Fourteen years after Édouard Berth, who at that time had rejoined the extreme Left, Lagardelle espoused the socialist-national synthesis that Valois continued to promote. He did not play an important role in the Faisceau, however, and did not really surface until January 1931, with the appearance of the monthly review *Plans*. By that time, Valois had also returned to the Left, leaving it to another representative of the revolutionary syndicalism of the beginning of the century to promote the cause of a planned economy, modernism, and syndicalism combined with antiliberalism and anti-Marxism.

The chief editor of *Plans* was Philippe Lamour, a veteran of the Faisceau, but it was the personality of Lagardelle that dominated this publication. The review was avant-gardist, modernistic—the almost ideal organ for a fascism oriented toward technology, the skyscraper, the cities of Walter Gropius and Le Corbusier, and the art of Fernand Léger. The journal at the same time strongly advocated an organic, harmonious society, the society of the "real" man, for there were two distinct tendencies in fascism. On one hand, there was the tendency represented by Drieu La Rochelle, who wished to defend the worker against the big city ("I say that the big city is capitalism"),[31] and on the other hand there was the tendency that found expression in the cult of the new city, the new aesthetics.[32] As might have been expected, this taste for modernist aesthetics was not confined to architecture; *Plans* published Marinetti, who explained "the elements of the futuristic sensibility that gave birth to our pictorial Dynamism, our unharmonic Music, our Art of noises, and our Words in liberty."[33]

Apart from these avant-gardist themes, Lagardelle's doctrinal reflections in this journal contained hardly any original elements. The criticism of capitalism, democracy, and parliamentarianism was always the same: the present crisis demonstrated the inability of the individualistic society to adapt itself to the conditions of modern life. Democracy, he wrote, "knows only the individual; it ignores the group." It divests "the individual of his sensitive qualities" and turns him into a "theoretical group."[34] The "defect of individualistic democracy," moreover, was to have "left the producer without defense." And finally, only syndicalism, which "has created the most pronounced type of the real man carried by the group to the surface of society," could bring about a true rupture with the established order and the "abstract" man.[35] With the "real" man, not only would a new society come into being, but also a new culture.

All this had already been said often, in exactly the same terms, thirty years earlier in the columns of *Le Mouvement socialiste*. *Plans* interrupted publication in 1933 when Lagardelle, at the request of Henry de Jouvenel, joined the French embassy in Rome. At the Quai d'Orsay, they knew the sense of intellectual debt that Mussolini had toward the former editor of *Le Mouvement socialiste* and his writers, and they also knew that most of the theoreticians of Italian revolutionary syndicalism belonged to the privileged circle of the founders of the regime. Moreover, in his celebrated article in the *Enci-*

clopedia Italiana which he had written in collaboration with Gentile, had not Mussolini mentioned Lagardelle and *Le Mouvement socialiste* as one of the major sources of fascism?[36] It was therefore quite natural that in Rome they would give the former syndicalist a particularly warm welcome.

In Rome, Lagardelle took a great deal of interest in social and economic questions. At that time he definitely came round to corporatism, which he identified with the objectives of his former syndicalism. This proved to be a good preparation for the post of secretary of state for labor that the Vichy government later offered him. Appointed to this position on 8 April 1942, he quit in November of the following year, shattered by an impossible undertaking.[37] For the last time, Lagardelle became a journalist; he took over the editorship of the Vichyist-syndicalist journal *La France socialiste*, where he found former syndicalists such as Georges Dumoulin, Georges Lefranc, and Francis Delaisi. Until the end, Lagardelle enthusiastically defended Italian corporatism, preached the necessity of a new socialism, and saw the advance of the Allies as representing the mortal danger of a victory of the "wild cult of money."[38] A quarter of a century earlier, Georges Sorel had seen the victory of those same Allies as a triumph of the plutocracy. In June 1940, Henri De Man, president of the Belgian Labor party, had said much the same.

APPLIED SORELIANISM

To the Sorelians, revolutionary revisionism was an original response to the phenomenon that at the end of the nineteenth and the beginning of the twentieth century was called the crisis of Marxism. In addition, it was considered to have had the special characteristic of being the only one to be compatible with the thought of Marx. Sorelians regarded this crisis as the logical outcome of a "divorce of theory from practice."[39] For that reason, they approved "the breath of intellectual revolution provoked by Bernstein"; like him, they wanted to make "theory and practice" coincide.[40] Only, the "practice" for which they wished to provide an ideological justification was that of a bellicose proletariat organized in combat formations, and not that of the socialist parties. The Sorelians, moreover, refused to accept the "decomposition" of Marxism resulting from the idealistic reaction "of which the return to Kant was the philosophical aspect." On one hand, Berth refused to soar "to the heights of an abstract, universal, eternal morality," or to substitute "for an inevitable economic evolution" a "no less inevitable democratic revolution."[41] On the other hand, if one wishes to rejuvenate Marxism, he wrote, "it is not so much *on the economic side* that one should concentrate one's efforts as *on the political side*," for what he felt to be essential in Marx was his "philosophy of action." Marx, he maintained, was "a great *philoso-*

pher of action," but "as an economist, his work will no doubt appear in many parts as more and more outdated." Here Berth supported his argument with reference to Arturo Labriola's demonstration of the weaknesses of the Marxist theory of surplus value and to Sorel's rejection of the concept of the preeminence of science as a factor of social change in the preface to his *Ruine du monde antique*.[42] The Sorelians saw the notion that "theory emerges from action and not action from theory" as "the main idea of Marxist socialism" and the only remaining chance of creating a revolutionary situation.[43]

Where the "new school" was concerned, this principle was all-important. For the Sorelians, "action" was "of primary importance," and "theory" was "only an a posteriori systematization of it." It followed that what was essential in Marx was "the sociological theory of class struggle" and not his economic analysis. The Sorelians believed not only that the Marxist economic theory was obsolete, but that in fact no "Marxist economic system" existed. Berth, like Sorel, noticed that "between the Manchesterian theories and the Marxist theories there was a striking similarity." Their sole difference—which Berth declared "enormous," but which in fact was not so great, for the good reason that its real importance was almost obviated in practice—was the fact that the liberals "took capitalism for an *eternal economic category,* while the others [the Marxists] took it for a *historical category.*"[44]

Here one finds the whole significance of the Sorelian revision of Marxism. For the Sorelians, Marxism was war, revolutionary action. Marx, they said, was neither an economist nor a philosopher, but a sociologist of class struggle. Socialism was thus reduced to a single element. As a result, as soon as it appeared that class struggle ceased to be a reality, all of socialism lost its raison d'être. At the same time, when the idea of class disappeared, activism and revolutionary struggle still remained. What changed was simply the *agent* of the revolution.

But at the time of which we are speaking (1905) one was still concerned with the war of the classes, which had to be preserved and developed by encouraging the conditions in which they could flourish. That was why Sorel asked the proletariat to oppose reformism by rejecting the rules of liberal democracy, to reject any measure that could hold back industrial development even when it was in the immediate interest of the workers, to spurn social legislation, and finally to oppose with all their might any move that "could reduce the class struggle to a rivalry of material interests."[45]

For the Sorelians, the proletariat was never anything other than a weapon of war to be used against the decadent bourgeoisie. They had no use for a proletariat that rejected a "*class struggle* worthy of the name" in order to take part in "the obscure and sterile rivalries of *democratic clans*" that caused the quarrels "around the always insufficiently filled troughs of the providential State."[46] This statement by Berth, whose modern connotations are striking, was made in 1913, but it only reiterated an idea expressed in

1904.[47] Where questions of principle were concerned, very little had changed between 1904 and 1913, and the positions of the Cercle Proudhon in the later period were merely the logical continuation of those of 1904–1905. The Sorelians always hoped that the proletariat, in liberating itself from democracy, would regain "a grandiose and epic quality that would bring both bourgeois society to its historical perfection and the working class to its full social maturity."[48]

One should also note that Sorel and his French followers refused from the very start to have anything to do with anticlericalism.[49] When the time came, this attitude facilitated their rapprochement with the Maurrassians, for whom Catholicism was an essential element in national tradition.

The fundamental aspect of the revision of Marxism, the one from which all the rest derived, was the critique of Marxist economics. Sorel, as we saw, began his criticism of Marxism at an early stage; Berth followed him in adopting as his own the conclusions of *Introduction à l'économie moderne*. For the Sorelians, it was a question of adapting "to our time Proudhon's ideas on the socialization of commerce and the State," but—and this was of prime importance—all this had to be done "without touching private property."[50] This axiom was never again questioned.

Sorel and Berth were not economists. Sorel made praiseworthy efforts, however, and he was well received by the Italian "liberists." Berth, for his part, was content to repeat a few Sorelian formulas on Marxist economics and the economics of the Manchester school. None of this went very far. The true critique of Marxist economics among European revolutionary syndicalists was confined to Italian academics. The autodidact of Boulogne-sur-Seine never looked so inadequate in the intellectual debates of the period as when set against the professional economists Enrico Leone and Arturo Labriola. Lagardelle was no doubt aware of this, and he asked Labriola for two long articles for *Le Mouvement socialiste* so that he and his readers could take stock of the question. Labriola simply presented in French the operational conclusions of a demonstration whose details were hidden away in the pages of Italian journals.[51]

Labriola regarded Marx the economist as a man of his time. In his period, he wrote, the theory of surplus value appeared to be "a completely irrefutable truth of common sense." Having passed through the physiocrats, Adam Smith, Ricardo, and above all the Ricardian school, it necessarily had to arrive at its Marxist formulation. It was thus not a discovery of Marx, as Engels had thought, and it certainly was not the source of Marx's scientific greatness. Rodbertus and Thompson could claim to an equal degree to be the systematizers of this common idea. But this was not the main point, which resided in the fact that "surplus value was an automatic phenomenon not of capitalist production, *but of the normal conditions of the labor market. . . . It was not the capitalist relationship*—that is, the existence of proletarians and capitalists and the contractual alienation of the labor force—that gave rise to profit, but the market conditions of the different factors of production." According to Labriola, this meant that the Marxist theory of surplus value was not exactly erroneous, inasmuch as surplus value always exists, but rather Marx's identification and description of the cause of this phenomenon was erroneous. On this error was built the entire edifice constructed first by petit bourgeois socialism and then by democratic reformism: an insipid, philantropical, and sentimental form of socialism. The theory therefore had to be rescued from this wrong direction in order to reestablish scientific truth (naturally), but above all in order "to prevent the practical degeneration of the labor movement." Similarly, Labriola rejected the famous laws of the collapse of capitalism and of pauperization. According to Labriola, these two ideas were in any case wrongly described as Marxist; in fact, they were indissociably connected with the fundamental ideology of the anticapitalist movement.[52]

Having thus virtually demolished the edifice as a whole, Labriola, in another major article, clearly stated: "It is not the economic principle of capitalist society that we are rebelling against." This amounted to a distortion of socialism, for, since it was the "heir to a society that brought the productive efficacity of human labor to its highest level," socialism, he wrote, "could only develop and apply on a still larger scale the economic principles of capitalism." Labriola admitted that not every type of socialism was capable of this—reformism was not, nor was that version of Marxism which soon came to be known as Leninism, because these two excrescences represented a kind of "socialism conceived in a unitary manner and in terms of the state," which was not in keeping with "the normal development of the contemporary economy." It was therefore essential never to impede the free play of economic forces; one should never, at the risk of incurring a "social disaster," touch the two principles by which capitalism had "achieved wonders"— "productive partnership and individual responsibility." For the same reason, one had to prevent measures "of social protection from impairing the vitality of capitalism and harming savings." Revolutionary syndicalism, he wrote, refused to "inherit an equality of penury."[53]

Finally, Labriola gave an explanation of the cause and nature of social antagonisms. The proletariat, he wrote, rebelled not against capitalism as such, but against "the principle of social—that is, hierarchical—organization proper to capitalism."[54] This assertion is of great importance for an understanding of the character of the Fascist synthesis. Let us listen to Labriola once more:

> The capitalist principle of organization makes capitalism look like *a boss* and capital like *an intellectual force of domination*, that is, like something transcendent to the body of workers. That is the essential fact which sets workers against

capitalists. The capitalist looks like a boss and the workers seem like a mass of slaves. Since intelligence and the power of organization and direction are extraneous to the body of workers, *the latter appear to be mere automatons in the hands of capital.*[55]

If that was all they believed there was to the question, it is easy to understand why most of the Italian theoreticians of revolutionary syndicalism were able, a few years later, to see corporatism as an adequate solution, and why Lagardelle remained convinced up to his last editorial on the eve of the Liberation of his fidelity to syndicalist principles. One can also understand why throughout the interwar period all these socialists who had become members of Fascist parties were able to consider corporatism an answer to the feelings of alienation of the proletariat. If one gave the worker the feeling of laboring for the good of the community and not for that of the employer, and if, within the framework of the corporate organization, one seemed to have radically modified the hierarchical relationships, was that not a great step forward? If the "aim of the socialist revolution" was "to abolish the separation between the worker and the instrument of production," if that was the aim and nothing else, and if one believed that there could be "an individual management of production, a regime of complete industrial liberty, within a collectivistic organization of economic life . . . a whole series of social forms within which the future society of freemen can be concretized," why should not corporatism have been one of these new social forms if one discovered that the state was something other than a mere instrument of the bourgeoisie? Was not this solution all the more legitimate in that revolutionary syndicalism regarded as disastrous any measure that would "impoverish the capitalists," and that would destroy "the marvelous fruits of capitalist civilization . . . together with the tree that produced them"?[56] Was this not precisely the argument the Italian and French Fascists employed against Soviet communism twenty years later? And, above all, do we not find here the true intellectual origins of the celebrated "intermediate regimes" spoken about by the neosocialist Déat, and of Henri De Man's idea that exploitation was far more a psychological problem than an economic phenomenon?

There remained the problem of the state. "The social revolution," wrote Labriola, "will not permit the existence above civil society of something it will have destroyed in the factory." This revolution "cannot be carried out without the decomposition of the state"[57]—not every form of state, however, and there was no question of transferring political power to the individual. Sorelism detested anarchism: it was individualistic only in the economic sphere. Berth wrote that "a real abyss" divided the ideas of the syndicalists from those of the anarchists.[58] Whether it was artisanal, agricultural, or high society in origin, whether inspired by Rousseau or Tolstoy, anarchism, according to the syndicalists, was an idealism, an intellectualism, a "metaphysical *simplism*," an "abstract and false rationalism." Anarchism was a "negation of the socialist idea," a "mere echo of the eighteenth century," and the "atomized individual,"[59] the "abstract man of anarchism," was only "Rousseau's savage or Diderot's cynic, the last representative of the eighteenth century, of the great bourgeois century."[60]

Berth and Labriola encompassed both anarchism and individualism in a single condemnation. One should not expect to find in these two men "a candid, idyllic optimism, an ingenuous belief in the beneficent instincts of man." The theoreticians of the "new school," deeply convinced that human nature is "not always likable,"[61] had confidence neither in liberal democracy, nor in social democracy, nor in any regime based on the principle of popular sovereignty. Their disdain for democracy and the law of numbers was never limited to its bourgeois and parliamentary manifestations; this criticism was aimed at the foundations of democracy. The cult of elites and of active syndicalist minorities instilled in them an absolute contempt for the childishness, as they believed, of thinking that people could govern themselves.

The theoreticians of revolutionary syndicalism detested the individual who refused to submit to social discipline, and they did not recognize any "absolute and transcendental liberty."[62] Berth denied the existence of an "abstract discrepancy between authority and liberty, between the state and the individual,"[63] and he took the further important step of asserting that the people feels and senses itself to be a collective social being. For Berth as for Proudhon, "to be is within the group."[64] Berth was only being consistent in recognizing "specifically that authority has hitherto been necessary" and that "civilization began and had to begin with constraint, and that this constraint was salutary, beneficial, and creative."[65]

The theoreticians of revolutionary syndicalism thus never proposed the disappearance of the state or of authority; they simply favored a process in which, as Labriola put it, "we *distribute* the authority of the state in the syndicates," whereas the anarchists "disperse it in the individual." Seen in this way, the "so-called antistate action of socialism" consisted of "this transfer of legal authority . . . from the state to the syndicate." In the development of this "new social organ," one saw "an objective necessity that made the syndicate into an authoritarian organ that gradually takes the place of the state."[66]

This clarified the question considerably. "Syndicalism no more wants to destroy the state, in the negative and reactionary sense that people imagine, than Monsieur Bergson wants to destroy science," wrote Berth.[67] The syndicalists were aware of the importance of the state in modern history, its unifying role, its function as an agent of modernization.[68] A rejection of the state and the abolition of private property were equally unacceptable to them. The state they opposed was the democratic state that existed or the socialist state the reformists wished to create, which, "suppressing all competition with the nationalists," consecrated "triumphant democracy"; the state they opposed was the one that developed a "pacifist protectionism" and impeded the free play of social forces.[69] They refused to replace capitalism with an "employer state" that would replace a multitude of individual employers; moreover, such a state, they believed, would be a "bad industrialist."[70] They rejected wholeheartedly what they called "state socialism," and since, in the conditions then prevailing, the development of the state could only mean the strengthening of liberal democracy or social democracy, Berth and Lagardelle coined an eloquent slogan: The Least State Possible![71]

In practice, they were true to the principles of economic liberalism to which, in this domain, revolutionary-syndicalist thought always returned. They vehemently opposed the "incessant interventionism" of the state in social relations, the truly hateful tendency of the democratic state to show the workers "repeated proofs of its solicitude" and to attempt to make "the employers see reason." Revolutionary syndicalism hated "this hothouse regime," which "renders anemic whatever it touches" and which "artificially sustains the weak, and above all necessitates its own extension."[72] This was undoubtedly a language that militant socialists were unaccustomed to and that made a bad impression on the traditional labor clientele. Berth, who was well aware of this, attempted to forestall criticism: "But, you will say, are you then for laissez-faire, laissez-aller? Your liberalism strangely resembles bourgeois liberalism! You are advocating a Darwinian struggle for existence. What a strange socialism!" To this argument, which, in order to be repeated in this way by Berth, must have been quite common in socialist circles, he had a necessarily somewhat weak but extremely characteristic reply: "The bourgeois concept," he wrote, "is an abstract concept. . . . It envisages individuals in isolation; the bourgeois social idea is one of an absolute atomism."[73] Revolutionary syndicalism sets against it the concrete person, the producer, and it founds upon the ruins of bourgeois culture a "culture of producers."[74] This culture of producers refuses to see the individual as the "motive force of the world";[75] it replaces the "abstract man" with the worker in the factory. This factory, a new sociopolitical cell, inherits the authority of the state.

That is why the syndicate arrogates to itself the right to speak on behalf of the entire working class: "A voluntary organism, it claims to tie up in a single bundle all the desires of the workers." Here Berth added an important element: the syndicate, he wrote, "is the government of the mass by the capable, the best, the labor elite."[76] This elitism, a fundamental principle of Sorelian thought, now clearly asserted itself and was immediately associated with the idea of struggle. While the anarchists wanted to turn the syndicate into "a sort of club of antiauthoritarian metaphysics,"[77] the Sorelians, for their part, conceived of the syndicates as fighting units that were disci-

plined, solidly organized, and led by an elite of enthusiastic militants. Lagardelle, moreover, described the idea of "class consciousness" as a "sense
that the cause of the whole takes precedence over the cause of the individual."[78] This idea of the primacy of the community over the individuals who
comprise it is absolutely necessary to an understanding of both Sorelism and
of the transition to fascism.

The workers in their syndicates—to quote Lagardelle again—desired "the
conquest of their dignity as man and the disappearance of a society of masters,"[79] but the characteristics of this new society and its principles were
described by Berth in images that leave no doubt about its real nature:

> "What we put in place of permanent armies," said Proudhon, "are industrial
> companies." And this is what Proudhon had to say about these companies: "Fi-
> nally we have companies of workers, *true armies of the Revolution*, in which the
> worker, *like the soldier in his battalion*, maneuvers with the precision of his
> machines; where thousands of wills, *intelligent and proud*, fuse into one supe-
> rior will, just as the arms they activate together produce a collective force
> greater than their multitude." Is this not a perfect transposition of the military
> order, as one might call it, into the labor order?[80]

It was undoubtedly such a transposition, and this was the ideal of the
perfect social organization proposed by the Sorelians.

But in *Les Nouveaux Aspects du socialisme*, a work published in 1908,
Berth had already made a fundamental distinction between the "productive
force" and "all nonproducers."[81] This distinction, an essential element in the
emergence of the Fascist synthesis, was greatly reinforced by another distinction made in the series of articles published in 1907–1908 that constitute
the major part of the volume *Les Méfaits des intellectuels*. According to this
source, one can speak not of capitalism as a single phenomenon, but of two
different forms of capitalism: "There is commercial capitalism and industrial
capitalism." The great enemy of the syndicalism of direct action is the "commercial and usurious capitalism, which is not favorable to a real progress of
productive forces," which "wishes to eliminate competition and stabilize the
market," and which requires a state that regulates social and economic relationships. Significantly, however, nothing of the kind is said about "industrial" capitalism. Far from it! Berth's distinction is so clear-cut, decisive, and
categorical that no one can be left in any doubt. It is accompanied by another
observation, which is no less clear: "If the idea of the state is a bourgeois
idea," he wrote, it is "a creation, as we said, of the commercial and intellectual bourgeoisie." These distinctions were already found in *Introduction à
l'économie moderne*, which Berth analyzed in January 1904 for the benefit of
the readers of *Le Mouvement socialiste*. They reappeared in *Les Méfaits des
intellectuels* in reference to another aspect of the fundamental distinction

between "the really productive part of the bourgeoisie" and the "nonproduc-ers" and "financiers," namely, that the former wished to break free of state control and fought the parasitism of the latter, who, on the contrary, con-stantly made demands on the state. It was therefore in no way surprising, wrote Berth, if one now saw "financiers professing socialist ideas, socialism naturally being for them state management taken to an extreme."[82]

This distinction between producers and parasites which now replaced the two classical categories of bourgeoisie and proletariat, this differentiation between a creative, fruitful capitalism and sterile finance, living at the ex-pense of those who labor, was not a Marxist distinction, but it played an important role in the thinking of the revolutionary revisionists at the begin-ning of the century. The socialist-nationalists took over this distinction, exac-erbating it, and it finally became one of the foundations of the social and economic doctrines of fascism. Lagardelle, for his part, also drew a sharp distinction between the "protective" state and the "warrior" state. His atti-tude to the two was quite different.[83] For the Sorelians, there was a funda-mental difference between authority in the service of democracy, whether liberal or socialist, and authority in the service of the syndicate, that strongly structured fighting unit with the characteristics of "a fully autonomous spiri-tual collectivity" in which "the masses are kept in a perpetual electric state."[84]

Lagardelle claimed there was a world of difference between a "political democracy, which recognizes only individuals," and a "labor democracy." Whereas the former was "uncertain and chaotic," the latter was "fixed and organic." Lagardelle was supremely contemptuous of the nonorganized in-dividual, the "human dust raised up by the opposing winds of politics."[85] He was quite convinced that the isolated worker was unable on his own to "pro-mote the principle of workers' government through professional groups" and believed there was a need for a "strong hierarchy" that would prevent the "uncertainties" and "oscillations of movements of opinion that exist in political democracies."[86] To this, Berth added a rejection of the "abstract and metaphysical concept" of people as "psychological atoms."[87]

Lagardelle was willing to envisage a "permanent control of the masses, insofar as they are organized," but he did not specify what form that control would take. He also stated that "socialist democracy will take its inspiration not from the laws of political democracy," but "from the rules of labor de-mocracy." This "labor democracy" was based on elitism and an absolute re-jection of equality. The first place was always given to those who were "most aware." "The concept of an abstract equality gives way here," wrote La-gardelle, "to the idea of a real equality based on the differences that in fact exist between the workers. They are not all on the same level because they do not all have the same aptitudes."[88] Finally, we learn that this very hierarchical, disciplined, elitist "labor democracy," which always favors the community over the individual, has the duty, "apart from electoral agitation, of regulating the smallest details of the workers' lives."[89]

The celebrated workers' liberty thus took on a very strange appearance, very close to a certain form of totalitarianism. Michels was able to claim in this framework that the elitist theory, which regarded the masses as a source of energy but denied them the capacity to determine the direction of social evolution, in no way contradicted the materialist conception of history and the idea of class warfare.[90] This framework also enabled the syndicalist leader Émile Pouget, who was not a Sorelian, to claim that direct action by the proletariat could "express itself in a benevolent and peaceful way or in a very forceful and violent manner," and that the great difference between syndicalism and "democratism" was precisely that "the latter, through universal suffrage, permits the unaware, the unintelligent to assume control . . . and stifles the minorities that contain the seed of the future."[91] Thus we see that the socialist extreme Left preached a contempt for democracy and parliamentarianism together with a cult of violent revolution by conscious activist minorities.

It was therefore not surprising that, speaking about the future of universal suffrage, Victor Griffuelhes should say: "It is clear to me that it should be relegated to the lumber room."[92] And Lagardelle was therefore correct in maintaining that "French syndicalism was born out of the reaction of the proletariat to democracy"—which, he claimed, was only a "popular form of bourgeois domination."[93] Émile Pouget declared that the methods of action of a confederal organization could not be based on the "vulgar democratic idea: they do not express the consent of the majority arrived at through the procedure of universal suffrage." Pouget believed that if democratic procedures were adopted in labor circles, "the lack of will of the unconscious and nonsyndicalized majority would paralyze all action. But the minority is not willing to abandon its demands and aspirations before the inertia of a mass that the spirit of revolt has not yet animated and enlightened. Consequently, the conscious minority has an obligation to act, without reckoning with the refractory mass." No one, he claimed, has the right to "recriminate against the disinterested initiative of the minority," least of all the "unconscious," who, compared with the militants, are no more than "human zeros."[94] This out-and-out elitism was very characteristic of syndicalist conceptions and linked up with that of some of the founders of the modern social sciences such as Pareto and Michels, whose work contributed a great deal to the development of fascism.

Throughout this period, Sorel, Pouget, and Lagardelle attempted to prove, each in his own way, that socialism could be built only "on an absolute separation of classes and on the abandonment of all hope of a political renewal."[95] Such a conception really meant the abandonment of the political, electoral, and parliamentary struggle and the paralysis of the Socialist party. If the opposition between class and party, between "class and opinion,"[96] was the guiding principle of syndicalism, and if, in identifying class struggle with the struggle of the party, the socialists were held to be guilty of a misconception, the syndicalists were necessarily driven into a position of neutrality that in practice eliminated the proletariat as an organized political force.

Ever attentive to the movement of ideas in labor circles, the Action française stressed its affinities with the revolutionary syndicalists. The CGT (General Confederation of Labor) failed to respond to its advances: it never really considered breaking its connection with social democracy. The only people in socialist circles to be attracted by the Maurrassian movement were those like Sorel, Berth, and Émile Janvion for whom democracy was in all circumstances the supreme evil. It would be a great mistake, however, to underestimate the depth of the antidemocratic and elitist reaction that involved not only the Sorelians, but also syndicalist leaders like Pouget and Griffuelhes who did not subscribe to the Sorelian theory of violence and were too preoccupied by the practical problems of the syndicates to be concerned with the question of bourgeois decadence. Among the Sorelians at that period, this convergence of views aroused inordinate expectations of the revolutionary potential of the French proletariat and the willingness of its leaders to lead it into battle.

Here we should point out the difference, very significant for the future, between French and Italian syndicalism. Whereas in France the secretaries of the CGT cautiously kept their distance from Sorel, in Italy Michele Bianchi, Alceste De Ambris, and Filippo Corridoni—famous syndicalist leaders whom one finds leading all the strikes of the period—were of one mind with the theoreticians. The French were sufficiently sure of themselves and confident in their followers not to need the conceptual framework that Sorel provided. This was not the case in Italy, where labor revolt had an urgent need of a mobilizing ideology that would impose solidarity and a unified objective on a mass of workers naturally divided by a multitude of local, regional, and cultural differences.

The Sorelians' primary concern remained the moral and intellectual delegitimation of the bourgeoisie and of democracy. Thus Berth, expressing a concept dear to Sorel, wrote that "the social idea" could not "be bourgeois." It "could hardly take any form except for two: it is *military* or *labor*." He insisted that war always remained "the source and principle of all virtue": ancient society collapsed "as soon as the heroic warrior ideal gave way."[97]

Like his master, Berth castigated "Socratic culture" and Socrates. To the teachings of this "first decadent," this "destroyer of the heroic Hellenic warrior society," he opposed a "tragic" conception "of life and the universe." Like Sorel again, he condemned the eighteenth century, which he saw as "licentious and already pornographic," decadent and corrupt. Berth extolled Bergson, "who destroyed intellectualism,"[98] and Nietszche, whose "superman . . . could adhere to revolutionary socialism."[99] He considered Comte and positivism, rationalism, intellectualism, and utilitarianism to be on the side of evil, while Nietzsche represented good. Nietzsche was regarded favorably because he taught that man "must overcome himself" and "becomes a hero only by participating in the great struggles whereby the heroic or divine work of history is accomplished," and Proudhon because he understood that war "raises everything to the level of the sublime" and makes man "larger than life."[100]

Berth wrote there was a need for *"a new philosophy of life"* and a new "hierarchy of values" in which "it was no longer science that had the dominant position, but action."[101] He believed that not abstract formulas about the socialization of the means of production would bring about the revolution, but "great, profound feelings that stir one's whole being."[102] For that reason, referring once again to Nietzsche, he too expressed his profound contempt for what the German philosopher called "English ideas"—liberalism and democracy—to which the reformists, headed by Bernstein, were unfortunately so attached. Berth thought the "will to power of the proletariat," bringing proletarian violence to a pitch, would give socialism a new face.[103] Thus, in order to improve and complete Marx, Berth, following in the footsteps of Sorel, drew on Nietzsche and Proudhon as well as other sources of inspiration[104] with the clear intention of proposing new structures for socialism. Before being able to organize the proletariat into combat formations, however, it was necessary to destroy its traditional political and emotional attachment to democracy.

The more Berth and Lagardelle fell under the influence of Sorel, the more pronounced their common attitude to democracy became. In 1902 Lagardelle wrote that if "the democratic principle, even more than democratic government, requires a socialist proletariat,"[105] it is nevertheless true that "socialism, which in certain respects is in agreement with democracy, is imperiled by it."[106] He strongly condemned the vision of socialism elaborated at the National Congress at Tours in March 1902, in which Jaurès won acceptance for the charter of the French Socialist party. This charter represented socialism as the necessary complement of the Declaration of the Rights of Man.[107] Lagardelle refused to accept the idea that "socialism is simply the logical outcome of democracy" and came to the conclusion that there was an essential contradiction between "the conception of class struggle, which is the basis of socialism," and democracy.[108] After the "Millerand experiment" (Millerand was the first socialist minister in France) and the moral collapse of the Dreyfus camp,[109] Lagardelle constantly attacked "corruption," which he believed he detected everywhere, and the fusion with extreme left-wing elements of the bourgeoisie implied by the program at Tours.[110] Moreover, this program represented, he wrote, the triumph of "state socialism," of the "new social democracy," of which Jaurès, the candidate of both the radical committees and of the socialist groups in the Tarn, had become the symbol.[111]

Two years later, the tone had hardened considerably. "Socialism has decomposed in France in contact with democracy," wrote Lagardelle.[112] "Present-day socialism cannot stand up to the test of democracy."[113] In Berth's view, if democracy was a sort of purgatory, a natural and necessary transitional stage between the ancien régime and socialism, the fact remained that between "socialism and democracy, there is an essential antagonism."[114] This was a basic problem about which the revolutionary syndicalists differed not only from the reformists, but also from those who in 1905 were regarded as orthodox, including Kautsky, author of a book entitled *Parlementarisme et socialisme*. Berth regarded this book as the most instructive example of orthodoxy's major error in maintaining that a triumphant socialism could impart new life to parliamentarianism and use it for different purposes. This, said Berth, was an illusion; parliamentarianism was the primary form of the political domination of the bourgeoisie and was doomed to disappear with it,[115] and the rules of democracy could not be said to apply in the world of labor.

The following text expresses the Sorelians' feelings concerning democracy and their conception of it. It is not, as might seem at first, a criticism of democratic practices, but rather of some of the fundamental principles of the democratic system.

> What is the law, democracy doing, with its mania for voting and its stupid cult of majorities? . . . The secret ballot—that is the perfect symbol of democracy! Look at the citizen, that member of the sovereign body, who tremblingly goes about exercising his sovereignty: he hides himself, he evades the scrutiny of society. No voting slip could be sufficiently opaque to veil his private thoughts, his act of sovereignty, from the eyes of the indiscreet: he enters into the voting booth like a thief. Here he is alone with his conscience, the supposed master of the moment: he ponders, he is alone—alone like Leibniz's monad, with all the doors and windows closed! For this is how democracy conceives of liberty in reality: it is the liberty of the monad, or, if one prefers, the liberty of Epicurus, withdrawn from the world in the peace of his selfish and solitary self-sufficiency, far from the cares and concerns of public life, free and sovereign in his solitude and nothingness. And this is how democracy views the People as King: of its collective power nothing remains, thanks to democracy, but a procession of timorous shadows who, trembling and in concealment in the silence of their conscience abandoned to its egoism and cowardice, exercise their so-called sovereignty![116]

This extreme rejection of democracy lay behind the Sorelians' ferocious campaign not only against "*reformist revisionism*," whether syndicalist or political, and the "moral degradation" and "parliamentary cretinism" it gave rise to,[117] but also against all "Guesdist" conceptions of socialism. No judgment was harsh enough, no sarcasm sufficiently injurious to condemn this *"socialism of the least effort"*[118] or to stigmatize the "nothingness and mendacity of reformist, democratic and idealist state socialism"[119]—that socialism, "bourgeois to the core," which could be observed in the celebrated international congresses with their lobbying, speeches by star performers, and all the "various manifestations usual in that kind of market or fair."[120]

The writers of *Le Mouvement socialiste* did not limit their hostility to France; they opened the pages of their journal to the Italian nonconformists and to Robert Michels. Arturo Labriola and Enrico Leone were eager to settle accounts with the "bastardized domestic socialism" that was trying to become established in the Italian peninsula, with the reformist leader Turati, whom they said was regarded by the Milanese bourgeoisie as a "sort of third local wonder, to be placed next to the Duomo and Leonardo's *Last Supper*," and with the "reformist farce" whose protagonists "bowed very graciously to the monarchy," while claiming that their approach was the "only truly . . . revolutionary conception of socialism."[121]

The year 1906 was important for the Sorelians. On one hand, their ideological corpus reached its maturity with the publication of *Réflexions*, and, on the other hand, a great confrontation was beginning in Italy between the revolutionary syndicalist intellectuals and the Socialist party. The struggle against the syndicalists had in fact begun in 1905, when Enrico Leone was dismissed from *Avanti!* Leone had supported the general strike of 1904 in this socialist daily. The editor of the journal, the centrist leader Enrico Ferri, who was very unenthusiastic about this mass action, obtained a unanimous vote of confidence from the party leadership and thereby forced him to resign. Michele Bianchi, Paolo Orano, and Tomaso Monicelli left together with Leone;[122] they all made an active contribution to the socialist-national synthesis of 1910 and eventually laid the foundations of the Fascist movement. At the same time, these people began to become aware of the true nature of socialist politics as well as of Italian social reality. They felt that a confrontation with the Socialist party had become inevitable, and simultaneously—and even more important—their doubts concerning the revolutionary potential of the proletariat increased.

With regard to relationships with the party, two currents manifested themselves in 1906: Arturo Labriola was still at the stage where, despite his bitter criticism of the Socialist party, he refused to leave it (in this he was in a way equivalent to Lagardelle), and he told the syndicalists they were "not responsible for his action."[123] At the same time Ottavio Dinale asked how long could the syndicalists, who believed in class struggle, continue to be associated with a party that had become a great electoral institution.[124]

The disillusionment was even greater when the nonconformists became aware of the existence of enormous structural impediments to the fulfillment

of their revolutionary aspirations. "The socialism of class struggle is ideologically much in advance of the historical conditions of our country," wrote
Labriola, adding that "experience seems to show that the mass of electors is
against the pure principles of class struggle."[125] Sergio Panunzio, for his part,
decided that the great theoretical problems of contemporary socialism did
not "unduly preoccupy the socialist consciousness of the masses"[126]—an
idea that Dinale expressed more bluntly when deploring the "passive psychology of the proletariat which causes it to remain weak and impotent every
time it undergoes a new bloodletting." Consequently, both Labriola and
Dinale came to the conclusion that only violence could inspire the proletariat with the "sentiment of heroism," which would turn it into a *revolutionary mass*," and that this was the sole "guarantee of a superior humanity."[127]
According to Paolo Orano, the aim of these revolutionaries was to be the
"barbarians of the monstrous secular empire built by reaction with the lime
of socialist democracy."[128]

The Italians, who always looked toward France and envied its labor movement given a special aura by the Commune of Paris, were beset with
enormous difficulties: regional rivalries and a degree of corruption in public
life unknown elsewhere in western Europe. Thus, the dark picture the Italian Sorelians painted and the virulence of their language hardly come as a
surprise. It is more surprising, however, that Robert Michels, for his part,
declared the total failure of the German socialist movement. His verdict of
failure on this great Socialist party—the party of Engels, Kautsky, Bernstein,
and Luxemburg—which had long dominated the international socialist
scene, was no less severe than that of the Italian nonconformists on theirs.
The nonconformists, whether French, Italian, or German, felt themselves to
be, and wanted to be, a single unit. This was first because the socialist parties
of their respective countries had rejected them, and second (and this was
their outstanding point of convergence) because they were convinced that
they represented all that was still valid in European socialism. "Parliamentarianism kills socialism," wrote Michels. "This is the case everywhere, in
France and Italy, just as it is in Germany."[129] To these revolutionaries, Germany was the laboratory of socialism, and its socialism represented a prefig-
uration of what was to happen elsewhere. Were not all the developing European socialist parties jealous of the might of Bebel's party?

The example of Germany, wrote Michels, illustrates precisely the fallacy
of this way of thinking, for what can be expected of democracy if a party that
has three hundred thousand members and obtains three million votes in
general elections reveals itself incapable of bringing about the slightest
change in its country? What is the use of universal suffrage if such a party is
unable even to influence the state in a liberal direction? What can be expected of a system that dooms to sterility a third of the votes cast? And
finally, what is the use of having a party, syndicates, money, newspapers,

schools, and sports clubs if the socialist masses prove to be "lazy and disinclined to action" for lack of a moral education?[130] Three years later, in 1907, Michels estimated the number of registered and regularly subscribing members of the SPD to be four hundred thousand. This gigantic party provided the spectacle of an enormous bureaucratic machine in which organization had become an end in itself.[131]

The same was true of the German syndicalist movement, which, with its three million members and magnificent bureaucratic apparatus, shared with the "Prussian state the sense of order, zeal, and good qualities of financial employees." The sole ideal of this syndicalism, which prided itself on being concerned only with economics, was to fill its coffers.[132] The great theoretical debates of a former time belonged to a past that was dead and buried. The Karl Johann Kautskys, Rosa Luxemburgs, and Clara Zetkins had become an uninfluential minority within a party that parliamentarianism had transformed into an extra cog in the machinery of the empire. If there was a war, whether against England or France, the socialists would publish a highly revolutionary manifesto against the government and would then go out and fight the enemy.[133] Michels condemned the German patriotism of the socialist leaders, another aspect of their moral and political decline. He was not afraid to adopt Gustave Hervé's view that the idea of dividing the phenomenon of war into "aggressive" and "defensive" warfare was childish. He then fought a courageous antimilitaristic campaign, which caused him great difficulties with his own party. After a series of lectures given in Paris, he was practically accused of treason.[134]

In about 1904 to 1905 there was nevertheless a moment when it seemed that the revolution might happen after all. The Italian general strike of 1904 was seen as a success (which in several respects it was), and the German social democratic congress at Jena in September 1905 was, in Michels's words, a "slight turn to the Left," representing a move toward the tactics of class warfare. At the other end of Europe, a rebellion had broken out in Russia. According to Michels, who remained the most violent critic of German socialism, the number of those who no longer believed in parliamentarianism as a means of achieving a socialist society was growing from day to day.[135] These hopes, however, were short-lived. In September 1906, the Berlin proletariat suffered a bitter defeat, which soon became a collapse of German syndicalism. Thirty-three thousand workers were dismissed as a measure of retaliation for a strike by a few hundred metalworkers. Faced with a self-confident body of employers, the syndicates led the proletariat to disaster.[136]

Michels now came to the conclusion that the cause of the trouble was not only in the apparatuses and oligarchies of the labor organizations, but also in the social reality represented by what in 1904 he called the "innumerable unconscious and blind proletariat."[137] This mass of workers, cowering with fear at the sight of a few policemen, had at least been known in the past for its taste for theoretical discussions,[138] and its leaders were at least supposed to be astute in electoral matters. In 1907 this too came to an end; it turned out that the party was no longer capable of even winning an election! Berth seized the opportunity, and the pleasure he had in rubbing salt into the gaping wound of that "vast socialist theological institute," which the German party—formerly so proud of its supremacy in theoretical doctrine, so convinced of possessing the truth[139]—had turned into, was exceeded only by the explosion of joy with which Lagardelle greeted the electoral defeat of the SPD in February 1907.[140]

A similar way of thinking existed in Italy. Ever since the socialist movement had "decided to become electoral," in Arturo Labriola's words, it had become more obvious every day, in his opinion, that there was no correlation between the electoral successes of socialism and its real achievements. Never, he wrote, "did socialist society seem so far from realization as when the socialists were close to gaining power." Finally, there were the electoral defeats, which showed that the compromises and changes of allegiance were not even effective. Socialism, concluded Labriola, "is something other than democracy."[141]

Lagardelle decided that all that now remained was direct action: "Class struggle," he wrote, "is the whole of socialism."[142] But here one came up against a problem that ended by dumbfounding the revolutionary syndicalists, namely, that class struggle was not a social reality. One had to create it out of nothing and develop in the proletariat those feelings of heroism, abnegation, and sacrifice which capitalism had failed to produce. Only "revolutionary idealism . . . enthusiasm for battle" could bring victory, Lagardelle told Jules Guesde at the congress at Nancy.[143] Michels added the following trenchant comment: A movement that seeks the emancipation of the working class "loses not only its effectiveness but also its raison d'être when it begins to weigh up sacrifices and to be afraid of them." The spirit of sacrifice, he wrote, is the precondition for the emergence of any "self-conscious force," which is the only kind that can be "a historical factor."[144] Lagardelle, for his part, asserted that one had to arouse the courage of the proletariat, "cultivate their will," "train them to action," and advocate "direct action," because it taught the proletarians that "there is no fatality, since men make their history themselves."[145] Three years earlier, Michels had already complained of the lack of a *"moral thirst"* among the German proletarians, the sinister consequence of an "ill-understood historical materialism."[146] This, then, was how the revolutionary syndicalist intellectuals applied Sorel's teachings in their own antimaterialistic revision of Marxism.

The various stages of the journey that led the Sorelians to the socialist-national synthesis are easy to distinguish. In the beginning, the dissidents wished to repudiate a certain kind of idealism, readily identified with utopianism, which they believed to be the alibi of the most vulgar opportunism and of economic determinism. Thus, they broke with both reformism and orthodoxy, regarding them as two different forms of an ill-understood and ineffective Marxism. In view of these "deviations," the Sorelians urged a return to Marx and authentic Marxism: the Marxism of class struggle, raised to the level of a moral value. The Sorelians, at that stage of their evolution, believed that Marxism rested on the postulate that there exist homogeneous social classes that are in a state of war, and they understood this situation of conflict to be the key to the future. Thus, they called for a relentless struggle against anything—such as political democracy, human rights, universal values, social Catholicism, or reformist socialism—that diminished, or that was capable of diminishing, this antagonism. They held that the relationship between the classes was a relationship of force: the Sorelians were not content with stating this as a fact, but declared that they wished to turn "this observation into a precept."[147] Force, wrote Lagardelle, "is the agent of the transformation of the world," and class struggle "the real stimulus of the modern world."[148] Berth wrote that Marx's true greatness was not that he had posed the problem of property (others had done that before him), but that in elaborating his theory of class struggle he had put "action, life, and development above abstract ideas."[149] With this understanding the French Sorelians adopted the formula of Panunzio, the future theoretician of fascism, that "syndicalism is the historical development of Marxism."[150] But they had also read *Le Dix-huit Brumaire* and knew that a social group that was passive and inert, even if it possessed the objective characteristics of a class, did not constitute a class in the Marxist sense of the term. It lacked the "awareness" and "unity of will" that could be formed only in struggle.[151]

In their formative years, the future Sorelians had already understood that "this class egoism is incompatible with high moral aspirations and constitutes in itself a depressing *diminution of the socialist spirit and consciousness*," but this was only one aspect of the essential problem. In 1900 Berth condemned a belief "in a mechanical and fatalistic evolution" and a blind confidence "in an alleged vertiginous decomposition of bourgeois society" that paralyzes revolutionary inclinations. Since the petit bourgeoisie and the peasantry were not part of the proletariat, and since capitalism was not too favorable to socialism, should not socialism, he asked, "be more favorable to itself?"[152] Did not this faith in a vulgar determinism, in the "dogmatic predictions of science," lead to the collapse of socialism, a total collapse that leaves behind "only a shameful reformism and that decks itself out in old revolutionary formulas"? This was precisely where revolutionary syndicalism came in. As Berth wrote, it "transfers the idea of catastrophe from the pole of capitalist fatality to the pole of proletarian liberty. Its great concern is to *bring the proletariat from passivity to activity*."[153] Direct action and the general strike were understood as an application of this voluntarism the

Sorelians advocated.[154] Thus Berth, following Sorel, in a significant passage that illustrates the true nature of this revolt, wrote: "It is necessary, in order that beings, like things, and collective beings, like individuals, attain their full judicial and metaphysical reality, that there should be violent oppositions. This is the very law of life, which is universal antagonism."[155]

To the Sorelian myth was now added this element of social Darwinism. With the myth of the general strike—a "grandiose and sublime myth"— Berth wrote that one was in the presence not of "an idea" but "of an absolutely new *collective state of mind*, an entirely new *social intuition*."[156] When he gathered into a volume the articles that made up *Les Méfaits des intellectuels*, he maintained that the Sorelian myth "is an *expression of the will*. . . . Sorel begins with the very simple observation that nothing would ever be done in the world if *there was only reason*. Reason is essentially relativistic, whereas action belongs to the absolute."[157]

This cult of activism, to which was added a visceral distrust of reason, was combined with a real veneration of war, held to be a source of greatness and virtue. Once again, Berth quoted Proudhon to the effect that antagonism is "the fundamental faith of the universe." Thus, industry was compared to a "battlefield," and war was described as "the most profound, most sublime phenomenon of our moral life."[158] Finally, conflict was said to give rise to the power of mobilization without which no mass movement is able to exist.

> The strike is a phenomenon of collective life and psychology. Here, very powerful, very contagious, almost electric sentiments come into play. . . . The will of each worker is submerged and absorbed in this unity: individual egoism, private interests, miserable personal preoccupations, and little secret weaknesses disappear. There is now only an electrified mass, a complex collective personality, transported all together with a single unanimous and powerful upsurge to the highest peaks of heroism and the sentiment of the sublime.[159]

The conceptual framework for the transition to national socialism and fascism was thus created long before the Great War. No theoretician of the interwar period had a better grasp of the relationship between the individual and the community proposed by fascism. No Fascist writer would speak in any other way of war, of heroism, of heroic values. Of Marxism, divested of its materialist and individualist content, deeply rooted in the rationalism of the eighteenth century, there remained only the conception of conflict as the motive force of history, the source of the beautiful and the sublime. All of socialism was reduced to this uncompromising struggle against the values and principles of liberal democracy. The instrument of this rebellion, the syndicate, was seen as the expression par excellence of all the virtues of a heroic proletariat regarded as the builder of a new civilization.

Thus reducing socialism to a single factor, however, meant dooming the whole edifice to certain collapse when this heroic, altruistic proletariat, organized in its syndicates in combat formations that take the bourgeois order by storm, was revealed as existing only in the imaginations, hopes, and wishes of theoreticians and intellectuals. This was shown to be doubly true, as it soon appeared that the syndicate, supposed to play the role of the liberator of the proletarians, was merely an organization like any other, guided and commanded like all organizations, including the socialist parties, by an oligarchy. Like all organizations, it developed a bureaucracy and had its own interests, which were unconnected with either proletarian internationalism or the future of humanity. The proletariat, at least in the industrialized countries, was only a crowd, and a crowd is amorphous and conservative by nature. In order to activate it, one needed a myth, one needed a revolutionary elite conscious of its duties.

Finally, the moment of truth arrived when it transpired that the proletarian path did not lead anywhere. The vast majority of the proletariat remained impervious to anything that did not touch its immediate material interests. The socialist parties and the syndicates accepted democracy and sought to benefit from it as much as possible. Anyone who wanted to persist in his revolutionary attitude had to find another solution. One had to replace the proletariat, which had absconded from its civilizing role, with another historical force.

THE EMERGENCE OF SOCIALIST NATIONALISM

By about 1907, the thinking of the dissidents was already overshadowed by doubts concerning the revolutionary capacities of the proletariat and hence the nature of socialism. Michels and the Italians were not the only ones to acknowledge this. In October 1906, Berth admitted that few labor movements were thus far animated by a heroic conception of class struggle. The proletariat, he wrote, "can fail in its mission. There is no objective necessity that socialism should be realized." However, one should not conclude from this deficiency that the working class is not the "necessary object" of socialism. The labor movement does not necessarily take a socialist direction, but "no socialism is possible without a labor movement."[160] Michels went still farther: he opposed the notion that the capitalist system, in "giving birth not to the proletariat, but to a *new form* of proletariat, brought socialism into being. Socialism as an ideology existed before it." Michels thought it was as useless to assert this opinion as to claim the opposite. It was no more the idea than it was the proletariat that produced socialism; instead—and this was the important point—"the socialist class movement . . . was born of a union of the proletariat with the idea." In the absence of a proletariat, there could not be a socialist movement, but "without the idea, there is no socialism either." He maintained that the whole significance of revolutionary syndicalism was precisely this "grandiose union of the *idea* with the *class*." The future writer of *Political Parties*, the unsparing critic of the German scene, understood rapidly that "class egoism alone is not sufficient to attain a revolutionary objective." On the contrary, he wrote, the economic egoism of the masses of workers employed in the Krupp armament factories led not to rebellion but to militarism. The more orders Krupp received from the sworn enemies of the proletariat, the more the wages of his workers increased. The same applied to the masses of workers occupied in manufacturing armaments and building arsenals in other countries. For that reason, he wrote, "without the *ethical elements* that raise brutal class egoism to the level of the socialist conception," the movement for workers' emancipation had no future.[161]

At the same time, Michels was aware that the social group commonly known as the proletariat was not a homogeneous entity. There were considerable differences not only between the industrial centers and the countryside but also between different industrial sectors. Corporative and professional interests easily worked against labor solidarity. This was a common idea in syndicalist circles, frequently repeated by Berth and Lagardelle.[162] The French Sorelians, however, were slower to grasp its immediate implications than the others, and unlike Michels they were even slower to understand that the syndicate was essentially far less different from any other social organism than those who had quasi-messianic expectations of it liked to imagine.

It soon became apparent that a class was not merely a group of people from the same economic milieu united by an awareness of their solidarity, nor did it represent the absolute opposite of a political party, regarded by the Sorelians as an artificial aggregate of disparate elements. All revolutionary syndicalism was thus called in question. Inasmuch as Michels attempted to show that the syndicate possessed the faults inherent in any organization and Berth believed that any representation "could only be a betrayal," one could assume that the same danger attended labor organizations, and the same fate lay in store for them. The masses of workers did not represent themselves, and the syndicates were not different from political parties. It was not political parties as part of the workings of liberal democracy that were responsible for bourgeois-mindedness and deviation, but the principle of organization itself.[163]

Even if the processes by which they reached it varied somewhat, the theoreticians of revolutionary syndicalism all came to the conclusion that a proletariat with a character of its own was an illusion. The proletariat did not possess the messianic qualities the revolutionaries had hoped for, and it had no intention of sacrificing its immediate interests in order to save the world from decadence. In the final analysis, the vast majority of the industrial proletariat of western Europe recognized itself in the great reformist parties of

Germany, France, and Italy. British trade unionism, which was satisfied with its lot and did not look for anything else, and the labor organizations of Germany, France, and Italy, which expressed dissatisfaction but nevertheless agreed to postpone the social revolution until some indefinite future, ultimately felt comfortable with the social-democratic consensus. The CGT became a vehicle for democratic socialism, and the labor syndicates proved to be anything but combat units. The rapprochement between the SFIO and the CGT pursued by Jaurès and Vaillant grew. The party made no concessions either in its principles or its reformist practices, and yet, when voting day came, the members of the CGT readily gave it their support. The position of revolutionary syndicalism now seemed to be a foregone conclusion: anyone who resisted integration into the bourgeois order (of which democratic socialism was now a part), anyone who wanted to persist in efforts to undermine the established order, necessarily had to find a new agent of revolution and to redefine the content and objectives of the revolution in question. It was now obvious that a proletarian uprising was inconceivable. The revolution would remain a moral revolution, an intellectual and spiritual revolution, but it would cease to be a proletarian revolution.

The Sorelians' disappointment was commensurate with the hopes they had placed in the proletariat. The theoreticians of labor revolt, captives of their absolute faith in the virtues of a proletariat fired by the myth of the general strike, had no other solution to offer. Among the socialists, they were the only ones to find themselves in this situation. Their intellectual position, because it rested on a single premise, was extremely fragile; this brand of socialism could not withstand the shock of experience. They who had brought everything down to the spontaneity of the workers' revolt were not in a position to beat a retreat or postpone the revolution indefinitely, nor were they able, like the Bolsheviks, to go in for conspiracy while awaiting the opportunity to make a final assault, nor could they fall back on democratic socialism. Moreover, the situation in western Europe did not seem to be changing much. While the Leninists and, more generally, the revolutionaries of central and eastern Europe, true to orthodox Marxist conceptions, felt the ground trembling beneath their feet and were able to await their hour, the French and Italian Sorelians, for their part, had no option but immediately to come to the conclusion that the void left by the collapse of revolutionary syndicalism had to be filled by another force capable of continuing the struggle.

When he was already committed to the socialist-national synthesis, Édouard Berth sought to draw the moral of the failure and reflected on its causes. If "syndicalism rapidly decomposed in the swampy environment of democracy," he wrote, it was because "the myth of the general strike, which should have played in the labor movement the role that the myth of the near return of Christ played in early Christianity, rapidly disintegrated as a result of political intrigues. The failure of the railway strike was its death blow."[164]

Democracy had proved to be to be too strong for revolutionary syndicalism, both in the sphere of intellectual competition and in political struggle. Defeated in the social sphere by the democratization of the regime and the introduction of social reforms, syndicalism was incapable of withstanding the power of mobilization demonstrated by democracy. Berth was aware, however, that the failure of the railway strike and the defection of labor activists were due to a far deeper cause. If "the syndicalist idea has so soon undergone the same process of degeneration as the socialist idea . . . ," he wrote, "it is because the working class has not yet made its *moral rupture* with bourgeois philosophy—that is, the philosophy of the eighteenth century."[165] Syndicalism had been ruined by disintegrating into socialism, and as Berth declared in 1913 of socialism as it then was: "With its innumerable variants, it is a pure and simple negation of civilization, an aspect of modern decadence, the contemporary disintegration taken to its ultimate conclusions and exceeding all limits."[166]

Therefore, in order to save syndicalism and civilization, one had to be conscious of two great truths. First, one had to recognize that there was a connection between *authentic* socialism—socialism as understood by syndicalism—and the sense of "historical grandeur" fostered by classical culture, just as there was a link between socialism and the "appetite for moral sublimity" promoted by a Christian education. There was "thus no contradiction, but rather a collaboration between tradition and revolution." This characteristic was lacking in socialism as it was, for it harbored the crazy ambition of wishing to construct an entirely new humanity while destroying the foundations on which any new construction could in fact be made. Was it not guilty of "arousing in the workers the most unhealthy sentiments: a taste for destruction, an appetite for enjoyment and well-being, an aspiration to that romantic and negative form of liberty which is to be rid of anything that constrains passions, instincts, and vices"?[167] For Berth as for Sorel, the essential problems were always of culture and morality. Their Catholic puritanism was simply an aspect of this outlook.

The second truth to be recognized was the importance of what Berth described as the "revival of heroic values that appears to be taking place among the younger bourgeoisie."[168] "Undoubtedly," he wrote, "something has changed in the bourgeoisie. . . . The bellicose and religious spirit is triumphing over the pacifistic and humanitarian spirit."[169] This "Catholic, patriotic, classical renaissance," which had been inconceivable less than ten years before,[170] had become a reality illustrated by Agathon's book (Agathon was the pseudonym of Henri Massis and Alfred de Tarde) and the writings of Péguy and Psichari, Renan's grandson, who rose up in defense of the church and the army. The eighteenth century, with Rousseau and the Encyclopedists, had fallen into oblivion; the century in favor was the Grand Siècle. Pascal, wrote Berth, quoting Sorel, had defeated Descartes.[171]

In other words, the bourgeois renaissance took place not only independently of the proletarian renaissance, which never happened, but also despite the proletariat's slow but continuous slide into degeneracy. Had the fate of civilization, then, ceased to depend on the antagonism of the classes, and did it now depend on the capacity of the proletariat to imitate the bourgeoisie? If this same revival of heroic values took place among the proletarian youth,[172] if "the bourgeois semiawakening that seems to be taking place at the present time" intensified and "in reaction forced the working class in turn into an awakening,"[173] would one not enter "into a new classical, bellicose, and revolutionary era"?[174] Here, then, the roles had been reversed: the bourgeoisie had snatched the torch of the revolution out of the tremulous hand of the proletariat. The new force for progress was the bourgeoisie, which had impressed its own image on the modern revolutionary movement.

This was clearly an important milestone in the Sorelians' development. On the eve of the war, a new conception of the revolution had appeared, just as a new idea of socialism had come into being. Once more it was Michels who blazed the trail, and in 1906 he crossed swords with Berth, who at that period was still true to the principles of revolutionary syndicalism. Berth reproached Michels with conceiving of socialism as merely an ideological construction, an aspiration to a more rational and just economic order. Michels, now convinced that the class interests of the proletariat were incapable of producing socialism and that the proletarian condition would not give rise to revolutionary idealism, maintained that socialism consisted of adherence to a system of ideas and was not dependent on a class situation. Berth rightly concluded that where Michels was concerned, the relationship between socialism and the proletariat was a purely empirical one.[175]

This, in fact, is what Michels's analysis suggested: socialism could exist independently of the working class. Not all the working class, in his view, was socialist, not all the workers' syndicates in the world were socialist, and not all socialists were workers. The relationship between socialism and the proletariat was therefore not essential. And since one could have a socialism without a proletariat, why should there not be a socialism for the entire nation? The socialist theoreticians Henri De Man and Marcel Déat subsequently came to the same conclusion, and, some five years after Michels, Berth also took this direction. If Michels had thought there could be a socialism without a proletariat, Berth now believed there could be a revolution without a proletariat, or in other words a moral, intellectual, and national renewal without a proletariat. On the eve of the Great War, Berth rejoined

Michels (who had meanwhile emigrated to Italy) and the Italian Sorelians; he now maintained that the bourgeoisie of the Action française, the representative of heroic values, would bring about a renaissance of civilization and the revival of the nation. An eventual resurrection of the proletariat depended on this bourgeoisie. Accordingly, he wrote, "Sorel and Maurras should be hailed as the two masters of the French and, I should add, the European regeneration."[176]

Far from being opposed to one another, Sorel and Maurras were said to complement one another like Apollo and Dionysus. Apollo and Dionysus had a common enemy, Socrates, the destroyer of tragedy, the ancestor of Voltaire, the archetype of the intellectual.[177] The alliance of Maurrassian "Apollonism" and Sorelian "Dionysism" meant the definite end of the reign of Socrates and Descartes, the defeat of the eighteenth century, and the victory of Pascal.[178] To this "dual nationalist and syndicalist movement,"[179] the Sorelians brought what they saw as the essence of their master's teaching: a belief in "the historical and civilizing value of violence," which they held to be "very beautiful, very noble, and very heroic." Thus, with regard to syndicalism, they stated their conviction that "it is in its revolutionary, untamed, and satanic character that its true social value is to be found." As for war, "that grandiose, sublime, and terrible reality," it denoted "a philosophy of life based on heroic pessimism" which could "scarcely be reconciled with the dull optimism of the eighteenth century."[180] That is what all the Fascists were to say.

To this new synthesis, the Sorelians brought the Proudhonian tradition: the cult of war, but also that of the family (a "*mystical institution*," according to Proudhon) and of indissoluble marriage, and an absolute respect for private property.[181] The syndicalist revolt contributed, finally, its horror of intellectualism and of intellectuals, who were condemned for their rejection of classical culture and heroic and martial values and for their participation in an "entirely bourgeois" creation "where everything, as Nietzsche said, is abstract." This taste for abstraction and this fight against classicism made the intellectual the pillar of democracy, the representative of an entirely negative revolt that corrupts and destroys "all the disciplines necessary for the education of humanity."[182]

The Action française, for its part, contributed "the beginning of a classical renaissance" that it had initiated, or in other words, "an insatiable appetite for heroic grandeur, political grandeur, and judicial grandeur,"[183] and sought "to establish a serious, organic, spiritual, living, and free order in opposition to the entirely mechanical and material order of façade" created by democracy.[184] On this common basis, "nationalists and syndicalists" agreed "to struggle against democracy,"[185] and against "the nauseous ideal . . . which is called a humanitarian, pacifistic, and rationalistic ideal."[186] On this common ground the Cercle Proudhon was founded in 1911.

Organized by Valois and Berth, the Cercle Proudhon sought, in Valois's words, to provide a common platform "for nationalists and leftist anti-democrats."[187] Placing itself under the authority of Proudhon, it also took inspiration from Sorel—the two great thinkers who had "prepared the meeting of the two French traditions that had opposed each other throughout the nineteenth century: nationalism and authentic socialism, uncorrupted by democracy, represented by syndicalism."[188] Indeed, the founders of the Cercle regarded Sorel as the truest disciple of Proudhon. They admired his anti-intellectualism, his antiromanticism, his dislike of Kant, his Bergsonism, and his contempt for bourgeois and liberal values, democracy, and parliamentarianism. Thus, Gilbert Maire stressed the great difference between a syndicalism based on an authentic Marxism, a "philosophy of arms and not of heads" that "saw the social revolution in a mystical light," and a democratic, Dreyfusard socialism, a socialism of unnatural alliances.[189] The Maurrassians welcomed Sorel gladly because he enabled them to invoke Marx against Jaurès, class interests against the solidarity of the "republican defense," syndicalism against socialism, and the new social sciences against Rousseau, the eighteenth century, democracy, and liberalism.

The Cercle was named after Proudhon because from the beginning the theoreticians of revolutionary syndicalism considered Proudhon the equal of Marx. The more their revision of Marxism developed, the more Proudhon eclipsed Marx, so that he appeared in Berth's writings, for instance, as the "father of modern socialism."[190] The Action française also, from its inception, regarded the author of *La Philosophie de la misère* as one of its masters. He was given a place of honor in the weekly section of the journal of the movement entitled, precisely, "Our Masters." Proudhon owed this place in *L'Action française* to what the Maurrassians saw as his antirepublicanism; his anti-Semitism; his loathing of Rousseau; his disdain for the French Revolution, democracy, and parliamentarianism; and his championship of the nation, the family, tradition, and the monarchy.[191]

The *Cahiers du Cercle Proudhon* took up the same themes, found more or less everywhere in Proudhon, but placed a special emphasis on his socialism. Moreover, like Maurras, who admired him because, "quite apart from his ideas, Proudhon had an instinct for French politics,"[192] the *Cahiers* were at pains to point out how worthy of respect was a man who, in addition to his passion for order, attempted to prove the supremacy of France and demanded for the French nation, "which has produced the finest flower of human civilization," the right to command the rest of Europe.[193] Valois, in turn, insisted on "Proudhon's revolutionary passion," which, instead of causing him to launch attacks against French society and property, made him turn against the true culprits: Jewish capitalism and the social order imposed by foreigners.[194] Berth, next, presented Proudhon as the representative of a "Gallic" socialism—a peasant, warrior socialism with a deep feeling for unity and order, a socialism drawn "from a pure French source."[195] Finally, Gilbert Maire wrote: "He dared to express more openly than anyone else the utility of direct action, the beauty of violence in the service of reason."[196]

The Sorelians and Maurrassians shared in the intellectual revolt against the heritage of the Enlightenment and the Revolution. They regarded Sorel as a disciple of Bergson and "an enthusiastic adherent of the intuitive philosophy."[197] And indeed, Sorel had never failed to come to the defense of Bergson,[198] just as he had always expressed his appreciation of Le Bon and Pareto.[199] The same was true of Berth and Valois, who were well acquainted with the works of Michels and Pareto and who referred to them in their writings.[200] All this helps to explain the "fundamental convergence" of "the ideas of the Action française and syndicalist aspirations,"[201] which was based on the conviction that "nationalism, like syndicalism, can triumph only through the complete eviction of democracy and the democratic ideology."[202]

Valois declared that the "junction" of syndicalism and nationalism had already been made, and Berth predicted that this "dual revolt" would necessarily lead to "the complete eviction of the regime of gold and the triumph of heroic values over the ignoble bourgeois materialism in which Europe is presently stifling. In other words, this awakening of Force and Blood against gold . . . must end with the total downfall of the plutocracy."[203] And this war waged by "these two great currents of national energy, . . . both of them antiliberal and antidemocratic" against "plutocracy," "big capital," and "high finance"[204] was at the same time a war against French decline and decadence.

In a classic work of national socialism written at the end of 1912, Édouard Berth summed up the despair and feelings of revolt of the Sorelians. He condemned "the ignoble positivism" in which "the bourgeoisie seems to have succeeded in sweeping along both the aristocracy and the people." "Pessimism, utilitarianism, and materialism," he wrote, "are eating away at all of us, nobles, bourgeois, and proletarians."[205] These words of Berth, a revolutionary syndicalist who was associated at that time with the integral nationalists, read like a text of Gentile. Did not the Italian thinker also see fascism principally as a revolt against positivism? The official philosopher of triumphant fascism not only expressed the same ideas, but employed exactly the same vocabulary as this French revolutionary syndicalist on the eve of the Great War. The essence of the future ideology of the Fascist movements of western Europe and that of the Mussolini regime was already in the pages of this review of the Maurrassians and French Sorelians.

Berth believed that positivism, which created the "regime of money, an essentially leveling, materialistic, and cosmopolitan regime," delivered up France to "the essence and quintessence of bourgeois materialism, the Jewish speculator and financier." Thus, "one saw socialism and syndicalism successively pass into the hands of the Jews and become the defenders of that nauseous and pestilential ideology of which Malthusianism, anti-Catholicism and antinationalism are the whole substance . . . and it would seem, in fact, that the people now aspire only to the state of well-being of the man who is retired and is completely uninterested in anything except his pension, and lives in terror of social or international unrest and asks for only one thing: peace—a stupid, vacuous peace made up of the most mediocre material satisfactions." Berth railed against "bourgeois decadence," against the "totally bourgeois pacifism" that infects "the people coming to birth with the corruption of the bourgeoisie coming to an end." Bourgeois decadence, he wrote, bequeaths to the people "a hypertrophied state, the product of a beggarly and half-starved rural and urban democracy," and it creates a "universal stagnation" in which the proletariat adopts "the worst ideas of the decadent bourgeoisie."[206]

To counteract the effects of decadence, then as in the past, Berth saw but one solution: war. "War," he wrote, "is not always that 'work of death' which a vain people of effeminate weaklings imagines. Behind every powerful industrial and commercial development there is an act of force, an act of war." War ensures the progress of civilization and at the same time raises the question of the state and the nation. Sorel's disciple quoted Proudhon— "War is our history, our life, our entire soul"—and Arturo Labriola, who claimed that "the sentiment of national independence, like the religious sentiment, leads to the most incredible manifestations of sacrifice." Only violence, he wrote, could save the human race from "becoming universally bourgeois," "from the platitude of an eternal peace." Thus, setting forth, like Sorel, on a crusade for the redemption of morality and civilization, Berth once again assailed the "international plutocracy" that is "pacifistic by instinct and interest," for this plutocracy, he wrote, feared "a revival of heroic values [that] could only hurt its purely materialistic domination." Berth quoted at length a text that Pareto had contributed to Sorel's journal *L'Indépendance*, in which the Italian sociologist accused this plutocracy of being "cowardly, as the Jews and the usurers had been in the Middle Ages. Its weapon is gold, not the sword: it knows how to scheme; it does not know how to fight. Thrown out on one side, it comes back on the other, without ever facing the danger; its riches increase while its energy diminishes. *Exhausted by economic materialism, it becomes increasingly impervious to an idealism of sentiments.*"[207]

After Pareto, Labriola, and Corradini, it was Nietzsche's turn. Like Nietzsche, Berth wrote he wanted to destroy "*the power of the average*, that is to say, of democratic, bourgeois, and liberal mediocrity (as Nietzsche said, the proper word to qualify whatever is *mediocre* is *liberal*)."[208] It followed, then, that to save civilization, one had "to persuade one group that the syndical ideal does not necessarily mean national abdication, and the other group

that the nationalist ideal does not necessarily imply a program of social pacification, for on the day when there will be a serious revival of bellicose and
revolutionary sentiments and a victorious upsurge of heroic, national and
proletarian values—on that day, the reign of Gold will be overthrown, and
we shall cease to be reduced to the ignominious role of satellites of the
plutocracy."[209]

The members of the Cercle Proudhon wished to replace the bourgeois
ideology with a new ethic that would totally supersede the liberal order as
well as democratic socialism. They sought to create a new world—virile,
heroic, pessimistic, and puritanical—based on a sense of duty and sacrifice,
a world where a morality of warriors and monks would prevail. They wanted
a society dominated by a powerful avant-garde, a proletarian elite, an aristocracy of producers, joined in an alliance against the decadent bourgeoisie
with an intellectual youth eager for action. When the time came, it would
not be difficult for a synthesis of this kind to assume the name of fascism.

In this national and social revolt against the democratic and liberal order
that was taking place in France, none of the classical attributes of the most
extreme forms of fascism were missing—not even anti-Semitism. In all periods since the days of Boulangism, including that of the Dreyfus Affair, anti-
Semitism had the aim of destroying both the conceptual and the political
structures of Jacobin democracy. It was a basic element of the revolt against
the liberal consensus and the social-democratic consensus: in periods of crisis, it was to be found among nonconformists of the extreme Left such as
Hervé and the writers of *La Guerre sociale*; it appeared in *Le Mouvement
socialiste*, and it played an important role in the thinking of Sorel and Berth,
both of whom were former Dreyfusards. At the time of the Cercle Proudhon,
anti-Semitism became a major element in the socialist-national ideology.[210]

Here one should draw attention to another factor necessary to an understanding of the Sorelians' contribution to fascism: their conception of the
state. It was not only the fundamental principles of democracy—materialism, rationalism—that they attacked and wanted to replace completely; they
also developed a conception of the state that became part of the original
fascism. The opposition of the theoreticians of revolutionary syndicalism to
the bourgeois state did not automatically render them impervious to the
attraction of integral nationalism. We demonstrated this at an earlier stage,
but here we wish to add certain observations. The state condemned by the
Sorelians was not the state as an institution, but the democratic, pluralistic
state, the much-denigrated state of universal suffrage, the state of the reviled
political parties. The state they wanted to destroy was that of political and
social reforms, the state formed in the crucible of the liberal democracy of
western Europe. We must repeat once again: the principle of authority was
never in question. On the contrary, the Sorelians did not condemn social
and political discipline or the primacy of the community over the individ-

ual—which explains why they never had any difficulty in creating a synthesis of revolutionary syndicalism and integral nationalism. The two ideologies had the same view of Western civilization and of the means to be used to arrest its decline, and they agreed on the political solutions to this problem.

The state that Berth opposed was "the modern democratic state," that is, an "abstract, centralized, pacifistic state" that, surrendering "the functions proper to the state, which are all related to its warlike nature (the army, diplomacy, law), arrogates to itself foreign, parasitic functions, economic and administrative functions." The state that had to be destroyed was one "that from being *bellicose* had become *pacifistic*, from being *political* had become *economic*."[211] Mussolini, on the eve of his seizure of power, would find nothing to change in these formulations. It was this degenerate institution that Berth had in mind when he returned to the slogan of the beginning of the century, the period of *Le Mouvement socialiste*: "*The least state possible* and *its absolute neutralization*."[212] It was the structures of the "*popular socialist state*," "which is the modern form of the utopia and a substitute for the old Providence," that needed, he wrote, to be overthrown.[213] However, this rejection of the "providential" state—the state of the weekly day of rest, old-age pensions, and compulsory education—was limited to a rejection of the social and economic functions of the state.

Thus, Berth said yes to the state, provided its character was not distorted. He insisted several times on this point: the state, he wrote, is a "warrior,"[214] and that is what it ought to be. This, he wrote, was precisely what the Maurrassians were trying to achieve. The state the Maurrassians were attempting to restore "no more resembles the modern democratic state than the constellation called the Dog resembles the barking animal called a dog."[215] The Action française had thus resurrected the state "whose death had been plotted by the whole of modern thought, stemming from the French Revolution"[216]—that is, "a *nonintellectual* state" whose true nature was "to be war made man [the personalization of war]."[217] This ideal state was a hereditary, authoritarian state freed from the encumbrances of democracy, political parties, pressure groups, universal suffrage, and the law of the majority.

In case anyone still harbored any doubts, the remains of an ambivalent past, Berth clarified his position further: "The syndicalists, in my opinion, ought to correct their initial assertions, for whatever people say or do, the problem of the state remains in all its cogency, being the same problem as that of the existence of autonomous countries and national civilizations."[218]

Finally, true to the economic conceptions all Sorelians shared, Berth gave a striking description of the objectives of the "dual nationalist and syndicalist offensive." This rebellion, he wrote, sought "the restoration of the state as a warlike entity and the expulsion of the state from the economy." Berth never missed an opportunity to stress this important aspect of national socialism:

"The restoration of a state worthy of the name," he wrote, would mean the creation of an authority whose power and manifestations would be unlimited in the political sphere but whose "encroachment in the area of economics" would be prevented by "a highly organized civil society."[219] It all depended, of course, on what was meant by a "civil society." In the opinion of the revolutionary syndicalists, economic and financial interests, monopolies, great concentrations of capital, and the privileges of the various professions could also represent a civil society. In this respect, the situation with regard to Italian corporatism was not very different. The hated political parties and opinion groups were eliminated, but the powerful and well-structured economic interests gave the state a free hand on condition that its economic policies worked in their favor. In revolutionary syndicalism and integral nationalism as in fascism when in office, liberalism was always confined to the economy.

The conception of the state thus arrived at after the long process of the revision of Marxism could hardly have been more clearly stated. Equally clear were the stated objectives of the "two synchronized and convergent movements, one on the extreme Right and the other on the extreme Left," which, "for the salvation of the modern world and the grandeur of our Latin humanity," had begun the "beleaguerment and assault" of democracy.[220] The world, wrote Berth in the conclusion of *Les Méfaits*, provided the spectacle "of a formidable revolt against God, against the state, against property, and against man. Secularism, democracy, socialism, and feminism are different forms of this universal insurrection, but this is merely a trial from which religion, the state, property, and male and paternal power must emerge strengthened and consolidated."[221] In order to foil this "universal insurrection," it was necessary that the revolutionary offensive launched by the Sorelians and Maurrassians should succeed. That, he wrote, was the significance of this "great modern revolt" through which "authority would emerge victorious all along the line."[222]

Berth was quite correct: authority did indeed emerge victorious "all along the line" from this "great revolt" against the eighteenth century, materialism, rationalism, liberalism, orthodox Marxism, reformist socialism, and democracy. In France and Italy, from the end of the first decade of this century, the revolt took the form of fascism. All the main elements of Fascist thought came to fruition before the explosion of August 1914. Everything that was of real importance in this synthesis of integral nationalism with post-Marxist socialism, emptied of its rationalist and Hegelian content, was elaborated before the first shot was fired. Well before the war, the Sorelians had completed this new conception of a revolution, one that had decided to mobilize the bourgeoisie to compensate for the deficiencies of the proletariat, one whose objective was the salvation of Western civilization rather than that of the working class, and one whose primary aim was the destruction of a whole liberal and democratic culture based on the preeminence of the individual.

This revolution, however, was also directed against the Marxist idea of a society that could eliminate inequality by means of a socialization of property. Advocates, as they were, of a market economy, the Sorelians, after having caused Marxism to undergo a veritable metamorphosis, remained true to Proudhon and the principle of private property. They thus produced an entirely new type of revolution: an antiliberal and anti-Marxist revolution whose adherents came not from one but from all social classes—a moral, intellectual, and political revolution, a national revolution. In the France of 1914, this convergence of the revolutionary syndicalist and nationalist rebels did not go beyond the stage of an intellectual synthesis, but on the other side of the Alps, in the atmosphere of distress that prevailed after the armistice, this synthesis became the great revolutionary force of the time.

CHAPTER THREE

Revolutionary Syndicalism in Italy

TWENTY YEARS: 1902–1922

In the last months of 1902, a number of nonconformists led by Arturo Labriola created a splinter group within the Italian Socialist party that claimed to be the party's revolutionary wing.[1] These people not only accused the reformist socialists of drawing their support from the industrial proletariat of northern Italy instead of from the masses in the country as a whole and especially the south, which constituted the majority of the population, but also insisted that the socialist revolution would come about only through the organization of the entire working class into fighting syndicates that, when the time came, would take over the process of production from the bourgeoisie. Because of this they were called the revolutionary syndicalists. The first group of revolutionary syndicalists came into being in Milan at the end of 1902, and in December of that year its intellectual leader, Arturo Labriola, founded the weekly publication *Avanguardia socialista*. This group of bourgeois intellectuals, deeply influenced by Sorel,[2] found a number of allies in Enrico Leone and Ernesto Cesare Longobardi's circle, which was very active in Naples.[3] The group's ideology was based on direct action by workers organized in syndicates, which at that period meant the idea of a general strike, perceived as both a mobilizing myth and a legitimate tool of combat.

The rapid spread of this ideology and the desire to put it into practice caused a split in the PSI (Italian Socialist party). Filippo Turati, the leader of the reformist socialists, accepted Bernstein's theoretical model and believed that it applied to the situation in Italy. He thought that socialism was justified in cooperating with the most progressive elements in the liberal system in order to obtain certain advantages for the industrial workers in the north of the country, who constituted the majority of the supporters of the PSI. The rules of the democratic system being what they were, the socialists needed to produce quick results, not only in order to be able to "deliver the goods" promised to their electorate, but also in order to ensure their continuous support. Reformism enabled them to achieve this objective directly.

The birth of Italian revolutionary syndicalism resulted from a movement of ideas that had originated outside Italy, but as soon as the ideology reached the peninsula it was subject to certain local sociohistorical factors that had a major influence on its development. These were: (1) The north-south dichotomy, especially in the sphere of economics. (2) The instability of the PSI, partly due to the lack of any long-established socialist tradition. (3) The relatively recent unification of Italy, which explained the almost complete absence of a tradition of political centralism, and to some degree the uneven geographical distribution of the rapid industrial development of the country. (4) The lack of a syndicalist tradition and the consequent weakness of labor organizations.

At the same time, 1900–1910, apart from the crisis of 1907, were years of rapid economic expansion and relative prosperity in Italy owing to a protectionist policy that greatly benefited the industrial north while hurting the agricultural south.[4] During almost all of this period Giovanni Giolitti, the leader of the liberals, led the government. His political acumen and his mastery of compromise brought the country considerable political stability and succeeded in neutralizing the Left.

Despite their violent opposition to liberal democracy and their hostility to the policies of the PSI, the revolutionary syndicalists did not leave the party until 1907. Previous to that date, despite the fact that they attempted to persuade the socialist Left to take the path of direct action, they participated actively in the organization of elections and presented themselves as candidates of the PSI in the parliamentary elections of 1904, which were held soon after the general strike. This movement, which declared itself to be antipolitical, was from the beginning very political in its conduct. It participated in the regional and national congresses of the party and took part in its electoral campaigns, with all the publicity it received in the socialist press as a result. Until 1905, Enrico Leone and Paolo Orano belonged to the editorial staff of *Avanti!* The revolutionary syndicalists even made an attempt to take over the party from within in collaboration with Enrico Ferri's orthodox faction.[5]

For all their intense activity, these radicals remained a minority group in the PSI. Nevertheless, they did not give up hope of imposing their views on the party and in fact had some success. At the regional congress of the party at Brescia in Lombardy in February 1904, Walter Mocchi, coeditor of *Avanguardia socialista*, joined Labriola in tabling a motion asserting the revolutionary and activistic character of socialism. Despite accusations of anarchism from Turati, the motion was adopted. A few weeks later, in April, at the national congress in Bologna, an alliance of the revolutionary syndicalists and the orthodox wing of the party enabled the radicals to gain acceptance for their ideas while defeating those of the reformists.[6]

At the same time, certain outstanding revolutionary syndicalist personalities—Arturo Labriola, Enrico Leone, Romeo Soldi—added their weight to the Anti-protectionist League (Lega antiprotezionista) founded in March 1904. There, together with the radical De Viti De Marco, the revolutionary syndicalists proclaimed the necessity for a "liberist" (free-market) economy, antiprotectionist by definition, which would make possible the establishment of a capitalist system in which socialism could develop.[7] From the revolutionary syndicalist point of view, the Lega antiprotezionista provided a possible solution to two intimately connected problems: The harm caused by the protectionist policy to the Italian economy and especially to the development of the agricultural Mezzogiorno, and its strengthening of both the state and the new bourgeoisie of the north in the process of industrialization—a strengthening that consolidated parliamentary and reformist socialism, which itself depended on the industrial workers, beneficiaries of protectionism.

The general strike of 1904 took place while the theoreticians of revolutionary syndicalism were in full intellectual ferment. This mass movement, surprising in its scale, was a turning point for them, especially as they could not fail to notice that the strike began as a spontaneous reaction to the death of workers in Buggerru, Sardinia, killed on 4 September by the police.[8]

Both in Italy and in all socialist circles in Europe, a debate on the purpose and revolutionary significance of the general strike was taking place—a debate that was halted with the adoption of the Rolland-Host motion at the sixth congress of the Socialist International, held in Amsterdam. This motion rejected the use of the general strike as a revolutionary weapon and permitted only its defensive use.[9] In Amsterdam, reformist socialism won; in general, the revolutionary syndicalist position was supported only by the French delegation.[10]

One day before the Buggerru incident, Hubert Lagardelle published an account of the revolutionary syndicalist position on the question in *Avanguardia socialista*. The general strike, understood as a supreme revolt of all organized producers against the capitalist regime in the sphere of production itself and thus identified with the concept of social revolution, was, he wrote, becoming the act of faith of an increasingly large segment of the revolutionary proletariat.[11] For Lagardelle, as for the other revolutionary syndicalists, the general strike represented a genuine weapon at the workers' disposal. They saw it as the essence of "direct action," a means of retrieving socialism from a path they felt to be false, and a perfect instrument for the training of the workers and for channeling their frustrations into a revolutionary goal. In short, they regarded a rejection of the general strike as quite simply a rejection of reformist socialism.[12]

The strike began in Milan on 16 September 1904 and spread rapidly throughout the country. The workers' acquiescence in the call of Dugoni, a syndicalist of Labriola's circle, to launch a general strike in response to further massacres of workers by the police or the army should be understood not as representing the success of syndicalism in penetrating the working class, but rather as a sign of its receptivity to the idea of the general strike. The question had been raised at the regional congress of the PSI in Brescia and at its national congress in Bologna in April 1904. Whatever the case, the strike began in reaction to events in Castelluzzo, Sicily, where on 14 September the local head of police gave orders to fire on a group of demonstrators: farm workers. Eight people were wounded.[13] The next day, all of Italy knew about it, and in Milan, when the Labor Chambers were still discussing what steps to take, five million workers stopped work. A general strike was decided on for 16 September.[14] The movement paralyzed the country: there ceased to be any public transport, bread, rice, or petrol.[15]

The *Avanguardia socialista* gave an account of the strike in an article entitled "The Five Days of the First Experiment in the Dictatorship of the Proletariat."[16] In fact, one was very far from a dictatorship of the proletariat! At the Milan Labor Chamber Labriola, who unlike Sorel, Berth, and Lagardelle was also a syndicalist leader, at least at the beginning of his career, was very skeptical about the way the strike would develop. He and his associates were aware of the effect that the lack of any political plan, coordination, or control could have on the strikers, and above all they knew that the leaders of the PSI were neither willing nor able to guide the movement in a revolutionary direction. For the revolutionary syndicalists, the course of events provided one more proof of the split between the essentially reformist Socialist party and the potentially revolutionary proletariat.

By 20 September it was clear that the strike was coming to an end. The cessation of the strike had nothing to do with the decision to end it taken by the leadership of the party two days earlier, since it had been massively rejected by the strikers.[17] Whatever the case, the revolutionary syndicalists had now witnessed an example of the application of the idea of the general strike in real life, and they drew the appropriate conclusions. They felt it was a good sign that the industrialized north had responded with a general strike to incidents affecting workers in the south. They also noticed that during the events the center of activity was the Labor Chamber and not the party. They took this as evidence that the theories of Sorel had begun to demonstrate their applicability to Italy. This explains their partial adoption by Labriola and his associates, who tried to adapt their ideology from one general strike to the next.

From September 1904 on, the revolutionary syndicalists engaged in constant antireformist activities. In June 1905, Paolo Orano and Enrico Leone were dismissed from the editorial committee of *Avanti!*[18] During the same period, the revolutionary syndicalist leaders succeeded in penetrating the local workers' organizations, especially in Ferrara, Parma, Piombino, and Apulia.[19] Generally speaking, however, the general strikes that followed that of September 1904 were disappointing. Labriola violently attacked the parliamentary wing of the PSI, which he accused of betraying the workers' interests by not supporting general strikes.[20] The PSI, for its part, appreciated neither the activism of the revolutionary syndicalists nor their positions on the general strike. Consequently, the reformist leadership of the party, which immediately took control of the General Confederation of Labor (Confederazione Generale del Lavoro, or CGL), created in Milan in 1906, had no rest until it had succeeded in expelling practically all revolutionary syndicalists, at least from national positions. The latter therefore decided to concentrate their energies on regional struggles and on the creation of a fighting syndicalist elite.[21] Thus, in the years following the general strike of 1904, the revolutionary syndicalists devoted themselves to refining their ideas and disseminating them. In Rome in 1905, Enrico Leone and Paolo Mantica began publishing a fortnightly journal of scientific socialism, *Il divenire sociale*. In Lugano in 1906, Angelo Oliviero Olivetti, a long-standing socialist turned revolutionary syndicalist, published *Pagine libere*. The first journal appeared until 1910 and the second, with a few interruptions, until the beginning of the Fascist period.

Despite these efforts, and despite the fact that it fought on every front, revolutionary syndicalism, ideologically opposed to party politics and parliamentarianism even if, on a day-to-day basis, it subscribed to the rules it rejected, was quickly marginalized in the socialist movement. The PSI rejected the idea of fighting the socialist battle from within the syndicates at its congress in Rome in October 1906. Those who proposed this idea found themselves isolated and in a minority. In July 1907, at a gathering of revolutionary syndicalists in Ferrara (where the syndicalist organizations were particularly strong and well organized and where they had led successful strikes in May and June of that year), it was decided that the movement would leave the PSI and would concentrate its efforts on "syndicalist politics." For this purpose, it rejoined the CGL with the aim of reconquering it from within. A few months later, in November, during a meeting in Parma, the revolutionary syndicalists decided to create the National Movement of Resistance in order to oppose the policies of the CGL, dominated by the reformists of the PSI. This time, a new generation, formed through constant frequentation of the Labor Chambers and experienced in the techniques of the strike, took over the leadership of the dissenting movements. Indeed, immediately after the strike of 1904, a number of labor activists began a process of moving to the Left, adopting as their own the revolutionary syndicalist ideology elaborated by Arturo Labriola and his collaborators. In this way, they gave revolutionary syndicalism, which hitherto had been merely a system of thought, its true historical importance. With these people, revolutionary syndicalism became a genuine social force. These activists, the most brilliant of whom became leaders of revolutionary syndicalism, led the great agrarian strikes of 1907 and 1908. Michele Bianchi, Alceste De Ambris, and Filippo Corridoni conceived of syndicalism as being exclusively radical, class-centered, and antiparty. They were convinced that a well-organized labor elite could always focus the conflict with the bourgeoisie upon itself and emerge victorious from the struggle.

The idea of a combatant syndicalist elite was put to the test of reality by the general agrarian strike in Parma in 1908.[22] This strike was the climax of a confrontation between the organized agricultural workers and the association of landowners. It began on 1 May and was the response of the body of workers to a landowners' lockout that was then in its forty-fourth day.[23]

The Parma Labor Chamber soon became the nerve center of the movement, as well as being a real center of solidarity. It was able to support the strikers by means of contributions collected from all members of syndicates. Discipline and organization were on a high level, enabling more than thirty-three thousand workers to cease all activity for more than eight weeks.[24] The strike ended only after the intervention of the army and the events of 20 June, when incidents with strike breakers led to the army's occupation of the Labor Chamber and its confiscation of the strike funds and various documents.[25] Official socialism reacted by the "excommunication" of the revolutionary syndicalists (to use the expression of Furiozzi, the writer of a remarkable study of the episode), and the PSI was quick to expel them, during the party congress in Florence in September 1908.[26]

Here it should be pointed out that despite the extreme positions the revolutionary syndicalists adopted, especially concerning the struggle against the system, their approach was to represent the process of social change as a gradual evolution. Their motives were primarily practical. Compared with the French labor movement of the first decade of the century, the Italian labor movement was still weak and badly organized. Indeed, as long as they remained in the sphere of ideology, the syndicalist theoreticians were undoubtedly extremists, and in political debate they were far more influential than their numerical importance might lead one to suppose. As soon as they left the world of ideas, however, their positions became far more flexible and often close to compromise. They could not have been otherwise without incurring the risk of political suicide. This attitude was reinforced by another important element: their lack of an electoral basis, due to the fact that the appearance of the revolutionary syndicalist ideology preceded the mass organization of the workers and the creation of a central organization, the CGL.

Another explanation—at least a partial one—of their distance from the revolutionary model of Marx, which required the acquisition of a class consciousness by the proletariat, was the fact that quite a number of the revolutionary syndicalist leaders came from bourgeois-socialist circles in the south. Although these people undoubtedly brought to socialism a tradition of rebellion, they also had a real desire to take the masses of agricultural workers in the Mezzogiorno into account. They therefore sought to find a model that would include both the industrialized north and the agricultural south in the scheme of revolution. For this purpose Labriola, Leone, and other revolutionary syndicalist intellectuals set about revising Marx's economic theories. The first reason for this move was clearly that Marxist determinism had not operated as expected. Then, in the case of Italy, the cooperation of reformist socialism with the liberal bourgeoisie meant not only the strengthening of the existing order but the deepening of the gulf traditionally separating north and south. The immediate consequence of this process was a massive emigration, especially from the undeveloped south—a problem that, at the end of the first decade of the century preoccupied both the revolutionary syndicalists and the radical nationalists. This fight against a system that accepted underdevelopment and encouraged emigration—that is, the loss of the very substance of the nation—became one of the major common denominators of the socialist-national synthesis.

Thus, around 1910, the nationalists and the revolutionary syndicalists shared an aversion for the existing political system. The idea that Italy was suffering from a fatal illness, the "liberal parliamentary democracy" personified by Giolitti, suggested to them a new solution: war. The radical nationalists and the revolutionary syndicalists—some of them in 1911, but most of them in 1914—now came to the conclusion that war was precisely the medicine that, if administered in a sufficiently strong dose, could eliminate the sickness undermining Italy.[27]

Assuredly, this position of the revolutionary syndicalists was far from their opinions on antimilitarism and the revolution a few years earlier. Sorel had regarded the army as "the expression of the state that is clearest, most tangible, and closest to its origins"—that is, of a state that, in the opinion of the revolutionary syndicalists, oppressed the workers and employed the army as the best means of practicing its tyranny. At that period, Sorel saw antimilitarism and antipatriotism as two manifestations of the confrontation between the revolutionary forces and the state.[28] This point of view was connected with the internationalism of the labor movement and the idea that by refusing a call to arms, the working class could prevent a war in Europe. International socialism proclaimed the solidarity of the working class as superior to national solidarity. In France, Gustave Hervé went so far as to urge the revolutionaries to refuse to serve under the colors and to reject any cooperation with the state.

Hervé's recommendations found a spokesman in Italy. In March 1907, Filippo Corridoni, who had already led a number of strikes, began publishing an antimilitarist leaflet, *Rompete le file!* (Break ranks!).[29] But the fact that Corridoni did not find any supporters, even among his friends, was indicative of the new mood. In fact, Labriola had already begun to contest Hervé's antiwar arguments.[30]

Labriola's attitude to war slowly began to change in 1907. Like other revolutionary syndicalist theoreticians (for example, Orano and Olivetti), he gradually began to maintain, but with an increasing insistence, that the concepts "nation" and "war" were not necessarily antithetical to those of "syndicalism" and "socialism," and that consequently they did not have to be automatically rejected. At the end of 1910, Orano began publishing in Rome *La lupa*, which threw open its pages to those who were trying to create bridges between revolutionary syndicalism and radical nationalism. In the previous year, a radical nationalist journal, *Il tricolore*, had appeared in Turin, which was the defender of a populist nationalism. This encounter was all the more natural in that radical nationalism was at that time seeking the support of the working masses who would give it an entry into modern politics. At the same time, revolutionary syndicalism was intent on clarifying the nature of the relationships among the state, the workers, and the nation.

The positions of the two schools of thought on the role of war and the idea of nation had reached this point when revolutionary syndicalism entered the controversy surrounding the Libyan crisis. In the months preceding the Libyan War, there had been a widespread debate on whether one should occupy Tripoli and enter into armed conflict with Turkey. The Catholic and nationalist press was in favor of the enterprise, and Enrico Corradini toured the country in an attempt to win support for the colonialist cause.[31]

On the political Left, there was an almost unanimous opposition to going to war, both in the PSI and the CGL. Thus, when Italy sent its ultimatum to Turkey, a general strike was declared for 27 September 1911. The action did not succeed in persuading the government to go into reverse. A large segment of public opinion, especially in the south, supported the operation.[32]

Those revolutionary syndicalists who backed the operation railed and vociferated throughout the year,[33] but they were nevertheless unable to prevent the Chambers of Labor from joining the socialists in their campaign against the war or from supporting the decision to call the general strike of 27 September. The disagreement between the intellectual wing of revolutionary syndicalism, led by Labriola, Orano, and Olivetti and the syndical leaders led by De Ambris caused the breakup of the editorial team of *Pagine libere* and the discontinuation of the journal at the end of 1911. This rupture, however, was short-lived.

Here the role played by the intellectuals of revolutionary syndicalism was clearly apparent. The theoreticians were always slightly ahead of the labor activists. They were quicker to dissociate themselves from the official party line, and they formulated policies that syndical leaders and politicians like Mussolini finally accepted after a longer or shorter period of hesitation. The theoreticians played the role of an avant-garde for all the militants, both in the syndicates and in the party.

The Libyan War did not really help the revolutionary syndicalists to solve the problems posed by concepts of nation and war. The general attitude of the movement, apart from the intellectuals, remained antimilitaristic, even if the conceptual difference between the nation and the state (the former being associated with the proletariat and the latter with the bourgeoisie) paved the way for a change in ideology that was soon to permit revolutionary syndicalism to support Italy's entry into the war on the side of France and Britain in 1914. It was not only on the question of war, however, that the theoreticians of revolutionary syndicalism differed from official socialism. During their united congress in Modena in November 1912, the revolutionary syndicalists decided to set up their own syndical union, thus quitting the party-controlled CGL. They wished, in accordance with revolutionary syndicalist principles, to render their organization totally independent, not only of the PSI and its outgrowth, the CGL, but also of all other political or syndical formations. Thus, the USI (Unione Sindacale Italiana) came into being, with more than one hundred thousand members at the end of 1912.[34] At that period, the CGL numbered three hundred thousand. The members of the USI were extremely active and took part in several conflicts, both in the agricultural sector and in the industrial and mining sectors. The USI adopted the traditionally antimilitaristic line of syndicalism, a line that it still adhered to at the time of the *settimana rossa* (red week). This week began on 7 June 1914, when the Left took to the streets to demonstrate against militarism; at Villa Rossa, the headquarters of the local Republican party in Ancona, the police and carabinieri fired into the crowd. Two demonstrators were killed on the spot and a third died in the hospital.[35] A general strike was immediately declared and was observed in almost the whole country. The PSI, the CGL and the railworkers' syndicate (the SFI) called for a stoppage of work. In Milan, Corridoni and Mussolini led a number of demonstrations. There were often manifestations of violence. In some places, the strike took on the characteristics of a real rebellion; in the Romagna, it almost became an armed revolt. The army had to intervene to reestablish order.

Italy had scarcely recovered from the shock of the settimana rossa when it had to face the problem of the war. Although bound by the Triple Alliance, in August 1914 it did not enter the war. However, even at the time of the worst quarrels over the Libyan affair, all elements of the revolutionary syndicalist movement agreed at least on one point: in the event of a general conflict, Italy should enter the war on the side of France and Britain. To the revolutionary syndicalists, the Prussian Empire allied to Austria-Hungary symbolized the direst reaction, and consequently, when war broke out, revolutionary syndicalism headed the left-wing interventionist camp. This caused unrest in the ranks of the USI, which in August 1914 adopted a resolution calling on Italy to remain neutral and threatening the government with a revolutionary general strike if it decided, despite everything, to involve the country in the conflict on either side.[36]

Thus, on 18 August 1914, Alceste De Ambris, speaking from the platform of the Milanese Syndical Union (USM), launched a violent attack against neutralism, urged the necessity of going to the aid of France and Britain in the face of German reaction, and equated the war with the French Revolution.[37] This declaration—supported by certain revolutionary syndicalists, members of the USI, such as Corridoni, leader of the USM, who was then in prison—caused a deep split in the organization. The majority, led by the anarchist Armando Borghi, opted for neutrality. The USM, the Parma Labor Chamber, and a number of revolutionary syndicalists now left the USI and at the beginning of October 1914 founded the Fascio rivoluzionario d'azione internazionalista. The manifesto of this movement was published by Olivetti in the first issue of a new series of *Pagine libere*, which began to appear in the same month. At that period Mussolini joined the movement, deciding to abandon the neutralist position of the PSI, and beginning to publish *Il popolo d'Italia* in November 1914.[38]

After months of agitation and negotiations between governments, Italy entered the war in May 1915. The left-wing interventionists had now achieved their first objective: to make Italy take part in the hostilities. The revolutionary syndicalist leaders, consistent with their political positions, volunteered for action. Only five days after Italy's entry into the war, De Ambris, Masotti, Coconi, and Fava volunteered and were sent to the front. Out of the fifty or so revolutionary syndicalist leaders who turned up at the recruitment centers (to count only the best known), thirty-six were conscripted and dispatched to the front. Six months after their country entered the war, nine were wounded and six killed.[39] A small number of leaders were asked, by common agreement, to stay behind to look after the syndicates.

At the moment the war broke out, the ideological development of revolutionary syndicalism had reached the point of no return. The socialist-national synthesis had come to fruition in the years before August 1914, but it is clear that this terrible ordeal greatly accelerated its evolution. The concepts of nation and socialism could now continue to develop only in the direction already indicated in *La lupa* and already proposed by Arturo Labriola, Orano, and Olivetti during the great debate on the Libyan campaign. The year 1917 played a major role in this process of sliding toward a socialism that was more and more "national," farther and farther away from its Marxist origins. The year 1917 saw the bombshell of the Bolshevik revolution, very threatening for the national interests of Italy, profoundly shaken by the defeat of Caporetto. Now more than ever, revolutionary syndicalism sided with the nation against a revolution that not only endangered the national interests, but also represented a model that the theoreticians of revolutionary syndicalism had always described as fundamentally erroneous.

This revolution destructive of capitalist gains could never have been to their liking, not even in the heyday of *Avanguardia socialista*.

Thus, it seems only natural that in May 1918 some revolutionary syndicalists should have joined independent socialists in founding the USI. This political movement was a synthesis of left-wing interventionist positions and nationalist and revolutionalist ideas—the whole bound up with revolutionary syndicalist ideology. At the end of 1919, the USI won twelve seats in parliament. Labriola was on that list and accepted the post of minister of labor, which Giolitti offered him.[40]

In the last year of the war, Alceste De Ambris founded *Il rinnovamento*, a monthly (and sometimes bimonthly) journal that soon overshadowed *Pagine libere* and became the organ of the theoreticians of national syndicalism. This review played an important role in the transition to fascism.

As was the case with *Avanguardia socialista* in the first years of the century, once again an intellectual review pointed the way for the movement. The Unione Italiana del Lavoro (Italian Union of Labor), founded in Milan in 1918, subscribed to the development of the revolutionary syndicalist ideology we have indicated. The journal of this union, *L'Italia nostra*, later called *Battaglie dell'Unione Italiana del Lavoro*, adopted the slogan The Fatherland Should Not Be Denied, It Should Be Conquered! In the critical years of the *biennio rosso* (the two red years, 1919–1920), the Italian Union of Labor was the focus of national syndicalist ideas.

The strike in Dalmine broke out in March 1919. For the first time, unionized workers tried to demonstrate their capacity to lead production themselves and their ability to manage the factory more efficiently than the owners, while achieving a fairer distribution of profits. A few days later the strike was broken up by the army. One year later, the leaders of the strike ascribed its failure to the ill-intentioned manipulations of the PSI and CGL.[41]

From that moment on, national syndicalist ideology supported the idea of workers' participation in management or of workers' self-management.[42] The lessons of the past, however, were not forgotten. When workers seized control of the industrial belt of the north in August–September 1920, the revolutionary syndicalists were aware of the danger an intervention of the authorities represented. Thus, they held that success could be assured only if workers took possession of the entire industrial sector and succeeded in making it function. Only in that way, they said, could the state, and hence its capacity of "reaction," be neutralized. Partial general strikes were thus by nature held to be ineffective and, worse, to inevitably lead to repression because of their failure to strike a blow at the machinery of the state.[43]

The national syndicalists presented their proposal for self-management in industry to the minister of labor, Arturo Labriola, and Prime Minister Giolitti succeeded in bringing the conflict to an end through a compromise. He won adoption of a plan for the reorganization of industry which recognized the right of workers to participate in the management of the enterprise that employed them and even granted them limited control of its finances.[44] Giolitti gave the industrialists back their factories while preserving the honor of labor organizations. He was convinced that in so doing he had averted a Soviet type of revolution.[45] In fact, he failed to understand that what he had done was to bring Italy one step closer to fascism. His compromise cut off large segments of the bourgeoisie from the liberal political system he represented.

The events of August and September 1920 were regarded in Italy as the scenario of a general strike that could bring the country to the brink of revolution and civil war. On the Left, the national syndicalists had simultaneously to confront the reformists and the maximalists. They were convinced that the real nature of the conflict was both political and economic. This conclusion seemed to have been confirmed by the spread of the workers' occupation of factories. In the opinion of the national syndicalists, this general strike, despite the fact that its causes were economic, would not be brought to a successful conclusion unless the solution was political and applied to the entire country. This view led to the idea of a corporatist and productionist model—a model remote from the Marxist socialism that less than twenty years before had been the starting point and theory of reference for the revolutionary syndicalists.

When the Fiume affair began in September 1919, the national syndicalists immediately supported D'Annunzio.[46] The UIL regarded Fiume as an integral part of Italy. De Ambris, who stayed there at the end of 1919, returned in January 1920 to take up the position of cabinet secretary of the command of the city.[47] In this post the syndical leader presented the famous nationalist condottiere with the outline of what a few months later became the constitution of Fiume—the Carta del Carnaro (Carnara Charter). This political document, claimed by many to be one of the main prefigurations of Fascist corporatism, in 1920 became the blueprint of national syndicalism.

The lack of success of the occupations of factories and the failure of the Fiume affair formed the background to the decision of several revolutionary syndicalists to go over to the Fascist camp. The Fascist movement was founded by Mussolini in Milan at a meeting in the Piazza San Sepolcro on 23 March 1919. Among the founding members were several eminent revolutionary syndicalist leaders such as Agostino Lanzillo and Michele Bianchi. In 1919 and 1920 the relationship between fascism and national syndicalism grew closer until the moment toward the end of 1920 when fascism became more violent and reactionary, especially in the agricultural sector.

The years 1919–1922 saw the strengthening of fascism as a political movement. For the national syndicalists, these were years in which they were faced with the question of whether to try to change fascism from within or whether to attempt to divide it in order to retrieve its left wing. The first

REVOLUTIONARY SYNDICALISM IN ITALY   143

solution finally triumphed, and many revolutionary syndicalists—theoreticians or famous leaders such as Panunzio, Orano, Olivetti, Bianchi, Cesare Rossi, Ottavio Dinale, Mantica, Livio Ciardi, Luigi Razza, Mario Racheli, Massimo Rocca, Amilcare De Ambris (the brother of Alceste), Tullio Masotti, Alfonso De Pietri-Tonelli, and Antonio Renda—became Fascists. They loyally served the movement and then the regime, even when very few of the original aims of revolutionary syndicalism remained.

THE PRIMACY OF ECONOMICS AND THE REVISION OF MARXIST ECONOMIC DOCTRINE

The most original aspect of the Italian contribution to revolutionary syndicalist theory was its revision of Marxist economics. With regard to the idea of the social function of syndicates or the advocacy of a "virile" socialism, or with regard to the criticism of democracy or the cult of anti-intellectualism, the Italians had little to add to the system of thought the French had created. But the economic analyses of Arturo Labriola and Enrico Leone conferred on revolutionary syndicalism a scientific dimension that Sorel and Sorelians of pure descent had shown themselves incapable of doing.

Like all revolutionary syndicalists, Labriola began by saying that "the autonomous management of production by a unified working class" remained the ideal of revolutionary syndicalism.[48] He opposed the economic character of this process—a revolution of structural relationships within society—to the superstructural character of the political activities of reformist socialism. The fundamental difference in the spheres of action in itself defined the difference between revolutionary syndicalist actions and those of the Socialist party. On one hand one had direct action in the economic sphere, and on the other hand and by way of contrast, indirect action in the political sphere.

While the reformist socialists regarded the syndicate as simply a professional body, the revolutionary syndicalists proclaimed revolutionary syndicates to be the necessary weapons of combat of the working class. Even though they did not deny the professional syndicate a positive role, revolutionary syndicalists like Labriola maintained that its field of action was extremely limited owing to the nature of the capitalist economy. Limits were set by the overriding need of capitalism to accede to workers' demands only to the degree that this concession would leave it with a profit. As soon as profit ceased, the capitalists moved on to some other sector where profit was assured, leaving the workers of the professional syndicates without employment. Labriola claimed that this kind of syndicate was incapable of posing a threat to bourgeois society. On the contrary, by easing local tensions, it perpetuated capitalism. Thus, once this type of organization had fulfilled its role of extracting as much as possible from capitalism, it could choose only one of two paths: to dissolve or to become an instrument of revolution.[49] Labriola added that if one seriously considers the fact that an oppressed social group or one that is in conflict with its superiors tends to organize its own social mechanisms, one can understand why the creation of the syndicate was inevitable for the workers. One can similarly understand why the formation of the syndicate preceded the formation of a stratum of socialist intellectuals.[50]

At that point, the objective of revolutionary syndicalism was the organization of a "society of free workers."[51] Its leaders concentrated their efforts on the economic sphere, for that, they believed, was where the revolution had to take place. The role of the state, in their view, was secondary, for the state was concerned only with administrative and noneconomic tasks. The only time when political action was regarded as having a positive aspect was in the intermediate stage before the struggle focused on the economic sphere. At that stage, they thought, political action could be of some use for the defense of the proletariat. In Marxist terms, what Labriola and his associates were seeking to achieve with their idea of an "economic revolution" was a change of infrastructure that would lead to a change in the superstructure. The syndicates had the task of remedying the deficiencies of the deterministic mechanisms described by Marx, which had been slow in creating conditions favorable for revolution. It was especially important to take action because the power and domination of the bourgeoisie were increasing, objectively aided in this by democratic socialism.

Here one comes upon a new element, of tremendous importance for the future. When Labriola proposed the revolutionary syndicalist ideal of a society of "free producers," he was describing consensual relationships representing the wishes of *all* producers.[52] Labriola spoke of "producers," no longer of a proletariat or workers. Deviating from Marxist conceptions and terminology, the term "producers" indicates a type of corporatist organization that appeared just after the war in the political writings of Lanzillo, Panunzio, and De Ambris. According to Labriola, the producers have to be grouped in corporations whose members are bound by a community of socioeconomic interests. It may happen that the interests of one corporation are opposed to those of another corporation. It is obvious that this concept is antithetical to Marxism, inasmuch as its fundamental criterion is not the relationship between the worker and the *means* of production (from which property and the exploitation of labor by the capitalist are derived), but the relationship between the workers and the *process* of production. Consequently, the class/category of producers could in the future include all participants in the productive process—workers, technicians, administrators, managers, directors, and even capitalist industrialists. To these "producers," the revolutionary syndicalists opposed the class/category of "parasites," consisting of all those who do not contribute to the productive process. The Marxist model of class struggle was thus replaced by that of a corporation formed from the bottom upward, beginning with the proletarians and some producers, and then including all producers. The revolutionary syndicalists believed that this model simply reflected reality, but above all it had the enormous advantage of providing an integrated solution to the social problem and the national problem. The fascism of 1919–1920 was based on this ideological evolution.

Moreover, to the declared necessity for a moral improvement and an administrative and technical amelioration that would prepare the workers for the day they took over the process of production, the revolutionary syndicalists added the voluntarist element. They believed that these three factors would cause the emergence of elites among the proletariat. These elites, organized in revolutionary syndicates, would lead the fight against bourgeois society and bring about a "liberist" (free-market) economy in which capital would have no legal privilege and where relations between capital and labor would be regulated by market forces. Here one is once more remote from the Marxist model.

Revolutionary syndicalism saw the syndicate as the nucleus of future society, the formative school that would give rise to "free producers." In the syndicate, the "new man" would become a creative inventor, full of initiative, capable of extricating himself from the slime of reformist socialism. Clearly, the image of the inventor-cum-producer-cum-artist brings one back to Sorelian thought. This character was supposed to demonstrate ingenuity, courage, and initiative—all qualities stifled by the antirevolutionary nature of materialism combined with calculating rationalism.[53] Here, revolutionary syndicalism stressed the irrational aspects of human nature, so foreign to the rationalism and dialectical materialism of Marx.

The subordination of politics to economics is apparent in the thought and work of Arturo Labriola and Enrico Leone.[54] This approach was conducive to an extreme "economism" where the Marxist dialectical relationship between infrastructure and superstructure could no longer be distinguished. The inclusion of elements taken from hedonist economics and that of mathematical models of neoclassical economics proposed by Jevons and Walras led Labriola and Leone to base their theoretical arguments on the economic aspect of the revolutionary process. The impossibility of incorporating the principles of economic hedonism into Marx's historical analysis now became clear to them; they thus chose to deck out the historical aspect of their theory with borrowings from the Sorelian revision of Marxism, which was concerned above all with its noneconomic aspects. The strong influence of Sorel's ideas on Italian revolutionary syndicalism may be explained by this combination of historical circumstances and theoretical problems.[55]

"The old tactics of revolutionary socialism, based on fallacious expectations of a class antagonism that grows deeper every day, have completely failed."[56] That was how Leone described the crisis of Marxism at the begin-

ning of the century. Internal pressures and recurrent crises did not bring
about the destruction of the capitalist system, nor did an awakening of proletarian revolutionary consciousness accelerate its disintegration. On the contrary, the crises and pressures contributed to the setting up of regulatory
mechanisms that even found political expression. In the socialist camp, this
was represented by Bernstein's reformism in Germany, Jaurès's in France,
and Turati's in Italy. In order to overcome this "crisis of Marxism," Labriola
and Leone decided to remold the criterion of Marxist economic thought—
the theory of value.[57]

Labriola was aware of the fact that the definition of economic processes
depends on the angle from which they are approached. He thought that
Marx's theory of value (surplus value) was undoubtedly an excellent description of the economic process as seen from the point of view of the proletariat.
But since metaphysics is superfluous in economics, which claims to be an
exact science, Labriola was less concerned with the moral principles underlying causes than with discovering the factors that condition value.[58] In
terms of neoclassical economics, it could be said that Labriola was searching
for a general equilibrium.[59] Labriola was also influenced by the marginal
utility theory of value of the Austrian school (Menger, von Weiser, Böhm-
Bawerk) which aimed at a better understanding of economic processes.
Pareto was a further influence, with his emphasis on the relationship between the general economic process and personal motives as a yardstick of
the utility and egoism of the individual as an economic performer.

Arturo Labriola and Enrico Leone made an attempt to combine the principles of "marginal utility" and the "hedonist maximum" with Marx's theory
of value.[60] Leone began by pointing out the differences in perspective between Marxist economics and modern scientific economics. The former considered the individual as the end, the culmination of a long process that
began with society as a whole, whereas the latter regarded the economic
behavior of the individual as the starting point of the analysis.[61] It followed
that if the science of economics wished to be true to reality, it would have to
start with a study of the *homo economicus*. Similarly, it would have to take
into account the principles of the general theory of equilibrium. The corrections Labriola and Leone proposed led them to the conception of a "society
of free producers"[62] in which the intervention of the state would be reduced
to a minimum, and the economy, which would function in totally free-market conditions, would have no extra-economic limitations. Leone knew that
the principal figures in socialism—Antonio Labriola and Antonio Graziadei,
for instance—wanted to have nothing to do with hedonist economics. He
therefore invoked the authority of Benedetto Croce, who saw hedonism as
a perfectly scientific approach to economics which could coexist harmoniously with Marxist doctrine even if it was not based on the same point of
view and did not have the same objectives. With his revision Leone was

trying to achieve "a better synthesis, a higher and more satisfying formulation of theoretical socialism, more in keeping with the most recent discoveries in economics." In his analysis, he wished to ignore any element unrelated
to economics and to concentrate on the hedonistic behavior of the individual.[63] In this way, he hoped to observe economic behavior in its pure state,
free from any outside interference. Like Walras, he was convinced that
"pure" economics was capable of proving that "social harmony can be attained only through the free functioning of the law of individual egoism."[64]
He added that the principles of hedonistic economics were universally applicable because they were in keeping with human nature. Individuals function in the economic sphere because they have needs. Social needs are the
sum of individual needs. Since the hedonistic principle of maximum profit
for a minimum effort is universal, it follows that value expresses the relationship between effort and profit. In other words, every individual—a worker
or an industrialist, a peasant or a landowner—wants maximum profit for
minimum effort. Consequently, in a truly free market, "an equality of expenses, efforts, and labor for all men, as well as an equality of profits and
salaries," is a realizable ideal. Leone, however, was aware that one problem
remained to be solved: How could one equate the results obtained in a free-
market economy—a relative equilibrium and equality—with the egalitarian
principles of socialism? Here, a distinction made by the Austrian economist
Sax between the economics of the individual and collective economics,
aimed at the satisfaction of different needs, helped him resolve the possible
contradiction between a liberist economy and socialism and permitted him
to conclude that both groups and individuals function according to hedonist
principles.[65]

Leone regarded the decision of working on an individual or a collective
basis as purely economic, one that could be explained only through hedonistic principles. He wished to prove that in a liberist economy it was possible
to attain an equality between producers, which would obviously lead to a
convergence between socialism and liberism. Such a scheme would mean
that everyone would be able to give free rein to economic egoism. And for
true socialism—the kind the revolutionary socialists aspired to—to be established, it was necessary that the state, parliament, the bureaucracy, the legal
system, reformist socialists, liberals, and above all intellectuals—in short, all
the structures and forces that bound the productive process to the narrow
interests of the bourgeoisie—be sidestepped. Leone and Labriola were convinced that with the help of the unionized workers, a free economic system
could bring things back on the right track.

Similarly, Leone thought that the practice of an individual and collective
hedonism not only was conducive to a general economic equilibrium but
would also resolve the contradiction between liberty and equality. Thus, the
application of an economic hedonism could take socialism out of the impasse

to which economic theories that had failed to work had confined it. Leone believed that proletarian socialism, to be effective, had to become an "integral liberalism."[66] Liberism was economic liberty; socialism aspired to political equality. In a situation of absolute economic liberty, a total economic equality can be attained. Leone explained this conclusion by means of the regulatory function of the mechanisms of the market which always tends, as in the principle of communicating vessels, to attain equilibrium. He wished to take socialism out of its metaphysical—or, as he said, "almost theological"—condition based on objective social power (the result of the organization of the proletariat on the basis of social consciousness) and bring it into the age of subjective and voluntaristic social power based on the energy of the proletariat. In short, he wanted to lead socialism in the direction indicated by the hedonistic desires of the mass of individuals who made up the working class.

Leone represented Marx's idea of suplus value as "the product of a conceptual abstraction to which a philosophical answer has been given."[67] This abstraction could conceivably serve as the basis for a political solution (the suppression of the phenomenon by the revolution), but could not be used as the basis of a scientific interpretation that would explain the harm surplus value causes the workers.

In order to explain surplus value in hedonistic terms, Leone traced the curves of pleasure and pain. He claimed that capitalism, because of its monopolistic character and its control over the means of production, could force the worker to produce beyond the point of equilibrium between pleasure and pain—a point that was also that of equilibrium between effort and utility. Leone called this point the "economic moment." Because capitalism required the worker to produce beyond the point of the economic moment, it was reasonable to say that the worker produced portions of a supramarginal utility that for the capitalist represented a product but had no value for the worker. In the curve of utility, this phenomenon was called "supramarginal effort" or "portions of supramarginal effort." It too became a product for the capitalist but remained valueless for the worker.[68]

Such a situation, he wrote, could not exist in an economy of natural equilibrium, because in that case capitalism would have no coercive power. In an economy of natural equilibrium, the worker would be stopped from producing as soon as the economic moment had been reached—that is, the point of equilibrium between effort and utility, between pleasure and pain. In such a case, the capitalist could therefore not expect any surplus value.

Here one must draw attention to an element of great importance for the evolution of revolutionary syndicalism. Leone claimed that the true conflict between class interests was the one he presented in hedonistic terms and that he held to be universally valid, because it was rooted in the inherent economic egoism of human nature. Marx's surplus value, he claimed, was only a conceptual category; owing to this fact, a social class whose identity and existence was defined by this concept was also regarded by Leone and many revolutionary syndicalists as a concept and not a reality.[69] Leone felt that Marx lacked scientific precision, at least in the economic sphere. He thought that Marx's theories were only a criticism of classical economics, not an alternative to them. Consequently, Labriola and Leone wished to produce a more functional economic analysis that would enable them to understand the workings of the market and find their way to economic equilibrium. In any case, they felt that the scientific imprecision of Marx's economic theories required that they be revised. This process, however, necessarily caused a profound change in the character of revolutionary syndicalism, for there was an enormous difference between this type of reasoning and Marxist demonstrations. Leone believed that in a situation of *relative* equilibrium, the capitalists benefited from a maximum hedonist surplus, the result of their capacity to oblige the workers to produce beyond the economic moment—that is, the moment when a balance between utility and effort was achieved. It followed that socialism had to attempt to bring the economy into a situation of *general* equilibrium in which the interests of the workers were respected, in other words, a situation that would not permit an accumulation of surplus value by the capitalists, and that, of course, was possible only in a liberist economy. The social consequence of a model of this kind would obviously be the abolition of the class struggle. Such a model required neither a proletarian consciousness nor a political revolution, for the economic tendency toward equality was both universal and subjective: universal because inherent in human nature, and subjective because of the particularity of the attitude of each individual.

Although Labriola and Leone were aware of the materialist substructure that this type of economic revolution could have in common with Marxist socialism, they were nevertheless attempting to describe a scheme of motivations that was essentially subjective and that took into account the irrational elements in human nature.[70] They claimed that their analysis was empirical and psychological, while Marx's economic objectivity was metaempirical and logical.[71] That, they said, was why Marx remained abstract, whereas they were not divorced from reality. The psychological method thus replaced the classical Marxist method.

According to the theoreticians of revolutionary syndicalism, the worker's motivation was not class consciousness but his economic egoism, and the only needs that existed were economic needs. Following this line of reasoning, these theoreticians denied the validity of theories that based their assertions on a study of history and that arrived at conclusions concerning individual economic behavior by not relating to people as economic agents. Finally, the revolutionary syndicalists saw the organization of workers as representing an accumulation of common hedonist forces that forced the proletariat to search for an equilibrium between labor and capital. They said that the labor syndicates took a revolutionary path only in order to break down the barriers erected by capitalism, protected as it was by a legal system erected by itself.[72] The end of the revolutionary process would therefore be reached only in a situation of general economic equilibrium, when the bourgeoisie and the proletariat would have the same possibility to control the means of production. The syndicate was the organization within which the labor movement had to function, and the revolutionary general strike was the recognized means of weakening and undermining the system.

There is no doubt that this body of ideology aimed to reduce the influence of the state. Liberism required the elimination of state intervention both in the economy and in economic legislation, but it also, and above all, rejected protectionism. In Italy, in the first decade, the protectionist policies of the government, as we have seen, favored the industrial north but were disadvantageous to the agricultural south. Revolutionary syndicalism was firmly antiprotectionist, first for political reasons and then out of ideology.[73]

In a two-part article entitled "The Limits of Revolutionary Syndicalism," which appeared in *Il divenire sociale* in 1910, Labriola described the society of "free producers" from the point of view of the liberist ideal. In this article he tried to demonstrate how quickly protectionist policies, despite their encouragement of industry, could become reactionary. The workers, he said, benefited from these policies as long as the economy was flourishing, but as soon as a recession appeared it became contrary to their interests to support the reformist socialism associated with protectionism. In this situation, the workers in industry would seek to change the way in which production was organized, and this could be achieved only by direct action in the best revolutionary syndicalist tradition. Labriola and Leone saw the struggle as taking place in the economic area: on one hand, one had the workers organized in syndicates and on the other, the bourgeoisie, whose utilization of the state and its legal system permitted it to retain control of the process of production. Only if the organized workers succeeded through their struggle in bringing Italy into a revolutionary crisis could they defeat the antirevolutionary front that had been created between reformism and the liberal system. In this way, the separate development of the two parts of the country would be prevented, as well as military waste, which in Italy meant a perpetuation of the underdevelopment of those sectors which were not connected through powerful interests with the establishment.

The liberist views of revolutionary syndicalism disintegrated, however, when the movement was confronted with the colonial question—closely linked to the north-south dichotomy and the problem of emigration—on the eve of the intervention in Libya. Like several revolutionary syndicalist leaders, Labriola was extremely conscious of Italy's problems of dependency and underdevelopment. A strict liberist policy, in allowing the importation of foreign capital to aid development, could only increase dependency. But a policy of independence had every likelihood of giving rise to protectionist practices and to lead to the intervention of the state in economic life. Enrico Leone, true to his liberist principles, was completely opposed to the Libyan War,[74] while Labriola, Orano, Olivetti, Rocca, and other revolutionary syndicalists favored the occupation of Tripoli. Because of its connection with the economic teachings of revolutionary syndicalism with its vitalist conceptions and its antistate and antimilitarist positions, the debate over the war and colonialism caused a quarrel among the leadership of the movement and prefigured the polemic over interventionism that took place in 1914–1915.

Here we should notice Leone's great consistency. His violent anti-intellectualism differed from that of Sorel or Berth in that it was rooted first and foremost in his economic analysis. Leone, like his master Achille Loria, believed that people do not act against their own economic interests. Thus, owing to the fact that the positions most of these intellectuals held in the government, the municipal administration, the press, and the university depended on the favor of the bourgeoisie, their loyalty toward the workers could not be trusted. And the role of intermediaries that they played in employer-worker relations could in the long run favor only the employers, even if in the short run it might seem to be the other way round.[75] Leone claimed that this underclass of intellectuals, in order to survive, would have to do the same as any other class and "become productive—that is, participate in the tasks of economic production." The revolutionary syndicalist ideology stated that "to the socialization of matter there corresponds a socialization of ideas,"[76] and consequently Leone believed in the principle of the participation of all producers in intellectual work, an area he wished to leave entirely open to anyone connected to the productive process. Leone, in fact, translated Sorel's anti-intellectualism into economic terms. He explained the political and moral justifications given for Bernstein's reformism as arguments used by socialist intellectuals to conceal their desire to subsist materially in dependence on the bourgeoisie.

Thus, the revision of Marx's thought was the cornerstone of the antireformist attitude adopted by revolutionary syndicalism. In the economic sphere, which they considered essential to Marxist socialism, Labriola and Leone attempted to offer a scientifically based alternative solution to that of Marx. They proposed new foundations on which a socialism of a different kind would be constructed. In so doing, however, and in their use of modern economics, they proved that it was possible to beat Marxism on its own ground. And as they were revolutionaries and not competitors of Böhm-Bawerk or Pareto, as they were "leftist" dissidents assailing the bourgeois order and democratic socialism and not bourgeois anti-Marxists, the socialism they proposed was both anti-Marxist and revolutionary. That was the real contribution of this revision.

SOREL, THE MOBILIZING MYTH OF THE
REVOLUTIONARY GENERAL STRIKE,
AND THE LESSONS OF REALITY

"The importance of Sorel in socialist historiography is in my opinion close to that of Marx and Engels and, beyond the shadow of a doubt, greater than that of Proudhon,"[77] wrote Lanzillo, who also compared Sorel with Antonio Labriola and Croce. He was aware of Proudhon's influence on Sorel, and especially on Sorel's perception of the conditions that divided and opposed the bourgeoisie and the proletariat. Through Sorel Proudhon's productional conceptions—increasing production and reducing consumption—penetrated revolutionary syndicalism. While keeping his distance from Marxist socialism, Lanzillo acknowledged the significance of Proudhon's ideas.[78]

The Italian revolutionary syndicalists hailed Sorel as the visionary capable of extracting socialism from what they called the parliamentary-liberal-bourgeois quagmire. His authority as a socialist was confirmed and even augmented by his correspondence with Antonio Labriola, his articles in *Le Mouvement socialiste*, and his writings on the socialist future of the syndicates.[79] Panunzio declared Sorel to be the man whose revision of Marxism had breathed new life into the mother ideology. He placed in the same intellectual family as Sorel the Frenchmen Hubert Lagardelle, Ernest Lafont, and Édouard Berth, the Germans Robert Michels and Raphael Friedeberg, and the Italians Arturo Labriola and Enrico Leone.[80] In a similar vein, Michels mentioned four important ideas that Sorel brought to Italian revolutionary syndicalism: (1) the concept of socialist purity, or rather the idea of the lack of purity from which socialism suffered, and the necessity of reorganizing the movement in order to achieve that purity; (2) a belief in the aptitude of revolutionary syndicalism to create a socialist economy; (3) the idea of the possible use of violence; and (4) a faith in the general strike as a means of training the masses.[81]

The two economists of the movement, Labriola and Leone, were influenced especially by Sorel's first formulation of his conception of syndicalism in "L'Avenir socialiste des syndicats." Yet one cannot say they were affected by his concept of the revolutionary general strike as expressed in *Réflexions sur la violence*. This was because ideas like "violence" and "myth" were hard to reconcile with the economic approach that predominated in their analysis. It was the other revolutionary syndicalist theoreticians who were not professional economists, like Lanzillo, Panunzio, Olivetti, and Orano, who adopted the idea of a moral revolution expressed by Sorel in his *Réflexions*. These pure Sorelians also were among the founding fathers of fascism, whereas the two economists prudently retired from the scene. The degree of attachment of these people to the Sorelian theory of myths and violence is not unrelated to the positions they ultimately adopted. The concept of syndicalism expressed in "L'Avenir socialiste des syndicats" was endorsed by all the Italian revolutionary syndicalists. (This concept was the organization of workers in revolutionary syndicates that would use the techniques of direct action, with the antiparliamentarian and antidemocratic orientation that it implies, as a means of political expression.) Yet the Sorel who held "creative violence" to be the motive force of history, who promoted the myth of the general strike as a metaphor for all socialist ideas and for the revolutionary feelings of the masses, the Sorel of *Réflexions sur la violence*, hardly influenced anyone except a group of intellectuals (Panunzio, Olivetti, Rocca, Dinale, Mantica, and Corridoni) whose intellectual development had taken place within a Marxism that had already been revised, by Labriola and Leone with regard to economic theory, and by Sorel with regard to historical theory. This permitted them to elaborate a position that, moving farther and farther away from Marxism, ended by being totally anti-Marxist.

That did not mean that there were not strong Sorelian echoes in Labriola, as in his description of revolutionary syndicalism as a "method of the conquering life," but a closer examination of the texts reveals that he favored a process of gradual progress through technical and moral improvement and economic development.[82] Similarly, Leone considered Sorel's "creative violence," like violence in general, an involuntary historical phenomenon. He opposed violence, whether spontaneous or planned. Although he regarded the acquisition and accumulation of power—essentially economic power—by the workers as creative and positive, he believed recourse to violence was destructive and negative.[83] Moreover, the fact that violence is not an economic concept made it difficult to integrate it into a system based solely on economic principles.

Ultimately, Italian revolutionary syndicalism became a far more pragmatic movement than a strict Sorelianism would have been. This was due to the fact that the leaders of the movement played simultaneously the role of ideologists and theoreticians and that of politicians and publicists. The contribution of labor chiefs who joined the national leadership of the movement also played a crucial part in this process. To the arguments of the theoreticians, men like De Ambris, Corridoni, Bianchi, Rossi, and Edmondo Rossoni added their long experience of organization and struggle gained in the Chambers of Labor. They also contributed their experience of the general strike, which for them was not a mere myth but a true weapon of combat. These men had a true idea of the power of the bourgeoisie, which they had known through government repression and the actions of the "white guards." They were also aware of the value of political alliances with other segments of the Left. This influence, superimposing itself on the Sorelian revolutionary ethics of which Olivetti, Panunzio, and Orano, for instance, were outstanding representatives, had the effect of postponing the hope of achieving the revolutionary syndicalist ideal, but it also rooted the movement in political reality.

Sorel and the French Sorelians occupied a special place in Italian intellectual life. For the Italian revolutionary syndicalists, France provided a counterbalance to the domination of German revisionism over the world of socialism. In addition to Sorel, *Il divenire sociale* and *Pagine libere* published Berth and Lagardelle a great deal, and also Griffuelhes and Pouget. Michels, who transmitted Kautsky's message to the Italians and had a strong influence on Italian revolutionary syndicalism throughout the first decade of the century, saw the works of Sorel, Berth, and Lagardelle as an attempt to create a synthesis of Marx, Proudhon, Bakunin, and Nietzsche.[84] The point in which the Italian revolutionary syndicalists greatly differed from the French was their knowledge of non-Marxist economic and sociological theory. Labriola, in particular, frequently referred to the great neoclassical economists—Walras, Edgeworth, Jevons, Cournot—but it was Vilfredo Pareto they mentioned most often.[85] Pareto, in turn, had a high opinion of Enrico Leone and said so.[86] Gaetano Mosca, a leading figure of modern political economy, was studied by Panunzio, who claimed that his *Elementi di scienza politica*—translated into English as *The Ruling Class* (1939)—had a number of points in common with revolutionary syndicalist doctrines.[87] One finds that Le Bon's social psychology had also been perfectly assimilated.[88]

However, it was Sorel who played the crucial role in the intellectual development of Italian revolutionary syndicalism. Through his correspondence with three of the most brilliant intellectual Italian figures—Francesco Saverio Merlino, Benedetto Croce, and Antonio Labriola—he won himself a reputation with the young revolutionary syndicalists as a socialist authority. His arguments against democracy and parliamentarianism particularly influenced people like Lanzillo, Orano, Panunzio, and Olivetti, and through them they spread to the whole Italian revolutionary syndicalist movement. It is true that Labriola, Leone, Mocchi, and Longobardi, who, with Gramsci, was to found the Italian Communist party, had always displayed an ambivalent attitude toward democracy and parliamentarianism.[89] They had no difficulty in absorbing Sorel's criticism.

The essence of Sorel's contribution to the critique of Marxism, as we have seen, was his idea of an ethical imperative that enabled the Marxist mechanism of revolt to fulfill its historical function. Precisely this use of an ethical criterion rendered Sorel, together with many revolutionary syndicalists, incapable of restricting his allegiance to the proletariat. Anyone who accepted the Sorelian model, the significance that Sorel gave to the general strike and the idea of violence, was finally bound to be cut off from the working class. The economists were no exception; when Labriola and Leone opened Marx's economic prototype to all "producers," a situation was created where Sorelian ethical criteria were used to explain the different paths that the various groups of operatives—producers organized in syndicates, "productive elites"—followed in order to attain the revolutionary syndical ideal of a "society of free producers."[90]

Finally, it is interesting to note that despite their different perspectives, Sorel, Arturo Labriola, and Leone all ended up in the antirationalist and anti-intellectualist camp. Sorel had called for an ethical and emotional change that could bring about a new heroic age. The intellectual-rationalist politician was obviously incapable of replacing the hero in making such a thing come to pass. The Italians arrived at a similar rejection of the intellectuals and their rationalism through an economic analysis that held egoistic motives ("the hedonistic maximum") to be the basic explanation of the *homo economicus*. Because the revolution could take place only in the economic sphere, it followed that the intellectual politician could not be a mediator who led or helped to lead the process to its final goal.

However, the major Sorelian concern that dominated revolutionary syndicalist thought was the idea of the general strike. In the first ten years of the century, the leaders of Italian revolutionary syndicalism made this idea a subject of reflection, from both a practical and a theoretical point of view. Arturo Labriola thought that Italy had not yet reached the socioeconomic maturity necessary to permit a revolution to succeed. As a result, he believed that the revolutionary syndicalists had the duty of restraining the enthusiasm of the advocates of the strike-here-and-now. Labriola suggested that strikes, even if they succeeded in overturning the monarchy and setting up a republic of "producers," would not have a lasting effect. This was because first the state of development of the country did not lend itself to this, and second a working class able to "carry" a republic of producers was still too small in numbers or nonexistent.[91] The course of events during the strike of September 1904 persuaded the revolutionary syndicalists that the path they had chosen was the right one. A general strike was possible, but not yet a republic of producers. They were now convinced that in the arsenal at the workers' disposal the general strike was the most effective weapon.[92]

Labriola hoped that the general strike would not only arrest the process of degeneration caused by the reformist approach, but confirm the central role of syndicalism in the class struggle and thus discredit the reformist approach that ascribed this role to the party.[93]

In voluntarism, in the dominant position given to syndicalism, in the vision of socialism as essentially a confrontation culminating in the general strike, one can see the influence of Sorel on Italian revolutionary syndicalism at this stage of its development. Walter Mocchi claimed that the Italians took from Sorel only those elements derived directly from Marx.[94] Antonio Polledro, another revolutionary syndicalist, who at the end of 1914 collaborated in the journal *Il popolo d'Italia*, wrote following the general strike of 1904 that the polarization of the social conflict, the widening of the gap between the classes, and the elimination of any possibility of compromise had been reflected in events and confirmed Marx's ideas on the intensification of social struggles.[95] However, he added, the general strike could not be transformed from a defensive into a revolutionary weapon until the workers reached a moral and technical level that allowed them to replace the bourgeoisie in the management of the productive process.[96]

In 1908 the revolutionary syndicalist leaders acknowledged that the "gymnastics of strikes"—as Paolo Mantica described the repeated use of them—had strengthened the organization of the workers in Parma, raised their level of social cohesion, and increased their capacities for sacrifice, initiative, and discipline—three qualities that Sorel regarded as indispensable for the syndical elite. These qualities, wrote Mantica, had enabled the workers of Parma to continue striking for so long.[97]

Another major consequence of this strike was, according to Orano, that it "brought to maturity the *education* of the combatant class, an education based on syndical struggle, energy, and concrete resistance—an education that should be the sole object of syndicalist doctrine and propaganda."[98] One should add that if the revolutionary syndicalists concluded the general strike had demonstrated the cohesion of the workers, they were also of the opinion that once it had begun the strike had accelerated and augmented that cohesion and had caused a polarization of wills conducive to the same end. These consequences were as much due to the combative spirit that mobilization had aroused as to the syndicates' increased detestation of a bourgeois society that seemed to understand only force and that drove them into confrontation.[99]

Orano thought that the strike in Parma was a confirmation of the character of a mobilizing myth that Sorel had recognized in the general strike: "It is necessary to believe in the general strike," he wrote. "In this way, we shall be able to bring it to the splendid dimensions it reached in the province of Ferrara and then in that of Parma. It is necessary . . . to believe deeply in the solemn and heroic desertion of organized masses who, for their part, have learned that a repeated resistance, each time a little more bellicose, each time a little more drawn out, can cause the erosion of that of the propertied classes and reduce it to its least significant expression."[100]

Agostino Lanzillo added that the general strike was a vigorous assertion of the antiparliamentary character of revolutionary syndicalism.[101] Labriola, however, felt it would be too dangerous to attempt to apply the revolutionary syndicalist theories during the strike in Parma and did not support De Ambris, Corridoni, and the other like-minded syndicalist leaders. He believed that it was necessary for the syndicalists first to try to convince the workers that an organized labor movement would unquestionably be more beneficial to them than the party system. Labriola feared that the strike would endanger this move.[102] He felt that this course of action was especially required because shortly after the congress of Ferrara the revolutionary syndicalists had decided to quit the PSI.

The experience of 1908 permitted the revolutionary syndicalists to draw a number of conclusions: (1) A strong and well-structured syndicalist organization (such as the Parma Chamber of Labor, for instance) could foster solidarity and coordination at the highest level among agricultural workers, industrial workers, and those in tertiary activities. (2) Given the existing regime, it was impossible to limit the conflict, because the adversary could always call upon the government and the army. (3) In order to wage the struggle against the united bourgeoisie, revolutionary syndicalism was unable to forgo the assistance of the Socialist party and other potential allies. (4) The years of education, propaganda, strikes, and organization had encouraged certain forms of behavior and consolidated certain attitudes among members of syndicates so that, when the time came, the syndicalist elite was able to draw from them the force and confidence necessary to permit the continuation and intensification of the strike. Six years later, Mussolini wrote: "The 'red bloc,' which today is an illusion and a dangerous 'absence,' may tomorrow be imposed through a revolutionary combination of circumstances. It would then arise spontaneously."[103] Despite the failure of his attempt to prevent the intervention in Libya by means of a general strike that he organized in September 1911, Mussolini declared that this instrument was "the most effective weapon of war the proletariat has,"[104] and De Ambris, while admitting that there had been no real preparation for the general strike of the red week, regarded the strike as a remarkable tool of psychological preparation.[105]

However, in the months before the First World War, there was a complete confusion among these revolutionaries. Previous to the outbreak of hostilities, all kinds of solutions began to be envisaged which were very far from the spirit of revolutionary syndicalism in its heroic period. One has the impression of people who were no longer bound by anything. De Ambris began to advocate the union of all forces of the Left—syndicalists, anarchists, and republicans.[106] Such a coalition, essentially political, was hardly compatible with the principle of direct action in the economic sector. Olivetti also, when he began the republication of *Pagine libere* in the summer of 1914, launched a new formula of "revision and adaptation" for the purpose of achieving an "integral revolutionism."[107] The economistic and mythical approach to the general strike had finally been abandoned for a politico-economic model regarded as more likely to lead to comprehensive solutions. This change was probably due to the political failure of the general strike, but especially to the impossibility of making full use of the weapon of the general strike without damaging the process of production. Labriola and Leone laid down the natural limits of the general strike when they said that the proletariat was not yet morally or technically capable of taking over the process of production. Until that happened, the existing system of production had to be preserved. In other words, for the foreseeable future, there was nothing that could replace capitalism. The full weight of this conclusion was felt during the war years and in the years following the armistice.

Indeed, revolutionary syndicalism remained true to the principle that it was absolutely necessary to prevent the revolutionary process from operating in a system of production that was destroyed or even disorganized. Just as they had in the past (in this they were true to their original principles), syndicalists stressed the necessity of maintaining production at the highest possible level. In the meantime, they added to this unchanging objective the idea of national solidarity and a little later of antibolshevism. The Sorelians wanted to inherit from the bourgeoisie, and in this they were true once again to an old Sorelian principle—the aspiration to a wealthier and more productive society. But it now appeared that they not only regarded themselves as heirs to the bourgeoisie, but preferred sharing with it a wealthier society to inheriting from it a poorer one. This was the essential reason for their antibolshevism: "Bolshevism, which causes the collapse of the bourgeois economic regime, disintegrates every productive organism, creates disorder in the industrial sector, and leads to disorder and poverty; it is the most antisocialist and most antiproletarian phenomenon in the world."[108]

De Ambris thought that bolshevism was not only destructive, but also incapable of creating a productive mechanism able to take over from the one it hoped to destroy.[109] In order to resist industrial lockouts and respond to the need of preserving the process of production, it was necessary, he believed, to invent a new type of general strike.[110] This new type of weapon would have to conform to the revolutionary syndicalist ideal of evolution, that is, it should raise the workers to a moral and technical level, enabling them to replace the bourgeoisie in the management of production or to share this management with the bourgeoisie.

Revolutionary syndicalism and later national syndicalism gradually abandoned the idea of the general strike because of practical failures, and also because their ideologists finally turned away from class and decided on nation as the motive force of the revolution. Now, a class could go on strike, but a nation went to war. Because it required a high degree of solidarity among producers, a productionist model did not have room for two conflicts. Finally, the idea of the revolutionary strike did not stand up to the test of reality but continued to survive as a mobilizing myth. This concept was also abandoned because Sorel had proposed it at a time when the Italian revolutionary syndicalists were preoccupied, above all, with the question of forming proletarian revolutionary elites and emphasized education and morale. National syndicalism, for its part, preferred the myth of the revolutionary war.

CHAPTER FOUR

The Socialist-National Synthesis

THE MYTH OF THE REVOLUTIONARY WAR

Despite their efforts in the first ten years of the century, the Italian revolutionary syndicalists did not succeed in bringing about any revolutionary change by means of the general strike. In the sphere of ideas, the Sorelian myth did not fare any better than the general strike did in the practical field. As for class struggle, it became problematic, to say the least, as soon as Labriola and Leone began, through their revision of Marxism, to introduce productionism into the revolutionary syndicalist idea. The new "producers" were supposed to combat all the unproductive elements—the parasites—of society, and it was in their interest to avoid any form of conflict that could paralyze the process of production.[1]

Nor did revolutionary syndicalism succeed in convincing the majority of the Left of the correctness of its ideas. That is what caused the split in Ferrara in 1907.[2] Little by little, the centrality of class struggle in the credo of the movement was replaced by elitist conceptions and a hope of raising the "moral level" of the working class. The revolutionary syndicalists, however, did not overlook the necessity, which they regarded as crucial, of proposing something else in place of the general strike. They knew that they would have to find another mobilizing myth with a wider scope, which would succeed in achieving the aim the general strike had failed to accomplish, namely, the destruction of the democratic-liberal structures. And since Italian society was incapable of giving rise to the internal conditions that could bring about such a destruction, one had to resort to external factors. The catalyst finally chosen was war.

For those theoreticians who made this choice first, it was by no means easy to do, nor did they find it simple to gain acceptance by the movement. At the beginning of the century, it was difficult for people of the revolutionary extreme Left to revise their positions on war, internationalism, or militarism or to change their attitudes toward concepts such as the "nation" or the "fatherland." When for years one has taught that war is contrary to the interests of the workers, it is difficult to suddenly support interventionism. This evolution did not take place without mishaps. Yet the idea that Italy was afflicted with "parliamentary democratic liberalism" as though with a fatal illness transmitted through the Giolitti virus made many people think that the only possible medicine was war. To an increasing extent, this conclusion became as common among the nationalists on the Right as among the revolutionary syndicalists on the Left.[3] Finally, in August 1914, the chief revolutionary syndicalist leaders agreed to press for Italy's entry into the war against Germany and Austria-Hungary.

Previously, syndicalists had attempted to penetrate army barracks with their traditional antimilitarism in the hope of developing "class consciousness" among the conscripts. Similarly, in order to anticipate the automatic support the army gave to the bourgeoisie in the "social war," the syndicalists tried to change the army's common perception of the worker as rebellious, strike-prone, and antinational, and for that reason they attempted to appeal to the "man and worker" in every soldier.[4] These attempts belonged to a rationalistic tradition that believed in the power of logical argument. By 1907, however, antirationalist currents had begun to influence revolutionary syndicalism, together with ambivalent ideas about the army and war. The concepts of "nation" and "fatherland" meanwhile took on different connotations.

Arturo Labriola began the debate by declaring war to be a mere instrument: "In the hands of a surgeon, a sharp blade confers health; in the hands of an assassin, it destroys life."[5] It is the aims and actors, he believed, that give a war its moral value. Labriola recognized the possibility of a war for a just cause; Hervé's pacifism at any price seemed senseless to him.[6] Influenced by Sorel's ideas, Labriola came to regard the fatherland and patriotism not as concepts but as sentiments inaccessible by reason or argument. This point of view nullified the contradiction between socialism and patriotism, especially when the latter regarded itself as the personification of a common language, tradition, and culture. Labriola explained the assertion of the *Communist Manifesto* that "the workers have no country" as a reflection of the hard living conditions of the workers in Marx's time. The common language and tradition, claimed Labriola, filter through to the working class only when it begins to derive some advantage from the state: social benefits, education, political rights, and so on.[7] But when the state uses the army for repressive purposes, then it is clear that from a socialist point of view "the degree to which we succeed in suppressing the blind automatism that makes the army a machine activated by the will of the state is precisely the degree to which socialism becomes a reality."[8]

This idea found an extreme expression in the concept of a striking army. Such a phenomenon would be an act of revolution. Looked at from the Sorelian point of view, a striking army was a no less revolutionary myth than that of the "classical" general strike. The fact that this myth was unrealizable in no way diminished its evocative power, for it implied the separation of the army from the bourgeois state. The right conditions for such a "moment" were more likely to occur in a war situation: war could therefore be beneficial to socialism. His adherence to the idea of a cultural-linguistic patriotism led Labriola to believe that in time of war workers would be willing to defend this type of national-cultural entity because it was indispensable to their own development. Once the opposition between patriotism and socialism had been eliminated, the way was open for the interventionist positions of Labriola and other revolutionary syndicalists at the time of the Libyan War.[9]

Labriola was not the only person to take this direction. Paolo Orano, at the second Syndicalist Congress in 1910, asked a question, to which he immediately provided the answer: "Can one believe in the possibility of abolishing war? Let us not delude ourselves! War is a necessity, the springtime of progress. And why should not progress require class warfare to be preferred to war between states?"[10]

Orano went on to say that true antimilitarism was that which succeeded in separating the bourgeois state from the army and which, owing to that fact, succeeded in truly neutralizing the army. Only class consciousness and syndical action were capable of achieving that form of antimilitarism, which had nothing in common with a hollow propaganda with sterile results. Orano believed that Italy, despite its glorious past, was in the process of disappearing, for it was not equal to the challenges the other powers posed. This was because Italian capitalism, which controlled the country through the liberal bourgeoisie, was interested only in the profits to be made from military expenses and failed to provide for the needs of the army and navy.[11]

Giuseppe Prezzolini, who with Giovanni Papini had laid the foundations of cultural nationalism in the first decade of the century, also subscribed to the syndicalist theory and sought to explain the lack of patriotic sentiment among the workers. "The syndicalist proletariat," he wrote, "is against the idea of the fatherland, against the fatherland of the bosses for which it is called upon to shed its blood, inasmuch as the bourgeoisie has taken from it anything that could have given it a patriotic sentiment."[12]

Prezzolini was convinced that an aggravation of the conflict between the bourgeois and the workers, encouraged and sustained by the syndicates, could give rise to the much-needed moral renewal in Italian society. This renewal would reach its finest expression in war, where "genius, audacity, poetry and passion, supreme justice, and tragic heroism" would be universal.[13]

The Sorelian conceptions of social war and moral revolution, as expressed in *Réflexions*, are clearly reflected in the writings of Labriola, Orano, and Prezzolini. For these three men, revolutionary syndicalism could not automatically be associated with antimilitarism. It was in war that moral qualities had their finest manifestation, and if social change, the revolution, could not come about by means of social war, a different scenario became necessary: war between nations.

FROM THE LIBYAN WAR TO THE INTERVENTIONISM OF
THE LEFT: THE IMPERIALISM OF THE WORKERS,
THE SYNDICATE, AND THE NATION

In October 1910, one year before the Libyan War, Paolo Orano began publishing *La lupa*. In the editorial staff of this journal, the names of Sorel, Hervé, and Peguy rubbed shoulders with those of Labriola, Michels, Missiroli, Pietri-Tonelli, and Fovel.[14] It should be pointed out that in 1910 Sorel was the object of attacks from the Italian Left, which reproached him for his close links with the Action française. Agostino Lanzillo, Sorel's closest disciple among the Italian revolutionary syndicalists, now took up a defense of the master in a series of articles in *Il divenire sociale*. While arguing in favor of the Sorelian concept of violence (in this case, proletarian violence), Lanzillo fiercely attacked Hervé.[15]

The fact that Sorel, the principal ideologist of revolutionary syndicalism, drew close to Maurrassian nationalism, adding to it antimaterialism and antirationalism, aroused the interest of the radical nationalist Corradini. Corradini had already seen a nationalist-syndicalist faction emerge and develop.[16] Corradini believed that revolutionary syndicalist "direct action" was indicative of a willingness to fight—a quality he held to be the precondition for the war through which Italian society would overcome its problems. He associated the syndicalist elites with aristocrats and antidemocrats.[17] This form of reasoning made the grafting together of nationalism and syndicalism seem conceivable and advantageous. Mario Viana and Enrico Corradini thus took it upon themselves to indicate the points in common of the two movements, publishing articles on the subject in the nationalist journal *Il tricolore*.[18] They pointed out that the two movements had parliamentarianism as their common enemy. Viana, for his part, tried to demonstrate the necessary identity of interests of capital and labor in a productionist economy, the only kind able to neutralize the inroads of foreign capital. In this connection, he reminded the syndicalists that they too sought an increased production.[19] Corradini saw syndicalism as a doctrine of class economic solidarity, while nationalism was the doctrine of national economic solidarity. He held that the nation was an intermediary between class and the international sphere. Because the nation was composed of individuals, the hedonistic principle of maximum profit for a minimum effort was as valid for the nation as it was for the class. For Corradini, however, the nation was and remained primarily a moral factor, and it was the dominant factor in historical development. It represented the largest functional unit of people able to coordinate their actions decisively and in full consciousness.[20]

Another common factor Corradini described was the desire for conquest, which according to him was shared by nationalists and syndicalists. On this basis, he saw a similarity in their call for a heroic spirit and for the necessity of developing the qualities this required. These resemblances gave rise to a joint aspiration: imperialism. Even though this manifested itself in two apparently different forms—national imperialism and labor imperialism—it was nevertheless the same beyond these two variations.[21] These two movements, he wrote, had the same purposes: to stop pacifism, oppose repression, and fight against bourgeois decadence. In order to facilitate the construction of a bridge leading from nationalism to syndicalism and vice versa, Corradini proposed the following synthesis: "There are nations that are in a condition of inferiority in relation to others, just as there are classes that are in a condition of inferiority in relation to other classes. Italy is a proletarian nation: emigration demonstrates this sufficiently. Italy is the proletarian of the world."[22]

The logic of Corradini's argument was that the antibourgeois struggle of revolutionary syndicalism could be transposed into the international sphere. In his opinion, Italy was in the process of becoming a proletarian nation. This tendency was increasing, especially as the country lacked colonies: territories it could populate with its citizens and from where it could draw the raw materials it needed so much and that could be markets for its industrial products. Italy had to raise itself to the level of the bourgeois nations, those colonial powers that controlled large segments of international commerce. Emigration was doubly dangerous for Italy, wrote Corradini, for not only did this drain deprive the country of a potentially useful work force, but it increased the power of the rival nations.[23]

War, he believed, was the only way out of this impasse. A victorious international and antibourgeois war would gain Italy the place it deserved. "In view of this," he wrote, "nationalism is inclined to wish a truce of God on all factions, including socialism and syndicalism."[24]

Heroism and the will to conquer were the moral values that had to be opposed to the mercantile values of the decadent bourgeoisie. These ideas were expressed in Corradini's *La patria lontana* (The distant fatherland), a book that discussed the relative significance of revolutionary syndicalism, liberalism, and nationalism. Nationalists and syndicalists, he wrote, found common ground in antiliberalism, an antiliberalism that aimed to eliminate the old bourgeois elite and replace it with a new elite actuated by imperialism—that is, the desire for conquest and moral renewal.[25]

Despite everything, in 1910 the revolutionary syndicalists were not yet ready to adopt an attitude that would cause them to use the general strike for the purpose of an international war or to exchange the principle of proletarian violence for imperialism. In the issue of *La lupa* in which Corradini wrote about nationalism and syndicalism, Labriola described what he perceived as two types of nationalism: "To the nationalism of the contractors and the military industries is opposed cultural nationalism, supported by the syndicalists, which creates a feeling of nationhood among the workers and interests them in the conservation of the assets they have in common with the whole country."[26]

Labriola was convinced that the social and economic integration of Italy could not come about without the participation of the workers. He held that Italy was only the linguistic union of a number of different regions whose disparity was particularly pronounced among the workers. The workers, he stated, ought to be concerned with the international situation of the country in that their economic situation was linked directly to the condition of Italian capitalism. The competition with Austria could seriously undermine the financial power of the country and in the long run even lead to the exclusion of its influence from the Mediterranean area. The question of the Adriatic should be taken seriously by the workers, because they too were concerned with it. Labriola regarded political nationalism as a regression. Nationalism was based on tradition, and in Italy tradition meant regionalism, internal rivalries, old suspicions, and long-standing enmities. Moreover, political nationalism implied the defense of a state that was simply "a parasitic bureaucracy, an inglorious army, and a Prince without a will of his own, a prisoner of circumstance."[27]

Such a state was incapable of bringing a great project to fruition. Everything, in fact, depended on the majority—that is, on the workers. Unfortunately, the working class did not seem able to fight, whether in a war or in a revolution. Labriola believed that this inability was due to a lack of inspired leaders: "Where Turati and Ferri triumph, there is neither a Napoleon nor a Garibaldi." Only the awakening of the Italian consciousness, maintained Labriola, could cure this paralysis. This consciousness—Labriola was really speaking of the Italian collective identity—was cultural, literary, and linguistic. If the workers acquired it, they would feel they were an integral part of the country. As soon as the workers identified with Italy through its culture, they would understand and automatically support its interests. For that reason, Labriola favored a cultural nationalism that would come from the bottom. He insisted, however, on the need for a separation between the nation and the state. Nationalism could not be imposed by the state through war or compulsory military service. The will to conquest would have to come from the working class; then, and only then, would the workers be able to fight. Labriola saw clearly the differences between his ideas and those of Corradini. Thus, he believed that violence and war were two different things.[28] The imperialism of the people could manifest itself only in a republican regime—certainly not in a monarchy, not even a nationalist one. It was nevertheless true that Labriola's search for an Italian cultural unity brought revolutionary syndicalism closer to nationalism.[29] This assertion of the preeminence of the cultural was a constant feature of revolutionary syndicalist thought; it was already found in Labriola's "Presentazione" of the movement in the first issue of *Pagine libere*.[30]

Thus, on the eve of the Libyan War, some revolutionary syndicalist intellectuals adopted positions close to those of the nationalist camp. Their main reasons for supporting the conquest of Tripoli were cultural and moral. War, they believed, was a training in violence, heroism, and sacrifice. In a war, one acquired the taste for risk, discipline, and hierarchy. In short, war was the school par excellence for those virtues which are necessary for greatness. These elementary lessons of Sorelianism were well learned in Italy, where, unlike France, an opportunity existed to apply them.

But there were also other reasons. When urging the occupation of Tripoli, Orano, Labriola, and Olivetti stressed the economic benefits that Italy and the Italian workers would gain from this conquest. They also pointed out the moral and pedagogical value of such an exercise as a training in revolution. Labriola wrote: "O my companions, do you know why the proletariat in Italy cannot make a revolution? I tell you it is because they are not even capable of making a war." This was a way of expressing the disillusion that had gradually overtaken some syndicalist leaders regarding the capacity of the working class to foment a revolution with the general strike. One sees here the first signs of an attempt to replace the myth of the revolutionary general strike with another formula for struggle, regarded as more mobilizing: revolutionary war. Labriola ended by preferring the experience of war to cultural nationalism. He wrote: "Let the bourgeoisie teach the proletariat how really to fight, and you will see how quickly the proletariat will learn to fight against that same bourgeoisie."[31]

Seven months before the war, Olivetti adopted Sorelian tones in describing the points in common between syndicalists and nationalists: "Now, the first coefficient of similitude between nationalism and syndicalism is that both are doctrines of energy and will which accept neither the idea nor the practice of compromise."[32]

In describing the content the two ideologies shared, Olivetti reminded his readers that it was already to be found in the philosophies of Schopenhauer and Nietzsche. He presented revolutionary syndicalism as a form of idealism in which the will to action and the will to power worked together toward the same objective: change. Moreover, nationalism and syndicalism rejected gradual change and compromise, which could only perpetuate the existing order. Both strongly opposed materialism: "Syndicalism and nationalism are thus antidemocratic and antibourgeois. And, one should say, they are both aristocratic tendencies in a basely materialistic society. One does everything to bring an elite of producers into being, and the other proclaims the domination of an elite of the race."[33]

The elitist and aristocratic character of this thought recalls Sorel, but also Corradini. Olivetti accused bourgeois society of lacking a sense of the tragic and of heroism. Nothing else, he wrote, was to be expected of a society controlled by the stock exchange and small businesses. Nationalism, however, was purely theoretical, divorced from reality; only a small elite could grasp its significance. The "fatherland" was an abstraction and as a result its power of attraction was limited. Production, on the other hand, was concrete. It could therefore serve as the basis for a functional myth. Precisely because of its abstract character, "mobile nationalism," as Olivetti called it, would necessarily remain the ideology of a few, for as soon as the time came to put it into practice, it would turn into an institutionalized militarism, the masses being incapable of reaching the level of abstraction needed for a comprehension of the idea of a fatherland.[34]

Corradini naturally rejected Olivetti's reasoning, but he understood that in order to become politically effective, nationalism would have to find its way to the masses. Now, the masses were the proletariat. The problem was therefore how to connect the workers' self-awareness with the syndical concepts of national solidarity and productionism. Corradini declared the politicians to be useless as intermediaries between the capitalists and workers for this purpose. If only the politicians were kept out of it, factory owners and workers would be clever enough to cooperate for their mutual benefit within the framework of a productionist economy.[35]

The attitudes we have described greatly facilitated a rapprochement over the question of Tripoli. Labriola, Orano, and Olivetti, however, explained that they made their choice in the hope of seeing an upsurge in the moral values to which a cultural nationalism (they insisted on this basis for their nationalism) could give rise. In any event, their objective remained social change, and one that was exclusively social. Unlike the "classical" nationalists, the revolutionary syndicalists claimed that a war could not be the expression, and still less the incarnation, of a national purpose; at best, it was a means by which social change could be accelerated. Despite the kinship that some intellectuals of the two movements recognized on certain essential points—the aristocratic character proposed for their respective elites, the belief in the spread of moral values as a precondition for change—the intentions of these two schools of thought were not yet interchangeable.

The anxiety with which the revolutionary syndicalists and nationalists regarded the massive emigration of Italians was another point in common. The syndicalists naturally saw it as an attempt to escape poverty, but economic distress could not explain everything. If the Italians had a slightly less fluctuating social ideology, the hemorrhage, they thought, would be less copious.[36] Even if they did not approve of emigrants, the syndicalists tried to understand them, knowing that poverty and suffering had led to their decision.

The nationalists, for their part, were mostly concerned with the economic and military implications of this movement of population for a country that was one of the most venerable on the European continent.[37] Some revolutionary syndicalists claimed that a victorious war in Libya would stop the hemorrhage. Others, while not denying the acuteness of the problem, maintained that war would not solve it.

The revolutionary syndicalists—even those who favored an intervention in Libya—continued to regard themselves as socialists. Olivetti spoke for all of them when he said that the growth of bourgeois capitalism was desirable only as a necessary stage in the social conflict between the working class and the bourgeoisie, and the Libyan War could play an important role in the development of that conflict.[38] Labriola, mindful of southern Italy, wrote: "The action in Libya is probably the most important and serious move in favor of the Mezzogiorno to be undertaken so far."[39] A colonized Libya, he believed, would transform the economy of the south. Moreover, if Italy did not take Tripoli, another power would, which in the best circumstances would use the conquered territory in a way disadvantageous to Italian economic interests. The working class would then inevitably be the first to be affected, as well as the one to be hurt the most.[40] Revolutionary syndicalists who called for a war in Libya did not fail to list the benefits that could result from a conquest of the region. There were material benefits, naturally—it was a source of raw materials, an outlet for finished products—but it also provided a solution to the problem of emigration. A colony to be settled close to the mother country was an ideal destination for those who were obliged to leave.[41] Olivetti saw this as an opportunity for the workers to develop an "aristocratic revolution" and a will to conquest, which were indispensable to their taking over the process of production: "The day the working class is ready for the great conquest, it will use the same language with the bourgeoisie as Italy employs with Turkey: the eternal language of force, confirmed in facts . . . the language of ancient Rome."[42]

A series of somewhat different arguments was put forward by Libero Tancredi (pseudonym of Massimo Rocca). Tancredi justified the Libyan enterprise in the belief that a world proletarian revolution was not about to happen. He therefore recommended deriving the maximum advantage from the existing state of affairs. The war, he believed, could at least serve as "(1) a lesson in revolution for the proletariat; (2) an opportunity of revival for the bourgeoisie; (3) the guarantee of a future field of expansion for the bourgeoisie or the proletariat, for whom it would provide economic resources; and (4) an opportunity to retrieve a land from the sterility to which its government and inhabitants had reduced it."[43]

Tancredi posed as a revolutionary while asserting that there was more to be gained from war and conquest than from peace and renunciation. As for the bourgeoisie, he claimed it would emerge from the experience matured and increased in stature because of the challenges it would have to face.[44] Foreseeing a conflict on a European scale, Tancredi called for a republican nationalism that, when the time came, would make Italy take the side of the camp of liberty: "The revolution must join the forces that will defend it against the Austrian monarchist-clerical-socialist feudalism."[45] This type of nationalism developed side by side with the other forms of nationalism that called for social change and condemned the reaction symbolized by the German and Austro-Hungarian emperors.

In the rapprochement between revolutionary syndicalism and nationalism, however, the Libyan War represented only the first stage. Most of the syndicalist leaders and Enrico Leone, a theoretician of the first rank, true to their socialist conceptions, were opposed to this expedition. They expressed opposition despite their reluctance to appear in agreement, even in this, with the reformist socialists. De Ambris, Corridoni, Mantica, Leone, Masotti, Barni, and Polledro took part in the general strike against the policy of intervention in Libya and the war with Turkey.[46] Leone threw himself vigorously into this battle. He vehemently rejected the idea that a politico-military colonialism could help achieve any of the objectives of syndicalism. Leone made a clear distinction between a natural economic expansion and an artificial expansion achieved by politico-military means.[47] Paolo Mantica likewise was unable to understand or justify sending workers to shed their blood to defend the interests of the Banco di Roma.[48] He held this establishment to be the very symbol of reaction and, worse, the objective accomplice of Austria-Hungary, that power which still controlled Italian-speaking territories. Tullio Masotti wrote that syndicalism had to oppose the war because it reflected the antiproletarian policies of the monarchy and of the Catholic and clerical bankers.[49] Giulio Barni, who also strongly opposed the war, nevertheless attempted to understand the position of people like Labriola, Olivetti, and Orano. He acknowledged that after many years of struggle and effort, the failure of the revolutionary strike and the inactivity and passivity of syndicalism in the period before the war might have influenced people dedicated to social revolution and made them search for other paths, other means. As for nationalism, he wrote, it had to choose: either it remained monarchical and lapsed into anachronism or it became republican and gained a new chance of viability.[50]

As was often the case at this period, it was De Ambris who led the group of revolutionary syndicalists opposed to the war. He remained true to the principle of class struggle and excluded for the moment any collaboration between workers and capitalists. He claimed that only through class conflict could the unionized workers gain the moral and technical training they needed in order to take over the process of production. He saw the Tripoli expedition as a new and more ambitious version of the attempt to conquer Ethiopia fifteen years earlier. De Ambris insisted: the workers should fight only to defend their own interests ("to break their own chains"), and not for military or financial objectives.[51] In his opinion, Labriola, Olivetti, and Orano, were more to be blamed than anyone else, for they knew the realities of the workers' struggles. They were false revolutionaries who, victims of their own specious arguments, supported an aggression whose results would benefit only the parasites and strengthen the bourgeois state.[52] Mantica also was opposed to a war from which, he wrote, only financial circles would benefit. But war as a manifestation of force might be desirable if the nation and the state did not coincide.[53] This opinion relates to the essence of cultural nationalism as defined by Labriola in his attacks on Hervé, namely, that the nation can be a model of reference provided the majority of the people—the workers—can identify themselves with it and find their place there.

In 1911 the revolutionary syndicalists opposed to the war compared it to a narrow stage where the state had agreed to be the understudy of Catholic financial circles. They thus represented it as an affair of the state and not of the nation. In 1914, however, the war was regarded as the affair of the entire nation. Between these two dates, the debate on this concept of war, as an element of political analysis, was very lively and held an important place in the thinking of the revolutionary syndicalists.

Replying to his critics, Labriola claimed that the syndicalist criterion applied only where class interests were concerned. However, there were considerations and general interests beyond those of class where syndicalism did not provide the answer.[54] Mantica immediately condemned this argument as reformism.[55] Next, it was Olivetti's turn to defend himself; accused by De Ambris of waving the flag of nationalism, he declared that his sole aim was to analyze the political facts from a purely syndicalist point of view, and certainly not to close ranks with Corradini's supporters.[56] While seeking to keep their distance from political nationalism, Labriola and Olivetti tried to retain their right to express themselves as theoreticians of revolutionary syndicalism and to analyze the situation in complete independence. They demanded this right with all the more insistence because they believed that the revolutionary syndicalist program did not have anything concrete to offer or anything applicable to the new situation.[57]

Finally, De Ambris and Mantica decided to leave the editorial staff of *Pagine libere*. De Ambris declared that he could not continue to work with people whose views about syndicalism were so different from his own. Mantica reproached the same people—Olivetti, Orano, and Labriola—of wanting to impose a philosophy of the proletariat totally at variance with daily syndical experience.[58] As for Enrico Leone, true to the liberist economic principles that had guided him in his revision of Marx ten years earlier, he expressed, as a good economist, the following argument: "Yes, young people, expansion is indeed necessary, but not when it is achieved by force of arms. Only commercial expansion is useful. As for military expansion, it is disastrous."[59] Leone thought military expansion was a parasitic phenomenon. Only when it was the outcome of economic growth and the free play of competition did expansion have a productive character. Leone concluded that because of overtaxation and increasing military expenditures, an politico-military expansion was economically damaging and unproductive, and thus negative from the revolutionary syndicalist point of view.

The real problem for revolutionary syndicalism, however, was not Libya, but the intrinsic value of war. The relationship between war and revolution, the lessons that revolution could learn from war, the nature of a new mobilizing myth to replace that of the revolutionary general strike, the attitude to adopt to the concept of nation: these were the questions debated in the movement in the years 1911 and 1912. The controversy that grew around the intervention in Libya concerning the purpose of war and the concept of nation no doubt contributed a great deal toward removing doubts and overcoming hesitations in revolutionary syndicalist circles in 1914. Revolutionary syndicalism approached the situation with a credo in which the myth of revolutionary war and interventionism overlapped.[60] The long, often bitter and violent debate that tore revolutionary syndicalism apart helped considerably to pave the way for the unanimity of the summer of 1914. It was not a complete accident that Alceste De Ambris, the fierce opponent of the "Libyan adventure," in 1914 headed the interventionist Left. Revolutionary syndicalist ideology, which had been refined at the time of the Tripoli expedition, was faced with circumstances where hesitation was no longer possible. All the revolutionary syndicalists now agreed about the revolutionary potential of the European war; all saw it as a war involving the entire nation, and not merely the bourgeois state. All the opponents of the Tripoli expedition, including leaders of the antimilitarist strikes of 1911 such as Corridoni and Mussolini, now pledged themselves to fight for the nation.

Between 1911 and 1914, the revolutionary syndicalist leaders who had opposed the Libyan War adopted a strongly antimilitaristic line of propaganda.[61] This was one aspect of their rejection of the liberal bourgeois state, and particularly of the use of the army by that state to break up strikes and disperse demonstrations. During the red week of June 1914, the government sent first the police and then the army against the antimilitarist demonstrators. The syndicalists immediately launched a general strike, and in certain places the movement turned into a rebellion against the established order. The revolutionary potential revealed by the red week caused the syndicalist leaders to reflect on the kind of catalyst that could transform that potential into a reality.

In the controversy surrounding the Libyan War, all the revolutionary syndicalists agreed on Europe: in their eyes, the countries of the Triple Alliance were the fountainhead of reaction. Thus it was quite understandable that in 1914 the people associated with *L'internazionale*—among whom were anarchists and republicans—should adopt the slogan Up with the Proletarians! Down with War![62] This cry, however, should not be interpreted as the watchword of some pacifist mystique. Indeed, an article with this title went so far as to speculate on the possibility of transforming the "shameful" war between nations into a "liberating" civil war. More than any other left-wing formation, the revolutionary syndicalists had no illusions concerning the ability of the workers to prevent mass mobilization once the European countries had ordered it. They had not forgotten the wave of patriotism aroused by the Libyan War and the failure of the general strike of 27 September 1911. De Ambris, like others, knew that only a few groups of selected, highly organized workers were able to measure up ideologically to the challenge of the war. The idea of transforming the war into a revolution, however, was entirely in keeping with the voluntarist and activist spirit of revolutionary syndicalism. The workers had to learn how to turn situations to their advantage:

> Let the governments blow up the ship!
> The explosion will sweep them away!
> Down with war! Long live the Revolution![63]

From the very beginning, this European quarrel did not seem to be simply a war like any other. There was a feeling that it would overturn social structures and transform the political and ethical situation of the peoples taking part.[64] Not wanting to let such an opportunity slip by them, the revolutionary syndicalists mobilized themselves as energetically as they could. They did not hesitate to represent this war as a confrontation between the forces of liberty and those of reaction. Corradini's argument was inverted: one had not a proletarian nation trying its luck on the battlefield, but rather a war that set the liberty-loving nations against the reactionary nations.

However, despite all this, the USI was still not unanimous. Many of its members, led by Armando Borghi, remained strongly antimilitaristic and thus true to the traditional position of the Left.[65] Likewise Enrico Leone, who in this situation too adhered to the revolutionary syndicalist model of a society of free producers, declared that state, politics, power, and war represented a single phenomenon whose source was the control of the process of production by the bourgeoisie. "Force is not only in the effect, it is the matrix," he wrote. "Whoever speaks of politics speaks of war, because he speaks of the state."[66] Leone believed that the army was there only to repress the proletariat. This body therefore had to be eliminated if a society of free producers was to be established. Interventionism was senseless, since war and the army were associated with the bourgeois mode of production, which revolutionary syndicalism wished to suppress.[67]

The leadership of the movement, however, had already made its decision. On 1 August 1914, Tullio Masotti declared the need to defend the revolution against reaction,[68] and simultaneously neutralism was abandoned in the name of peace. There was a growing hope that Europe would emerge from the war purified. Paolo Mantica was so bold as to predict that "tomorrow will be the finest page of history in the golden book of humanity, when the genius of war will have killed war and given birth to peace."[69]

At the same time, Alceste De Ambris, a tireless propagandist, launched out against the position of the PSI and the CGL and called on the workers to defend Western civilization against German imperialism.[70] De Ambris was now convinced that a war would result in a revision of outmoded political classifications and would compel old modes of thought to give way to others better suited to the evolution of society. He considered socialist internationalism as irrelevant as bourgeois pacifism. His most violent attacks, however, were directed against Germany. He believed that Fichte's historical mysticism had penetrated all levels of German society, without even excluding the workers and their representative, the Socialist party. A German defeat, he wrote, would do away forever with the relics that had found refuge in Prussian militarism and would destroy the Austro-Hungarian Empire, at the same time solving the problem of Italian irredentism and of the right of peoples to self-determination. Another consequence of this defeat would be to liberate German socialism from a belief in the superior destiny of the German nation and to restore it to the socialist path. Above all, wrote De Ambris, "it has been said that a European conflagration is equivalent to a great and true revolution. That is a fact."[71] The human losses and ravages of a war, he wrote, would be bearable only if the war was revolutionary or precipitated a revolution. De Ambris drew the conclusion that Italy ought to ally itself with France against Germany.

Sergio Panunzio reasoned in a similar manner: "Anyone, whatever his nationality, who wants to see the triumph of socialism *must* take part in the destruction of the power of the main obstacle to that triumph: the German feudal and military hegemony."[72] Panunzio did not see any contradiction between socialism and the war. On the contrary, he could not conceive of the permanent survival of socialism without a military intervention. In another article he tried to prove that the revolution was only a continuation of the war, and he referred the reader to his reflections in the *Avanguardia socialista* of 6 August 1904, where he declared: "If one perceives the war as a sudden and violent solution *necessary* for the determination of sociopolitical relationships, it seems to us as something that can rapidly advance the socialist cause *quicker than any reformism*."[73] Arturo Labriola, for his part, in a book published in 1915, proposed the democratization of the army as a possible solution to the crisis of socialism. He suggested that the army should suppress its officer caste and sever its connection with the monarchy. In that way, it would be closer to the people.[74]

For revolutionary syndicalism, the polemic of 1914–1915 was simply a continuation of its antireformist positions. True to form, the syndicalists chose an activist-voluntarist position opposed to the general line of official

socialism. Once again, the dialectical interaction between ideology and political reality was highly fruitful. Revolutionary syndicalism, that regarded
its ideology as a force that through syndicates, Chambers of Labor, direct
action, and politics was capable of molding reality, had created a network of
reciprocal relationships and influences between the ideology and practical
politics which allowed a great deal of room for ideological adaptation. So it
was during the theoretical debate on the revolutionary general strike that
had preoccupied syndicalism for so long during the years 1903–1904. When
the strike of 1904 erupted, it created for the movement a situation propitious
to ideological reflection, and at that time its ideology expanded to include
the idea of the mobilizing myth. The revolutionary general strike now became a central theme of revolutionary syndicalist thought and action. The
idea of the revolutionary war in many respects had a similar history. In 1907
Labriola made his criticism of Hervé, which led him, together with Olivetti
and Orano, to a cultural nationalism that dissociated nation from state. At the
time of the Libyan War, particular emphasis was laid on the pedagogical
value of the war as a school in which activists would receive an education
they would find indispensable in the revolutionary struggle that lay ahead.
At that time, finally, the idea of a workers' imperialism was put forward—
that is, the idea that the war simply gave the proletarians the opportunity of
exercising their heroic, conquering virtues. In 1914 revolutionary syndicalism had no choice but to remove any ambiguities that might exist concerning
its position with regard to the war. The result was left-wing interventionism
and the adoption of the myth of the revolutionary war.

This mobilizing myth provided a short-term concrete solution and means
of action, even if its true objective remained the society of free producers—
the long-term aim of revolutionary syndicalism. The mobilizing myth served
equally as a bridge between real events and an ideal whose realization was
relegated to a distant future, for in order that the ideal should come to pass,
not only a revolutionary situation was needed, but also an elite that possessed the qualities necessary to bring it about. The activists and leaders
grouped around Alceste De Ambris in 1914 wanted to be that elite. As for
Labriola, the former editor of *Avanguardia socialista*, seeing the total failure
of internationalism, invoked cultural nationalism and claimed that in time of
war ties of class were less important than national ties, especially when the
population had reached a certain level of education and consciousness.[75]
Internationalism was relegated to a future when, once reaction was defeated, it could no longer serve the interests of a German socialism enslaved
to the empire and reaction.[76]

At the same time, the war was represented as a means of weakening capitalism. Thus, a new argument was put forward against neutralism: "Anyone
who supports the cause of peace is unconsciously supporting the cause of
the conservation of capitalism."[77] One sees that two characteristic socialist
attitudes, internationalism and anticapitalism, if taken separately, without

reference to the other, could lead to the opposite positions of neutrality and interventionism.[78]

In October 1914, Olivetti renewed the publication of *Pagine libere*. The journal was naturally presented as the organ of the revolutionary syndicalist theoreticians. In the October issue, a favorable position was adopted toward the stand of the Revolutionary Fascio for Internationalist Action, which in a manifesto published a few days earlier had for the first time called upon the workers to take the side of the interventionists.[79] As in the purest revolutionary syndicalist tradition, the manifesto of the Fascio was a combination of theoretical principles and pragmatic ideology: "Major historical contradictions are resolved not by being denied in ideological terms but by being transcended in practice. One cannot fight war with words or with sterile verbal negations but through an elimination of the initial cause or a diminishment of the factors that give it strength and validity."[80]

Olivetti thought that if it was necessary for revolutionary movements to attempt to solve ethnic and national problems, that was so that they should not be obstacles in the path of social revolution. The war, he believed, might also offer the chance of a solution,[81] because, according to revolutionary syndicalist thinking, Europe had not yet reached the point where capitalism everywhere had the same interests and the same aspirations. It followed that it was still too early to advance the universal interests of the workers as a dialectical response to a situation that did not yet exist. This explained the failure of proletarian internationalism. Olivetti observed that many societies were still preoccupied with noneconomic conflicts such as religious differences and problems connected with tradition, culture, and language. Hence the oppression of some peoples by others and the resulting multiplicity of struggles of national liberation. He concluded: "The struggle for complete human liberty is more than a struggle for the redemption of the wage earner."[82]

In 1914 the revolutionary syndicalists were already engaged in an attempt to find a theoretical solution that would embrace both nationalism and socialism. This move, they said, was necessitated by the realities of the situation revealed by the European war, and also, and in particular, by the failure of their original conception of achieving a syndicalist revolution by means of the general strike. If the working class was incapable of achieving revolution on its own strength, the nation, for its part, was able to do so. This way of thinking coincided with the productionist character of syndicalist socialism. Lanzillo, for example, was convinced that a new order of production necessarily required national independence and autonomy, economic liberty, the application of the law, and an improved technology.[83] A strong nation could satisfy all these requirements.

The reality of a general war forced the revolutionary syndicalists to develop their arguments and to propose a conceptual system that not only fitted the situation but provided guidance for thought and action.[84] The myth of the revolutionary war as they had developed it now provided them with the analytical means necessary to support their point of view in the polemic over interventionism. They declared that war, and not the general strike, would overthrow the existing structures. Direct action, or extraparliamentary activity—the only form of politics they recognized as expressing the popular will—could take the form of only campaigning in favor of the war or of taking part in the war. The myth of the revolutionary war was an instrument of political mobilization and a call for action to take society out of its immobility. The revolutionary syndicalists therefore denounced all those who opposed the war, whether liberals, reformist socialists, or anarchists, as conservatives: "Today we see, on the one side, all the conservatives from the king to the anarchists—all made from the same clay, all baked *ejusdem farinae* [from the same flour]. And on the other side we see those who hope for something new, who seek to surpass themselves in an act of force, willpower, and justice."[85]

From the functional point of view, myth served as the link between concepts elaborated by the intellectuals and leaders of revolutionary syndicalism—De Ambris, Olivetti, Panunzio, Lanzillo, and Corridoni among others—and the masses to whom their call was directed. In the case of the myth of the revolutionary war, its imagery sought to combine the idea of the necessity of defending Italy as a nation with the idea of a need for a social justice that would strengthen the nation. In this way, the revolution would be realized by means of the nation and the nation would achieve realization by means of the revolution. Since this objective could not be achieved either through Italian society perceived as an entity or by rallying the internal forces that composed it, another means had to be found, and that was war. The general strike and war were both political realities that attained mythical expression in revolutionary syndicalist ideology and practice. If both were utilized as mobilizing myths, it is because they were given social connotations, and as a result they found an echo in certain groups in Italian society. Their contents were variable although interconnected, being conceived in accordance with the requirements of a changing reality.

Olivetti, more than any other syndicalist interventionist, represented the Sorelian encounter between nationalism and syndicalism. He believed that the revolution which would follow the war would foster ethical ideals held in common by the syndicates and the nation—heroism, voluntarism, the will to conquer, and a willingness to sacrifice[86]—qualities the workers needed in order to achieve social justice, and the nation in order to establish national justice.[87] With all this, the revolutionary syndicalists showed themselves consistent with their faith in the myth of the revolutionary war: on the day that Italy decided to enter the war, they enlisted en masse.[88]

The Great War therefore succeeded where the Libyan War had failed: by erasing the long disagreement that war, in its finality, and the concept of the nation had caused in revolutionary syndicalism. The political failure of socialist internationalism and the total lack of political influence of the myth of the general strike upon the background of class struggle made the theoreticians shift from class to nation and from the revolutionary strike to the revolutionary war. For the revolutionary syndicalists, good propagandists that they were, a revolutionary war had at first to be directed against reactionary Germany, which threatened every social gain achieved since the French Revolution. The war was also expected to complete the national integration of Italy and deprive the bourgeoisie of its stranglehold on society, and it was finally to bring about a social revolution as conceived by revolutionary syndicalism.[89]

The myth of the revolutionary general strike took shape in the course of the antireformist polemic that the revolutionary syndicalists had conducted in the socialist movement. The myth of the revolutionary war emerged from the continuation of the same polemic when, in conformity with the traditional position of socialism, the PSI opted for a neutralist line, although it was clear that the idea of internationalism had become obsolete. Activism (direct action) and strikes had been directed against gradualism (parliamentarism); now, interventionism attacked neutralism. The voluntarist element, always present in the revolutionary syndicalist ideology, found its expression in myths, whether that of the strike or that of war, and, in war as in the strike, the revolutionary syndicalist elite sought a moral elevation. The myth of the general strike represented the type of socialism adopted by revolutionary syndicalism—a socialism of class struggle combating reaction. In its new transposition, the myth changed in scale and became more extensive, at least in its geographical dimensions. It was nevertheless carefully pointed out that it was directed against reaction (international) and that it remained the expression of a militant socialism. From 1914 on, this socialism had a great deal of influence on the process that transformed revolutionary syndicalism into national syndicalism.

The myth of the revolutionary war was the product of an ideology that every day had to face two different situations: a social reality close to revolution and an international war. This conjunction created an atmosphere where in the postwar crisis, the conditions existed in which a national socialism—a mutation of revolutionary socialism—could contribute to the formation of the original fascism and become one of its main elements.

NATIONAL SYNDICALISM, THE PRODUCTIONIST SOLUTION, AND THE PROGRAM OF PARTIAL EXPROPRIATION

At the end of the war, revolutionary syndicalism, that had assimilated the changes that made it deserving of the title "national syndicalism" (The Fatherland Should Not Be Denied, It Should Be Conquered),[90] had an ideological orientation whose "constitutional" expression was the Carta del Carnaro.[91] This manifesto, indeed, was preceded and followed by other theoretical texts of no less importance, published at the same period by Olivetti, Panunzio, De Ambris, Orano, and others in reviews such as *Pagine libere* and *Il rinnovamento*.[92] Other publications, like *L'internazionale, L'Italia nostra*, and a number of local journals, contributed in one way or another to the propagation of the ideology and positions of national syndicalism and the UIL. Revolutionary syndicalism had traveled a long road, which took it very far from its original socialist ideology of class struggle. It had become patriotic and adopted the principle of national solidarity as its own.

One of the main indications of the dividing line between Left and Right and between revolutionary syndicalism and fascism (passing through national syndicalism) was the kind of revolution that some syndicalist theoreticians sought to create. As is always or nearly always the case, the dialectic of ends and means determined the extent to which the line could be crossed. In the case of someone like De Ambris, who became a militant anti-Fascist, the importance he gave to the Italian national question should not blind us to the fact that he considered the true nature and purpose of the revolution to be socioeconomic change. From his point of view, elitism, moral superiority, and nationalism were merely functional means of accelerating the mobilization of Italian society in readiness for a revolution. On the other hand, others, such as Lanzillo, Orano, Olivetti, and Panunzio, who became Fascists, saw the revolution in terms of ethical change. They believed that the only function of the corporatist and productionist models was to support the process that led to the moral revolution that Italy required. This group had accepted the Sorelian idea that a society, if it wishes to avoid stagnation and decadence, has to live in a state of perpetual change—a change that is the essence of history.

They believed that the existence of an elite, activated by the will to conquer, that perfect manifestation of voluntarism, and practicing the other ideal virtues of altruism and heroism, was immanent and certainly not functional in nature. They described their revolution as being above all an ethical mutation. Only an elite that had undergone a change of spiritual values was able, they thought, to set up the corporatist-industrial system that would bring Italy out of the impasse into which it had been led by political liberalism.

During the red years (biennio rosso) of 1919–1920, when Italy experienced one crisis after another and Italian society was shaken by convulsions, national syndicalism manifested its mixture of anti-Marxist socialism and nationalism. During that period, however, syndicalism—arguing the need for a national solidarity to save Italian society from disintegration and from a chaotic, sterile Soviet-type revolution—showed itself finally to be less and less socialist and more and more nationalistic. This distancing from socialism was the outcome of a long process initiated with the revision of Marxism in the first years of the century. The controversy that began just before the war between interventionists and neutralists helped to bring matters to a head. In 1918, when Lanzillo published his book on the defeat of socialism, one reached the point of no return. For years revolutionary syndicalism had studied Marxism very selectively, seeking only material that could support its own vision of social change—a vision that, according to De Ambris, was influenced by Mazzini, Marx, and Bakunin. "From all these masters," De Ambris wrote "we take whatever is true, good, and possible, and it is on this that we build our revolutionism."[93] Marxist socialism, in the view of the revolutionary syndicalists, had failed to provide a complete solution either in the economic sphere (hence the need to incorporate hedonism and the theories of general equilibrium) or in the political sphere (hence the need to abandon internationalist ideas and to adopt interventionist positions). Already in 1914, Lanzillo denied the deterministic logic of a socialist solution. The success of socialism, he claimed, depended on the state of capitalism, which still needed a national framework in which to develop. Thus, Lanzillo described his voluntaristic socialism as "a class movement confined to national borders whose modest objective is well-being and prosperity."[94]

Panunzio denied the scientific and materialist validity of socialism, placing it in the idealist current of the German philosophical tradition.[95] In the view of this theoretician, socialism could only be national, idealistic, and voluntaristic—a socialism undoubtedly very remote from the determinism and materialism of Marx! An idealist socialism of this kind became utopian at the very moment it ceased to depend on a class and referred itself to the nation. At all times, but particularly in time of war, the nation, wrote Panunzio, could not dispense with a high degree of national solidarity. The only economic system that allowed a socialism for the entire nation was productionism, where the syndicate played a central role owing to the fact that the workers were the soul of the nation. Lanzillo, for his part, claimed that the war provided the universal revolutionary solution that would eliminate the social crisis created by capitalism and democracy, which had been rampant for nearly one and a half centuries.[96] Revolutionary syndicalism was then in the process of formulating an ideology that combined the ideas of Maurras, the conceptions of Vico and Proudhon, the philosophies of Bergson and James, the sociology of Pareto, and all the theories that at that period emphasized the importance of spirit and will to power.[97] The antimaterialism that linked this syndicalism to the Sorelian view of the world was expressed in the following declaration by Lanzillo: "The war has shown that *materializing life means going against life, denying it.*"[98]

This conception of life went together with a type of social altruism and an exercise of the will derived from Sorel's idea of the moral revolution. Thus, according to Lanzillo, the only people who formed part of the collectivity were those who produced, contributed to the good of society, and were ready for personal sacrifice. The producers were undoubtedly an economic group, but in order to exist they needed certain moral attributes that placed them on a higher ethical level than was generally encountered in a democratic regime or in the capitalist system.

Lanzillo now made a lengthy analysis of the relationship between capitalism and socialism, while reflecting on the reasons for the failure and defeat of socialism. He concluded:

> In attempting to identify the consequences of the decadence of the socialist movement, one can say, precisely, that the passivity that has destroyed the edifice of the socialist struggle has been due to:
>
> 1. The existence and development of socialist parties.
> 2. Social legislation.
> 3. The absence, in the proletariat, of an idealistic and voluntaristic conception of its own power.[99]

The first two points were in a direct line of descent from the antireformist struggle waged by syndicalism from the beginning of the century. The third point was connected with the idealistic character of the type of syndicalism that emerged immediately before and during the war—a syndicalism in the process of cutting itself off from its socialist and Marxist past. Lanzillo believed that the war had not only destroyed all that socialism had built, but undermined its theoretical foundations as well.[100] Another beneficial consequence of the war was that it had destroyed the alliance between syndicalism and capitalism. In the final analysis, claimed Lanzillo, a revolution could not succeed if it adopted the paternalistic principles of reformist socialism. As for internationalism and its offshoots, neutralism and pacifism, they simply revealed a lack of revolutionary capacity.[101] The war was a manifestation of collective passion able to inspire the people with a spirit of sacrifice; one should not seek to explain it through practical considerations or economic arguments. It had "destroyed the most visible and dramatic aspects of class divisions, bringing all classes together into a single unit sustained by a transcendent ideal and capable of the supreme abnegation: death."[102]

Lanzillo rejected the materialism of capitalism no less than that of socialism; he also denied the principle of equality. On this point, he agreed with the conclusions of Pareto and insisted on the necessity for an elite (in this case, a syndicalist one), which he believed was the only element that could combat decadence and prepare society for a moral renewal.[103] In his book *La disfatta del socialismo: Critica della guerra e del socialismo* (The defeat of socialism: criticism of war and socialism), published first in 1917 but containing ideas formulated as early as 1914, Lanzillo, reflecting the evolution of revolutionary syndicalism, expressed a preference for an ethical nationalism over the materialist internationalism of socialism. In his opinion, the modus vivendi that had been arrived at between reformist socialism and finance capitalism had taken socialism up a blind alley. This was the primary cause of the war, which was the best and indeed the only way of extricating oneself from the impasse. The war would lead to the emergence of values that would bring about a change—fundamentally antimaterialist values, of which the highest was the unrewarded sacrifice offered in war. Lanzillo was convinced that once a people—in this case, the Italian people—had chosen this path, there could be no return to the previous situation. Each individual was too involved in the tragedy of war, and the price exacted was too high to permit society to repeat the mistakes that had caused it.

Lanzillo's point of view was not only shared by the syndicalists, but was also expressed by those who founded the Fascist movement in 1919.[104] Nevertheless, Lanzillo's book, because it formulated only general idealist principles of the theory of the revolutionary war and the necessity for a moral and social transformation, could not serve as a platform that would provide a basis for a positive ideology and a political program. The war had undoubtedly confirmed some of the hypotheses of revolutionary syndicalism—the failure of reformist socialism, the importance of the nation, the necessity for a spirit of sacrifice—but it had also brought in its wake new crises. A no less important aspect of the conflict was the events in Russia in 1917, which, in the beginning at least, seemed to justify the concept of the revolutionary war.[105]

Essentially, however, the war confirmed the central role of the nation in the historical process. It also revealed the capacity of the state to discipline society, control the economy, and direct the war. Such a state, which worked for the national interest and opposed exploitation and speculation, could appear attractive. This being the case, the syndicalists now accepted that an institution of this kind should govern postwar Italy.[106]

It was agreed that if the war was to be truly revolutionary, it would have to lead to some social improvement. In 1917 De Ambris launched the slogan The Land to the Peasants, and from then on he frequently observed that when the war broke out, it was the peasants, the largest social group in the country, who had borne the heaviest burden. He estimated that they constituted up to eighty percent of the troops sent to the front. It was they who, with their own bodies, had stopped the Austro-German advance. With their corpses, they had built a defensive wall that had protected Italy. This fact alone gave them the right to the Italian land—that land which they and their ancestors had worked for centuries. The country, wrote De Ambris, owed a debt to its soldier-peasants, and it was obliged to honor this debt by giving them the land for which they had already shed and would continue to shed their blood, probably to a greater extent than any other social group.[107]

During the last year of the war, the syndicalists feared that the deplorable condition of the peasants might diminish their readiness to go to the front. Moreover, they believed them to be devoid of national consciousness. Only in regions such as Parma where syndicalism was deeply rooted did agricultural communities develop that type of consciousness. Thus it appeared that the syndicates were capable of arousing the sentiment of belonging to the nation. In rural areas they had succeeded in doing so all the more effectively and rapidly because they fought to grant land to the peasants.

"In order to bind the peasants to the nation, one has to give them the land."[108] Italy existed; it was time to create the Italians. Here there was a clear nationalist overtone. The syndicalists were convinced that a law that gave land to the peasants who did not possess any would stimulate their desire to fight for Italy.[109] The question of the distribution of land played a leading role in the program of partial expropriation that De Ambris proposed after the war.

Following the war, the syndicalists declared that the economic crisis in Italy demanded a radical solution, but one that would not destroy the system of production.[110]

The productionist ideal, one should recall, demanded increased production, a strengthening of the nation, and an organization that would permit the workers to take an active part, together with the propertied classes and the administrators, in the management of industry and all other areas of national activity.[111] According to De Ambris, since the war had allowed people he called sharks to make scandalous profits, any profit above a certain level should be expropriated to create an investment fund. This money would be used to create jobs in all sectors, especially for demobilized soldiers, those disabled in the war, and the families of soldiers killed in battle.[112] This program which he published in 1919, was entirely in keeping with the productionist conceptions of national syndicalism.

De Ambris knew that the normal, classic solution to the financial crisis caused by the enormous growth of the national debt due to the cost of the war was increased taxation. But in that case, he argued, it was the ex-soldiers who would have to work hardest. Once again, it was they who would have to shoulder the major part of the burden in extracting the country from its economic crisis, just as they had paid the highest price by defending the country. Moreover, tax money would cover only the interest on state bonds held by those who had not taken part in the war but who nevertheless had profited from it. In any case, the debt was too large for a simple increase in fiscal pressure to mop it up. This way of reasoning, in which economics was mingled with moral considerations, led De Ambris to conclude that "it would be rash to consider us excessively pessimistic if, faced with such a situation, we claimed that the producing masses would prefer to run the risk of a revolution, even if the venture did not have a happy ending, rather than accept the certitude of a stark misery that would infinitely prolong the misery of the trenches."[113]

Thus, a program of partial expropriation was the only possible answer, and not some revolutionary fantasy of a Bolshevik type that a number of national syndicalists, like De Ambris, believed would probably destroy the capitalist system of production without necessarily replacing it with a better one. De Ambris wanted to tax capital, not labor; the amount to be taken would depend on the needs of the nation. Partial expropriation, he wrote, should target speculative capital but spare capital directly invested in production, for one had to avoid creating or increasing unemployment.[114] This meant that, as the revolutionary syndicalists had known for a long time, there was nothing that would replace capitalism!

What were the limits of partial expropriation? In order to answer that question, De Ambris, according to a method he often used, divided the national debt into two: the debt to the capitalists to whom the country had sold treasury bonds in order to finance the war and the debt to the soldiers who had offered up their bodies and souls for the sake of victory. This second debt, in the opinion of De Ambris, was far more significant than the ninety billion liras owed as national debt: "This moral debt which, for lack of a better means, has to be evaluated financially, is too sacred for one to dream for a single moment of repudiating it."[115]

There could be no question of the state's not repaying its moral debt. It therefore had to keep the promises made to the people during the war and at the same time seek to resolve the most pressing socioeconomic problems. It had little choice; the only way was through the partial expropriation of financial capital, which is to production what acid is to iron. This expropriation had to take place in the agricultural sector as well as in industry.[116]

This program was drawn up with a view to increasing production and was meant to benefit all the parties concerned—workers, technicians, managers, and the propertied classes. It was also necessary that it should be voluntarily accepted by everyone. It stipulated that the state and the municipality should participate in the management of industries, which would bring about a better understanding among all the participants in production. The result would be a reduction in taxes and where possible profit sharing by the workers. Moreover, if the state and the municipalities were involved in the management of enterprises, paralyzing bureaucratic procedures that were characteristic of the indirect relationships prevailing in capitalist regimes would automatically be simplified. Thus, true to their productionist economic philosophy and their desire to take the role of incentives into consideration, the national syndicalists were not afraid to demand a reconstruction of private property and a redistribution to the benefit of those whom they held to be productive and to the disadvantage of those whom they considered parasitic. It seems that sometimes even an abolition of private property was considered. Thus, national syndicalism went farther than the revolutionary syndicalism of the beginning of the century. One also sees how revolutionary syndicalism, whose economic conceptions had stressed the dynamics of market forces and the techno-moral aspects of change and revolution, was now transformed into a national syndicalism was willing to give politics a central role and even with a political program, one of whose main points was the plan of partial expropriation.[117] This dominant position given to politics was one of the main features of the transition to fascism.

This was the program that on 9 June 1919 De Ambris presented to the Fascist cadres assembled at the Porta Romana School in Milan. The meeting, which was held under Mussolini's auspices,[118] brought the Fascists nothing new. Indeed, the socioeconomic platform in their program, published in June 1919, was almost an exact replica of De Ambris's plan of partial expropriation.[119] Other parts of the Fascist program borrowed ideas defended by the UIL.[120] Thus, the article on the nation in arms recalled the spirit of Olivetti's slogan of 1914: Arms to the People![121] In 1921 De Ambris was careful to remind the Fascists of the ideological positions to which they were committed.[122]

In 1919 and in the period that followed the foundation of the Fascist political movement, national syndicalism and fascism found themselves in the political camp common to all the interventionists of the Left. Both shared the same anti-Bolshevik attitude, drew the same lessons from their experience of the war, and were convinced that something had to be done quickly to bring Italy out of its crisis and to gain it the position it deserved among the European powers. De Ambris said at that time that if he had not been secretary of the UIL, "I would have joined the Fasci di Combattimento. Not that I find all their actions acceptable, but because, despite their deficiencies and their errors, they are today the only Italian political movement that energetically and effectively opposes the incompetence of the ruling classes and the social-neutralist demagoguery."[123]

In 1919, in short, syndicalists and Fascists had the same views on social change and ways of achieving it, and both were productionists and nationalists. At the same time, one must insist here on the fact that the red years finally convinced the national syndicalist leaders that a revolution in Italy was not possible for the time being, not even in the near future. Moreover, their antimaximalist point of view made them reach the conclusion that the wave of strikes then sweeping the country played into the hands of foreign powers, which did not wish to see an Italy that was economically strong and thus competitive. These syndicalists maintained that the liberal system was bankrupt, yet they were no less convinced that the Communist threat was to be taken seriously and had to be held at bay by "a group of men sufficiently stouthearted to confront the Bolshevik troupe and compel it to mend its violent revolutionary ways."[124] A man like Alceste De Ambris was well aware that national syndicalism did not grant a dominant role to the working class, which had become simply one actor on the political stage among others, but he thought that this was the price to be paid if one wished to reach a comprehensive solution without lapsing into revolutionary impotence. In any case, he maintained that it was absolutely essential for all forces of the interventionist Left to unite around a common minimal program supporting partial expropriation, disarmament, and the convocation of a constituent assembly.[125] At the time that he made these proposals, De Ambris still considered fascism a branch of the realistic Left capable of working for the salvation of Italy. In fact, if fascism in 1919 was regarded as belonging to the Left, it was because of its ideological dependence on national syndicalism and because it adopted similar positions on certain questions. When the Fiume adventure took place, however, De Ambris drew away from Mussolini and from Fascist ideas and methods of action.

National syndicalism had come a long way from the "old days" when the "economistic" theories of revolutionary syndicalism flourished and when this movement called for revolution through direct action. When the ideologists and leaders of syndicalism were convinced that the working class possessed neither the bellicose spirit of the bourgeoisie nor the ability to manage the process of production, and when they were convinced that the war had had the integrative effect on society that they hoped for, they drew the only conclusion that seemed logical to them: namely, that politics is an essential factor of change. They now felt the need to create a new type of political structure, better suited to the problems of a society undergoing a process of productionistic industrialization and directed toward the nation rather than a class.[126] Here the primacy of politics had become evident.

In March 1919, Sergio Panunzio presented his "Program of Action," by which he intended to solve the problem of both property and production. This plan proposed a society organized according to a corporatist model, in which the state, which had abolished private property, granted owners recognized as capable of producing the use (utenza) of the land, factories, and all other means of production. The idea was to associate the right to property—in fact, the right of using it in order to produce and reap the benefit of it—with the act of producing. Those who did not wish to produce, described as parasites, were not only to be excluded from the process of production but also to be deprived of their right to property. Panunzio went on to describe the reorganization of political structures. He proposed setting up a restricted, aristocratic central parliament that would function in accordance with a preestablished division of tasks, in coordination with local parliaments established according to socioeconomic criteria. For this division to be effective, it was necessary that

Article 5.   The entire population be divided into "organic classes."
Article 6.   The classes be organized into corporations.
Article 7.   The administration of social matters be transferred to the
             corporations.[127]

The organic class of corporations was the backbone of this political system, whose dual objective was to suppress individualistic liberalism and to prevent a collective class socialism. In reserving the state the rights of arbi-

trage and allocation where production and property were concerned, Panunzio's corporatist program considerably increased its prerogatives at the
same time as attacking private property. Once again, it is evident that national syndicalism had moved away from the revolutionary syndicalist model
of a state reduced to purely administrative functions. In the new scheme, the
state was a central factor in politics. As for relations with what was to become
the Fascist movement, Panunzio had already written in 1918:

> The national syndicalism of Mussolini, which is a syndicalism five or more years
> behindhand, but which is also the only social movement to have integrated the
> immense historical experience of the war, is undoubtedly a sign of the times
> and should in my opinion be their watchword.[128]

Panunzio wanted an integral syndicalism, different from labor syndicalism, which would reunite workers, owners, officials, businesspeople, peasants, and all those involved in production.[129] Owing to the fact that each
person was a member of a syndicate-corporation, the nation would be made
up of syndicates and no longer of individuals solely concerned with their
personal profit. The special function of the corporatist political structure was
to stress the importance of the relations between the state and the syndicates.[130]

The model Panunzio put forward retained the classic system of political
representation. Nevertheless, he referred to two articles by Agostino
Lanzillo in *Il popolo d'Italia* in which a corporatist system of representation
was proposed.[131] Lanzillo's plan was that political rights would be exercised
by citizen producers organized in corporations. He proposed a bicameral
system in which the lower chamber would have the task of debating and
deciding on the questions directly concerning the corporations, while the
senate, elected by the lower chamber, would debate and decide on questions concerning the general interest and the state. The new ideology of
national syndicalism formulated by De Ambris, Panunzio, Lanzillo, and
other syndicalist theoreticians thus placed economic production parallel to
political representation:

> The syndicates will have to regulate production; above them, the new legisla-
> tive institutions, solemnly designated with the name of the social republic, will
> be the expression and the guardian of the national synthesis.[132]

FROM THE CARTA DEL CARNARO TO
FASCIST SYNDICALISM

The Carta del Carnaro (the Charter of the Carnaro) was promulgated by
Commandante Gabriele D'Annunzio on 28 September 1920 as a constitutional text for the regency of Fiume.[133] The document was drafted by De

Ambris, whom D'Annunzio appointed secretary for civil affairs of the Command of the Fiume Army of Liberation.[134] D'Annunzio examined the document before its publication. He made a few stylistic corrections, but above all he introduced his philosophic-aesthetic interpretation of life.[135]

For the national syndicalists, the Fiume enterprise served a dual purpose. It was a catalyst that could precipitate a national revolution and it prevented any movement toward a Bolshevik type of revolution. Moreover, the regime set up in Fiume could serve as a model for a society that wished to live as a nation within a republic based on the revolutionary syndicalist principles of autonomy, production, communalism, and corporatism—all ideological elements in the national syndicalist program discussed earlier. De Ambris, who noticed the strong irredentist character of D'Annunzio's enterprise, also saw how readily the situation created in Fiume could be molded and how easily it could lead to the rapid development of a revolution. Finally, he was of the opinion that the course of events in Fiume was bound to have a positive effect on Italy.[136]

Fiume was an area of confrontation between the interventionists of the Right and the interventionists of the Left. The influence of socialists, liberals, and Catholics was practically nonexistent. D'Annunzio's legionnaires had been joined by many nationalist radicals who also hoped to accelerate social change. Among these people, who rejected both liberalism and democratic socialism, De Ambris wished to implant national syndicalism. For this reason, after the failure of negotiations between D'Annunzio and the Italian government, he went to Fiume to see to what extent the city was ripe for revolution. He carried a letter from Mussolini in which the Fascist leader advised D'Annunzio not to march on Rome. De Ambris then returned to Milan, from where he was recalled by D'Annunzio, who on 13 January 1920 appointed him to the post of secretary for civil affairs (that is, head of cabinet, or chief of staff) of the Command of Fiume.[137]

De Ambris's favorable attitude to D'Annunzio's action should by no means be construed as the position of one isolated individual. The national syndicalists and interventionists did all they could to encourage it, giving nationalist and revolutionary motives.[138] The fact remains, however, that it was De Ambris who carried the message of the national syndicalist ideology to the banks of the Carnaro. It was there that, according to his own testimony, he drafted the text called the Carta del Carnaro, of which he said: "Materially, it was I who prepared it, but under the inspiration and direction of the Commandante. All I did was to interpret his political thinking with great fidelity and a loyal intelligence."[139]

After the promulgation of the charter, De Ambris wrote to D'Annunzio to tell him that act three of the drama *Fiume* had now begun but that the final act would have to take place in Rome.[140] The charter was a political document in which the corporatist productionism of national syndicalism coexisted harmoniously with D'Annunzio's philosophical ideas and aestheticism.[141] These two ways of thinking succeeded in general in harmonizing with one another because each related to a different aspect of politics—that is, the economic and the cultural aspect. Moreover, each approached the question of alienation in a manner that respected the similarities between the theories of revolutionary syndicalism and those of radical nationalism. This common element included a social altruism extending to the entire nation, an antimaterialism that rejected both liberal and Marxist values, and finally a voluntaristic and by definition aesthetic conception of revolution— one that was intended to be entirely different from the conceptions of the established religion and system of politics. Corporatism, productionism, and the importance given to the criterion of work in the Carta del Carnaro were all intended to eliminate the distance between the individual and the state (and hence the alienation of one from the other), as well as that between the producer and the economic system in which the producer lived and worked. The corporation became the bridge between producer and state as well as the institution able to structure and regulate production. Work was both a constitutional right and a duty. People had to produce; the constitution had to take it upon itself to ensure them both the means and the possibility of fulfilling this duty. The constitution of Fiume sought to lay down the conditions that would enable the individual, once capitalist egoism and socialist bureaucratism were eliminated, to freely produce, create, and benefit from life. Accordingly, article nine of the charter described the state as the product of the common will and an institutional phenomenon expressing the desire of the people to combine its efforts in order to achieve an even higher degree of material and spiritual vigor.[142] Thus, only producers capable of creating such wealth and power would be full citizens in Fiume.[143]

In De Ambris's corporatist model, business and property owners had a special corporation of their own. He wanted to limit the tendency to try to lead each corporation from within. He knew that the fact of possession could cause owners to promulgate an order of priorities that did not correspond exactly to the general need.[144] Despite the communal autonomy provided by the charter and all the guarantees of democracy it contained, it was a document that expressed above all a nationalistic and organic view of society. The mechanisms envisaged by this "constitution" were suited to a political "age of the masses" whose vocation was to invigorate the producers. This corporatism, intended to facilitate industrialization and permit a politics of the masses, was later adopted by fascism, but in a more statist and authoritarian form.

From the national syndicalist viewpoint, the Carta del Carnaro provided the solution to both the social problem and the national problem. If the new class of producers lived and acted within corporations, it would be automatically identified with the state. In this way, the conflicts between class and state—between the working class and the bourgeois state—would disappear without the necessity to abolish the right to private property.

The charter affirmed not only the Italian character of the city of Fiume, but also its revolutionary status. The Italian government had every reason to be wary of this combination, first because of the international implications of D'Annunzio's action, and second because it feared that Fiume, having become a symbol for all opponents of liberal democracy, would focus and encourage all revolutionary tendencies. Thus, on 20 December 1920, Giolitti put an end to the regency of Fiume, and the Carta del Carnaro had no opportunity of passing beyond the stage of a project.

Many groups within the Fascist movement—especially those that came from the interventionist Left—saw the Fiume "constitution" as a suitable model for Fascist Italy. However, this heritage of revolutionary syndicalism, now transformed into national syndicalism, to which the Fascists who came from the Left of the beginning of the century continued to lay claim, faded away during the process of the fascistisation of the state. At the end of 1920, fascism began to move to the Right. After D'Annunzio's failure in Fiume and the compromise reached between Giolitti and the syndicates, fascism, which was still theoretically grouped with left-wing interventionists, violently attacked the socialist Left.[145] Henceforth, the primary enemy was socialism, and the delicate balance that the initiators of national syndicalism, the regency of Fiume, and the interventionism of the Left had sought to maintain was definitely upset.

Conscious of this evolution, De Ambris soon realized that fascism was in the process of becoming an antirevolutionary instrument manipulated by the bourgeoisie. He remarked on this to D'Annunzio.[146] Olivetti thought differently; like many other syndicalists, he believed that the confusion and internal contradictions that characterized the social ideas of fascism were due to the fact that it had not yet clearly defined its ideology.[147] This, he said, was a sickness of youth. These different views, which reflected the growth of fascism, gradually created divisions within the ranks of revolutionary syndicalists. Panunzio, for instance, argued that if Italy claimed to be a proletarian nation, an internal struggle between classes was no longer acceptable. De Ambris, who always retained his revolutionary syndicalist reflexes, was quick to reply that only a struggle between classes could lead to a perfect mode of production.[148] While Panunzio increasingly accepted an ethical concept of revolution where moral elevation finally replaced the struggle of classes, De Ambris returned to the socioeconomic arguments that gave birth to the vision of a "society of free producers."

Edmondo Rossoni, one of the leaders of national syndicalism, who joined the Fascists and was one of the founders of Fascist syndicalism, considered the antisocialist reaction a necessary stage in the salvation of Italy.[149] He was of the opinion, however, that the national idea was not sufficient for this purpose; thus, he continued to defend the social ideas of national syndicalism. The syndicalist leaders knew the differences of opinion in fascism and tried to take advantage of them. De Ambris launched an urgent appeal to the "socialistically inclined" and the militants on the left of the movement to rejoin national syndicalism.[150] For a long time, some syndicalists continued to hope that fascism would finally return to the left-wing principles of its beginnings.[151]

Despite the "reactionary" character of the positions fascism adopted and the actions it perpetrated, there were some, such as Olivetti, who tried to convince themselves that the influence of the masses would still prevail in its final orientation: "Fascism would like to be conservative, but it will end by being revolutionary."[152] De Ambris, for his part, said that one should not confuse the two aspects of fascism: its agrarian aspect, dominated by land-owners whose sole objective was to prevent any attempt at organization among the agricultural workers, and the other aspect, by definition urban and revolutionary because derived from ex-servicemen—the very ones who in 1919 had been the vital constituents of the original fascism. The former aspect was characterized solely by economic and conservative considera-tions—the worst kind—while the latter was aflame with idealism and the patriotism that distinguishes students and those who have experienced war and sacrifice. De Ambris saw conservatism gradually replacing idealism, and he saw nationalism becoming increasingly bourgeois.[153] This theory of the two "faces" of fascism was taken over by *Pagine libere*, and especially by Enzo Ferrari, who explained the duality by the fact that fascism was aban-doning the principles of Fiume and becoming a political formation like any other. The final stage of this process would be the subordination of the syn-dicates to the political control of the party apparatus—something totally op-posed to the idea of the syndical economy that was one of the articles of faith of the original fascism.[154]

Among syndicalists, a close association with fascism was not always re-garded with the same degree of enthusiasm or indulgence. Alceste De Am-bris, who was in a minority position on the eve of fascism's accession to power, was deeply rooted in the tradition of Mazzini and remained true to the original conceptions of the revolutionary syndicalism of Labriola and Leone. Despite Labriola's flirtation with the ideas of Sorel, these two Nea-politan economists remained attached, like De Ambris, to the fundamentally economic nature of revolutionary syndicalism as conceived and expressed in their revision of Marx. Like De Ambris, they opposed fascism when it was in power.

Labriola—who left revolutionary syndicalism after the Libyan War, was elected to parliament as an independent socialist, and in 1920, the year of crises and occupations of factories, was appointed minister of labor under Giolitti—was also opposed to fascism and also went into exile. He returned to Italy only in 1935, at the time of the Ethiopian War. He maintained that this war represented the same ideals as the Libyan expedition: a labor impe-rialism and a defense of Italy's interests.[155] Enrico Leone, for his part, returned to socialism and refused to compromise with fascism. It is difficult to say what form his struggle would have taken if he had not passed the major part of the Fascist period in a psychiatric hospital.[156]

The most famous of the revolutionary syndicalist opponents of fascism was Alceste De Ambris. In 1919 and 1920 he had been closely associated with Mussolini, but the attitude of the latter in the Fiume episode had greatly disappointed him. Moreover, he had come to the conclusion that Mussolini was in the process of betraying the ideals of national syndicalism and that he was moving farther and farther to the right.[157] It should be remembered that the "economistic" view of syndicalism held by De Ambris accepted nationalism only within the limits necessary to productionism. This view owed a great deal to the theories of Labriola and Leone and remained within the Mazzinian tradition of social justice and national identity. When fascism became openly antileftist and still more violent after 1920, other syndicalists such as Ugo Dalbi, Elio Laceria, Enzo Ferrari, and Ulisse Lucchesi joined De Ambris in his opposition. These were the very people who had once believed that Fascist syndicalism had a positive aspect, inasmuch as its labor component would be bound to cause a division between the socialistically minded and the reactionaries in the movement. In 1922, when fascism came to power, De Ambris and his group went into opposition. De Ambris finally went into exile.[158]

However, these people were only a minority among the great names of revolutionary syndicalism. All the other prominent theoreticians and activists belonged to the hard core of the founders of the Fascist movement. Cesare Rossi became deputy secretary-general of the Fasci, and Edmondo Rossoni was the founder of the Fascist Group of Affiliated Syndicates.[159] Michele Bianchi, the famous labor leader from Ferrara, belonged to Mussolini's intimate circle. In 1921 he became secretary-general of the National Fascist party and in 1922 was one of the *quadrumviri* (quadrumvirate, four-people council) who attempted to share the running of the party with Mussolini. In 1924 Bianchi became a Fascist deputy, and in 1929 he entered the government as minister of public works.[160] This eminent personality of the Italian labor movement was followed into fascism by people like Ottavio Dinale, Tullio Masotti, and Umberto Pasella.

With the exception of Arturo Labriola and Enrico Leone, the revolutionary syndicalist theoreticians of the first rank committed themselves enthusiastically to fascism. Most prominent among them was Angelo O. Olivetti, editor of *Pagine libere*, writer of the "Manifesto dei sindacalisti," and one of the principal ideologists of the movement. He was a member of the National Council of Corporations and one of the eighteen members of the commission charged with proposing a reform of the constitution. He taught in the Fascist Faculty in Perugia; he was Jewish. His death in 1931 spared him a knowledge of the racial laws of Fascist Italy.[161]

Sergio Panunzio, who was a socialist, a revolutionary syndicalist, and then a national syndicalist, became a fascist deputy in 1924. He belonged to the leadership of the PNF, and he too was a member of the National Council of Corporations. It was as a theoretician of corporatism, however, that he played the most important role in fascism. Together with Rocco and Gentile, he is regarded as one of the main ideologists of the Fascist party. He directed and taught at the Fascist Faculty of Political Science in Perugia[162] in the company of Paolo Orano. Orano, who was chief editor of *La lupa* in the years 1910–1911, had begun, like Panunzio, as a socialist (he was on the staff of *Avanti!* until 1905), becoming a revolutionary syndicalist and a national syndicalist before finally joining fascism. He was a declared anti-Semite. In 1924 and 1925 he was responsible for the Roman edition of *Il popolo d'Italia*. In 1939 he became a senator of the kingdom.[163]

Agostino Lanzillo, Sorel's most faithful Italian disciple, joined Mussolini in 1914. From that time on, he wrote continually for *Il popolo d'Italia*. This former revolutionary syndicalist was still at the side of Mussolini when the Fasci were founded in Milan in March 1919. He then entered Parliament as a Fascist and was a member of the National Council of Corporations.[164]

The name of the German Robert Michels should again be mentioned here. His association with Italy for a third of a century and the role he played in the movement of ideas that led to Italian fascism quite naturally earn him a place in the list of those we have just mentioned. He joined the PSI in 1902; at the same time, he was a member of the SPD, which enabled him to participate in the national congresses of both parties. In Italy, he joined the revolutionary syndicalist movement and wrote in *Avanguardia socialista* and *Il divenire sociale*. His book *Political Parties*, published for the first time in Germany in 1911, forms an integral part of the revolutionary syndicalist critique of socialism. Like Labriola, he upheld the theory of proletarian imperialism. In 1925 he published *Sozialismus und Fascismus in Italien*, in which, using the analytical classifications of Sorel and Pareto, he attempted to demonstrate that from Pisacane and Garibaldi to fascism Italy preserved the same social and national ideology. In 1929 he began teaching in Perugia. One year earlier he had joined the PNF, of which he was a member until his death in 1936.[165]

One last question remains: What was the criterion that determined which revolutionary syndicalists would participate in the founding of fascism, remaining faithful to it until their deaths, and having contributed to setting up the movement, that would retreat and even go into exile? As long as the productionist ideology had not been tested by events, the proponents of an ethical revolution could coexist with creators of economic theories like Leone or Labriola, or with syndicalists like De Ambris who wished to form a synthesis of socialism and nationalism but who rejected a total substitution of the nation for the idea of class. When the hour of reckoning came, however, adherents of the ethical and voluntaristic conception of social change gave economic analysis only second place. They believed in the dominant role of elites and held willpower to be the real source of change.

Until 1920 national syndicalism was still able to accommodate both tendencies: that of the economists and "structuralists" and that of the ethical revolutionaries. But the crises that broke out that year—the Fiume affair and the occupations of factories—forced the movement to decide whether productionism was primarily for the benefit of members of syndicates or whether it was intended to benefit the whole nation. The Right had already launched its campaign against the Left; it had recruited dependable and determined allies in the antisocialist and activistic wing of fascism. This campaign had two objectives: to destroy the PSI and to destroy the labor organizations.

The second objective divided the syndicalists into two groups: those who, like De Ambris, had long been antisocialist and especially anti-PSI but were neither against the workers nor opposed to labor organizations and the group of intellectuals characterized by the Sorelian concept of an ethical revolution. The latter had long before distanced themselves from Marxist-socialist analysis, with its materialist implications. They had replaced the working class with the nation—a voluntaristic nation in which the process of social change was entrusted to activist elites. They held that socialism had completely lost its revolutionary spirit and that materialism had succeeded only in poisoning the party and the labor organizations. Olivetti explained how the replacement of the idea of class consciousness by an ethiconational vision was to be understood. In his "Manifesto dei Sindacalisti," drafted in the first half of 1921, he declared: "The producer, in achieving his moral liberty and in accomplishing his whole duty, will realize the social revolution, which is above all a national revolution and a moral revolution." Olivetti left no room for doubt about the relative importance of class problems and national problems. "The nation is above classes," he declared, "and all considerations of class should give way before things of a national character."[166] Olivetti wished syndicalism to be an aristocratic doctrine that would improve the moral fiber of the people, a doctrine from which it would draw the will and strength to surpass itself continually.

Thus, revolutionary idealism replaced historical materialism, and ethical change replaced the voluntaristic economic change characteristic of De Ambris's productionism, which itself had replaced economic determinism. Revolutionary syndicalism had come a long way since the beginning of the century, the period when it had started out as one of the movements of the socialist-Marxist family. After passing through the stage of the revision of Marxist economics by Labriola and Leone in the first decade of the century, it opted for the method of direct action and the revolutionary mobilization of the masses.[167] Sorel influenced the movement through both his early reflections on syndicalism and his ideas on violence, the mobilizing myth, and the spiritual revolution. By 1910 the revolutionary syndicalists had already broken away from traditional socialism and were convinced of the inability of the proletariat to act as a revolutionary agent. They had begun to exchange ideas with radical nationalists like Corradini and Viana. They then became productionists and voluntarists, which brought them into conjunction with the new nationalists, whose contempt for liberalism and democracy they shared.

Certainly, unlike the new nationalists, not all revolutionary syndicalists had an irrepressible hatred for socialism, and when they did have it, it was not for the same reasons; nor did it have the identical objective. Where the syndicalists hated the party, the nationalists rejected the very idea of socialism. All, however, were opposed to rationalist materialism. This was the common denominator that permitted the ideological "dialogue" between nationalists and syndicalists, which, if it did not lead to a joint venture or even a definite political exchange, was a new and truly revolutionary phenomenon in the realm of ideas. The next stage was the search for a mobilizing myth that would replace that of the general revolutionary strike. This was the period when the concept of the nation was introduced as the criterion of history. The Libyan War and the Great War played a crucial role in gaining acceptance for the idea of the nation in syndicalist theory. War was now seen as a revolutionary factor, and syndicalism became integral and national. Finally, after the First World War, national syndicalism, developed by people like De Ambris, Lanzillo, Panunzio, Orano, and Olivetti, provided the ideological definitions and program of the original fascism of the years 1919–1920.

The Mussolini Crossroads: From the Critique of Marxism to National Socialism and Fascism

WITHIN THE ORBIT OF REVOLUTIONARY SYNDICALISM

There is no need today to insist on the historical importance of Benito Mussolini, his qualities of leadership, his sense of opportunity, or the role he played in the rise to power of the Fascist movement. Yet the central position he occupied among the Italian revolutionaries, whether intellectuals or syndical leaders, who after the war called for the destruction of the existing regime, is always ill understood or underestimated because it is little studied. After the war, he was the point of convergence of all tendencies in the new revolutionary movement that rebelled against the government while rejecting the Left-Right alternative.

It was around Mussolini, the former editor of *Avanti!*, that his former associates from the left wing of the Socialist party and from revolutionary syndicalism, nationalists looking for a chief and futurists looking for a condottiere, grouped themselves. Mussolini brought the Italian leftist and nationalist dissidents something their French counterparts had always lacked: a leader. He was a leader from the Left, a socialist familiar with all the mechanisms of party politics, but also a nonconformist, a charismatic chief, brutal and unscrupulous, and at the same time an intellectual capable of speaking to Arturo Labriola or Marinetti, of impressing Michels or Mosca, and of being regarded with indulgence or even admiration by Pareto and Croce.

This man who in 1912 conquered the Italian Socialist party from within and who in 1914 was recognized as the undisputed head of the party by both the Socialist Youth and a figure like Gramsci was the same man who in March 1919 presided over the foundation of the Fascist movement in which revolutionary syndicalists, futurists, and various left-wing dissidents took part.[1] Mussolini did not take this step on a sudden impulse, nor out of opportunism, and still less out of self-interest. The postwar situation did not turn him into a Fascist, nor did the war cause this metamorphosis. In reality, this move was the result of an intellectual evolution and a growing awareness of European and Italian realities that existed before the war, and it was unconnected with it. We will now try to retrace this path.

From the beginning of his political activities, Mussolini developed within the groove of revolutionary syndicalism. Exiled to Switzerland between July 1902 and November 1904, he collaborated in *L'avvenire del lavoratore*, the Italian Socialist party weekly in Switzerland, and then in *Il proletario*, an Italian socialist weekly published in New York. In October 1903, when he was living in Lausanne and probably attending Pareto's lectures (Pareto was a professor in Lausanne), Mussolini began to write in Arturo Labriola's *Avanguardia socialista*. His first article in the journal was about two lectures that the celebrated French anarchist Sébastien Faure had recently given in Lausanne.[2] Mussolini's ideas at this period were not yet formed. He was sympathetic to anarchism,[3] but in the end he opted for the theories of revolutionary syndicalism. In April 1904, Mussolini attended the Congress of Italian Socialists in Switzerland, where he met Angelo Oliviero Olivetti, president elect of the congress. He placed himself resolutely in the antireformist camp and expressed his position in a violent critique of Italian parliamentary democracy published in July in *Avanguardia socialista*.[4] On the eve of the general strike of September 1904, Mussolini was a defender of class struggle in the purest revolutionary syndicalist tradition.[5]

But the preoccupations of this young revolutionary were not purely political. He wrote two historiographical articles in *Avanguardia socialista*, one about the night of 4 August and the other on Ferdinand Lasalle.[6] At the same time, he studied the teachings of Vilfredo Pareto, whose theory of elites was strongly to influence his own thinking, just as it influenced that of all revolutionary syndicalists. Mussolini then attempted an analysis of Italian syndicalism in relation to Pareto's theoretical model.[7]

This period of formation, intellectually very rich, came to an end in December 1904, when Mussolini decided to return to Forlì in his native province of the Romagna to do his military service. During a period of leave in March 1905 (his mother had just died), he wrote his last article for *Avanguardia socialista*.[8] While serving in the army, he was unable to do more than that; he was not permitted to participate in a political publication, and this put an end to his collaboration in Arturo Labriola's journal.

His activities in revolutionary syndicalist circles opened new horizons for him and decisively influenced the development of his thought. From that time until after the Great War, Mussolini recognized and deferred to the authority of Arturo Labriola and Enrico Leone. In those years, he also showed the greatest respect for Pareto's sociology. The influence of the great Italian academic on Mussolini was both direct—especially during his exile in Switzerland—and indirect, through the syndicalist theoreticians. He accepted unquestioningly the idea of the fusion of the principle of class struggle with the theory of elites. Mussolini saw the revolutionary proletariat as the new social elite that had been formed in the syndicates and would eventually replace the bourgeois elite, just as the bourgeoisie, at the time of the

French Revolution, had replaced the nobility and clergy: "Do you recall Vilfredo Pareto's theory of elites?" he wrote. "This theory, which teaches us that history is simply a succession of dominant elites, is probably the most brilliant sociological concept of modern times."[9]

Mussolini explained the social and political crises in Italy by bourgeois decadence and by the inability of the governing elite to rule the country and to deal with its problems. He believed that to an equal degree this bourgeois degeneracy affected reformist socialism, which was continually going down-hill.[10]

Like all self-respecting revolutionaries, Mussolini considered himself a Marxist. He regarded Marx as "the greatest theoretician of socialism" and Marxism as "the scientific doctrine of class revolution."[11] This young activist was not a Marxist theoretician, however. Marxism reached him in a revised and predigested form, first via Arturo Labriola and Leone and then via Sorel. His writings also reveal other influences: that of Luxemburg especially, but also those of Guesde and Jaurès.[12] The views expressed by Mussolini on all the main ideological questions of the period—whether internationalism, militarism, war, class struggle, or the general strike—in no way differed from those of a number of other socialist intellectuals.[13]

However one would today describe the Marxism professed by Mussolini during the period he was a member of the Socialist party, it is undeniable that his approach to these questions was first determined by the theory of class struggle and by his conviction that the socialist revolution was in prog-ress. In those days, Mussolini never failed to demonstrate his support for the international socialist movement and the Socialist International. Like any other socialist militant, he claimed that militarism was merely one of the consequences of capitalism, and war was one of the means used by the bour-geois to retain their power and to exploit the proletariat to the maximum degree.

Mussolini made no distinction between the foreign and Italian bourgeoi-sie.[14] In December 1910, when Corradini founded the Nationalist Associa-tion, he condemned both Italian nationalism and militarism, seeing them as attempts to delay the collapse of the bourgeoisie.[15] In order to curb these two phenomena, Mussolini appealed to the socialist solidarity of the prole-tariat. He said it was not "bourgeois and democratic pacifism" that could prevent war, but only internationalistic socialism.[16] The fight against war and militarism was at that time one of the things to which he was most enthusiastically committed in his battle for socialism, making it a focus of his journalistic and literary activity.

Already in the first years of the century, he had praised the atmosphere of the internationalist congresses and their antimilitarist resolutions. In 1903 he described the years after 1871 as an idyllic period when internationalism had supplanted militarism. As a result of the enthusiasm with which the workers of Paris had joined hands with the workers of Germany, war had become impossible in Europe. And if a war nevertheless did break out, the proletariat would refuse to go out and be killed without reacting. It would apply the principles of Jules Guesde and launch a general strike, which would be the beginning of a social revolution.[17]

Moreover, if the proletariat did not succeed in preventing war, it would do everything to exploit it for its own revolutionary purposes and to seize power by means of the general strike. This conception was neither original nor innovative. Mussolini was only adopting an idea common in socialist circles at that time.[18] He was equally true to the socialist line of thought when he said that the proletariat had no country because it had never derived any benefit from possessing one. It was therefore quite natural that the proletariat should seek to take advantage of a war in order to hasten the outbreak of a civil conflict.[19] All these ideas, in fact, were banal and conventional for that period.

Such were Mussolini's positions when Italy began the Libyan campaign in September 1911. True to his ideas, he tried to launch a general strike in protest against the war.[20] It was a total failure. Mussolini was arrested and sentenced to a year's imprisonment. By the time of his release in March 1912 (his sentence had been reduced by five and a half months), he had gained considerably in stature. Within the party, he rapidly became a national figure and leader of its revolutionary wing—which was victorious at the congress in Reggio Emilia in July 1912.[21] This turn of events had two immediate consequences: the thrusting aside of the reformists and the appointment of Mussolini as chief editor of *Avanti!* in November of that year.

From his abortive action against the Libyan War, Mussolini learned one lesson he never forgot: the necessity of mercilessly opposing the reformist socialists, whom he accused of having caused the failure of the strike. As we know, his revenge against these people was not long in coming. At the same time, he began to have serious doubts about the ability of the proletariat to fulfill its historic role. In this, his conclusions were similar to those of Sorel, Michels, and the Italian and French revolutionary syndicalists. However, unlike these people, who like Sorel had never been activists of a socialist party or who had been rejected from such a party for dissent, Mussolini was a man whom the party assured of a splendid future. This, precisely, was one of the most important and interesting stages of his development. Just when his party had cleared the way for his uninterrupted progress to the top, when it had eliminated his enemies on the Right, and when he was showing himself to be one of the leaders capable of drawing the party toward more radical positions, Mussolini began a slow process of rupture with the traditional positions of socialism. One could see him beginning to undergo an ideological transformation that was to lead him to fascism.

Even if other influences are discernible in his writings, that of the theoreticians of revolutionary syndicalism always remained paramount. In 1909 Mussolini was careful to point out that his Marxism was not the original Marxism known in Germany but a Marxism revised by Sorel.[22] This socialist militant therefore had no difficulty, after quoting Paolo Orano, in subscribing to the syndicalist criticism of Marxism as a whole: "We acknowledge, like the 'socialist critics' of Marx, that certain ideas in his economic theory are erroneous, but we cannot join the dubious chorus of those who declare the failure of Marxism."[23]

To the intellectual baggage acquired through his association with Italian revolutionary syndicalism (that is, the theory of elites and the "socialist criticism" of Marxism) was now added the knowledge gained from reading Sorel. Together with Pareto, Arturo Labriola, and Leone, Sorel was the other source of inspiration for the fiery young revolutionary from the Romagna. "With regard to the concept of violence," wrote Mussolini in June 1908, "my modest ideas have found a sufficiently authoritative confirmation in the article of Georges Sorel which I am giving an account of farther on—an article that appeared in the last issue of *La guerra sociale* of Turin on this last 29 May."[24]

A year later, Mussolini reviewed *Réflexions sur la violence*, which had just appeared in Italian. He noticed the weakness of this work—its lack of a proper structure—but he had no reservations about its contents. On the contrary, Mussolini maintained that only violence, only an all-out struggle against democracy, would enable the proletariat to fulfill its historic mission. Mussolini saw Sorel as a salutary antidote to the perversions that Marxism had undergone in Germany.[25]

In May 1909, Mussolini published his most important article on revolutionary syndicalism—a review of *La teoria sindacalista* by Giuseppe Prezzolini. In this article, Mussolini described himself as having been "a syndicalist for the last five years."[26] In making his adherence to revolutionary syndicalist ideas go back to 1904, he was faithfully reconstructing the reality of his first years as an activist. In Mussolini's opinion, Sorel was a far more important influence on revolutionary syndicalism than Bergson. He saw Sorel as the real link between Marx and syndicalism; like the French thinker, he too regarded violence as a historical necessity, the only effective weapon against the ruling bourgeoisie.[27]

Mussolini did not only accept the authority of Sorel. He also respected the other intellectual leaders of revolutionary syndicalism: Robert Michels, Paolo Orano, and, as we have said, Arturo Labriola, whom he saw as both a great theoretician and a political leader with a promising future, the only person able to stand up to Turati.[28] As for Enrico Leone, Mussolini regarded him as the theoretician par excellence. His admiration for him never changed, not even at the time of the rise of the Fascist movement. Not until a Soviet offensive was stopped near Warsaw in August 1920 did Mussolini attack him for the first time. Leone took the side of the Bolsheviks, which, for the Fascist leader, was no longer acceptable.[29]

It is necessary to point out here, once again, the importance of praxis for the revolutionary syndicalists. In this respect, Mussolini had every reason to consider himself one of them. If he admired Sorel so much, it was precisely because "for Sorel Marx's work was to be understood as advice and not as theory, as a practice and not as a science." In fact, like all the revolutionary syndicalists of that period, Mussolini, around 1909–1910, began to have doubts about the revolutionary capacities of the proletariat. Mussolini said that syndicalism was perfect as a system of thought, but it lacked the battalions that could make the theory victorious. These battalions had to be trained and prepared if syndicalism was not to become a mere intellectual and literary fashion.[30]

If we wish to understand the nature of the relationship between Mussolini and the revolutionary syndicalists, we must bear in mind one essential fact: this former schoolmaster was above all a politician and a journalist. He was an educated journalist who read an enormous amount and who was interested in Nietzsche and Bergson and liked the German poet Klopstock.[31] He did not, however, claim to be a theoretician, nor did he consider himself a thinker to be ranked with Arturo Labriola, Leone, Orano, Panunzio, or Michels. In fact, the milieu of the syndicalist theoreticians—all eminent intellectuals and, for the most part, professional academics—did not offer this activist a suitable soil in which to develop his talents. Mussolini also was not a syndicalist leader like the De Ambris brothers, Corridoni, and Michele Bianchi, true heroes of the proletarian struggles whom he admired and with whom he had no intention of entering into competition. This young activist did not take part in the great labor struggles of the first decade of the century. He did his military service in 1905–1906, and he was not present in Ferrara in 1907 or in Parma in 1908 when the militant activism of the revolutionary syndicalists reached its climax. He did not participate in their attempt to conquer the Socialist party from within, nor did he follow them when, after the Ferrara congress in 1907, they came to the conclusion that the party no longer offered them any future.

Unlike these syndicalist leaders and intellectuals, Mussolini was convinced that Italian socialism had nothing with which to replace the party. At a quite early stage, he ceased to believe in the messianic virtues of the autonomous organizations of the proletariat, and he refused to break away from the Socialist party. An activist on its extreme Left, strongly opposed to reformism, Mussolini regarded revolutionary syndicalism as an extraordinary tool of action. The theory of proletarian violence, of an out-and-out class struggle, corresponded perfectly to his own conception of socialism. And yet, for all that, he did not believe in a rupture with the party. This was his first point of disagreement with the revolutionary syndicalists, a disagreement that was purely tactical, for he never questioned the Sorelian ideology. Having rapidly been appointed secretary of the Forlì branch of the party, Mussolini was quick in finding an area in which to exercise his particular talents. An incomparable party man, an extraordinary tactician, he knew marvelously well how to take advantage of all the opportunities the Socialist party offered him. He rose quickly through the ranks, and when he finally found himself face-to-face with the great names of revolutionary syndicalism, it was already as a leader of the revolutionary Left, a leader who had succeeded where his mentors had so lamentably failed: in conquering the party from within.

During the five years preceding the Great War, an ambiguous relationship developed between Mussolini and his intellectual mentors. With regard to immediate political choices, including the Tripoli expedition, the relationship was one of conflict, and it often degenerated into violent verbal confrontations. The revolutionary syndicalists who had left the party or who had been dismissed from it took up positions that Mussolini regarded as dubious. Had not these people joined themselves to nationalists and futurists? Did they not support the Libyan War, a classic colonial expedition? True, they advocated general strikes, but at the same time they were willing to come to terms with universal suffrage. Mussolini found it easy to condemn a behavior that he conveniently described as incoherent. At the same time as opposing these "leftists" who fought the party from outside and who befriended the national Right and supported its worst imperial follies, Mussolini fought the good fight within the socialist consensus. Nevertheless, his intellectual dependence on syndicalist doctrine had by no means diminished. Consequently, after the Italian-Turkish War and especially at the time when he founded the review *Utopia* at the end of 1913, Mussolini had no difficulty in renewing his intellectual collaboration with the theoreticians of revolutionary syndicalism. In reality, the relationship of the strongman of the revolutionary Left, steadily rising within the party mechanism, with the dissidents who took up their position outside the party, was a two-sided one.

Thus, in conformity with his attitude, Mussolini avoided touching the doctrine when he launched his first attack on the revolutionary syndicalists in November 1909. What he really reproached these rebels for—whose long-term objectives and temperament he shared—was their successive failures. He did not like to see an aging revolutionary syndicalism falling into literary dilettantism.[32] He was angry at its compromises and turned his criticism on the writer of *Réflexions*, guilty of forming an alliance with L'Action française:

We have known Georges Sorel for a long time. We have never believed in the revolutionary character of this library-devouring pensioner. His syndicalism is only a movement of reaction.[33]

Elsewhere, he wrote:

At one time he was an assiduous collaborator of the perfidious *Resto del carlino*. . . . I am beginning to believe that the accusation made against him that he is vain and a poseur (thus, for example, he attaches much importance to the Legion d'Honneur) was neither exaggerated nor without foundation.[34]

In December 1910, Mussolini passed judgment on the case of Sorel by simply declaring: "The 'master' has definitely gone over to the service of the ancien régime and of force."[35] Then, commenting on the role revolutionary syndicalism played in the political scene, Mussolini concluded:

Today syndicalism is at the service of nationalism, futurism, imperialism, mysticism, warmongers, and clericalism. Sometimes, it places itself at the service of landowners [agraria], in a way comparable to the articles of Paolo Orano and Georges Sorel calling for strike breaking [crumireschi], or the lectures of Labriola.[36]

But Mussolini did not stop there. He attacked nearly all the other revolutionary syndicalists even more fiercely.[37] The only ones he spared were those like Leone and De Ambris who in 1911 opposed the Tripoli expedition.[38] But when Alceste De Ambris decided to stand as a parliamentary candidate in 1913, Mussolini exploded again.[39] He could find no words harsh enough to condemn the four revolutionary syndicalist theoreticians who suddenly took part in the electoral agitation of October–November 1913. So Olivetti had become an election agent for Bossi, observed Mussolini; Enrico Leone was campaigning in Ferrara for Michele Bianchi; and Paolo Orano supported the electoral initiatives of his friends, of whom some—and not the least important among them, since one was speaking of Alceste De Ambris, Ottavio Dinale, and Arturo Labriola—were candidates themselves![40]

Mussolini said that in addition to fighting the party by trying to use the votes of its supporters against it, in 1912 these people had caused a new split, this time in the General Confederation of Labor. Nor was this all; Mussolini thought his rivals used the strike weapon ineffectively. All the striker movements launched during these years had ended badly and had inevitably led to humiliating compromises for the proletariat.[41] Again, one must point out here that Mussolini no longer believed in the revolutionary virtues of a heroic proletariat exclusively organized in its autonomous strongholds and eager to throw itself into battle in order to save civilization.[42] Like all the activists of the socialist parties in western Europe, he never forgot that the worker was also a citizen and that consequently there could be no question of abandoning the weapon of the political general strike.[43] It was thus quite logical that Mussolini defended the party against the dissidents as vigorously as a few years earlier Jules Guesde had defended it against Lagardelle. In a text of great clarity, he explained his attitude to the revolutionary syndicalists. The basic difference between himself and them, he wrote, was his "skepticism concerning the revolutionary capacity of economic organizations. Syndicalism asserts the uselessness of the Socialist party: I think precisely the opposite. But syndicalism, in the last ten years, has produced a whole body of doctrine and a whole mass of proletarian experience that a revolutionary socialist cannot ignore."[44]

In reality, Mussolini, in writing these lines in 1914, was forcing a door open. The syndicalists had long before ceased to regard the proletariat as the messianic force that Sorel had dreamed of, and they had long before abandoned the hope of a regeneration of humankind via the proletariat. In refusing to accept the myth of a proletariat that saved civilization, Mussolini was simply seeing reality, but when accusing the revolutionary syndicalists of being locked in an imaginary world, he was making unjustified charges.

In fact, far from losing themselves in a dream about a hypothetical future, the syndicalists displayed a great deal of pragmatism: they were simply trying to force their way out of a blocked situation. They did not merely wait for an opportunity: they did all they could to create one and made many attempts at rebellion. No one could know which strike would cause the real explosion. All means were good to end the baseness of a political system in which bargaining and compromise vied with treachery. The means could just as well be the Tripoli expedition as some strike. In other words, from the point of view of the revolutionary syndicalists, a foreign war or a workers' rebellion could, all things considered, be equally beneficial.

This was the main difference between Mussolini and the syndicalist leaders. In reproaching them of irresponsibility, the socialist leader was not entirely wrong. He did not consider all opportunities to be valid. Indeed, in the summer of 1913, the general strike in Milan, led by Corridoni, having been badly prepared, was an absolute failure. Despite his criticisms, Mussolini, contrary to the wishes of the party, supported the striking Lombard metalworkers. He wanted to show solidarity with the workers' struggle.[45] Once the strike was over, however, he settled accounts with the Unione Sindacale Italiana, the revolutionary syndicalist breakaway from the CGL, which bore responsibility for this new fiasco.[46] The polemic with and against Filippo Corridoni continued until the first months of 1914,[47] but the dispute, often violent in tone, in no way affected the mutual respect of these two men. Moreover, they collaborated in the red week of June 1914 and then in the interventionist movement.

Such was the nature of the problems that Mussolini debated with the revolutionary syndicalists. Despite this verbal violence, very common in the Italy of that period, where insults were bandied about even more freely than in France, these exchanges never exceeded the limits of a political and tactical debate of a purely circumstantial nature. Never, during these four years of animosity, did Mussolini attack the principles of revolutionary syndicalism. The antimaterialist revision of Marxism with its antirationalist and vitalist accretions remained a permanent part of his thinking. Similarly, the function of violence or of myths as generators of political and social activity was never questioned. This scathing polemicist never said a single word against socialism as a system of thought, which explains the ease with which the revolutionaries joined forces in the first months of the war. It should be pointed out that at the very moment he was engaging in a polemic with Corridoni, Mussolini had already begun publishing *Utopia*, a nonconformist review that threw itself wide open to the theoreticians of revolutionary syndicalism. Thus, the respective attitudes of both parties in June 1914 only confirmed the fact that the controversy concerned purely tactical issues. It was really only a question of deciding on the most suitable opportunity for launching the revolutionary process.

When the first demonstrations and strikes began of those days known as la settimana rossa (the red week), Mussolini thought that the moment had come. This is no doubt explained to a great extent by the extraordinary atmosphere of tension prevailing at that time. Despite the official interdiction of the party, Mussolini threw himself into the battle with enthusiasm; he believed it was the beginning of a real insurrection.[48] In the streets of Milan, the head of the revolutionary Left, known for his physical courage (he had fought several duels), gained the reputation of a determined leader. Using his fists in the pitched battle with the forces of order, struck by the police, and thrown on the ground, Mussolini saw Amilcare De Ambris, the brother of Alceste, Filippo Corridoni, and Cesare Rossi form a human wall to protect him. A new stage had been reached in the relationship between Mussolini and the syndicalist leaders. However, even though he agreed with the syndicalists about the significance of this mass movement, he complied with the CGL's orders to stop the strike. Like all those who descended into the streets of Milan, he was surprised by the large scale of the mobilization and saw in it great possibilities for the future. In June 1914, Mussolini too had come to the conclusion that the moment to overturn the ruling elite was approaching.

But the European crisis intervened, giving no time for these ideas to mature and still less to be put into practice. For one last time, Mussolini, following the party line, resisted the pressures of those "leftists" who, in accordance with their conception of the revolutionary war, launched a huge campaign under Alceste De Ambris in favor of intervention.[49] This new opposition lasted only a few weeks. In the autumn of 1914, Mussolini openly and unreservedly espoused the revolutionary syndicalist position. On 18 October 1914, he published an article in *Avanti!* advocating the abandonment of an "absolute" neutrality in favor of an "active and committed" neutrality.[50] Disowned the next day by the party leadership, he resigned that evening. A few days later, he officially joined the syndicalist leaders who were agitating in favor of intervention.

Clearly, Mussolini had not acted on a mere impulse. The speed and ease with which he had abandoned his tasks and his strategic position at the head of the Socialist party and the facility with which he had joined the revolutionary syndicalists were the outcome of a long process. Between the Tripoli expedition and the outbreak of the Great War, Mussolini, although working as an activist, had passed through an intellectual crisis that began the second phase of his development, at the end of which he abandoned the leadership of the revolutionary Left of the Socialist party to become the head of emergent fascism.

On 1 October in Milan, a new organization was created: the Revolutionary Fascio for Internationalist Action. On 5 October, the Fascio published a manifesto addressed to the workers of Italy. It stated that henceforth the social revolution would come about through a national revolution:

> We, revolutionaries who remain true to the teachings of our masters, believe that it is not possible to go beyond the limits of national revolutions without first passing through the stage of the national revolution itself. . . . If each people does not live within the framework of its own national frontiers formed by language and race, if the national question is not resolved, the historical climate necessary to the normal development of a class movement cannot exist.[51]

This text was signed by the members of a "Comitato d'iniziativa" made up entirely of revolutionary syndicalist leaders. Among the signatories were Corridoni, Michele Bianchi, Amilcare De Ambris, Olivetti, Cesare Rossi, and Libero Tancredi. Michele Bianchi became general secretary of the movement of Interventionist Fasci in 1915 before becoming general secretary of the National Fascist party. National socialism thus became a social reality, and the agitation in favor of the war, which was depicted as a great revolutionary war, must be seen as the birth pangs of fascism.

At that time, Mussolini was still editor of *Avanti!* He waited two weeks before joining these national socialists, who, on the thirteenth of that month, were described by the prefect of Milan in a report to the ministry of the interior as "people without a country" who wanted a war "solely in order to fish in troubled waters." The people in question were the activists of the managing committee of the Fascio of Milan: Corridoni, Olivetti, Dinale, Masotti, Ciardi, Mantica, Rocca, and Rossi. On 24 November 1914, an appeal by the Revolutionary Fascio for Internationalist Action was made "to the workers, to the revolutionaries of Rome." The text was signed by Francesco Pucci, Paolo Mantica, Agostino Lanzillo, and Nicolo Fancello.[52]

The creation of the first Fascio thus preceded Mussolini's break with the Socialist party. When the head of the revolutionary Left went over to the national socialists, events gathered momentum. Mussolini immediately took over the leadership of the new organization. He was well known, and he was not a man who was willing to take second place. His only potential rival, Filippo Corridoni, was also an outstanding personality, but this great syndicalist leader did not have the savoir faire of the incomparable "politico" who was the former editor of *Avanti!* Scarcely a month after his resignation from the Socialist party, Mussolini launched *Il popolo d'Italia*, which succeeded *Utopia*, whose last issue appeared on 15 December 1914. In the editorial room of the new daily, one found former writers of *Avanti!* and *Utopia*, but also former opponents. Revolutionary syndicalism was represented by Lanzillo, Dinale, Panunzio, Mantica, Poledro, and a few lesser-known activists.

For these people who had fought so much and who, from the great strikes of the very first years of the century to the Tripoli expedition and the red week, had done all they could to disrupt the status quo, for these people for whom anything, from a general strike to a foreign war, was acceptable if it overturned the existing order, the great European conflagration came as a deliverance. In May 1915—the celebrated "radiant May"—Italy entered the war, and on 31 August Mussolini joined his regiment of *bersaglieri*.

For the next three years, his revolutionary activities were greatly limited. He was on the front or in the hospital, or convalescing from his wounds, but he seized every opportunity to write or express himself. After the armistice, he no longer had any real rivals: Corridoni had been killed in action.[53] Neither Alceste De Ambris nor even Gabriele D'Annunzio, an authentic hero who in Italian military history was of incomparably greater importance than Sergeant Mussolini, was able to dispute the leadership of the Fascist movement with him.

THE INTELLECTUAL REALIGNMENT OF A SOCIALIST MILITANT

During the strike of 1911, intended to prevent Italy from entering the Libyan War, the new elements of Mussolini's intellectual evolution became apparent. One may recall that he had been greatly disappointed by the inability of the organized proletariat to shape history. This disillusionment only increased and by November 1914 was irreversible. Two years later, Mussolini began to question the theory that regarded war and revolution as mutually beneficial. From that time onward, his terminology ceased to be derived solely from the Marxist vocabulary and his arguments were based on sources other than Marx, whom a few years earlier he had described as "the greatest theoretician of socialism." His attitude changed, not only with regard to the questions already referred to, but as new questions arose.

Thus, when he was about to become editor of *Avanti!* he said at a meeting of the Socialist International in Milan to protest against a possible intervention of the European countries in the Balkans: "Another illusion has just been shattered—an illusion that we cherished until only yesterday: the illusion that led us to believe that a war could no longer break out between European countries." As well as demonstrating a clear perception of European realities, this opinion showed that at that time Mussolini had a correct idea of the real importance of the International. In the same speech, he added: "If at least it were true that war preceded and prepared the revolution! But that is an illusion, a deception." If it was now apparent to him that war did not necessarily serve as a path to revolution, it was because "war cannot arouse a revolutionary sentiment where one does not exist. On the contrary, where it does not exist in the first place, it can only repress and stifle it."[54] Mussolini ended his speech, as was proper at a socialist gathering, by urging the proletariat to summon the moral courage to arrest any tendency toward war in Europe. But if a conflagration nevertheless did occur, the proletariat, he said, should know how to take advantage of it. This concession to socialist opinion, probably motivated by a desire not to shock to excess, too soon, or too many people at once, could not conceal the doubts Mussolini began to have following the strike of 1911 about the ability of the working class to turn a war into a social revolution.

At that period of his career, however, Mussolini preferred to devote his energies to preventing a renewal of the Triple Alliance, an agreement he believed to be contrary or even disastrous to Italian interests. From then on, he began to favor an argument that had never been associated with him before. For the first time, he claimed that the interests of all of Italy had to take precedence, and precisely these national interests forbade Italy to throw in its lot with Austria and Germany. It was no longer a matter of the interests of the international proletariat or of the Italian proletariat: it was Italy first of all![55] He decided to turn himself into the spokesman of a nation betrayed by its leaders, whose policies could only make Italy dependent on Germany and Austria. Naturally, his terminology changed as well; in articles he published from the end of 1912, the terms "popolo" and "nazione" replaced "proletariato." Mussolini explained this substitution by the fact that the concepts "the people" and "the nation" also embraced that of "the proletariat."[56] At that period, Mussolini also began to pay much attention to the problems of the Italian minority in the Austro-Hungarian Empire. He already approached the subject from a national point of view, even if he continued to employ a socialist terminology in his argumentation.[57] In fact, throughout these years before the war, Mussolini was continuously moving, slowly but surely, away from orthodoxy. Little by little, the nation replaced the proletariat. At first, the substitution was veiled and almost imperceptible, but the more definite the threats of war became, the less verbal reticence was used and the less tortuous the ideological convolutions became.

The clearest sign of this development was Mussolini's decision to bring out his own review, *Utopia*, whose first issue appeared on 22 November 1913.[58] That the spokesman of the Socialist party (was he not editor of its daily newspaper?) and its leading personality should want to have another forum caused great astonishment. Mussolini recognized the controversial nature of this move and thus hastened to explain that it was not to be interpreted as the sign of an ideological disagreement or some "crisis of conscience." At the beginning of his presentation of the review, he was careful to protest his fidelity: "In Marxism, which, of all the socialist doctrines, is the most organic system, everything is open to controversy but nothing has gone bankrupt." The key words of this declaration were clearly "everything is open to controversy" (tutto è controverso).[59] There was one reality, but its interpretation had split the labor movement into factions. Mussolini then exploited the opportunity provided by the need to discover the best and most exact interpretation in order to make a severe criticism of European socialism. In his opinion, the failure of international socialism was connected with the failure of reformism and the crisis of positivistic philosophy. He condemned the reformist leaders who supported the participation of their respective parties in government, thereby stopping any antimilitarist action, and the leaders, like those in Germany, who went so far as to endorse huge military budgets.

There was therefore an urgent and pressing need to make "a revision of socialism from the revolutionary point of view." This, said Mussolini, was the task that *Utopia* had taken upon itself. It is interesting to note that Mussolini referred to a "revolutionary revision of socialism"—a formula favored by the revolutionary syndicalists—at the very moment when he was beginning to move away from Marxism! Mussolini did not use this expression by chance; it already formed part of the intellectual development of the Italian and French revolutionary syndicalists. Indeed, one can readily understand Mussolini's need to possess his own mouthpiece when one reads the article he published in the second issue of *Utopia*. In this article, Mussolini launched an appeal "To Young People," both socialists and nonsocialists, calling on them to rally around him.[60] The purpose of the new journal was thus not only to give a new interpretation to ideological questions but also to recruit people of the Left who were not socialists. In *Utopia* one saw the beginning of a conception of revolution that was regarded as belonging to the Left but that was not necessarily socialistic. Even under Mussolini's editorship, *Avanti!* would not have accepted such a language.

Prezzolini was quite correct when in his journal *La voce* he congratulated Mussolini on the appearance of *Utopia* as representing the action of a man who had chosen to be whole, or, as Mussolini said, to be more "himself." On 15 January 1914, Mussolini thanked Prezzolini and confirmed the accuracy of his judgment.[61] As he said in a text of great significance,

> Elsewhere I present the collective opinion of a party that can be, and that nearly always is, my own. Here I present my opinion, my vision of the world (*Weltanschauung*) without worrying about whether it conforms to the predominant opinion of the party. Elsewhere, I am a soldier who "obeys" orders, but here I am a soldier who can "discuss" orders. So, one of two things must be true: either I am no longer a soldier, or else they are no longer orders. The fact is that in an army there are "orders" that are not discussed, just as in the church one does not polemicize truth or heresy. If one acknowledges that truth is a woman, as Nietzsche has suggested, it is clear that she has her modesty. It is not possible, it is not advisable to display her suddenly to the public. She has to be revealed discreetly, silently, to be possessed in the shadows, and to be presented to the public only when it is initiated.[62]

This was the function he intended for *Utopia*: to allow this incipient heresy to express itself freely, independently of the party and outside it. It would provide a support for the "revision of socialism" to which one was invited to give one's adherence; it would bring together revolutionary forces of a new kind. For this purpose, Mussolini addressed an appeal to the younger generation, encouraging it to give a new interpretation to socialist thought.[63] In January 1914, employing arguments very close to those of revolutionary syndicalism, he launched an all-out attack against Marxism in which he established the main lines of his future offensive.

As usual, and as had happened with all the revisionists before him, Mussolini began by stating that capitalism by no means seemed to have entered a period of decline, and that he did not accept the Marxist view of society as being divided into two classes. On this occasion, this socialist activist introduced an element that for him was new: socialism, he said, had not taken into account the psychological factors in human behavior. One therefore had to ask oneself whether there were contradictions between the theory and the historical reality.[64]

This question, which the revolutionary syndicalists had debated publicly since the time Mussolini had collaborated in Arturo Labriola's *Avanguardia socialista*, could be asked around 1914 without causing any immediate scandal. Mussolini, as an experienced politician, now proceeded carefully with the aim of going farther. He immediately summoned his former revolutionary syndicalist friends. He knew that in major ideological debates, where there was always a great danger of too obvious a deviation from the party line, they were afraid of nothing and had nothing to lose. He also knew that they excelled in this kind of controversy.

One of those who joined this struggle was Sergio Panunzio, who was a professor in Ferrara. He was careful to point out that his opinions reflected those of the editor of the review. With him, one was immediately—and deeply—immersed in an antimaterialist revision of socialism. "Socialism," he wrote, "is idealism, not materialism, and, if this is true, socialism is utopia. Mussolini, for his part, is well aware that insofar as it claims to be a science, socialism is a false one." Moreover, "The revolutionary philosophy cannot be materialistic." The lesson to be drawn was clear: if the Socialist party did not want to abandon its revolutionary aspirations, it had to adopt an idealist philosophy. Then, declaring once again that his ideas reflected those of Mussolini, he went on: "We learn from history that all revolutionary movements have been absolutist, intransigent, intolerant—one might say Jacobin, for Jacobinism is an absolute moment of the idea."

And finally: "We will go farther: on one hand Mussolini's position is both a threat and a danger (and what a danger!) for the reformists and realists who still remain within the party; and, on the other hand, for us syndicalists who have placed ourselves outside the party, it is a promise that the disagreements will neither be suppressed nor, at best, hardly even whispered, and that they will soon end by exploding."[65]

This conclusion illustrates the character of the ideological opposition of the people grouped around Mussolini in the spring of 1914 to the Socialist party as a whole. The staff of *Utopia* already included revolutionaries who for several years had taken up a stand outside official socialism. From now on, these people, pleading the necessity of an antimaterialistic revision of Marxism, were to oppose both Turati's "centrists" and the "maximalists." The materialist-scientific interpretation of Marxism was at that time the common denominator of all trends of Italian socialism.

This heresy was in reality by no means new. This time, however, it did not belong to the dissidents alone: the most powerful figure in the Socialist party, through the agency of Panunzio, had taken it upon himself to sponsor and propagate it. For Panunzio, the future revolution could never be a revolution of a Marxist type. For a long time, he and his associates had no longer considered the proletarians to be a revolutionary force. The revolution, he said, would be a Jacobin revolution led by Mussolini. It was then May 1914.

Mussolini undoubtedly intended *Utopia* to be the breeding ground of the intellectual leadership of a revolution that, for want of a better title, was called a Jacobin revolution. The term was not entirely inappropriate, since Jacobinism also suggested nationalism, an appeal to the people, a call for the defense of the country in danger. Among the collaborators of *Utopia*, one notices on the one hand people like Amadeo Bordiga, Angelo Tasca, and

Karl Liebknecht, and on the other hand Arturo Labriola, Panunzio, Lanzillo, Leone, and Massimo Rocca. The common denominator of this team of activist intellectuals was a total rejection of the existing order and a merciless criticism of the socialist parties, their ideology, and their methods. All these people were convinced that a revolution did not happen on its own, but they differed on one essential point: the first group sought to make a revolution that would overthrow capitalism, and the second believed in the permanence of capitalism and had no intention of touching private property. This was the dividing line between the future founders of Communist parties (Bordiga and Tasca in Italy, Liebknecht in Germany) and the future founders of the Fascist movement: Mussolini, Panunzio, Lanzillo, and Rocca.

The differences between these two groups began to become apparent in November 1913, despite the fact that all the founders of *Utopia* were on the extreme revolutionary Left. They were all either members of the Socialist party or—in the case of those who had been excluded from the party for their radicalism—revolutionaries. But, at the same time, their views differed on the final objective and the nature of the regime that would one day replace the existing order. As time went on, these differences increased; in the last issues of *Utopia* one sees a growing number of revolutionary-syndicalist bylines, while that of the party members decreased. The positions both groups adopted were as radical and revolutionary as ever, but the "revolutionary revisionist" current clearly gained ascendancy. The antimaterialist revision of Marxism gave rise to an unprecedented revolutionary current whose special character was not clearly discernible in its beginnings and asserted itself only progressively. Ten years after the appearance of *Utopia*, the liberal historian Luigi Salvatorelli, a shrewd observer, noted: "Apart from popular and democratic sources, we have a whole series of manifestations of fascism to which, despite and beyond its assumption of power, one can and must ascribe a 'leftist' character. Despite their leftist vocabulary, however, these actions have always had 'rightist' results."[66]

Thus, in this way, in the immediate prewar period, Mussolini's thought developed and took on substance. The failure in 1911 of the general strike led to a period of reflection in which Mussolini again drew close to the revolutionary syndicalists. He remained a revolutionary, he was more of one than ever, but meanwhile he had greatly modified his Marxism. Moreover, while he was growing increasingly aware of the inertia of the proletariat, he was also becoming conscious of the power of nationalism. If in January 1914 he did not yet by any means share the position of the nationalists on the question of Trieste, a city claimed for Italy by Corradini's followers, his views were no longer those traditionally held by the Socialist party.[67]

On the Right, they were aware of the evolution that was taking place in the thinking of the most celebrated of socialist leaders. An interview Mussolini gave to *Il resto del carlino*, a moderate right-wing daily, in April 1914, was correctly evaluated by the journal: "We on the Right who strive earnestly for political honesty cannot be unaware that the same is being done on the Left by people of the same generation—people who have the same moral preoccupations and are motivated by the same ideals."[68]

After the armistice, this newspaper made its columns generously available to Georges Sorel.

The major event that definitely put an end to Mussolini's socialism was the failure of the famous red week. At the time when the antimilitarist demonstrations began in Ancona on 7 November 1914, Mussolini, despite his misgivings and in spite of the experience of 1911, felt that the long-awaited opportunity had arrived to resort to a general strike in order to overthrow the regime. He was ready for a real armed insurrection. These hopes, however, were short-lived. Four days later, in a speech in Milan, Mussolini suggested terminating a strike that had no chance of success. He believed that official socialism, which had become a pillar of the established order, would never allow the revolutionary process to get started. At the same time, he expressed his faith in the necessity and possibility of a revolution; the red week had been a revolution thwarted by the Socialist party and its syndicates. He claimed that this revolution or near revolution had become inevitable because there was "too much electricity in the air." Alas, the quasi-messianic hopes for a major change had been betrayed by the socialist leaders and, indirectly, by the other European socialist parties. However, it was only postponed until later. "Italy needs a revolution," wrote Mussolini, "and it will have one!"[69]

As formulated in July 1914, this conviction no longer fitted into the classical Marxist scheme. For Mussolini, this expectation expressed a deep psychological need: the whole of his article on the red week in *Utopia* was based on it. The earth, he felt, was shaking underfoot; on the day the right conditions existed, the Italian boiler, whose steam was constantly rising, would explode. The revolutionary process no longer depended on European socialism, and this explains the enthusiasm with which the socialist leader threw himself into interventionism and nationalism. The first step in this journey that led first to national socialism and then to fascism was Mussolini's intellectual rupture with social democracy on the eve of the outbreak of war:

> "Modern" international socialism is a meaningless phrase. A single socialist gospel to which all nations must conform on pain of excommunication does not exist. Each nation has created its own socialism. The period of German domination of the socialist movement is now coming to an end; defiance toward the German socialists is increasing. What are they doing in Germany today? In journals and reviews, they are heatedly discussing whether the socialist parliamentary group should continue sitting in the Reichstag or whether, on the

contrary, it should leave at the end of the session at the moment of the imperial declaration. They are also talking about a general strike, but who is talking about it? The radicals (socialist revolutionaries). Worse, only Rosa Luxemburg still mentions it, a Polish Jewess for whom the self-righteous among the socialists do not spare their harsh criticisms.[70]

Thus, on the eve of the war, Mussolini's political thinking was in the midst of change. The leader of the left wing of the Socialist party questioned the overly schematic nature of the Marxist explanation of social and national realities. War broke out at a time when the cracks in the orthodoxy of this system of thought were beginning to deepen and multiply; on hearing Mussolini speak of the illusion of socialist internationalism and on reading his vilification of German social democracy, one has the impression of being confronted with one of Michels's many diatribes of a few years earlier. Before the first shot was fired, Mussolini had joined the revolutionary syndicalists in their criticism of democratic socialism, of internationalistic verbiage, of the inability to act displayed by the leaders of the party. Coming on top of all this, the red week was the straw that broke the camel's back. It was the final incident that, leading to a verdict without appeal, marked the end of traditional socialism.

In August 1914, the evolution of Mussolini's thought had already reached the point of no return. The traditional Marxist positions, eroded during the three or four final years of peace, now belonged to a past that was dead and buried. With the collapse of the Socialist International, which Mussolini had foreseen (and Michels and Panunzio had also expected), only the nation was still viable. Therefore the national interest would now be paramount, and it was in accordance with that interest that Mussolini would henceforth determine his line of conduct.[71]

Such were the results of the profound intellectual crisis that had been brewing since the antimilitaristic campaign of 1911. From that time on, Mussolini entered a process of revision of Marxism based on an evaluation of new realities that caused him to lose faith both in the revolutionary virtues of the proletariat together with the organizations by which it was represented and in internationalism. This evolution, slow and gradual, accelerated with the beginning of hostilities. In the second half of August, Mussolini launched a violent attack upon the International which he signed with his usual pseudonym, "the man who searches." The article was published in *Utopia*. From the outbreak of hostilities, Mussolini drew the only possible conclusion: that everywhere socialism was losing out to the nation.[72]

Indeed, the working class in France and Germany, led by the social democratic parties and reformist syndicates, responded promptly to the appeals of the bourgeois governments; they threw themselves into the battle without any noticeable hesitation or reservation. It is obvious that in such a situation

Mussolini, who had led two unsuccessful attempts at a general strike, had no wish to initiate another such action.[73] It only remained for him to accept the facts, namely, that the process of the disintegration of socialism, whether "orthodox" or "reformist," was now completed.

In October 1914, the revolutionary syndicalists Massimo Rocca and Tullio Masotti turned to the Italian socialist leader and asked him to resolve the contradiction that, they said, existed between Benito Mussolini, a politician convinced in his heart of hearts of the need to join the interventionists, and the editor of *Avanti!*, an official personality obliged to follow the party line.[74] Replying to Rocca, who was soon to join him in founding the Fascist movement, Mussolini admitted that he had passed through an intellectual crisis. As he was a man of action, this self-examination immediately led to a practical conclusion: a possible intervention in the war had to be considered "from a purely national point of view."[75] He had no doubt about the outcome of the struggle: in this gigantic confrontation, the Franco-British alliance would be victorious. Since this was only a conflict of two imperialisms and not a struggle for democracy, liberty, or justice or an attempt to change the nature of European society, Italy had to promote its national interests by joining the strongest side.[76]

Throughout this period of waiting that preceded his leaving the Socialist party and his founding of the celebrated daily *Il popolo d'Italia*, on 15 November 1914, Mussolini's thought was dominated by nationalism, but a nationalism of a new type. In his opinion, the inability of socialism to perceive the nature and power of nationalism was simply due to blindness and dogmatism, and the failure of the Socialist International derived from a refusal to take the national question into consideration.[77] Did not the situation demonstrate that "the nation represents a stage in human progress, a stage that has not yet been passed"? A little farther on, he added: "The sentiment of nationality exists: one cannot deny it! The old antipatriotism is gone, and those beacons of socialism that are Marx and Engels wrote things about patriotism that are quite shocking!"[78] Consequently, he concluded, "the socialist criticism of the future could try to find a force of equilibrium between the nation and the class."[79] This force of equilibrium was the new kind of socialism evolved by Mussolini: national socialism. The content of this national socialism determined concrete political choices. The whole question of interventionism depended on Mussolini's perception of the importance of national sentiment and national identity in the life of the collectivity. It is nevertheless necessary to point out that this clear realization of the fact of nationhood never caused Mussolini to abandon the idea of socialism as a continuous process of social reform. Thus, national socialism sprang up, at once a political movement and an ideological orientation—a real transitional phase in the development of fascism.

NATIONAL SOCIALISM

Mussolini's theory of national socialism, as we have seen, progressed in stages and evolved together with a process of revising Marxism. But, as always, this evolution took place in accordance with the realities of the period: it accelerated from the winter of 1914. Originally, Mussolini's national socialism was an offshoot of the antimaterialist revision of Marxism, but it gradually acquired its own character. As an independent phenomenon, Mussolinism was an amalgam of elements that, blended together in a kind of "mixer," produced something very different from any of its original components. Mussolini himself played an important part in this process.

It is necessary to insist on one point. Contrary to the belief held by as competent a historian as Roberto Vivarelli, for instance, the nationalism of Mussolini was very different from classical nationalism.[80] Mussolini was not a traditional nationalist, and he did not espouse all the usual nationalist causes. Where territorial problems and postwar frontiers were concerned, he demonstrated by his support for the principle of the creation of a Yugoslavian state that he had his own ideas, which differed considerably from those of the nationalists. In the postwar period, he displayed a lack of enthusiasm for the Fiume expedition, which aroused the openly expressed irritation of Alceste De Ambris, chief of staff and second in command of Gabriele D'Annunzio. Despite his protestations of fidelity toward the Commandante and his men, Mussolini in fact abandoned the cause of the "Italian Regency of the Carnaro." That is why De Ambris, when he published the constitution of the regency in September 1920, did not even take the trouble of showing it to Mussolini before bringing it to the attention of the other Italian newspaper editors. Mussolini complained of this in *Il popolo d'Italia*, but he did not change his attitude. Less than three months later, he expressed his support for the Treaty of Rapallo. By the end of December 1920, the Fiume affair ended without Mussolini's having done anything to help D'Annunzio and De Ambris. The Fascist leader did not adopt this course merely to rid himself of two rivals. Indeed, Mussolini was both a highly experienced politician and acutely aware of realities: he knew that Italy did not have the means to fight another war.[81] But Mussolini—and this is the important point—never practiced a simplistic and purely chauvinistic nationalism; his vision was far more complex. Similarly, the former leader of the revolutionary Left was not, as De Felice thought, a simple socialist who drew close to the nationalists only in November 1916.[82] In reality, this development had begun much earlier and was an important aspect of the formation of national socialism, that is to say, of a new and comprehensive vision of the aims assigned to society as a whole.

At first, Mussolini represented nationalism as an instrument for the promotion of socialism. Since the international solidarity of the workers could not function because of national rivalries, and since the national question held back revolutionary tendencies, the path to social revolution, he claimed, passed through the solution of national problems.[83] Revolution still remained the final objective, and Mussolini sought to demonstrate that there was no contradiction between nationalism and socialism. To illustrate the point, he made much use of the example of Blanqui. A veteran of all the revolutions of the nineteenth century, did Blanqui not call upon the people to defend the country when the bourgeois Right was ready to capitulate?[84]

There were periods, said Mussolini, when patriotism and socialism were perfectly compatible. This was the case at the beginning of 1915: intervention in the European war would serve the interests of the nation and also those of socialism. However, in relation to his earlier statements, there now was a difference. Mussolini no longer claimed that the war and the revolution would coincide, and he no longer considered calling a general strike as a prelude to the revolution. Now the results of the war would decide the fate of the revolution, indefinitely postponed.[85]

In May 1915, a few days after the declaration of war, the tone grew harsher. By then, Mussolini and his associates, excluded from the Socialist party, had launched their own journal and were able to express themselves freely. The targets of their abuse were no longer the reformist leaders, but the founding fathers of socialism. Marx and Engels were accused of having always identified themselves with their German fatherland and worked for its interests. Both were now represented as tools of Germanism and of Bismarckian diplomacy. German social democracy was the same: it had wanted this war, which had just broken out, and it had done all it could to prepare the people morally to play an active part in it.[86] Attacks on Marx and Engels multiplied throughout 1915. Mussolini, an extraordinary "political animal," was not a man for half-measures: he literally became unleashed. To hear him, one would think that if anyone bore responsibility for the war, it was Marx, Engels, and the German socialists, who had always been allies of Bismarck and Hindenburg.[87] Very soon, these attacks on Marxism, whose failure on an international level had been demonstrated and which had been represented as one of the vehicles of pan-Germanism, developed into a comprehensive criticism of the system.

It was obvious that the principle of class struggle no longer applied, and praises of the Italian proletariat and condemnation of the Italian bourgeoisie were bestowed in accordance with only one criterion: their respective patriotism. If the proletariat was deemed worthy of praise, it was because it had proved its superiority by its capacity to work for the good of the country.[88]

These were the classic themes of national socialism. Mussolini, like all his predecessors, like all those who were to take this path after him, and like the revolutionary syndicalists who replaced the category of "proletarians" with that of "producers," continued to abhor a fraction of the bourgeoisie that he described as "parasitic." He always considered himself a revolutionary,[89] but the nature, significance, and aims of the revolution had altered. The envisaged revolution was national and anti-Marxist, but at the same time it was not a bourgeois revolution. Contrary to the opinion of Renzo De Felice, Mussolini in 1915 was no longer a "dormant" socialist,[90] but a national, anti-liberal, and anti-Marxist socialist who was undoubtedly a revolutionary, but a revolutionary of a type hitherto unknown.

This, among other things, explains his fierce opposition to Lenin and bolshevism, objectively allies of the Reich and hence enemies of the Italian fatherland. In Mussolini's view, Lenin could only continue the work of Marx, the German patriot of 1870, and the Bolshevik revolution was merely a prolongation of German militarism.[91] But if Lenin and the German socialists who acclaimed the October Revolution with joy were simply enemies, the Italian socialists, for their part, were traitors.[92] Mussolini harped on this theme from the beginning of 1915.[93] Subservient to the kaiser, the Italian socialists lightheartedly delivered up their country, Europe, and the rest of the world to the foreigners.[94] When in power, Mussolini continued to express this opinion.

However, Mussolini's violent opposition to the October Revolution was not due simply to the Russian withdrawal from the war against Germany. His total rejection of bolshevism dated from before the revolutionaries' seizure of power, and it was not motivated solely by strategic considerations. Mussolini rejected the Russian Revolution because it was a Marxist revolution. Contrary to the view of De Felice, it was neither the October Revolution nor the defeat of Caporetto that drove Mussolini to the Right.[95] Mussolini did not abandon Marxism all at once and under the impact of catastrophic events; he abandoned it as a result of several years' development. The political and intellectual factors that caused the most powerful figure of the Italian Socialist party to break with Marxism had already begun to operate at the time of the Libyan War. This process, very similar to the development of the revolutionary syndicalists, was connected from an early stage with their own synthesis of socialism and nationalism.

Mussolini saw Marxism fail first on the home front. Neither the class consciousness of the proletariat nor its inner cohesion nor the policies of the socialist parties corresponded to Marxist theory. After having suffered a series of reverses in Italy, Marxism finally collapsed internationally. That, at least, was Mussolini's interpretation of prewar history.

In accordance with a now classic development, Mussolinian national socialism implicitly recognized the permanence of capitalism. Six months before the first shot was fired, the editor of *Utopia* expressed himself with great clarity on this subject:

Capitalism—that is, the economic-political system of the modern nations—confronts us with its reality. It is various and multiform: it is a reality in movement. At a certain moment, the socialists became victims of a very serious error. They believed that capitalism had had its time. Capitalism, however, is still capable of reversals, and its series of transformations has not yet come to an end. Capitalism presents us with a reality with many facets, especially economic ones.[96]

This idea, which had been developed for a long time by the revolutionary syndicalists and which amounted to a defense of the existing economic order, now served as the starting point of national socialism, a link in the chain leading to fascism.

In August 1917, Mussolini visualized the main outlines of the postwar situation. His main concern was the modernization of the country, which would not only permit the economic development of Italian society, but would also raise Italy to the level of a major power. He believed that the Slavic countries, like the eastern Mediterranean, were a natural area of expansion for Italy. He said that in order to exploit this fact, one had to destroy the German political and economic influence in these countries and support the Slav independence movements directed against the Austrian empire.[97]

In this process of industrialization and economic growth, the proletariat was given a role of great importance. Certainly, it was a question not of a proletarian revolution, but, on the contrary, of national solidarity; according to Mussolini, the interests of the nation and those of the proletariat coincided.[98] At the same time, Mussolini took the principle of the identification of the interests of the individual with the national interests very far—far beyond the national-socialist synthesis the revolutionary syndicalists formulated. Whereas the national syndicalists of *Pagine libere* and *Il divenire sociale* always regarded the interests of the workers as the proper objective of collective action and saw the nation only as a necessary means to achieve this goal, with Mussolini this order of priorities was reversed.[99]

On 1 May 1918, Mussolini reacted to events in Russia. He saw the Soviet revolution as proof of the failure of the proletariat in both the political and the economic sphere. Lenin's revolutionaries had now demonstrated to the entire world that the proletariat was incapable of ruling and did not deserve to rule. The fact that it constituted a majority gave the proletariat no special rights; power should go to those who are best and not necessarily to the most numerous. Perhaps a time would come, he wrote, when a fraction of the proletariat, properly prepared and somehow purified, would prove itself worthy of playing the role of a ruling elite. For the time being, this was not the case. Consequently, the regime that national socialism and national syndicalism hoped to set up would not be egalitarian, and there would be no question of a socialization of property. The new economy, he wrote, would be directed entirely toward growth, efficiency, and the "productivization" of the masses. Only a highly hierarchic regime embracing a society ruled by a powerful elite would be capable of leading the country on the path of growth.[100]

The French and Italian Sorelians had for a long time advocated more or less the same principles. There was no alternative, they said, to capitalism or to a system of government by elites. Democracy had always been an object of disdain for the syndicalists, and these sociologists, jurists, and economists had always been extremely doubtful about the capacity of people to govern themselves. As time passed, these ideas were taken to an extreme: with national syndicalism, the theory of productionism constituted an antithesis to Marxism. Even the idea of a "national proletariat" was abandoned in favor of that of "producers." The producers came from all social classes; they were found in all strata of society, and they represented the new Italy. These assured the modernization of the country and consequently its future. Like his former mentors, the economists Arturo Labriola and Enrico Leone—in fact, like all the intellectuals of Italian revolutionary syndicalism who had thought much about economic problems, and many of whom had come from the undeveloped Mezzogiorno—Mussolini was extremely conscious of Italian backwardness. An economically weak Italy, he wrote, would be an eternal prey for more powerful neighbors; the idea of revolution was now replaced by that of "renovation."[101] Renovation required the collaboration of the classes: this idea dominated Mussolini's thinking increasingly. From being a cardinal principle of productionism, the idea of "collaboration" became a fundamental tenet of corporatism. An essential instrument of modernization, the collaboration of the classes also involved social reforms. The sole objective of this social policy, however, was now to ensure the smooth functioning of the system and the absolute loyalty of the workers to the nation.[102]

Thus, it was not, as De Felice claimed, the fear of the possible spread of bolshevism or the danger of a Communist revolution in Italy that made Mussolini take up the defense of capitalism.[103] Certainly, Mussolini was determined to prevent the Bolshevization of Italy, but the Communist danger did not underlie the productionist theory. Productionism was the result of Mussolini's fusion with the revolutionary syndicalists; in January 1914, when he was still the undisputed leader of the Italian socialists, Mussolini declared his support of the capitalist system.[104] In October of that year, he reiterated the necessity of modernizing industry, agriculture, and transportation and of driving the productive capacity of the Italian economy to its limits to ensure the country the status of a great power. All these objectives, he wrote, could be achieved only—as the revolutionary syndicalists had long maintained—within the framework of the capitalist system.

After the war, Mussolini and his associates—especially the revolutionary syndicalists and the futurists—were convinced that with national syndicalism they had found a "third way," the way so earnestly sought between a Marxism that was bankrupt and a liberalism whose moral and political defects no longer required any proof. Mussolini, as a disciple of Hegelian Marxism, liked to speak of the synthesis of two antitheses, class and nation. "We take our stand on the nation, which embraces all classes, whereas the class does not embrace the nation," he declared on the eve of the foundation of the Fascist movement.[105]

While laying down the social and economic principles of what soon became the Fascist program, he also indicated its political conceptions. Referring to the French Revolution, Carnot, and Napoleon and drawing the moral of the Russian Revolution, Mussolini came to the conclusion that the defense of the country, the promotion of its influence, and the requirements of a revolution in the true sense (that is, one like the French Revolution or the first stage of the Russian Revolution, which was patriotic and took up the defense of the nation) necessitated a dictatorship. In July 1917, Mussolini unambiguously described the character, significance, and objectives of this type of revolution:

> A revolution is not chaos, it is not disorder, it does not affect all activities and all aspects of social life as extremist idiots in certain countries maintain. A revolution has a meaning and a historical significance only when it represents a superior order, a political, economic, and moral system of a more elevated kind. If this is not the case, the revolution is reaction, it is la Vendée. A revolution is a discipline that replaces another discipline, it is a hierarchy that takes the place of another hierarchy.[106]

Mussolini's thought assumed its final form when the Russian Revolution had already taken place. Mussolini was undoubtedly fully conscious of this great event, but it would be erroneous to imagine that his ideas were a direct reaction to what had happened or was happening in Russia. Most of the ideas he put into practice after Lenin came to power had been envisaged by Mussolini several years before October 1917. But as time passed and the international situation changed, Mussolini's thinking also altered. In a heated discussion with his former socialist friends at the beginning of October 1917, Mussolini made the following declaration:

> But the fatherland ought not to be denied! And, above all, the fatherland ought not to be betrayed, especially when it is engaged in a struggle for existence. If one speaks of the fatherland, one speaks of discipline, and if one speaks of discipline, one acknowledges a hierarchy of authority, functions, and intelligences. And wherever this discipline is not freely accepted, wherever the necessity for it is not understood, it has to be imposed through violence, if necessary: if necessary—if the censor permits me to say so—through the kind of dictatorship that the Romans of the First Republic set up at critical moments of their history.[107]

The war, wrote Mussolini, was to bring about a national renaissance, a collective self-awareness; it represented a historic opportunity to sweep away the old world with its decadent politicians and outmoded ideologies. This salutary cleansing would be the work of new elites: a national proletariat,[108] especially "a new and better elite" that had fought in the trenches and would "govern the Italy of tomorrow"[109] and preside over the fusion of opposites on which the entire future depended.

> One is surprised at those people who in their simplicity still desperately cling to the old mental stereotypes. They are missing the train! The train goes by, and they remain standing on the platform with an expression of mixed stupefaction and anger. The words *republic, democracy, radicalism*, and *liberalism* have no more meaning than the word *socialism*. They will have one tomorrow, but it will be the meaning given by the millions of *ritornati* [soldiers returning from the front]. This meaning could be quite different. It could be an anti-Marxist and national socialism, for instance. The millions of workers who will return to the furrows of their fields after having lived in the furrows of the trenches will establish the synthesis of the class-nation antithesis.[110]

All this was said before Lenin seized power, or in the first weeks following the fall of the Kerensky government. It simply represented the outcome of ideas developed in nonconformist leftist circles not only before the fall of the czar, but before the German invasion of Belgium as well. These ideas, which originated before the war, gained substance and were consolidated during and because of the war. The Fascist ideology developed in an organic and logical manner and determined Mussolini's political actions.

If Mussolini detached himself progressively from socialism some time before the war, he by no means relinquished his revolutionary propensities. What had changed was the significance and purpose of the revolution. Mussolini had learned from the revolutionary syndicalists that one should not interfere with capitalism: after the failure of the general strikes and before 1914, he realized that the proletariat of western Europe would not produce a revolution. If one wanted to overthrow the existing order, which was one of underdevelopment in the south and enslavement to German money in the north, one of corruption and *combinazione*, if one wanted to cleanse parliament and the administration, the church and the army, the political parties and the reformist syndicates, so that they would become something other than cogs in a great mechanism for exploiting the people, one would have to create a revolution, but a revolution of a new kind.

Moreover, it soon became apparent that a systematic opposition to the propertied classes was no longer acceptable: the future of the proletariat was linked to that of the productive bourgeoisie. Mussolini welcomed with great satisfaction the productionist principles that Alceste De Ambris had strongly advocated in the final months before the armistice.[111] He adopted Lanzillo's slogan of a permanent "social armistice" subsequent to the national union confirmed by interventionism. At the same time, Mussolini did not forget that the final aim of revolutionary syndicalism was for the proletariat to be able to replace the bourgeoisie in the process of production. He wanted to give the proletariat the largest share in national wealth and even proposed a direct workers' participation in the Peace Conference in order to ensure that the interests of labor would be given the proper consideration.[112]

During the last months of the war, the ties between Mussolini and the revolutionary syndicalists grew even stronger. The former editor of *Avanti!*, who did not renew contact with the Socialist party, tried to create a political tool of his own. He attempted to set up a broad coalition of interventionists of the Left.[113] Bianchi, Lanzillo, Rocca, and Dinale were very active at his side. Mussolini regarded the Unione Italiana del Lavoro (UIL)—founded by the revolutionary syndicalists in June 1918 to counterbalance the CGL, dominated by the socialists—as a natural ally. At the same time, he unhesitatingly endorsed the Italian expansionist and irredentist objectives expressed by Panunzio.[114] Mussolini saw irredentism as an excellent means of political mobilization, and he did not fail to make use of it. He regarded irredentism as the successor to the interventionism of the Left, a sequel to the "war of the masses" which he hoped would end in a "victory of the masses."[115] Similarly, he thought that the terrible war that had just been experienced and that had involved the entire people could result only in profound changes in social life, in the relationships between rich and poor. The people had not fought the war so that things should remain as they were in August 1914, he said in effect to the metalworkers of Dalmine, who on 16 March 1919 took over the Franchi-Gregorini factory but, in accordance with productionist principles, did not stop work.[116]

A week after his speech at Dalmine, the Fascist movement was founded in Milan. Among the seven founders who were present at a preparatory meeting on 21 March were three former socialists—Mussolini, Ferrari, and Ferradini—and two syndicalists—Michele Bianchi and Marco Giampaoli. On 23 March, the founding meeting of fascism, at which Marinetti was also present,[117] took place in the Piazza San Sepolcro. Mussolini reasserted his adoption of the positions of the UIL: he took over its productionist ideas and demanded the confiscation of wealth illegally acquired during the war. His program, as he rightly said, represented a national syndicalism.[118]

Undoubtedly the intellectual heritage of revolutionary syndicalism formed the basis of the Fascist ideology in the beginning. Alceste De Ambris, secretary general of the UIL, whose regulations forbade membership of a political party, was careful to point this out. On 9 June 1919, De Ambris gave a lecture to the Fascists of Milan, who, as we saw, included his celebrated proposal of partial expropriation in the official program of their movement. In a speech following this lecture, Mussolini expressed himself in a forthright manner. "The Italian nation," he said, "is like a large family. The cash boxes are empty; who is going to fill them? We, perhaps? We, who possess neither houses, nor vehicles, nor banks, nor mines, nor land, nor factories, nor money? Whoever is able to, must pay. Whoever is able to, will have to pay up. . . . The hour of sacrifices for all has come. Whoever has not given his blood, will give his money."[119]

With regard to the internal problems of Italian society and the question of the territories still claimed by Italy, revolutionary syndicalism provided nascent fascism with its ideological content. De Ambris with regard to partial expropriation and Olivetti with regard to Fiume and Dalmatia faithfully reflected the positions adopted by Mussolini. The Fascist program of June 1919 still included corporatist, communalistic, and regionalistic principles previously expressed in *Il rinnovamento* and *L'internazionale*.[120]

However, in 1920, the year of factory occupations, the Italian internal crisis assumed dramatic proportions. Both among the old socialist Left and among the nationalist Right the idea gained ground that the solution to this crisis would have to be a radical one. On the Left, the consensus began to shift in the direction of a Communist type of solution; on the Right, there was opposition to any reform that would interfere with the rights of property owners. The liberal center, for its part, in the best Giolitti tradition, wanted some kind of compromise. The interventionist Left, which included fascism and sought to be a movement for reassembling and redeeming the entire nation, refused to allow the affluent to crush the workers, just as it would not countenance a social revolution.

But the hour had passed for half measures, and the moment had come when a choice had to be made. By the summer of 1920, it had become obvious that fascism had begun to move away from its left-wing revolutionary origins. Mussolini asked the workers, on behalf of the nation, to make the same sacrifices as he had demanded of the industrialists.[121] Finally, productivism was regarded as all-important. If the national interest required that socialism be opposed, if modernization, economic growth, and the capacity of the country to maintain its position in the world required the suppression of labor organizations, if the landowners had to be supported in order to prevent the breakup of society and the outbreak of a social revolution that could only lead to civil war and a national disaster, then it followed that fascism had to become an apologist for the bourgeoisie—for the entire bourgeoisie. As a result of this evolution, which reflected not only the pressure of events but also a very powerful internal logic, the National Fascist party, founded in November 1921, bore little resemblance to the original Fasci of 1914 or to those of 1919. From being an elitist movement, still very close to its origins, it became a great mass party. This change recalls that which took place in the socialist parties at the beginning of the century: a shift to the Right is the usual price of success. Like all political parties preparing to take office, fascism toned itself down considerably. Thus, on the eve of coming to power, the movement had a very different appearance from that it had displayed in the Piazza San Sepolcro.

In 1919–1920, the revolutionary syndicalists and socialists who had followed Mussolini in leaving the Socialist party still represented the core of the movement. They were the only professional politicians in the original fascism, and their experience was invaluable. From their syndicalist background, these people brought to the movement a revolutionary enthusiasm and a faith in the power of active elites. They had no doubt about the matter: it was the determination of a minority, they held, that had drawn the inert masses into the European conflict, and the will of a revolutionary avant-garde had forced the hand of democracy. There was no reason to stop when things were going so well. These syndicalists, however, were soon obliged to acknowledge the fact that the masses would not follow them. The elections of November 1919 were proof of it, and at the second congress of the movement, in May 1920, Cesare Rossi drew the practical conclusion: it was futile to try to detach the proletariat from socialism.[122] This meant that an old idea, conceived long before the commencement of hostilities, had proved to be more valid than ever: if one wished to make a revolution, one would have to find the manpower somewhere other than among the proletariat.

The idea that the concept of nation would have to replace that of the proletariat began long before August 1914. The first to invent it were the French Sorelians. But the war, that school for those qualities of sacrifice and abnegation so admired by the revolutionary syndicalists, nationalists, and futurists, created a new reservoir of energies, hopes, and mingled sentiments. It was thus to these men who had learned not only how to obey but also, and more especially, how to command, that Mussolini now addressed himself. In August 1919, *Il popolo d'Italia*, ceasing to describe itself as a socialist journal, became "the journal of the combatants and the producers." Two years later, fascism turned toward the leaders of the combatants, especially the officers of the shock troops, the celebrated *arditi*. These young officers henceforth played a highly important role in the progressive transformation of the movement. A little later, the development of agrarian fascism demonstrated this evolution in an even more obvious manner. The expansion of the movement and its transformation were also greatly assisted by the mobilization of certain hitherto little politicized strata of the petit bourgeoisie.[123] Thus, the shift to the Right continued.

But this process resulted not only from the changes that had taken place in the social composition of fascism, which continually embraced new elements that had never had any connection with revolutionary syndicalism or the Socialist party, but also from a decision on the part of Mussolini to transform his movement into a party—a massive party of government. As an experienced politician, he knew that nothing could be achieved in the Italy of his day in opposition to the traditional social forces: the army, the bureaucracy, the legal system, business circles, the monarchy, and the church. The former leader of the revolutionary Left had learned his lesson from the failure of all the revolutionaries: the occupations of factories had hardly proved any more successful than the Fiume adventure, and the dream of a republic of Soviets had been swept away by the same winds as had carried off the Carta del Carnaro. He therefore began to seek the support of the real centers of power.

Moreover, Mussolini had to deal with the divisions that, following the elections of 1921 and the Pact of Pacification—the truce with the socialists—appeared in the movement between "left" and "right"; the agrarians, the city dwellers, and the "provincials"; the "politicians" and the "military." The latter were in confrontation over who was to control the Fascist shock troops. In this confusion of tendencies, pressure groups, and temperaments, Mussolini's powers of leadership were severely tested; the opponents of normalization, led by Dino Grandi and Pietro Marsich, the provincial leader of the Fascists of the Veneto, wanted a great revolutionary movement that would remain extraneous to parliamentary politics.[124] In opposing Mussolini, they exploited the D'Annunzian mystique. That was one more important reason to transform the movement as quickly as possible into a respectable party, capable of filling the political vacuum that was coming into being. In October 1922, this was accomplished.

Mussolini's seizure of power, as we know, was not the result of a coup d'état but the outcome of a political process lasting several months. This process was possible not because of an abdication of the state to Fascist violence and cunning, but owing to the comprehension and even sympathy shown to the Fascists by a large segment of the politicians, the intellectuals, the molders of opinion, and the social elites in general. Fascist agitation, whether in the industrial centers or in the countryside, the high schools, the universities, or among war veterans, did not pose any real problem to the authorities; the balance of forces that existed allowed this agitation to be stopped at any moment. The same applied to that grotesque expedition called the march on Rome. Poorly equipped, badly fed, floundering in the mud amid torrential rain, the Fascists, faced with the well-organized forces of order, would have had no chance of succeeding had they not encountered political authorities with little determination to resist. In other words, it was necessary that on 28 October 1922 someone should have had sufficient willpower to assume responsibilities. Someone had to want to stop fascism, just as in the years 1921 and 1922 someone in Rome should have had the courage to support those determined provincial prefects who quite easily thwarted Fascist initiatives.

The authorities' lack of decisiveness in opposing fascism may be explained neither by the weakness of the state (the means of control worked sufficiently well when anyone cared to use them) nor by Mussolini's ability to maneuver. It is true that this outstanding professional managed things marvelously. In the strange and bizarre quagmire of Italian parliamentary democracy, he swam like a fish in water. The Fascist movement was not exempt from the rules of Italian politics: Mussolini had to face a possible collapse of the bases of his own power. He had to neutralize the danger that D'Annunzio represented for him, and he had at all costs to prevent the formation of an anti-Fascist front. In relation to these difficulties one can perceive the depth of the impregnation of the political and social elites by the Fascist ideology.

If the collapse of liberal democracy in Italy was due to a deficiency of willpower and a lack of confidence in the capacity of the regime to resist pressures, these very weaknesses were due to the esteem in which fascism was held. Among the politicians and intellectuals many did not like its "squadrista" methods, but far fewer did not sympathize with certain objectives of fascism or certain aspects of its ideology. This explains, first, how the king could call on Mussolini, on behalf of the liberal establishment, to end the crisis of the regime, and second, how the Fascist leader was subsequently able to maintain himself in office.

Indeed, before 30 October 1922 and in the two years after he came to power, Mussolini's situation was often precarious. The Fascist adventure sometimes nearly came to an end, at least provisionally. The first occasion was in 1922; when there was a possibility, at that time, of forming a broad anti-Fascist coalition with socialist participation, a letter from Giolitti to the editor of the journal *Tribuna* brutally snuffed out this final manifestation of energy. From that time onward, the question was no longer whether the Fascists would be represented in the government but whether they would demand the most important posts or be content to be less conspicuous.[125]

A second opportunity of ousting the Fascists occurred two years later. The assassination on 10 June 1924 of the socialist deputy Matteotti, whose famous speech on 30 May was much resented by the Fascists, resulted in a serious crisis. Matteotti's strength of character and courage were legendary. His abduction in the heart of the capital gave rise to strong feelings. Reactions to the event threw the entourage of the head of government into a panic, and even moderate Fascist ministers became rebellious. If liberals had intervened with the king, it would no doubt have been sufficient to persuade him to replace Mussolini, but Giolitti's friends were as yet still too well disposed toward fascism to demand the departure of its leader.

However, the position adopted by Benedetto Croce, the country's leading intellectual, and, where the outside world was concerned, the most celebrated representative of Italian culture, was most significant. At that critical moment, Croce believed that fascism, despite everything, had done a great deal of good, and that it would be inadvisable to work for its downfall. On the contrary, he claimed, one should give it time to sober down and complete the process of normalization. On 26 June, the senator gave the Mussolini government a vote of confidence.[126] This raised hand of one of the most famous Europeans of his time in favor of the dictator to be, already two years in office and guilty of a horrible crime, at a time when the regime (whose true nature could no longer be ignored) was particularly vulnerable, is revealing. It was an outstanding symbol of the ambivalent attitudes to fascism of that European intelligentsia, so cultured and refined, whose faith in the virtues of liberal democracy had long since disappeared.

THE STATE AND DICTATORSHIP: FROM NATIONAL
SOCIALISM TO FASCISM

Of all the main elements of the Fascist ideology, the concept of state was the last to be formed. There were historical as well as purely ideological reasons for this. The generation of politicians who had fought in the war had discovered the almost unimaginable power of the state. But those people who came from Marxism—even a Marxism revised and re-created by the Sorelians—accustomed themselves only with difficulty to the extensive use of political power. Revolutionary syndicalism gave an important place to authority and was profoundly disdainful of democracy, but its intellectual makeup did not include the exercise of state terrorism. This was a course of action that the Fascists, like the Communists, learned on the job. In this domain, the experience of the war was decisive: there one learned that the state's capacity to intervene was practically unlimited.

However, where the delimitation of the essential functions of the state was concerned, there was a continuity in this sphere as in others. Like his revolutionary syndicalist mentors who had now become his partners in launching the Fascist movement, Mussolini based his conception of the state on his idea of capitalism. Not only did he not question private property, but, having assimilated the teachings of Sorel and Arturo Labriola, he sought to divest the state of all economic functions. "The state ought not to be a 'producer,'" wrote Mussolini in July 1919, "for whoever speaks of a state necessarily speaks of a bureaucracy, and a bureaucracy is antiproductionist and parasitic by definition. The state must not create obstacles to the resumption of economic life."[127] For Mussolini, politics and economics were two separate spheres. Mussolini's analysis was sufficiently subtle to assert that the state could remain unchanged while the regime was radically transformed.[128] What he wished to indicate was that capitalism was not tied to any particular political regime.[129] It followed that it was possible to liquidate political liberalism with its "bourgeois" values of political freedom and respect for the rights of people while preserving the economic aspects of capitalist civilization. This conclusion led Mussolini, in January 1921, to state the following principles, which remained unchanged throughout the Fascist period: "The state must exercise all possible and imaginable controls, but it must renounce any form of economic management. Even the so-called public services must not be its sole monopoly." And again: "In short, the position of fascism where the state is concerned is as follows: the struggle against the economic-monopolistic state is indispensable for the development of the forces of the nation. One must return to the political-judicial state, for those are its true functions. In other words, one must strengthen the political state and progressively dismantle the economic state."[130]

In his first speech in parliament in June 1921, Mussolini reiterated these principles in two concise formulas: "But I tell you at once: we oppose with all our might socialization, state ownership, and collectivization." And, as against this: "We must reduce the state to its pure and simple judicial and political expression."[131] If this concept of the state was not modified in the years before Mussolini came to power, it was nevertheless filled out. The idea of the "political-judicial state" was developed in a speech on the occasion of the founding of the National Fascist party at the congress of Rome on 8 November 1921. The state was described as the sole source of sovereignty, the unquestioned arbiter of national policies. In this speech one can already find the first concrete elements of corporatism.[132] This was the moment when Mussolini described the outline of the future Fascist state, based on the ideological principles of the Fascist party. Once again, he referred to his two great intellectual mentors and fellow travelers, Arturo Labriola and Enrico Leone. "The syndicalist writer," he wrote in November 1921, in reference to the latter, "has understood that fascism is a potential state that tends to replace an existing state."[133] Indeed, Leone, the theoretician of revolutionary syndicalism, had few doubts about the nature of the coming revolution or about the results it would produce. On this point, intellectuals like Leone were in agreement with the political leaders, including the one who at one time appeared to be the rival of Mussolini: Dino Grandi.

According to Mussolini, the Fascist conception of the state differed from the Communist one only in its substitution of the terms of reference; thus, nation replaced class. The state had to be centralistic and unitarian.[134] As the Fascists conceived it, the state was the "judicial incarnation of the nation,"[135] but one that was solely judicial. These principles were spelled out in the "Programs and Statutes of the National Fascist Party" of December 1921. By and large, they demonstrated a vision similar to that of the national-socialist synthesis of *La lupa* or the Cercle Proudhon.

There was a remarkable continuity between the works of the revolutionary syndicalists, published at the beginning of the century, and those of Mussolini. A similar continuity existed between Mussolini's writings in *Utopia* and those in *Gerarchia*, a doctrinal review of the Fascist party founded at the end of January 1922 with the purpose of clarifying the ideological principles of the new party. In an important programmatic article, published in June 1922, Mussolini explained the basic principles of his action.[136] All his ideas have been extensively expounded in *Utopia*. In the same way, elitist, authoritarian ideas and opposition to the "monopolistic" state in the economic sphere had already characterized the thinking of the new leadership of the National Fascist party, which made its declaration of principles in November 1921. Fascism now felt itself properly equipped to respond to the crisis of the state.[137] A few weeks after the appearance of Mussolini's article in *Gerarchia*, Giacomo Lumbroso expounded these ideas in another issue of the Fascist review. The party, he wrote, announced its readiness to take over the government and proceed to the fascistization of the state.[138] Throughout the summer and autumn of 1922, Mussolini and his associates declared their intention of liquidating the existing regime and replacing it with a system that would provide a total alternative to both democracy and socialism.[139] This was the substance of the two famous programmatic speeches Mussolini delivered in Udine on 20 September 1922 and in Milan on 4 October.[140] These two harangues prepared the way for the speech in Naples in which Mussolini called upon his troops to march on Rome.

On the eve of Mussolini's nomination as head of government, Camillo Pellizzi, a professor of philosophy and a disciple of Gentile, described in *Gerarchia* the conceptual framework of the great antimaterialist revolution that was about to take place.

> Fascism—that is, the practical negation of historical materialism and, still more, the negation of democratic individualism, of the rationalism of the Enlightenment—fascism is the affirmation of the principles of tradition, hierarchy, authority, and individual sacrifice in view of a historical ideal. It is the practical affirmation of the value of the spiritual and historical personality (of man, the nation, humanity) as opposed to and in opposition to reason and the abstract and empirical individuality of the men of the Enlightenment, the positivists, and the utilitarians.[141]

The philosophy of fascism was thus fully elaborated even before the movement came to power. One finds in it all the elements of integral nationalism combined, in a synthesis developed over a long period, with the antimaterialist and antirationalist revision of Marxism carried out by French and Italian revolutionary syndicalism. In this respect, Mussolini's political actions no more represented a coarse pragmatism or a vulgar opportunism than did those of Lenin or Léon Blum. Indeed, the realities of the Italian regime of the interwar period were a faithful reflection of the principles that Mussolini and his associates professed at the moment when they were the first people in the twentieth century to terminate a liberal democratic regime.

Italian fascism—as can be clearly seen—was the product of a number of different but convergent elements. It should be pointed out that the very important ideological contribution of the nationalist movement also reached maturity before fascism came to power. After the synthesis represented by *La lupa*, there came the contribution of Alfredo Rocco. This highly regarded nationalist jurist to whom Corradini always paid tribute and who was minister of justice from January 1925 to June 1932, played a major role in the codification of fascism and the translation of its principles into legislation. His conception of the state and his antidemocratic, totalitarian ideas were also virtually formed by 1914; the Italian specialists in the field have known this for several years.[142] The heir to Corradini, he soon eclipsed Corradini. Founder of the Nationalist Association, a mediocre writer but a gifted orator, Corradini had now completed his task. When the state became Fascist, it was no longer a time for speeches, especially as it was now the Duce who harangued the crowds. What the regime needed was a codification of the nationalist and Fascist principles and their transposition into laws and structures of government. No one was more suited to this undertaking than Alfredo Rocco. Mussolini's and Rocco's ideas began to converge from the first months of 1914 and came together with the foundation of the National Fascist party in November 1921. Only then were the Fasci di Combattimento, founded in March 1919 by Mussolini with the collaboration of the revolutionary syndicalists and futurists on the one hand and of the members of Corradini's Nationalist Association on the other, able firmly to establish the new movement. The essence of Alfredo Rocco's thought was a mystical and organic view of the nation, an absolute affirmation of the supremacy of the collectivity over the individual, and a total rejection of liberal democracy, its principles, and its institutions.[143] This was quite sufficient to serve as an ideological common denominator between these two men of totally different backgrounds. It only remained to do as Mussolini urged and to replace the principle of popular sovereignty with that of the sovereignty of the state for the primacy of the state to be ensured.[144]

Throughout the summer and autumn of 1922, the collaborators of *Gerarchia* tried to translate the philosophical principles of fascism into concrete terms; no political party more brilliantly described its objectives and the means by which they could be achieved. Never until that time, it would seem, was a more open political debate engaged in by a revolutionary movement preparing to assail democracy. Not only were general principles formulated, but a veritable program of government was proposed before Mussolini had crossed the threshold of the Presidency of the Council.[145] When in power, the Fascist party used the full apparatus of the state to put into practice its vision of the politically ideal. When the Duce was facing innumerable difficulties and was attempting, with his usual brutality and determination, to set up the Fascist dictatorship, Camillo Pellizzi, during the great crisis of 1924, described the revolution in progress as follows:

> For the moment, we conceive of the State neither as an association of individuals/citizens nor as a quasi-contract that would be fulfilled in the course of history. But if we have to describe this institution, we see it as the concretization of a predominant historical *personality*, as a social instrument usable for the realization of a myth. The state is thus not a fixed reality but a dynamic process that cannot lay claim to movement unless, in another way, it is its own continuation. Nor can it be the *renewal* of a myth unless it represents the dialectical and tragic unity of previous myths.
>
> This word "state" is inapplicable to our concept. In our nonstate, the law is dependent on the final myth, not the initial myth, and the final aim can only be, in its way, a new unity of previous myths.[146]

This mythical conception of politics, or rather this faith in the power of myth as the motive force of history, is the key to the Fascist view of the world. In effect, everything else derived from it. However, in attempting to apply its principles, fascism, like every political movement that comes to power, encountered innumerable obstacles: the hour of triumph is also necessarily a time of compromise.

In this, fascism did not differ from any other political movement that attained office. Mussolini came to terms with the existing social forces, and the process of the fascistization of the state and society lasted throughout the 1920s. The obstacles to be surmounted were tremendous, and the imposition of dictatorship met endless difficulties. To the degree that fascism increased its hold, the socialist revolutionary heritage was weakened. Fascism in office no longer resembled the fascism of 1919 and still less the revolutionary syndicalism of 1910. The Duce also found great difficulty in remaining consistent, ten years later, with his speech of 23 March. But was bolshevism in office an exact application of the ideas that, ten years before the fall of the Winter Palace, had preoccupied Plekhanov, Trotsky, and Lenin? Coming to terms with reality, however, did not mean that the National Fascist party came to power without an ideological framework. Quite the contrary. From the beginning of their political activity, Mussolini and his associates possessed a clear idea of the objectives they wished to attain. They came to power equipped with a coherent ideological system that was intended as a total alternative to liberalism and Marxism. Their conception of the structures to be set up in place of liberal democracy was one of great coherence, and they set to work without delay. Mature fascism was composed of elements created before the war and synthesized into a solid whole in the course of the war and in the first years following the armistice.

Undoubtedly, as fascism became the state, resistance to its revolutionary-syndicalist heritage greatly altered the relative proportion of the national and the social within it. The Mussolinian dictatorship, steeped in the holy horror that all the components of fascism in all periods felt for democracy, finally produced a regime from which all elements of socialist origin were banished. Yet the Mussolini regime of the 1930s was much closer to the ideological synthesis of *La lupa* or the Cercle Proudhon than the Stalin regime was to the original Marxism. The evolution of fascism throughout the 1920s took place in relation to primary objectives fixed, ten years before the march on Rome, by the protagonists of an unprecedented type of revolution, one that was antiliberal, antimaterialist, and anti-Marxist—a political, moral, and spiritual revolution, a revolution for the entire nation.

From a Cultural Rebellion to a
Political Revolution

ON THE EVE of the accession to power of Italian fascism, its ideological corpus still bore some of the revolutionary and nonconformist characteristics of its origins. There was great uncertainty at the beginning of the 1920s, when a general permutation of people and ideas confused a public opinion already disoriented by the postwar crises. Once again, it was Sorel who more than anyone else embodied the complexity of reaction and intellectual confusion of a generation that saw any remaining certainties disintegrate. In September 1919, he published his celebrated "For Lenin" as an appendix to the fourth edition of *Réflexions*. The October Revolution, he declared, meant that a new opportunity for bringing down the "bourgeois democracies" had presented itself.[1] Eighteen months later, another young revolutionary force was assailing democracy. "The Fascists are not entirely wrong to invoke my opinions," wrote Sorel, "for their power very clearly demonstrates the value of triumphant violence."[2]

Undoubtedly the cult of violence united all the dissident groups—futurists, Sorelians, and nationalists—that were attempting to set up fascism. All these nonconformists came together in their rejection of the established order, the existing ideologies, and the prevailing aesthetics. Sorel and Marinetti were very close to one another; they were subject to the same influences and often drew from the same sources. Marinetti was undoubtedly influenced by Marxist and anarchistic doctrines, by the aesthetic theories of avant-garde movements such as *art nouveau*, the *Jugendstil*, and *Die Brücke*, and by the new poetics. But the founder of futurism was above all affected by Nietzsche, Bergson, and William James[3]—three people whose thought had molded that of Sorel in a decisive manner.

According to Noémie Blumenkranz, it was Bergson, with his philosophy of *élan vital* (life force) and its adjuncts—the dynamism and continuity of matter, the duration of psychic states, the infallibility of instinct, the superiority of intuition to discursive intelligence, and, above all, the role assigned to pure perception—who had the greatest influence on Marinetti. Marinetti also took a great deal from Nietzsche and, later, from the pragmatism of William James, whom Papini introduced to Italy in 1905. James influenced Marinetti through his conception of action (which he regarded as superior to thought) and through his idea that truth was defined by the practical possibilities of action in the actual world.[4] One recognizes that these were also some of Sorel's main sources.

In Europe in the first years of the century, Sorelianism and futurism constituted two aspects of the revolutionary current. However, unlike other cultural movements also engaged in political rebellion, futurism, thanks to Marinetti, became a political force in the strict sense of the term.[5] The synthesis that fused Sorelian revolutionary syndicalism, radical nationalism, and futurism was clearly not the product of sympathy alone and was not restricted to affinities of language and temperament. No, this was a synthesis on a truly basic level. It is not difficult to understand, wrote Giovanni Lista, why futurism recognized its image in the current known as anarchist-syndicalist, where it found the myths of action and violence that it wanted, rather than in pacifist anarchy. Marinetti, for instance, detested the utopian reveries of the anarchists, their "sweet tenderness, sister of cowardice."[6] In this, he was entirely in agreement with Sorel and his disciples. Moreover, throughout the first decade of the century, his calls for struggle, for violence, and for a forward-looking orientation found an echo or were quite naturally taken up in the revolutionary syndicalist journals, whether it was *Avanguardia socialista*, *Il divenire sociale*, or *Pagine libere*. Marinetti actively collaborated in *La demolizione*, an anarchist journal with a revolutionary-syndicalist orientation which Ottavio Dinale published first in Switzerland and then, from 1907 on, in Italy. On 15 March 1909, Dinale's journal published the "Futurist Manifesto," and close relations were established between the two men in the first year of the futurist movement. Dinale, it should be recalled, was a major figure of revolutionary syndicalism, one of the organizers of the first Peasant Leagues. A friend of Mussolini, he undoubtedly had a certain influence on the young socialist leader. A new series of *La demolizione* began in 1910; among its principal collaborators were Marinetti, Paolo Orano, Alceste De Ambris, and Luigi Fabbi.

It is probable that Marinetti, who had just ceased publication of his review *Poesia*, now participated in the financing of the revolutionary syndicalist journal. In February 1910, he once again proclaimed his religion of violence: "We must love and encourage war, the world's sole hygiene, a superb upsurge of enthusiasm and generosity, a noble bath of heroism, in the absence of which the races slumber in a lazy egoism, in economic arrivism, in a leprosy of the spirit and of the will."[7] A month later, he took another important step in publishing in *La demolizione* a text steeped in Nietzschean rhetoric in which, in the name of a violence creative of the future, he proposed setting up a common front uniting futurist revolt with Sorelian revolutionary aspirations. This text exemplifies not only the Nietzschean side of Marinetti's thought, but also its Sorelian aspects: Marinetti regarded the idea of the future as an absolute myth and thus as an image that generated the action necessary for further development.[8]

Like Sorel, Marinetti did not make a proposal for a new society. Nothing was said about the world that would come into being as a result of revolutionary action. With both men one remains on the level of the "aesthetization of politics," to use Walter Benjamin's expression, which leads directly to fascism. The manifesto of 16 March 1910, noted G. Lista, was quite explicit in this respect:

> Friends, brethren, let us recognize once and for all the light of our incendiary flames! We want a fatherland, we want a fatherland that is great and strong. Do you not instinctively sense that you have a weapon with you when you feel especially fired by your wonderful ideal? Does not anyone amongst you feel himself to be the soldier of an approaching battle? Are you really sure that your children will not one day reproach you for having brought them up in neglect and disdain of the greatest of aesthetics: that of frenzied battalions armed to the teeth?[9]

The Marinettian explosion of nationalism left the revolutionary syndicalists behind. After the appearance of this last manifesto, entitled "Our Common Enemies," Dinale's journal ceased to publish Marinetti and confined itself to a cautious review of his novel *Mafarka le futuriste*, which had just been translated into Italian. A few weeks later, however, in May 1910, *La demolizione* initiated an inquiry concerning the "foundation of a revolutionary party." This move was motivated, once again, by the need to respond to the crisis of Italian revolutionary syndicalism.[10] But most interesting of all was the fact that at that precise moment some circles of the nonconformist extreme Left began to move away from their traditional antipatriotism and to reject the antimilitaristic extremism of Gustave Hervé. These people were beginning to become aware of the mobilizing power of the idea of the fatherland and wished to place it at the service of the proletariat and the revolution.

At that moment, when the "revolutionary nationalist" trend began to come into being within revolutionary syndicalism, Marinetti decided to give a lecture on "the beauty and necessity of violence" and to canvass for a seat in parliament in an electoral constituency in Piedmont. Within that constituency, a political current was in the process of being formed around the journal *Il tricolore*, advocating an alliance between nationalism and revolutionary syndicalism. Marinetti gave his lecture in Naples, Milan, and Parma, where Alceste De Ambris published his weekly journal *L'internazionale*, the organ of the revolutionary syndicalist movement. Printing the more or less complete text of Marinetti's lecture, De Ambris praised this "magnificent and superb hymn to violence," this splendid incitation to life "in the midst of the cemetery of Italian existence." Essentially, this lecture was a defense of war and a hymn to the fatherland, condemning the mean and petty utilitarianism of reformist democracy and, finally, extolling the "destructive gesture of the anarchists," the general strike and the revolution.[11]

La demolizione ceased to appear when Marinetti ended his lecture tour. Two months later, in October 1910, Paolo Orano founded the weekly journal *La lupa*. Also in October 1910, another initiative, originating in nonconformist circles, resulted in the creation of the Associazione nazionale d'avanguardia. Marinetti was one of the founding members. Finally, in December of that year, the Associazione Nazionalista Italiana was founded, with Corradini as its leading figure. Marinetti joined the new organization, which later became the Italian Nationalist party. In many ways, Marinetti was the point of connection between all the rebels and dissidents who were organizing themselves at that period in order to overthrow the existing order.

The Marinettian form of revolution was based on the revolutionary orientations of the Sorelians from the time they discovered the uprooting power of nationalism. It was in fact in revolutionary syndicalism and nationalism that Marinetti found the only genuine subversive forces of Latin Europe. Thus, there can be no doubt about the matter; some years before the explosion of 1914, the Fascist synthesis was already taking shape. The new aesthetics to a considerable degree explains both the power of attraction of fascism and its ambiguity. Not all futurists became Fascists; at the end of 1924 Marinetti made an attempt to bring the futurists together, but this only served to demonstrate the breakup of the movement and the refusal of some of his associates who had followed him into antisocialist, anticlerical, and antimonarchist interventionism to involve themselves in fascism.[12]

The Russian futurists, for their part, under Marinetti's approving eye, participated in the revolutionary ferment of their country. Malevitch, who was not a futurist but whose written work shows undeniable signs of Marinetti's influence, was so bold as to defend, right into the revolutionary period, one of the principal founders of fascism. In 1923 he still quoted whole passages of the "Futurist Manifesto" of 1909. He referred specifically to Marinetti in 1929 in his didactic work *Le Nouvel Art*, which appeared in several issues of a Ukrainian futurist journal.[13] For both of these men, inventors and promoters of the movement of rebellion in the arts and profoundly involved in the political battle, the main thing was the possibility that had appeared of dealing a fatal blow to the existing system.

In the four years preceding the war, Marinetti traveled a great deal and was untiring in his efforts. There were lectures and meetings, and his militancy in favor of the Libyan campaign was as great as his enthusiasm at the time of the siege of Adrianople. During the long period of agitation in 1914–1915, he was everywhere and was present at all demonstrations. The moment Italy declared war, he asked to be conscripted; he returned from the front wounded and decorated. Everyone agrees he was a courageous and highly competent officer.

Some of the most gifted futurists died in the war, among them the architect Sant'Elia, who heralded Le Corbusier and was one of his sources of inspiration, and the painter Boccioni. Many fought bravely in elite battalions, including the famous Explorers of Death, the core of the *Arditi* corps. They all had the feeling that they had gained the right to offer their opinion on politics and society. But the avant-gardist war heroes did not lead the great postwar movement of revolt: the futurist phase of fascism did not last beyond its seizure of power. Nevertheless, despite the increasingly conservative character that fascism was to adopt throughout the 1920s, Marinetti remained loyal to Mussolini right to the end. A volunteer for the Ethiopian campaign and then for the Russian one, Marinetti never ceased to sing the praises of the Duce.[14]

In June 1914, the appearance of the review *Blast* officially announced the birth of vorticism, another avant-gardist movement, connected to futurism. The term originated with the poet Ezra Pound, who compared the London art world to a vortex. Later, he used the term to describe the art of Wyndham Lewis.[15] Vorticism helps to illustrate the nature of the affinities between the cultural revolt and the rise of fascism. The career of Ezra Pound, an American who emigrated to England and then, in 1925, to Italy is well known. One of the most influential and controversial figures of twentieth-century poetry and today universally recognized as a great name in modern literature, Pound became known to the public at large through his propaganda broadcasts on behalf of fascism and Nazism during the Second World War. Found guilty and confined to an American mental hospital, he returned to Italy in 1958.[16]

Having written a book to Hitler's glory in 1931,[17] the writer and painter Wyndham Lewis decided, on the eve of the Second World War, to opt for an irreproachable anti-Nazism. Yet he never denied any of the convictions that had formerly led him to sing the praises of the future German chancellor. An American who, like Pound, had emigrated to England, Lewis was one of the most imaginative British writers of the first half of the century.[18] Certainly, he never represented himself, like Marinetti or later Drieu La Rochelle or Brasillach, as a committed Fascist intellectual, but he was a good example of the fellow traveler, the modernist intellectual drawn by the vitality, energy, and power of that phenomenon of antimaterialist, antibourgeois, and anti-Marxist rebellion that was Nazism.

To Lewis, Nazism was first a response to communism, and he felt that the concept of race was a welcome antidote to the idea of class. In his opinion, the Nazi program was something that all the ruling classes in Europe should have welcomed, as it constituted an excellent plan of defense of the old continent against the danger posed by the non-European world. Moreover,

Lewis found in Nazi ideology some of his favorite themes, notably, a hatred of parliamentary and bourgeois democracy, a horror of money and finance, and a cult of youth. On all these points, as in his view of class struggle and his disdain for bourgeois culture, he never altered his opinion until his death in 1957. And even when he changed his verdict on Hitler's personality—not until 1939—Lewis remained convinced that fascism (he did not always distinguish between fascism and Nazism) constituted the most adequate and complete expression of the opposition to the status quo.[19]

Strictly speaking, futurism and vorticism were two distinct movements. Their respective styles and some of their convictions often brought them into opposition. Moreover, the vorticists were eager, especially after June 1914, to differentiate themselves from the futurists. Yet, at the same time they sought to benefit from the extensive publicity that Marinetti gained for futurism. Thus, they participated in the great futurist demonstrations, banquets, and parades. It is true that, where political thought was concerned, the differences between futurism and vorticism were not of great consequence. It would be wrong, however, to imagine that differences did not exist, even if, outside the circles of writers, painters, and musicians, few people in 1914 really troubled to distinguish between futurist violence and vorticist brutality. Violence, wrote Laurette Veza, is unbridled passion, impetuosity, vehemence, whereas brutality is primitive harshness. Less pure than brutality, violence is tainted with empathy. Like the philosopher and art critic T. E. Hulme, Lewis and Pound rejected the phenomenon of empathy.[20] They regarded themselves as primitive precisely to the degree that they refused to appeal to the affectivity of the spectator or reader. To futurist intuition, the vorticists opposed instinct. Vorticism professed to represent energy and a tendency to austerity and nudity. In making this claim, it set itself against futurism, which it considered superficial, romantic, spectacular, melodramatic, and sentimental. Lewis and Pound reproached Marinetti for his romanticism. For all these reasons that were known to the initiated, and also because of a natural desire to assert their own character, in June 1914 Lewis and Pound decided to break officially with Marinetti.

Despite these differences, however, futurism and vorticism appeared as two parallel movements, very close to one another. Both made a frontal attack on decadence, academicism, frozen aestheticism, tepidity, and softness in general. Futurism and vorticism had the same watchword, *energy*, and the same objective: to cure England and Italy of their languor, their aesthetic leprosy, and to revitalize through violence the sick sensibility of an apathetic generation.[21]

Even if vorticism cannot exactly be regarded as an offshoot of Italian futurism, it is probable that without the enormous interest Marinetti's ideas aroused, without his expansionism, his lecture tours, and his boundless energy, the idea of an English vorticist movement producing its manifestos, its journal, and its own exhibitions would never have come into being, let alone taken hold.[22] In March 1910 Marinetti gave his first lecture in London. He praised the patriotism of the English and their love of freedom but condemned their hypocritical prudery and snobbery. He returned to the British capital in April of that year and then in the following year to speak, this time, about Italy and the Libyan question. In March 1912, Marinetti, accompanied by Boccioni, Carrà, and Russolo, was again in London for the first futurist exhibition, which was held at the Sackville Gallery. He displayed, on this occasion, his usual patriotism and nationalism. Two years later, in the spring of 1914, he appeared once more on the banks of the Thames: Lewis hailed him as the "Cromwell of our time."[23]

This enthusiasm did not last long. Soon Lewis launched a counteroffensive to gather English artists under a non-Italian banner. In that spring of 1914, he founded the Rebel Art Center, and in June he decided to create a movement that would be separate from futurism.[24] However, what really matters for the historian of ideas are two elements of far greater importance than mere national susceptibilities.

In the first place, futurism could not escape time, and its very name suggested that the movement was situated within time. Writing on the subject of time and Western man in 1928, Lewis said of the futurists that "they were thorough adepts of the time-philosophy: and Marinetti, their prophet, was a *pur sang* bergsonian."[25] In the second place, Marinetti was an iconoclast who broke with the entire cultural legacy of the past. The vorticists viewed him as a romantic and an impressionist. Ezra Pound, for his part, always remained attached to the cultural heritage, as did T. E. Hulme, who was a real theoretician of revolutionary classicism. In fact, these differences were unimportant compared to the fact that in the political sphere they had no real significance. Marinetti and Pound were Fascists to the end, and Wyndham Lewis, less committed and more clear-sighted, never denied a single one of his ideas. Marinetti the Bergsonian futurist and Pound the vorticist developed a rejection and hatred of what exists, whether political, aesthetic, or moral. Vorticists and futurists were in all respects avant-garde revolutionaries: the former traditionalistic and "classical," and the latter impenitent romantics. They all glorified the violence extolled by that other traditionalist and "classical" revolutionary, the writer of the famous *Réflexions*. It was no accident if Hulme took the initiative of translating *Réflexions sur la violence* into English, Hulme who was the intellectual mentor of Lewis and Pound, and also of W. B. Yeats and T. S. Eliot, two other fellow travelers of fascism.

Killed in the war in September 1917 at the age of thirty-four, Thomas Ernest Hulme was an exceptional personality. Even if it would be excessive to compare him as a thinker to Socrates and Plato, as his friend, the well-known sculptor Jacob Epstein did, there is no doubt that this young philosopher was marked out, in the words of Bergson, "to produce interesting and important works."[26] In describing Hulme as one of the most influential minds of his generation and as the leading figure of the intellectual scene of his time, his present biographer seems only to be repeating an opinion that was widespread in Anglo-American circles of that period.[27] To be sure, he was not an original thinker in that he did not invent a system of thought, but he was an extraordinary transmitter of ideas who compelled recognition through the force of his personality. All those who left memoirs describing the intellectual life in London at the turn of the century remarked on the impact of his presence.[28] The translator of Bergson and Sorel and an admirer of the anti-intellectualist philosophy of the end of the nineteenth and the beginning of the twentieth century, Hulme, said T. S. Eliot, writing in 1924, was the great precursor of a new state of mind, characteristic of the twentieth century.[29]

At the center of his thought was a violent opposition to humanism, the concept of human perfectibility and the idea of progress. His harshest criticisms were aimed at that "on which everything really depends": "these abstract conceptions of the nature of man" and the idea that existence is, or should be, the source of all values.[30] Hulme condemned the spirit and art of the Renaissance—Donatello, Michelangelo, Marlowe—an era in which a new psychology and a new anthropology gave rise to a harmful philosophy that in turn passed on its conceptual framework to ethical and political systems that were no less injurious: Descartes, Hobbes, Spinoza. Hulme did not deny that this humanism could possess a certain attraction and that it had heroic origins, but he claimed that it could lead only to "a sentimental, utilitarian romanticism" and that it "was bound sooner or later to end in Rousseau. There is a parallel development in art," he wrote. "Just as humanism leads to Rousseau, so Michael Angelo leads to Greuze."[31] Hulme's disdain for Rousseau was equaled only by his admiration for Pascal. Humanism, for him, represented what was false; the antihumanistic vision represented what was true. Fortunately, he wrote, the humanistic vision seemed to be coming to an end. Humanism was disintegrating, and one saw a "revival of the anti-humanistic attitude" and the "subordination of man to certain absolute values."[32]

To the humanistic conception of human nature, to the faith in the perfectibility of the individual and in progress, Hulme opposed a religious concept based on the idea of original sin, the fall of man, and the existence of ultimate values.[33] That is why he was so hostile to romanticism: underlying romanticism and the French Revolution, he believed, was the Rousseauist concept of the individual. Rousseau, he wrote, taught the people of the eighteenth century "that man was by nature good," that he was "an infinite reservoir of possibilities," and that the source of all evils was "bad laws." According to Rousseau, the destruction of the existing oppressive order would open up infinite possibilities of progress. Classicism, wrote Hulme, was defined by an

opposite conception, namely, that "man is an extraordinarily fixed and limited animal whose nature is absolutely constant. It is only by tradition and
organization that anything decent can be got out of him." In maintaining this
attitude, Hulme was adopting—as he explicitly said—the positions and definitions of Maurras, Lasserre, and the representatives of the Action française.
The romantics, he wrote, believed in the infinitude of man, the classicists in
his limitations.[34]

The young philosopher thus concluded that there was a necessity for a
strict religious discipline, which implied a political discipline and obedience
to the state. Hulme rejected the idea that the individual should aim at the
spontaneous development of his personality. Such a conception, he thought,
deformed the nature of ethical values, in that it made them derive from
subjective and therefore egoistical phenomena such as individual desires
and sentiments. It was a conception that, being simply the logical result of
humanism, led to romanticism. The antihumanistic revival was expressed in
a transformation of both literature and society in accordance with principles
that were "classical" in the sense that the Action française gave to the term.
Such was the conceptual framework that, in the years before the Great War,
Thomas Hulme passed on to Yeats, Pound, Lewis, and Eliot. They were all
agreed in rejecting the humanistic tradition, and they all rebelled with extreme violence against democracy.[35]

An adherent of the intuitive philosophy of Bergson,[36] Hulme immediately
grasped the importance of Sorel. At the time when he had begun to exert his
authority in the avant-garde circles of London, he had already assimilated
the main arguments of *Reflections on Violence*. No one has given a more
precise account of the place of Sorel in the history of ideas, describing him
as "a revolutionary who is also antidemocratic, an absolutist in ethics, rejecting all rationalism and relativism, who gives great importance to the mystical
element in religion which he knows 'will never disappear,' and who speaks
contemptuously of modernism and *progress*, and uses a concept like *honor*
with no sense of unreality."[37] For Wyndham Lewis as well, Sorel was "the
key to all contemporary political thought," "a symptomatic figure whom it
would be hard to equal."[38] In a very similar way, T. S. Eliot described Hulme
as "classical, reactionary and revolutionary, the antipodes of the eclectic,
tolerant and democratic mind of the last century."[39] These two succinct por-
traits of Sorel and Hulme, when viewed side by side, amount to a classic
definition of revolutionary conservatism, which in some cases is synonymous
with fascism.

Hulme was a protagonist of this new type of revolution. What appealed to
him in Sorel was precisely the profoundly antihumanistic, antirationalistic,
and antidemocratic quality of *Reflections on Violence*, and, of course, the
pessimism and classicism of the work. He also perceived Sorel's wisdom in
dissociating the working class from democracy, that two-centuries-old bour-

geois ideology.[40] Sorel's pessimistic conception of man, wrote Hulme, underlay his conviction that "the transformation of society is an heroic task requiring . . . qualities . . . which are not likely to flourish on the soil of a rational and skeptical ethic." Thus, in Hulme's view, the regeneration Sorel hoped for could result only from an ethic that, from the point of view of a narrow rationalism, could only seem irrational, being relative. An understanding of the classical side of this antithesis, wrote Hulme, "entirely removes the strangeness of Sorel's position."[41]

Thus, the significance of the Sorelian revolution was clearly revealed. Hulme realized that Sorel's main arguments were already to be found in *Le Procès de Socrate*, but felt that his antidemocratism became explicit only after the Dreyfus Affair. Because the characters and events referred to in *Reflections* might seem obscure to the English or American reader, Hulme insisted on the universality of the work. Hulme, finally, understood that the alliance between Sorel and the Action française was by no means accidental but concerned the very basis of Sorelian thought, which sought and expected a revival of the classical spirit through class struggle and proletarian violence. With Sorel, wrote Hulme, the pacifistic, hedonistic, and rationalistic system of ideas that still dominated the intellectual scene would be swept back. Hulme concluded by saying that for all those who were beginning to be disenchanted with liberal democracy, Sorel, whom he regarded as one of the most remarkable writers since Marx,[42] would appear as an emancipator.

Judging by his penetrating intelligence in the sphere of political thought and by his collection of essays entitled *Speculations*, Thomas Hulme was well suited to becoming the successor of Sorel both as a theoretician of the antirationalist viewpoint and as an opponent of hedonism, utilitarianism, and liberal democracy. He quickly perceived that Sorel was not a Marxist theoretician like the others, but one of the first and most important representatives of the cultural revolt taking place all over Europe, heralding the birth of a new spirit that was soon to take the name fascism.

That spirit was abroad in Europe even in places where the Fascist movement did not endanger liberal democracy. The small membership and political ineffectiveness of Oswald Mosley's British Union of Fascists are well known, but who today could deny the importance of Lewis, Pound, Eliot, Lawrence, and Yeats in the culture of the twentieth century? At this period at the beginning of the century, the cultural revolt preceded the political. A desire to cleanse the world of the defilements of the eighteenth century and to introduce various forms of discipline such as classicism and nationalism, no less than a rejection of liberal and bourgeois "decadence," united in a single tide of sentiment some of the most important literary and artistic avant-gardes in Europe. Sorel's role in this movement of ideas of the beginning of the century appears ever more significant, not, of course, on account of his contribution to Marxist theory, but because of the part he played in this cultural revolt, without which the emergence of fascism would not be comprehensible. His cult of violence as a generator of morality contributed to the rise of the vorticists as well as that of the futurists, the revolutionary syndicalists, and the nationalists.

Moreover, a contempt for democracy was undoubtedly encouraged by the fear that cultured circles felt for the masses. Here a certain form of elitism reflected the theory of elites propounded by Pareto, Mosca, and Michels. Indeed, the vorticist and futurist avant-garde found logical support in the theories of the new social sciences, and its preoccupations coincided perfectly with the elitism of the revolutionary syndicalists. The sovereign disdain of the latter for the inert and disorganized masses, the law of numbers and democracy, and their cult of minorities, violence, and direct action made them the natural allies of the writers, painters, architects, and musicians who proclaimed the birth of a new world.

All these elements that contributed, each in its own way, each to its own degree, to this cultural and political revolution, to this national revolution that was fascism, already existed in the last years before the Great War. Pacifism, antimilitarism, and an extreme internationalism were the last obstacles to a moral mobilization in view of this conflagration that now threatened. This barrier fell with the conversion of Gustave Hervé.

Today, Hervé's celebrity seems incomprehensible to us. In the collective memory of the French, he seems to have been only the winner of a famous "competition" organized during the war by *Le Canard enchaîné*. On that occasion, Hervé was given the title "foremost dispenser of eyewash" in France. Second place was given to Barrès. His unbridled fanaticism from the time of the Battle of the Marne to the time of the armistice, his clumsy actions as the leader of a small Fascist group in the 1920s, and his celebrated call for a savior ("It's Pétain we need!") in 1936 have obscured the main point: namely, that in the first years of the century, Hervé was a major figure of the European Left.

An apostle of antimilitarism and internationalism, his devotion to his cause was boundless. He spent several years in prison for violating press laws. He was cast in the mold of those nineteenth-century revolutionaries who for the sake of a cause would shrink from no sacrifice. Behind this pious image, however, lurked a dangerous megalomaniac, yet this image of an infinitely self-sacrificing activist helped to make "Hervéism" the symbol of an unsparing struggle on behalf of socialism and against the bourgeois state. Even within the respectable SFIO, led by Jaurès, one had to reckon with this leftist agitator whose popularity with the militants continually increased despite the distrust and antipathy of quite a number of the party's leaders. In February 1912, Marcel Sembat offered him his seat as a deputy in order to enable him to leave the Santé Prison. True to the principle of extraparliamentary struggle, Hervé flatly rejected this compromise, which he deemed unworthy of a true revolutionary.[43] He was liberated, together with all others guilty of press offenses, on 14 July of that year. On leaving prison, Hervé made headlines by exclaiming "And I say to you, merde!"[44]

This was the man who, in the summer of 1912, was expected to take up his position again as the leader of the antimilitaristic and antipatriotic campaign. One can therefore understand the consternation of his followers when, on his liberation after twenty-six months in prison, he described in a major article three important points on which his thinking had evolved. First, he advocated solidarity with the Socialist party; henceforth, he said, one should avoid any polemics that could diminish people's confidence in French socialism. Next, he declared that he recognized the Socialist party as valuable a means of preparing the way for an egalitarian "social republic" as the CGT, a realization that made him call for a "disarmament of hatreds" between the syndical movement and the party. In other words, this intransigent revolutionary, the sworn enemy of parliamentarianism, bourgeois democracy, and the Third Republic had thrown in his lot entirely with social democracy. Finally, there was the third revelation, "revolutionary militarism." Hervé urged the socialists to conquer the army from within in order to transform it, when the time came, into an instrument of revolution.[45] In plain terms, he was asking his friends to renounce antipatriotism and antimilitarism and to accept integration with national collectivity. All in all, Hervé had fallen in line with the most conventional positions of the SFIO.

At the end of September, Hervé, faced with a revolt by some of his followers, tried to explain his thinking. He organized a huge meeting in the Salle Wagram. There, in front of an audience that cried treason (shots were exchanged), he reaffirmed his new positions: he attacked the anarchists, advocated a close alliance with the Socialist party, and ended by redefining patriotism: "Antipatriot! A disturbing word, an ambiguous word, a word that kills!" Hervé explained that his antipatriotism had never been anything other than a hatred for the bourgeois domination of the fatherland, and that he had been attacking only the exploiters of patriotism.[46]

One is therefore not really surprised to find that two years later, when the war broke out, Hervé displayed a patriotism that would have put Déroulède to shame and was filled with a hatred of Marxism which only Léon Daudet then equaled. Hervé was not acting under the impact of the war when he transformed *La Guerre sociale*, which he edited, into *La Victoire*; he had simply arrived at the end of a process lasting several years. With a similar logic, in July 1919 he founded the National Socialist party.[47] He was soon joined by Alexandre Zévaès, a former Guesdist deputy from Isère, who in the interim had become the defender of Villain, Jaurès's murderer. At that time, Zévaès headed a small faction, the Action republicaine socialiste, which had come into being as the result of a regrouping of activists opposed to the "Marxist" character of the SFIO, which had split the party in 1910.[48]

From that period on, Hervé was a great admirer of Mussolini and continued to demand for France a strong regime based on the Italian model.[49]
Hervé's most spectacular and significant success, however, was in winning
the support of Jean Allemane. On 2 August 1919, *La Victoire* published a
letter in which the former Communard declared his readiness to "enter the
phalanx of national socialists" in order to "enlighten the working class about
its true interests" and show it "that they were identical with those of the
nation."[50] The founder in 1890 of the Parti ouvrier socialiste révolutionnaire,
known for his labor exclusivism, an advocate of the general strike, and an
antimilitarist, in 1894 Allemane was condemned to two months' imprisonment for insulting the army. This anti-Boulangist, this Dreyfusard who was
among the first to enter the fray, this witness of heroic times was, at the
period when he ended his career as an activist on the eve of the Great War,
one of the great figures of French socialism. His rapprochement with Hervé
was one more example of the evolution of thinking that one must bear in
mind if one wishes to understand the birth and development of fascism.

This process whereby socialist intellectuals, polemicists, and political
leaders thus came to contribute to the theories and swell the ranks of the
Fascist movements continued throughout the interwar period. In this respect also, the Great War ought not to be seen as a genuine watershed. If the
methods were modernized and adapted to the realities of the 1920s and
1930s, the phenomenon remained the same. As before the war, it was always
a matter of refining or improving the antimaterialist revision of Marxism.
Only the social and psychological conditions were different.

The first generation of revisionists questioned the revolutionary capacities
of the workers and ended by losing faith in them. The generation that
emerged from the trenches did not even trouble to ask the question. Certainly, in many respects, the dissidents of the 1920s and 1930s retraced the
path traveled by the "revolutionary revisionists" of the first generation. Like
them, they proposed original solutions based on an antimaterialist revision
of Marxism, like them they detested democracy, and like them they advocated a national socialism fused with corporatism. The difference was that
whereas between 1912 and 1922 Michels, Panunzio, Dinale, Lanzillo, Olivetti, Bianchi, and Rossoni could not know what their synthesis of socialism
and nationalism would lead to, the new revisionists already had several
years' experience of a Fascist regime.

Of all the theoreticians who in the 1920s and 1930s attempted an antimaterialist revision of Marxism, Henri De Man was the most important.
Although trained in Germany, he was the most authentic heir to French and
Italian Sorelianism. More than anyone else in the interwar period, this great
Flemish bourgeois, won over to socialism when he was still in high school,
continued the tradition begun by that other nonconformist reared in the
school of German social democracy, Robert Michels. His career is of particu-

lar interest, for he was not just anybody. Vice president of the Parti ouvrier belge (POB, Belgian Workers' party), and then, on the death of Emile Vandervelde in 1938, its president, De Man was one of the leading socialist theoreticians of the period, even if he was the most controversial. Among his contemporaries, only Gramsci and Lukács could claim to be his superiors. His development, as reflected in his successive theoretical works, was not very different from that of the revolutionary-syndicalist founders of fascism, and it ended in a way that was also not totally dissimilar.

Mussolini made no mistake. When the Italian translation of De Man's *Au-delà du marxisme* appeared, a veritable landmark in the antimaterialist revision of Marxism, Mussolini expressed his interest in the work in a letter to the author. He immediately put his finger on the salient point: this criticism, he wrote, destroys "whatever 'scientific' element still remains in Marxism." Mussolini was particularly appreciative of the idea that a corporative organization and a new relationship between labor and capital would eliminate "the psychological distance in which—more than in the clash of economic interests—you rightly see the germ of class warfare."[51] Having, like the revolutionary syndicalists of his milieu, been through it himself, the former editor of *Avanti!* perfectly understood the character and importance of this new wave of revisionism. He knew that the work of the most brilliant representative of the new generation of socialists (Gramsci and Lukács, for their part, were Communists) provided fascism with an invaluable reinforcement: that of the people who had come to Marxist theory and socialist militancy after the war.

In his reply, De Man did not feel that he had to correct the Duce when he made an intelligent attempt to point out the similarity between the arguments of *Au-delà du marxisme* and fascism. On the contrary! Although not concealing his objections to fascism, De Man was ready to acknowledge that there were aspects he found positive.

> Having said this, I beg you to believe that no prejudice prevents me from following daily, insofar as one can from reading, with an ardent concern for objective information, the doctrinal and political work that you are undertaking. . . . It is precisely because, belonging like you to the "generation of the front" and influenced, like you, by the ideas of Georges Sorel, I do not close my mind to any manifestations of creative force, it is precisely because I am not afraid to do justice to certain organizational aspects of the Fascist enterprise, that I follow its progress with a passionate interest.[52]

With a quite conscious intention De Man invoked the memory of Sorel and stressed the long-term influence of *Reflections on Violence* on the author, in full awareness that he was expressing his views to the head of Italian fascism. De Man was well aware of the fact that Sorel's reinterpretation had always been the common denominator of the antimaterialist revisionists of

Marxism. He had never hidden his objectives. "In order that there should be no doubt about my apostasy," he wrote in 1919, "I will call it: the revision of Marxism."[53] A few years later, in presenting his most famous work to the reader, he was even more explicit: at the end of the 1920s, he envisaged quite simply "the liquidation of Marxism."[54] In *Après Coup*, published in 1941 in occupied Brussels, the former president of the POB recalled his primary objective of fifteen years earlier: to destroy the system by attacking its very roots, "economic determinism and rationalistic scientism."[55]

In the development of his thought, De Man proceeded in a now classic manner. He began by assaulting the theory of surplus value and the Marxist concept of "class consciousness," and he put forward a conception of socialism that required no structural changes in social and economic relationships. This new variant of socialism was based on a new view of the idea of exploitation which is of great importance for an understanding of the role that this revision of Marxism was to play both in the formation of the Fascist philosophy and in the practice of fascism. "The concept of exploitation is ethical and not economic," wrote De Man,[56] and socialism, he maintained, was unable to fight bourgeois egoism with a labor materialism and hedonism.[57] The idea that the concept of exploitation is ethical and not economic was strongly emphasized in the development of the Fascist philosophy both before and after the First World War.

All this therefore led to one major conclusion: if exploitation is a psychological and not an economic phenomenon and if class relationships are likewise the reflection of subjective feelings, the solution to social and economic problems must also necessarily be of a psychological nature. In practice, with De Man, psychological, emotional, and affective problems took precedence over economic questions, and aesthetics played at least as important a role in peoples' lives as economics. Thus, by satisfying the workers' psychological needs one was spared having to deal with structural problems; that was the practical implication of this point of view.[58] That was also the Fascist attitude, based on the conviction that existential questions are essentially cultural, emotional, and affective. It was this view of the nature of individual motivations that underlay the Fascist revolution. Fascism therefore sought to demonstrate that one can profoundly alter peoples' lives without touching economic structures in any way. Since human motivations were affective, since one was concerned not with the actual standard of living but with the "instinct of self-esteem" or a "complex of social inferiority," since it was now a question not of the place of the individual in the system of production but of his or her dignity,[59] one could create a revolution without changing the foundations of the system.

A very pronounced elitism and the idea that people have a profound need for inequality and a no less deeply rooted need to obey—these were natural concomitants of Henri De Man's "theory of motivations." The result was hardly surprising: there could be no question of touching the structures of capitalism, private property, profit, or the market economy in general. What De Man attacked was the great bankers, the lords of finance, large-scale capital, which he described as "hypercapitalism." He proposed an alliance of the working class with all the victims of "finance capitalism," a category that included the "middle classes in revolt against the hypercapitalism of large-scale banking."[60] This was a variation, expressed in similar terms, of the idea of an alliance of all "producers" against all "parasites." This move was not surprising; from the first years of the century, it was one of the main routes of migration of the Left toward fascism.

Finally, after a defense of a certain type of corporatism,[61] De Man took up the idea of a "strong state."[62] In 1938 he expressed his thinking as follows: "In the future, we shall have to be more determined in realizing a socialist order at the same time as setting up an authoritarian state, the one conditioning the other."[63] The development of his thought reached its logical conclusion on 28 June 1940, when the president of the Belgian Workers' party published a manifesto addressed to socialist activists, asking them to accept the Nazi victory as the starting point for the construction of a new world. This piece is in all respects a classic of Fascist literature.[64]

A similar development took place in France in the neosocialist circles led by Marcel Déat and among Doriotists from various backgrounds. They violently criticized the "Marxist spirit" and its "materialist" conception "of man and history." Marxism, "because of its inhuman and repulsive quality, has sterilized the labor movement." Thus, Georges Roditi, one of the leading representatives of the younger generation of neosocialists, reproached Marxism for its "*scientific* fatalism, its lack of hierarchical sense, its inability to arouse and utilize personal qualities in individuals," opposing to it "the socialist and national outlook."[65] In the same way as De Man, the "neos" invoked the authority of Proudhon, Sorel, and Péguy, opposing them to Marx, and called for "the constructive spirit of pre-Marxist French socialism," a sense of "order and responsibility," and a "Nietzschean" socialism.[66] Like De Man, the "neos" propounded the theory of an authoritarian and corporatist national revolution based on an "anticapitalist" alliance.[67] By then, the idea was certainly no longer new. The Italians already had proposed that a distinction should be made between "producers" and "parasites" in the integration of classes and the creation of national solidarity.

Here it is necessary to explain a point that is not always clearly understood. If neosocialism provoked such a strong reaction in France, if De Man appeared so suspect (even in the Belgian Socialist party, whose leadership had no choice but to pretend not to see what his revision of Marxism could lead to), it was because in the 1930s democratic and reformist socialism had not yet repudiated Marxism. If one overlooks or misinterprets this indisputable historical fact, one risks being led astray by an anachronism.[68] The socialism of those years still clung to the principles—not all the details, but the major principles—of the Marxist analysis. It objected to the sectarianism of the Communist parties and their totalitarian methods, but it never rejected Marxism as such. On the contrary, during this period of crisis when Italian, German, and Austrian socialisms were destroyed, French socialists led by Blum increased their fidelity to Marxism. Just as at the beginning of the century Antonio Labriola and Rudolf Hilferding, Jean Jaurès and Max Adler had sought only to improve and modernize Marxism when offering their interpretation of the system, so Gramsci and Lukács, Blum and Vandervelde, despite all their reservations about communism as was then practiced in the Soviet Union, refused to countenance any non-Marxist form of socialism.[69]

In this rivalry between the two types of revolution—that of the "classical" socialists and that of the "néos"—the hearts and minds of the European intelligentsia tended to side with the great antimaterialist rebellion. That is why, at the hour of testing, liberal and democratic Europe did not find a larger number of staunch defenders among its famous intellectuals. It was in the often unconscious attraction of its ideology of rupture that the great power of fascism resided. That was also the reason why the phenomenon of fascism could not be explained in terms of postwar crises.

These crises only accelerated or caused the emergence of a favorable environment, but they did not and could not give rise to an ideology of rupture as powerful as that of fascism. Explanations in terms of circumstance can result only in banalities. In certain German academic circles, the Bolshevik danger is nowadays used as the great argument to explain both the Nazi ideology and its practice.[70]

But this tendency to describe fascism and Nazism, their origins and the reasons for their emergence as isolated, incidental phenomena, completely detached from their general, cultural context, is not confined to Germany. In Italy and especially in France this tendency serves the interests of an apologetic approach to national history. The marginalization of fascism relieves those that deal with the necessity of relating to the broad cultural context, which was its true intellectual seedbed. Those who choose the easy path are spared the need to answer many perplexing questions, including that of the intellectual, emotional, or political connection that existed in a given period between broad circles of the intelligentsia and the Fascists or Nazis, or other advocates of a "national revolution." The apologetic interpretation of events consciously disregards the cultural history of Europe in the last hundred years, the fact that toward the end of the nineteenth century the opposition to optimism, universalism, and humanism developed into a general struggle that affected all areas of intellectual activity. At that time, an alternative political culture came into being; it sought to rescue Europe from the heritage of the Enlightenment, and, naturally, when the crisis reached its peak at the beginning of the twentieth century, the attack was directed first against rationalism and humanism.

In 1929, this general conflict between the two schools took the symbolic and unusual form of a face-to-face confrontation between Martin Heidegger, a standard-bearer of antiuniversalism and one of the prophets of postmodernism, and the German-Jewish philosopher Ernst Cassirer. This harsh and bitter debate, which ended with a complete rupture, took place in Davos, Switzerland, and became famous. The ostensible subject of the debate was Kant, the most outstanding and brilliant representative of the eighteenth century, but in reality the future of Europe was the subject of the discussion. A few years later, another, final attempt was made to sound the alarm bells. In 1935 Edmund Husserl, whom some regarded as the most important philosopher since Hegel, gave a lecture in Vienna. Because he was Jewish and for fear that his words may harm the Jews in Germany, Husserl had been careful to keep silent since the Nazis had come to power. On this occasion, however, he responded to an invitation to appear in public. His address was an outstanding declaration of principles entirely devoted to the defense of rationalism and universalism. Husserl did not refrain from attacking a wild and reckless nationalism that trampled the values of the Enlightenment underfoot.[71] When Husserl spoke in Vienna, Cassirer was already in exile in Oxford and Martin Heidegger was making speeches about the greatness of Nazism and the spiritual truth it contained. Thus, we learn once again that theoretical discussions never take place in a vacuum and there can be no philosophical thought without political consequences.

In the period between the two world wars, the antiuniversalistic trends became an especially destructive historical force. But this would not have been possible without the emergence all over Europe, from the nineteenth century onward, of a cultural outlook that supported the political struggle against liberal democracy. Throughout western Europe there developed at that period an acute sense of cultural degeneration, of frustration, disintegration, and regression, and the entire blame for the negative phenomena was placed on rationalism and materialism, on Kant, Rousseau, Marx, and the French Revolution. From the end of the nineteenth century, the French Revolution—"the last great slave rebellion," as Nietzsche called it—had been responsible for the domination of the masses over Western culture. To those critics of that culture, the eighteenth century had given birth to the new type of "man of the herd," the representative of the masses par excellence who demanded for himself rights equal to those of the natural elites. This demand for equality was regarded as inevitably and necessarily leading to the destruction of Western culture.[72]

In Germany, France, Italy, and Spain in the period between the two world wars, the rebellion against the basic values of the nineteenth century took an extremely dramatic form, but from the doctrinal point of view it had changed very little since the years before the First World War. When Mussolini attempted to define fascism in 1932, he described it as a revolt against "the materialistic positivism of the nineteenth century."[73] A year later, when the Fascist movement was founded in Spain, its leader, José Antonio Primo de Rivera, began by launching an attack on Rousseau.[74] In 1940 the French Fascist writer Pierre Drieu La Rochelle declared that "France had been destroyed by rationalism."[75] The French Catholic leftist Emmanuel Mounier wrote that he regarded the fall of France as the overthrow of liberalism.[76]

Mounier was not alone in his belief, and this was the heart of the matter: not only Fascists but also broad circles of the European intelligentsia looked with sympathy and sometimes admiration at the rebellion against liberal, bourgeois, materialistic, and utilitarian order. They included Jews and converted Jews, and also people who a few years later were to become victims of Nazism or would oppose it by the force of arms. French dissidents of the Left and Right, nonconformists from the London cultural avant-garde, philosophers of history like Benedetto Croce and founding fathers of the modern social sciences like Michels and Mosca, representatives of the "conservative revolution" like Spengler and Jünger, philosophers like Heidegger, whose influence only increased with the passage of time—all of them fell victim, at some point in their lives, to the attraction of the cultural revolt against the universalistic heritage of the eighteenth century. They all took part in the obsessive criticism of democracy and of the demand for equality that had grown ever more clamorous since the end of the last century. They all saw fascism or Nazism as an expression of the hoped-for antihumanistic rebellion, a kind of return to the basic values of a heroic society led by natural elites.

They all had a fear of the masses, but the masses who inspired such dread in them were not the masses of fascism. The Fascist and Nazi mass movements were elitist movements whose raison d'être was to deny universal values. The masses who so terrified Spengler in Germany, Maurras in France, and Luigi Pirandello in Italy were those who took part in the demonstrations of the first of May and the miners' strikes, those who stormed the czar's Winter Palace and who expropriated the factories in Italy and set up the Popular Front in France.

Of course, sympathy with the great revolt against the liberal or socialist "slave morality" was one thing and support of a police state, concentration camps, and political assassinations as a system of government was quite another. It is true that not everyone who applauded the overthrow of the bourgeois and liberal decadence supported the extermination of the Jews or was part of the machinery of oppression. In this context, the question arises of the responsibility of the intellectual. No writer or artist should be held accountable or responsible for any consequences of his or her work other than the intended ones, but each thinker functions within a certain historical context, and from the moment the work goes out into the public domain it has an influence and consequences. Among the thinkers mentioned in this work, not a single one could claim to be apolitical. Even the most abstract ideas of Nietzsche and Heidegger had immediate political application, and they knew it. How much more did this apply when the statements were made by writers, poets, artists, philosophers, historians, and social scientists—among the most important and original of their generation—who negated the humanistic heritage of the Enlightenment, providing a cultural and political alternative? The political revolt that reached its climax in the period between the two world wars (we are referring not only to fascism and Nazism but to all the expressions of the "national revolution" in France, Spain, and Portugal) would not have been possible without a long period of intellectual preparation. The cultural revolt preceded the political one in every part of Europe. Fascism was the hard core of the cultural revolt and succeeded in translating it into a political force.

Fascism, therefore, was not content to criticize the existing state of affairs; it also sought to provide the nucleus of a comprehensive, heroic, and violent political culture. Fascism wished to create a new human being, activist and dynamic, and even when it assailed the universalistic principles of modernity—that is, of the heritage of the Enlightenment—it did not eschew cultural avant-gardism of a futuristic, nationalistic, and violent variety. Futurism, as we have seen, was one of the elements of fascism in its initial form, and it played an important part in the power of attraction of Italian fascism. This futurist and romantic element, however, was only one aspect of the many-sidedness of fascism; another was classicism, which extolled the asceticism and heroism of Pascal and reviled Descartes and his legacy, this being yet another weapon in the mighty struggle against the heritage of the Enlightenment.

The elitist element of the Fascist ideology was another reason for its power to attract. Nietzsche and Pareto taught that noble qualities are present in all strata of society. It was one's mental capacities that counted, not one's social position. Anyone who felt capable and worthy could form part of the elite, which had the right, by virtue of the law of natural selection, to govern society. An elite, claimed the Fascists, was not a social category determined by one's place in the process of production; it simply represented a quality of mind. Already in Sorel, the idea of class embraced not all of the industrial proletariat, but only an activist elite ready for every sacrifice. This cult of altruism, of renunciation for the good of the collectivity, had an importance for the people of the beginning of the century that today one can hardly imagine. The idea that the individual came into the world to serve the community and that life is a struggle on behalf of nonmaterial values was very common, especially in intellectual circles, but one had to await the postwar period for them to become mandatory.

In the first years of the century, the idea that the resistance of the world as it existed could be broken by the force of willpower, by faith, by myths, was also prevalent. The educative power of myth, which mobilized energies and created consciousness, was felt to be self-evident. Indeed, nearly all great political concepts of the period, including those of class and nation, began to be perceived in terms of myths. Similarly, the revolt against historical materialism cannot be dissociated from this awareness of the place of myth in history. The revolt began with a criticism of Marxist economics and then took the form of the introduction into Marxism of irrational elements that completely changed its character. When this revision was completed, none of the original components of Marxism remained except for activism. Hence the ease with which this revision of Marxism joined forces with nationalist activism and futurist activism. The synthesis that grew out of this encounter now provided the conceptual framework for what in the last years of the nineteenth century was still no more than an aspiration expressed in the original national socialism. And what had been no more than an often ill-articulated sentiment now became a conviction: that the key to a correct social engineering was not class struggle but the organic unity of the nation. This conclusion led the theoreticians of protofascism and then of fascism to adopt and refine corporatism.

Corporatism, as we know, was in the air at the turn of the nineteenth and the twentieth centuries. It was much discussed in Action française circles. Indeed, as a social ideal, it had never been entirely forgotten throughout the nineteenth century. The first generation of Fascists who came from the Left adopted the principle of collaboration between the classes, a fact that was correctly interpreted by the Fascists who came from the nationalist Right as an acceptance of corporatism. The readiness of the former socialists to assimilate corporatism greatly increased after the extent of the economic bankruptcy of the Soviet Union became apparent. Against this background, might not corporatism, based on the principle of "producer" versus "parasite," be regarded, they wondered, as an original and bold solution to the sickness of the capitalist system? Might this not be a new, modern solution that made it possible to correct the distortions of capitalism without destroying the whole structure? Did not Arturo Labriola, Enrico Leone, and Sorel himself, so appreciated by the "liberists," teach that there was no substitute for capitalism? Corporatism was one of the mainstays of a regime that achieved the tour de force of giving vast sections of the population the feeling that life had changed and that entirely new opportunities of promotion and participation had arisen without the necessity of touching existing socioeconomic structures. Fascism in office succeeded in reducing economic and social problems to questions of a primarily psychological nature. To serve society while being at one with it, to identify one's interests with that of the nation, to share in a cult of heroic values, was a far more satisfying way of participating in the life of the community than slipping a voting paper into a ballot box.

This is why political style was so important in fascism. But one has to insist that the style did no more than express the ideological essence of the movement. It translated into concrete terms its activist values and demonstrated its supreme disdain for bourgeois values. There too one had an instrument for the mobilization of the masses on behalf of an ideology and not a mere vulgar expedient. This nonconformist style, at once elitist and egalitarian, expressed the cult of violence as a permanent value. The inflammatory vocabulary of fascism, its incessant attacks on the ideas and practices of the bourgeoisie, its cult of comradeship and team spirit, naturally attracted the avant-gardist artists, but also all the young intellectuals who, rejecting the Marxist solution, also loathed the established order. For all of that generation, the spread of fascism throughout Europe was proof that a culture could exist based not on privileges of birth or wealth but on the spirit of the group so well described by Brasillach.

This revolt of the feelings and instincts, of energy, of the will, and of primal forces, this search for new values could ensure the integrity of the community, this rejection of materialism, excited, impressed, and influenced a great many Europeans, including some important ones. Freud, for instance, regarded Mussolini as a cultural hero.[77] If Mussolini in 1933 was a hero of culture for the founder of psychoanalysis, why should Croce have voted against him in 1924, and why should Pirandello have refused the offer of a seat in the Italian Academy, established in 1929? It is true that in 1925 Croce entered into dissidence and launched the "battle of the manifestos"; his celebrated "Anti-Fascist Intellectuals' Manifesto" cannot, however, hide the support he gave the regime in the crucial years when it came to power. Croce always found it extremely difficult to account for either Italian fascism or his own positions at a certain period in the history of fascism. Twenty years after his vote of confidence in 1924, he fell back on an extraordinary explanation of events. Mussolini, he wrote, was just a "poor devil, ignorant and unintelligent," who had succeeded in laying his hands on "a free and civilized Italy"![78] Here one is not very far from the postmortem explanations of Nazism given by Meinecke, Ritter, and Nolte.

Contortions of this kind, however, cannot conceal the reality. Mussolini would probably never have entered the Quirinal Palace if people like Croce had not initially seen fascism as something positive. The historian of ideas cannot overlook or regard as unimportant the hesitations, contradictions, and ambiguities that characterized Croce's attitude until 1925. The same principle applied to Germany, Spain, and the Vichy regime in France.

Spengler and Ernst Jünger, for example, were contemptuous of the Austrian corporal who took over their country, but they and their friends from the "revolutionary conservative" school of thought gave Nazism the legitimacy it needed in the eyes of the upper middle class. It was they who brought the elite of the German Reich into the arms of Hitler. Carl Schmitt served the regime faithfully and Heidegger spoke of the "great inner truth of Nazism."[79] In this connection, the contemporary German philosopher Jürgen Habermas was correct in saying that if a Nazi intelligentsia as such never came into being, it was for one reason only, namely, that the Nazi leadership was incapable of appreciating the intellectuals and thus unable to exploit their readiness to serve the regime.[80]

An outstanding example of the importance of ideological preparation in generating revolutionary political change is provided by the "national revolution" in France in 1940. The liquidation of French liberal democracy in less than six months, despite its deep roots, could not have been achieved without the position of dominance that the new ideology had gained in society. It was precisely the elites that collapsed most quickly; this was the most significant immediate factor in creating the conditions for the realization of the revolution. This fact was an eloquent demonstration of the success of the ceaseless destructive criticism directed every morning for fifty years against both the principles of liberalism and the functioning of the democratic regime. The call for a strong government that would put an end once and for all to the horse-trading in votes by voters and representatives broke democracy's power of resistance. The fact that horse-trading was an element of a regime that by its nature was a system of compromise operating according to complicated rules intended to ensure the freedom of the individual and equality before the law did not carry much weight with the nonconformists. In 1940 the political elite collapsed and delivered up the country to a dictator. Most of the important intellectuals, politicians, people of the media, senior officials, members of parliament, members of the Académie française, university professors, artists, journalists, and judges joined the ranks of the national revolution. This was the real problem: it was not the common citizen but the social leadership that betrayed democracy. That is how the oldest and most deeply rooted democracy on the European continent fell.

Above all, the national revolution reflected one basic fact: the political ideology and political forces that had assailed the liberal-democratic order since the end of the nineteenth century had finally achieved their major victory. The fall of France was regarded first and foremost as the defeat of a political culture. It was not an army that prepared for war according to the rules and principles of the one before that was considered to have been defeated, nor was it a conservative, hidebound, and impotent high command, but a liberal and democratic political culture rooted in the principles of the French Revolution. In this respect, the national revolution in France was simply an aspect of the European revolution that overtook Germany and Italy, and to a great extent Spain and Portugal as well. It was in France, however, that the national revolution had its greatest success, because there the victory had a particular significance. There it meant the defeat of the liberal and democratic order in a society that at the end of the eighteenth century had laid the foundations of the modern world and bequeathed its principles to all of European culture. In 1940 it was possible to put the last nail in the coffin of 1789.

In the view of the people who came to power in the summer of 1940, France had been overcome not by the most perfect and effective war machine ever known in military history, but by a political culture that was the antithesis of the rationalist, humanist, and individualist political culture that sprang out of the soil of the eighteenth century. The materialism and egoism underlying liberalism and socialism, the principle of equality introduced by the revolution—these had been roundly defeated by a political culture based on the organic conception of society and its definite priority with regard to the individual. The victorious ideology refused to define society as a collection of individuals, regarded only blood relationships as natural to human beings, and denied the validity of relationships deriving from the will and decisions of the individual.

Benedetto Croce in Italy and Emmanuel Mounier in France were typical representatives of the cultural elite that in periods of crisis responded, if not with full collaboration then at any rate with a sympathetic neutrality, to the continuous assaults, from the end of the nineteenth century, on the liberal democratic order. Mounier participated in the Vichy educational system until the end of 1942. In January 1943, he joined the underground, together with the whole teaching staff of one of the schools of Vichy activists. His admirers wish only to recall his heroic period of struggle against the German occupation and make every effort to diminish the importance of his period of collaboration with the regime of the national revolution. The great Italian anti-Fascist intellectual whose persistent hostility toward the democratic order caused him to support fascism until 1925 and the French Catholic intellectual who was also disdainful of democracy, liberalism, and the principles of the French Revolution and decided in favor of collaboration with the Vichy regime are subject to one and the same ambiguity. Precisely this composite picture throws the strongest light on the process of the rooting of fascism in Italy and of the national revolution in France. Today anyone who seeks a comprehensive explanation of the causes of the liquidation of freedom in western Europe will find that a reading of the writings of Spengler, Jünger, Miguel de Unamuno, Croce, and Mounier will be no less useful than a study of the works of the founders of fascism.

The realities of the interwar period were not all of a piece. Italian culture in the 1920s and 1930s was represented as much by Gentile, Marinetti, and

Pirandello as by the anti-Fascist Croce, and the anti-Fascist Croce was no more representative of the Italian intelligentsia than Senator Croce had been. Not only celebrated anti-Nazis like the Mann brothers spoke on behalf of Germany, but also Spengler, Moeller van den Bruck, Ernst Jünger, Heidegger, Gottfried Benn, and Arnolt Bronnen. Moreover, the France of Gide and Camus, Sartre and Malraux was also that of Maurras and Drieu La Rochelle, Brasillach and Céline.[81]

These two contradictory but nevertheless real aspects of European culture present themselves each time one examines the problem of antirationalism. Consequently, we have to make one last observation: one must always be aware of the tremendous difference between an attitude that recognizes the importance of irrational factors in human behavior and rejects a narrow, vulgar materialism or an arid, often stultifying positivism and one that is purely antirational. A recognition of the existence of an area not controlled by reason and an acknowledgment that it cannot be explored by rational means alone is one thing; the intellectual and political exploitation of antirationalism is quite another.

Here one finds the essential difference between thinkers who recognized the existence of irrational factors and their influence on society and those who made irrationalism the core of their teaching and an intellectual and political tool to win the support of the masses. Husserl also recognized the weakness of the naive rationalism of the seventeenth and eighteenth centuries, but, faced with the essentially irrationalistic approach of Heidegger and his followers, he made a spirited defense of the essential value of rationalism: "I too think that the European crisis derives from the perversions of rationalism," he wrote, "but there is no reason to say that rationalism is bad in itself or that it is of secondary importance in human life as a whole."[82] This basic conception placed on one side of the fence Heidegger, Spengler, Jünger, the whole German "conservative revolutionary" school, Pound, Lewis, Lawrence, Eliot, and Yeats and on the other side Husserl, Jaspers, Thomas Mann, and Joyce. This was the demarcation between Sorel, Barrès, Montherlant, and Brasillach on the one hand and Gide and Anatole France on the other. They all recognized the importance of irrational factors, they all criticized the existing political and social order, but not all were Fascists or sympathizers of fascism. Not all criticism of the existing order necessarily develops into fascism; not all sensitivity to the institutional weaknesses of democracy necessarily leads to a denial of its principles.

Fascism becomes a conceptual system when the rejection of materialism and rationalism becomes the essence of a total political outlook, a focus for enlisting the support of the masses and an instrument of attack against the principles of liberalism, Marxism, and democracy. The emergence of fascism became inevitable when this comprehensive rejection of the heritage of the Enlightenment was accompanied by a strong cultural pessimism, well suited to the age of technology, and a cult of elitism and violence. Cultural rebellion was not in itself fascism, but its undermining of the principles of modernity as they were formed in the eighteenth century and put into practice at the time of the French Revolution laid the path to fascism. And indeed, more than any other historical phenomenon, the emergence of fascism forces us to notice the part played by its numerous allies and sympathizers, both active and passive, and the destructive potential of a rejection of the rationalist utopia of the Enlightenment. Much has been said and written in recent years, especially on the occasion of the bicentenary of the French Revolution, about the dangers of attempting to realize such utopias. Many people have pointed out the destruction of freedom that necessarily results from a desire to achieve the impossible. But, to the same degree, it is useful to insist on the greatness of the destruction resulting from a conscious abandonment of the rationalistic dream of the eighteenth century.

Thus, if a conclusion is needed now, at the end of our century, to the great cultural rebellion that swept over Europe in the first half of the twentieth century, it is that to this day no better basis has been found for a human order worthy of the name than the universalism and humanism of the Enlightenment.

Notes

Introduction

1. See B. Croce, "The Fascist Germ Still Lives," *The New York Times Magazine*, 28 November 1943. In this article, Croce warned the Western world against a possible renewal of the Fascist infection in the body of our civilization, in consequence of that other war which was still in progress. About Benedetto Croce's conception of fascism, see also *Scritti e discorsi politici (1943–1947)*, vol. 1 (Bari: Laterza, 1969), pp. 7–16; vol. 2, pp. 46–50, 361–63. Renzo De Felice's excellent work, *Interpretations of Fascism* (Cambridge, Mass.: Harvard University Press, 1977), led me to these texts of Croce.

2. F. Meinecke, *The German Catastrophe, Reflections and Recollections* (Boston: Beacon Press, 1967) (translation of *Die Deutsche Katastrophe,* published in 1946). See particularly chap. 7, entitled "Mass Macchiavellianism"; G. Ritter, "The Historical Foundations of the Rise of National-Socialism," in *The Third Reich* (London: Weidenfeld and Nicolson, 1955), pp. 381–416. This was one of the most apologetic works produced by a professional historian. In a work published a few years later, *The German Problem: Basic Question of German Political Life, Past and Present* (Columbus: Ohio State University Press, 1965), pp. 199ff., Ritter was a little more subtle, but he still explained Nazism by Hitler's personality and by the impatience of the Germans to see their country extricated from the crisis, rather than by their nationalism.

3. E. Nolte, *Three Faces of Fascism: Action Française, Italian Fascism, National Socialism* (New York: Holt, Rinehart and Winston, 1966) (translation of *Der Faschismus in seiner Epoche*, published in 1963). Ernst Nolte's book remains a classic, despite the fact that it tends to minimize, if not to trivialize, the Nazi phenomenon. For a more detailed criticism of his work and his connection with the interpretation of Nazism as an aspect of a European "philosophy of evil," see Z. Sternhell, "Fascist Ideology," in W. Laqueur, ed., *Fascism: A Reader's Guide. Analyses, Interpretations, Bibliography* (Berkeley and Los Angeles: University of California Press, 1976), pp. 369ff. See also J. J. Linz, "Some Notes Toward a Comparative Study of Fascism in Sociological Historical Perspective," in W. Laqueur, ed., *Fascism: A Reader's Guide*, pp. 15–25, and A. J. Gregor, *Young Mussolini and the Intellectual Origins of Fascism* (Berkeley: University of California Press, 1979), p. xi.

4. J. M. Cammet, "Communist Theories of Fascism (1920–1935)," *Science and Society* (winter 1967): 149–63. See also a work very representative of the 1930s: M. H. Dobb, *Political Economy and Capitalism: Some Essays in Economic Tradition* (London: Routledge, 1940). On fascism, see pp. 259ff.

5. Works devoted to the questions that concern us here have abounded in recent years. A complete multilingual bibliography was published a few years ago: Philip Rees, *Fascism and Pre-Fascism in Europe, 1890–1945: A Bibliography of the Extreme Right* (Totowa, N.J.: Barnes and Noble Books, 1984).

Karl Dietrich Bracher's excellent book *The Age of Ideologies: A History of Political Thought in the Twentieth Century* (New York: St. Martin's Press, 1984) (original title: *Zeit Der Ideologien*) should be consulted first. Jacob Leib Talmon's posthumous work, *The Myth of the Nation and the Vision of Revolution: The Origins of Ideological Polarization in the Twentieth Century* (London: Weidenfeld and Nicolson, 1981), deserves a special mention. The records of the international symposium of June 1982 in memory of this great historian (he died in 1980), *Totalitarian Democracy and After* (Jerusalem: Magnes Press, 1984), should also be consulted. The most recent and important effort at providing an explanation of generic fascism is Roger Griffin's *The Nature of Fascism* (London: Pinter Publishers, 1991). A few older works in English remain the best in the field. See in particular A. James Gregor, *The Ideology of Fascism: The Rationale of Totalitarianism* (New York: Free Press, 1969), and *Italian Fascism and Developmental Dictatorship* (Princeton: Princeton University Press, 1979); George L. Mosse, *Masses and Man: Nationalist and Fascist Perceptions of Reality* (New York: Howard Fertig, 1980); Stanley G. Payne, *Fascism: Comparison and Definition* (Madison: University of Wisconsin Press, 1980).

In Italian, the work of Renzo De Felice is more important than ever; see his monumental seven-volume biography of Mussolini, published by Einaudi in Turin from 1965 to 1990. Four other excellent works should also be consulted: Emilio Gentile, *Le origini dell'ideologia fascista* (Bari: Laterza, 1975) and *Il mito dello stato nuovo. Dall'antigiolittismo al fascismo* (Bari: Laterza, 1982); Pier Giorgio Zunino, *L'ideologia del fascismo. Miti, credenze e valori nella stabilizzazione del regime* (Bologna: Il Mulino, 1985) and *Interpretazione e memoria del fascismo. Gli anni del regime* (Roma: Laterza, 1991).

In French, Pierre Milza's synthesis, *Les Fascismes* (Paris: Imprimerie Nationale, l985), can also be read with profit.

6. De Felice, *Interpretations of Fascism*, pp. 19–25.

7. Here I refer the reader to two of my earlier works: *La Droite révolutionnaire. Les Origines françaises du fascisme* (Paris: Ed. du Seuil, 1978) (new paperback edition: *Points-Histoire*, 1985) and *Neither Right nor Left: Fascist Ideology in France* (Berkeley: University of California Press, 1986).

8. See K. D. Bracher, "The Role of Hitler: Perspectives of Interpretation," in Laqueur, ed., *Fascism: A Reader's Guide*, pp. 217ff.

9. On the Action française, see V. Nguyen's remarkable *Aux Origines de l'Action française. Intelligence et politique à l'aube du XXᵉ siècle* (Paris: Fayard, 1991); C. Capitan Peter, *Charles Maurras et l'idéologie d'Action française* (Paris: Ed. du Seuil, 1972), and E. Weber, *Action française* (Stanford, Calif.: Stanford University Press, 1962). See also Z. Sternhell, *Maurice Barrès et le nationalisme français* (Paris: A. Colin, 1972; new paperback edition: Brussels: Ed. Complexe, 1985), and *La Droite révolutionnaire*.

10. M. Barrès, "Que faut-il faire?" *Le Courrier de l'Est*, 12 May 1898.

11. E. Corradini, "Principii di nazionalismo," *Discorsi politici (1902–1923)* (Florence: Vallechi Editore, 1923), pp. 100–101. These ideas were expressed in a speech that Corradini gave on 3 December 1910 at the Nationalist Congress in Florence. See also another speech that Corradini gave in several Italian towns in January 1911: "Le nazioni proletarie e il nazionalismo," pp. 105–118. On the idea of peace between the proletariat and the nation, see "Nazionalismo e democrazia," a

speech Corradini gave in Rome on 9 February 1913 and repeated in several other Italian towns (p. 154).

12. E. Corradini, "Il nazionalismo e i sindacati," a speech given on 16 March 1919 at the Nationalist Congress in Rome, *Discorsi politici*, p. 421.

13. E. Corradini, "Nazionalismo e democrazia," *Discorsi politici*, pp. 155ff. See also "Proletariato, Emigrazione, Tripoli" (speech of May 1911), pp. 119–34; "La morale della guerra" (speech of 10 January 1912), pp. 137–50; "Liberali e nazionalisti" (speech of December 1913), pp. 183–96; "Le nuove dottrine nazionale e il rinnovamento spirituale" (speech of 13 December 1913 in Trieste and Fiume), pp. 199–209.

14. On Bernstein's intellectual development, see Peter Gay's excellent *The Dilemma of Democratic Socialism: Eduard Bernstein's Challenge to Marx* (New York: Collier's Books, 1962).

15. K. Kautsky, *Le Chemin du pouvoir* (Paris: Anthropos, 1960; French translation of 1911 edition).

16. G. Lichtheim, *Marxism: An Historical and Critical Study* (London: Routledge and Kegan Paul, 1974), pp. 260–61.

17. 16. C. Schorske, *German Social Democracy, 1905–1917: The Development of the Great Schism* (Cambridge, Mass.: Harvard University Press, 1955), pp. 7–16.

18. The idea of revolutionary revisionism was widespread among the Sorelians from 1904 onward. See, among others, H. Lagardelle, "Le socialisme ouvrier," *Le Mouvement socialiste*, no. 142 (1 November 1904): 5, 8; R. Michels, "Le Congrès des socialistes de Prusse," *Le Mouvement socialiste*, no. 149 (15 February 1905): 51; Arturo Labriola, "Plus-value et réformisme," ibid., pp. 216–17, and "Syndicalisme et réformisme en Italie," *Le Mouvement socialiste*, nos. 168–69 (15 December 1905): 411–12.

19. Lichtheim, *Marxism*, pp. 268–69.

20. Max Adler, *Démocratie et conseils ouvriers*, translation, presentation, and notes by Yvon Bourdet (Paris: Maspero, 1967); *Otto Bauer et la Révolution*, texts selected and presented by Y. Bourdet (Paris: Études et Documentation internationales, 1968); and above all R. Hilferding, *Finance Capital: A Study of the Latest Phase of Capitalist Development*, edited with an introduction by Tom Bottomore, from translations by Morris Watnick and Sam Gordon (London: Routledge and Kegan Paul, 1981).

Useful biographical information may also be found in *Le Dictionnaire biographique du mouvement ouvrier international*, ed. Jean Maitron and Georges Haupt (Paris: Les Éditions Ouvrières, 1971), vol. 1 (Austria).

There is an excellent anthology in English, with a good introduction, notes, and bibliography: *Austro-Marxism*, texts translated and edited by Tom Bottomore and Patrick Goude (Oxford: Oxford University Press, 1978). Daniel Lindenberg's contribution, "Le débat marxiste au tournant du siècle," in P. Ory, ed., *Nouvelle Histoire des idées politiques* (Paris: Hachette, 1987), pp. 275–83, is also useful.

21. Lichtheim, *Marxism*, p. 313.

22. Y. Bourdet, Introduction to R. Hilferding, *Le Capital financier, étude sur le développement récent du capitalisme*, translated from the German by Marcel Olivier (Paris: Editions de Minuit, 1970), pp. 9–13.

23. R. Luxemburg, *The Accumulation of Capital*, with an introduction by Joan Robinson (London: Routledge and Kegan Paul, 1951). The personality of Luxem-

burg, the quality of her work, and her tragic end fascinated the interwar generation and still attract scholars. Peter Nettl's masterly biography, *La Vie et l'oeuvre de Rosa Luxemburg*, 2 vols. (Paris: Maspero, 1972), remains unsurpassed.

24. See the English translation of Böhm-Bawerk's chief work, *Zum Abschluss des Marxschen Systems*, 1896, published by Paul Sweezy, a Marxist economist, with a reply by Hilferding: *Karl Marx and the Close of His System by Eugen von Böhm-Bawerk* and *Böhm-Bawerk's Criticism of Marx by Rudolf Hilferding* (New York: Augustus M. Kelly, 1949), pp. vi–x.

In his reply to Böhm-Bawerk, Hilferding, who was then less than thirty years old, produced one of the most important works of Marxism since *Das Kapital*. In many ways, his work and his career epitomized the greatness, weaknesses, and final tragedy of German socialism. A Vienna-born Jew who came to the notice of Kautsky at an early age, Hilferding rose like a meteor in the world of European socialism. Later, he voted against military funding and in 1917 participated in the founding of the Independent Social Democratic Party (SPD). At the time of the split, which resulted in the founding of the Communist party, he returned to the right and rejoined the SPD. During the last ten years of the Weimar Republic, Hilferding, regarded as the party's leading intellectual, was twice appointed minister of finance. Despite his vitality and his eminence as a theoretician, he failed in his ministerial post and was totally mistaken in his assessment of Nazism. Exiled to Switzerland and then to France, he was handed over to the Germans by the Vichy police. Consigned to the Santé Prison, Hilferding died at the hands of the Gestapo.

25. See Pareto, Introduction to *Karl Marx: Le Capital, extraits faits par M. Paul Lafargue* (Paris: Guillaumin, 1897). This introduction was 77 pages long, as compared with the 165 pages of extracts from Marx's text and the 8 pages of Paul Lafargue's notes. See in particular, with regard to the theory of surplus value, pp. xxvii–xxix; xxxix–xlix, lx–lxiii.

26. Ibid., pp. xxix, lxxi, and lxxix.

27. V. Pareto, *Les Systèmes socialistes*, 2d ed., vol. 2 (Paris: Giard, 1926), chaps. 14 and 15. See in particular p. 398.

28. Ibid., p. 408. Concerning Pareto, see also R. Cirillo, *The Economics of Vilfredo Pareto* (London: Frank Cass, 1979).

29. B. Croce, *Matérialisme historique et économie marxiste* (Paris: V. Giard et E. Brière, 1901), p. 101.

30. Ibid., pp. 55ff. His first essay, "The Historical Theories of M. Loria," was published in *Le Devenir social* of November 1896 and followed by another important essay dating from 1899: "Recent Interpretations of the Marxist Theory of Value" (pp. 209–34). See also pp. 101 and 220–221, where Croce both paid tribute to the Sorelian critique of Marxism and replied to the countercriticism of Antonio Labriola.

31. M. Charzat, *Georges Sorel et la révolution au XXème siecle* (Paris: Hachette, 1977), p. 8. See also pp. 52, 251ff.

32. Antonio Labriola, *Socialisme et Philosophie (lettres à Georges Sorel)* (Paris: V. Giard et E. Brière, 1899). This work consists of a series of long letters written by Antonio Labriola to Sorel between April and September 1897. See the English translation: Antonio Labriola, *Socialism and Philosophy,* trans. E. Untermann (St. Louis: Telos Press, 1980), p. 94. See also P. Piccone, *Italian Marxism* (Berkeley: University of California Press, 1983), p. 1.

33. Antonio Labriola, *Socialisme et Philosophie*, p. iv. Sorel did not forget this rupture. Years later, he complained about it bitterly: "Ten years ago . . . ," he wrote in 1909, "he not only broke off all relations with me, but solemnly excommunicated me."; see his "Préface" to the work of Antonio Labriola, *Karl Marx, l'économiste, le socialiste*, trans. E. Berth (Paris: Rivière, 1910), p. xxxiii.

34. See P. Nettl, *La vie et l'oeuvre de Rosa Luxemburg*, vol. 1, pp. 44 and 246, and vol. 2, p. 484.

35. O. Bauer, *La Marche au socialisme* (Paris: Librairie du Parti Socialiste et de *L'Humanité*, 1919).

36. Arturo Labriola, "Syndicalisme et réformisme," *Le Mouvement socialiste*, nos. 168–69 (15 December 1905): 412.

37. H. Lagardelle, "Les Revues," *Le Mouvement socialiste*, no. 243 (July–August 1912): 153.

38. F. Marinetti, *Enquête internationale sur le vers libre et Manifeste du Futurisme* (Milan: Editions de "Poesia," 1909), pp. 9–12, 16.

39. J. Joll, *Intellectuals in Politics: Three Biographical Essays* (London: Weidenfeld and Nicolson), 1960, p. 134.

40. See A. Y. Kaplan's remarkable work *Reproductions of Banality: Fascism, Literature, and French Intellectual Life* (Minneapolis: University of Minnesota Press, 1986), p. 26.

41. See P. Bergman, "L'Ésthetique de la vitesse. Origines et première manifestation," in *Présence de F. T. Marinetti. Actes du Colloque international tenu à l'Unesco*, ed. Jean-Claude Marcade (Lausanne: L'Âge d'Homme, 1982), pp. 20–25; G. Lista, "Marinetti et les anarcho-syndicalistes," in *Présence de F. T. Marinetti*, pp. 84–85.

42. Lista, "Marinetti et les anarcho-syndicalistes," p. 84.

43. B. Mussolini, *La Doctrine du fascisme*, vol. 9 of *Édition définitive des oeuvres et discours de Benito Mussolini* (Paris: Flammarion, [1935]), p. 76.

44. See Ch. Péguy, *Notre jeunesse*, *Cahiers de la Quinzaine* (Paris, 1910), pp. 21, 27, 39, 56; *L'Argent*, vol. 3 of *Oeuvres complètes de Charles Péguy, 1873–1914* (Paris: Gallimard, 1928), pp. 398–99, and *L'Argent* (*suite*), vol. 14, p. 133.

Chapter One

1. G. Sorel, "Mes Raisons du syndicalisme," in *Matériaux d'une théorie du prolétariat* (Paris: Marcel Rivière, 1921; reprint, New York: Arno Press, 1975), p. 286. This collection was ready for publication in June 1914.

2. Works on Georges Sorel abound. In France Sorelian studies are now promoted by a society of that name, founded in 1983, with Jacques Julliard as its president. The Sorel Symposium of May 1982, which gave birth to the Society of Sorelian Studies, resulted in 1985, on Julliard's initiative, in a collective volume published by Éditions du Seuil, *Georges Sorel en son temps*, which is not without value, and which includes an excellent bibliography. This volume, however, still has the character of the publication of a clique with loyal followers, together with one or two unbelievers. One particularly regrets the absence of the American scholars who have made remarkable contributions to the subject, which should have been brought to the attention of the French reader: Michael Curtis, *Three Against the Third Republic: Sorel, Barrès, and Maurras* (Princeton: Princeton University Press, 1959); Irving L. Horowitz, *Radical-*

ism and the Revolt Against Reason: The Social Theories of Georges Sorel (London: Routledge and Kegan Paul, 1961); A. James Gregor, *The Ideology of Fascism: The Rationale of Totalitarianism* (New York: Free Press, 1969); *Roberto Michels e l'ideologia del fascismo* (Rome: Giovanni Volpe, 1979); Gregor, *Young Mussolini*; Jack J. Roth, *The Cult of Violence: Sorel and the Sorelians* (Berkeley and Los Angeles: University of California Press, 1980); John. L. Stanley, *The Sociology of Virtue: The Political and Social Theories of Georges Sorel* (Berkeley and Los Angeles: University of California Press, 1981); R. Vernon, *Commitment and Change: Georges Sorel and the Idea of Revolution. Essay and Translations* (Toronto: Toronto University Press, 1978).

There is one more observation to be made. When reading some of the contributions to the *Cahiers Georges Sorel*, one cannot avoid a certain irritation. From what the contributors say, one would think that Sorelian studies had only just been invented. However, most of the "discoveries" of recent years, especially those concerning the different aspects of Sorel's relationship with Marxism, already exist in works that are little known in France. One should mention, for example, James H. Meisel's book, *The Genesis of Georges Sorel* (Ann Arbor: Georg Wahr, 1951), which contains most of the elements of the debate on the interpretation of Sorel. Meisel refers with great expertise to all the articles, pamphlets, and letters that some people present today as material they have discovered: pp. 16–19, 26–27, 58–61, 79–92, 106–107, 114–17, 120–25, 132–33, 150–53, 216–31, 259–68. One should also mention the work of Richard Humphrey, *Georges Sorel, Prophet without Honor: A Study in Anti-Intellectualism* (Cambridge, Mass: Harvard University Press, 1951).

3. Sorel, "Avertissement" to "L'Avenir socialiste des syndicats," in *Matériaux*, p. 55. See also p. 5.

4. Sorel, "Avant-propos," in *Matériaux*, pp. 3, 5.

5. Ibid., p. 17 (Sorel's italics).

6. G. Sorel, *Réflexions sur la violence*, 11th ed. (Paris: Marcel Rivière, 1950), pp. 453–54.

7. G. Sorel, "Science et Socialisme," *Revue philosophique de la France et de l'Étranger* 18, no. 5 (May 1893): 510, 511.

8. These articles were gathered together into a volume by Édouard Berth: see G. Sorel, *D'Aristote à Marx (L'Ancienne et la Nouvelle Métaphysique)* (Paris: Marcel Rivière, 1935), p. 94.

9. G. Sorel, *La Ruine du Monde antique. Conception matérialiste de l'Histoire*, 3d ed. (Paris: Marcel Rivière, 1933). With a Foreword by Edouard Berth (1st ed. in 1901), p. 159.

10. Sorel, *D'Aristote à Marx*, p. 96.

11. P. Andreu, "La Préparation morale à l'absolu marxiste," in *Georges Sorel en son temps*, p. 168.

12. E. Berth, "Avertissement," in G. Sorel, *D'Aristote à Marx*, p. 3. See also p. 1.

13. P. Piccone, *Italian Marxism* (Berkeley: University of California Press, 1983), p. 80.

14. W. L. Adamson, *Hegemony and Revolution: Antonio Gramsci's Political and Cultural Theory* (Berkeley: University of California Press, 1980), p. 24.

15. Preface to Antonio Labriola, *Essais sur la conception matérialiste de l'Histoire* (Paris: V. Giard et E. Brière, 1897), p. 3. (italics in original).

16. Ibid., pp. 6–10, 16–19 (italics in original).

17. G. Sorel, "Superstition socialiste," *Le Devenir social* 1, no. 8 (November 1895): 757 (italics in original).

18. G. Sorel, *Introduction à l'économie moderne*, 2d ed. (Paris: Marcel Rivière, 1922), p. 392.

19. Sorel, "Superstition socialiste," p. 757.

20. G. Sorel, "L'éthique du socialisme," *Revue de métaphysique et de morale* 7 (May 1899): 286, 288. See also pp. 291ff.

21. Ibid., pp. 292, 294.

22. G. Sorel, "La Crise du socialisme," *Revue politique et parlementaire* 18 (1898): 596–600.

23. P. Lafargue, "Idéalisme et matérialisme dans l'Histoire," *L'Ère nouvelle*, 1 July 1893. See also C. Willard, *Le Mouvement socialiste en France (1893–1905): Les guesdistes* (Paris: Éditions Sociales, 1965), p. 160.

24. G. Sorel, "Idées socialistes et faits économiques au XIXe siècle," *La Revue socialiste* 35 (January–June 1902): 399.

25. Sorel, "L'éthique du socialisme," p. 292.

26. Sorel, "Préface pour Colajanni," in *Matériaux* p. 178. This preface was written in 1899 for the work of the Italian deputy Napoleone Colajanni, *Le Socialisme*, published in Paris in 1900 (italics in original).

27. Sorel, "Bases de critique sociale," in *Matériaux* p. 170. Sorel was quoting the preface he wrote to Saverio Merlino's book, *Formes et essence du socialisme* (italics in original).

28. Sorel, "L'éthique du socialisme," pp. 292–93.

29. Sorel, "Mes Raisons du syndicalisme," in *Matériaux*, pp. 177–78.

30. Sorel, "L'éthique du socialisme," pp. 293, 301. See also "Préface pour Colajanni," in *Materiaux*, pp. 177–78.

31. Sorel, "Préface pour Colajanni," pp. 177, 179. Sorel based himself on Bernstein (italics in original).

32. G. Sorel, "Y a-t-il de l'utopie dans le marxisme?" *Revue de métaphysique et de morale* 7 (March 1899): 167, 174–75. See Engels's letter to Lafargue of 11 August 1884, in F. Engels, P. Lafargue, and L. Lafargue, *Correspondance*, vol. 1 (Paris: Editions Sociales, 1956), p. 235. In speaking of Marxism in France, Marx went so far as to say, "What is certain is that I am not a Marxist." This pleasantry of Marx's, related by Engels in a letter to Bernstein of 2–3 November 1882, was published in *Le Mouvement socialiste*, no. 45 (1 November 1900): 523.

33. Sorel, Préface to *Essais sur la conception matérialiste de l'Histoire* by Antonio Labriola, pp. 13–14.

34. Sorel, "Mes Raisons du syndicalisme," in *Matériaux*, p. 253.

35. Sorel, Préface to *Essais sur la conception matérialiste de l'Histoire* by Antonio Labriola, pp. 13–14.

36. Sorel, "La théorie marxiste de la valeur," *Journal des Économistes. Revue mensuelle de la science économique et de la statistique*, ser. 5, vol. 30 (April–June 1897): 222–31. See also p. 225.

37. G. Sorel, "Les polémiques pour l'interprétation du marxisme: Bernstein et Kautsky," in G. Sorel, *La Décomposition du marxisme*, an anthology compiled and edited by Thierry Paquot (Paris: PUF, 1982), p. 149. See also pp. 145–48.

38. G. Sorel, "Économie et Agriculture," *La Revue socialiste* (March–April 1901): 440, 411 (italics in original). See also Sorel, "Idées socialistes et faits économiques au XIXe siècle," p. 389 n. 2: "It would be very useful for the history of socialist ideas always to distinguish between Marx's contributions and those of Engels."

39. G. Sorel, *Insegnamenti sociali dell'economia contemporanea. Degenerazione capitalista e degenerazione socialista* (Milan: Remo Sandron, 1907), pp. 17–20.

40. Sorel, *Introduction à l'économie moderne*, pp. 138–41.

41. Ibid., p. 11 (italics in original).

42. Ibid., pp. 11–12. A highly significant review of this work by Sorel in *Le Mouvement socialiste*, nos. 162–63 of 1 and 15 September 1905, presented this question in the same way: "The writer does not wish to reconstruct the world, nor does he wish to satisfy the wishes of all those who see socialism as a matter of a fairer distribution of the public wealth: this is a good preoccupation for *idealists*. He takes the social scene as it presents itself, with *private property as a basis*, and simply investigates the way in which there develop, or in which there can develop, institutions of partial socialization that can rid production of the obstacles that hinder it and prevent it from improving the life of the People on account of the stranglehold of the state or of private individuals on the mechanism of this production, but without touching the production itself, and he restricts himself to the problems in the modern economy that are simplest and easiest to solve," pp. 110–11 (italics in original).

43. Sorel, "Idées socialistes et faits économiques," p. 519 (italics in original).

44. Ibid., p. 531.

45. Ibid., pp. 520–21 (italics in original).

46. Ibid., pp. 520–23.

47. Ibid., p. 523.

48. Ibid., p. 540 (italics in original).

49. Ibid., p. 529.

50. Ibid., p. 541.

51. Sorel, *Insegnamenti*, pp. xiii–xiv.

52. G. Sorel, *La Décomposition du marxisme* (Paris: Marcel Rivière, 1908), pp. 44, 61–62.

53. Sorel, "Idées socialistes et faits économiques," p. 401.

54. Ibid., p. 519. See also p. 541, where Sorel asked people to have the courage to acknowledge that "Marxism has now been abandoned by the majority."

55. Sorel, *La Décomposition du marxisme*, pp. 8, 11.

56. G. Sorel, "Les polémiques pour l'interprétation du marxisme: Bernstein et Kautsky," in Paquot, ed., *La Décomposition du marxisme*, p. 182.

57. Ibid., pp. 154–63 (italics in original).

58. Ibid., pp. 182–83.

59. Sorel, *Réflexions sur la violence*, p. 60 (italics in original).

60. Sorel, *La Décomposition du marxisme*, p. 12; see also pp. 28–32, 47.

61. Ibid., p. 12.

62. Ibid., pp. 56–60.

63. Ibid., pp. 63–64.

64. Sorel, "Idées socialistes et faits économiques," pp. 519–20.

65. M. Rubel, "Georges Sorel et l'achèvement de l'oeuvre de Karl Marx," in *Cahiers Georges Sorel*, vol. 1 (1983), pp. 27, 18; L. Kolakowski, "Georges Sorel: Jansenist Marxist," *Dissent* 22 (1975): 78.

66. Sorel, *Matériaux*, p. 184.

67. G. Sorel, Préface to the work of Arturo Labriola, *Karl Marx, l'économiste, le socialiste* (Paris: Marcel Rivière, 1909), p. xxxviii.

68. G. Sorel, *Saggi di critica del marxismo*, quoted in Paquot, ed., *La Décomposition du marxisme*, p. 214.

69. G. Sorel, *Les Illusions du progrès* (Paris: Marcel Rivière, 1947), p. 9. This work was first published in the form of a series of articles in *Le Mouvement socialiste* from August to December 1906 (italics in original).

70. Ibid., p. 2.

71. Sorel, "Idées socialistes et faits économiques," p. 389.

72. Sorel, *Les Illusions du progrès*, pp. 94–95.

73. Ibid., p. 104 and "Avant-Propos," in *Matériaux*, pp. 284–85.

74. Sorel, "Mes Raisons du syndicalisme," in *Matériaux*, pp. 284–86.

75. G. Sorel, "Le syndicalisme révolutionnaire," *Le Mouvement socialiste*, nos. 166–67 (1–15 November 1905): 274.

76. G. Sorel, "L'Avenir socialiste des syndicats," in *Matériaux*, p. 123.

77. Ibid., pp. 131–32.

78. Sorel, "L'éthique du socialisme," p. 299.

79. Sorel, "L'Avenir socialiste des syndicats," in *Matériaux*, pp. 102, 105, 113–14, 118–20 (italics in original).

80. Sorel, "Idées socialistes et faits économiques," p. 519.

81. Sorel, "Bases de critique sociale," in *Matériaux*, p. 171.

82. Sorel, "Idées socialistes et faits économiques," p. 520.

83. Sorel, *Matériaux*, p. 2.

84. Sorel, "Le Syndicalisme révolutionnaire," p. 265.

85. M. Rebérioux, *La République radicale, 1898–1914* (Paris: Éd. du Seuil, 1975), pp. 88–93.

86. On economic growth in France at the beginning of the century, see Jean-Charles Asselain, *Histoire économique de la France du XVIIIe siècle à nos jours*, vol. 1, *De l'Ancien Régime à la Première Guerre mondiale* (Paris: Éd. du Seuil, 1984), pp. 171ff.

87. J.-M. Mayeur, *La Vie politique sous la Troisième République, 1870–1940* (Paris: Éd. du Seuil, 1984), pp. 202–203.

88. Sorel, "Préface pour Colajanni," in *Matériaux*, pp. 184–89 (italics in original).

89. Ibid., pp. 188–89. See p. 189 n. 2, added in 1914.

90. Sorel, *Introduction à l'économie moderne*, pp. 386, 384. See also P. Kahn, "Mythe et réalité sociale chez Sorel," *Cahiers internationaux de Sociologie* 11 (1951): 133.

91. Sorel, *Introduction à l'économie moderne*, pp. 386–87, 390.

92. Kahn, "Mythe et réalité sociale chez Sorel," p. 134.

93. Sorel, *Introduction à l'économie moderne*, p. 394. In the second edition of this work, the one we have quoted here, Sorel added a footnote: "In *Réflexions sur la violence*, the theory of myths took on a more definite form."

94. G. Sorel, *Le Procès de Socrate. Examen critique des thèses socratiques* (Paris: Alcan, 1889), pp. 344–55.

95. Kahn, "Mythe et réalité sociale chez Sorel," p. 133.

96. Sorel, *Introduction à l'économie moderne*, p. 389.

97. Ibid., p. 394.

98. G. Sorel, "La Valeur sociale de l'art," *Revue de métaphysique et de morale*, 9 (1901): 275.

99. Sorel, *Introduction à l'économie moderne*, pp. 395–96 (italics in original).

100. Ibid., p. 390 (italics in original).

101. Ibid., p. 394.

102. Sorel, "Mes Raisons du syndicalisme," in *Matériaux*, p. 285.

103. See Kahn, "Mythe et réalité sociale chez Sorel," p. 151. Paul Kahn claims that the Sorelian theory of myths is based on a misunderstanding: the confusion between myth and mysticity. See p. 153. See also S. P. Rouanet's excellent article "Irrationalism and Myth in Georges Sorel," *Review of Politics* 26 (1964): 45–69. The most recent work on this subject is Michael Tager's article "Myth and Politics in the Works of Sorel and Barthes," *Journal of the History of Ideas*, October–December 1986, pp. 625–39.

104. Sorel, *Réflexions sur la violence*, pp. 32–38.

105. Ibid., pp. 177, 180.

106. Ibid., pp. 32–33.

107. Ibid., pp. 44, 47, 49.

108. Ibid., p. 179. Sorel added the following footnote: "I have tried to show how this social myth, which has disappeared, was succeeded by a devotion that has retained a capital importance in Catholic life. This evolution from the social to the individual seems to me quite natural in a religion" (*Le système historique de Renan*, pp. 374–82).

109. Ibid., pp. 180–81. See also p. 185:

> We must now go farther and ask ourselves if the picture provided by the general strike is really complete: that is, if it includes all the elements of struggle recognized by modern socialism. But, first of all, the question has to be stated exactly, which should be easy on the basis of the explanations given previously of the nature of this construction. We have seen that the general strike has to be regarded as an undivided whole; consequently, no detail of execution is of interest for an understanding of socialism. One should even add that one is always in danger of losing something of that understanding if one attempts to break up this whole into pieces. We shall attempt to show that there is a fundamental identity between the main theses of Marxism and the total picture of the general strike. (italics in original)

110. Ibid., pp. 39, 45–46, 48.

111. Ibid., p. 172.

112. Ibid., pp. 40, 42–43, 48.

113. Ibid., pp. 43–44.

114. Ibid., p. 46.

115. Ibid., p. 173.

116. Ibid., p. 182: "An organization of images capable of instinctively evoking all the sentiments that correspond." See also p. 177.

117. Ibid., p. 47.

118. Ibid., p. 177.

119. Ibid., p. 182.

120. Ibid., p. 49.

121. Ibid., pp. 173–77. On Sorelian irrationalism, see Rouanet, "Irrationalism and Myth in Georges Sorel," pp. 60ff.

122. Ibid., pp. 186–89 (italics in original).

123. Ibid., p. 206. See also pp. 204–205 on *"The bourgeois conception of science"* (italics in original), based on the idea that science could not only predict the future but guide it, and could create universal happiness.

124. Ibid., pp. 208–209. See also p. 207.

125. Ibid., p. 220.

126. Ibid., p. 217 (italics in original).

127. Ibid., p. 208.

128. Ibid., p. 39.

129. Ibid., p. 50.

130. Ibid., pp. 46–47.

131. Ibid., p. 189.

132. Ibid., p. 329.

133. Ibid., pp. 189–93.

134. Ibid., pp. 192–93, 200, 202. Concerning Le Bon, see Serge Moscovici's excellent work *L'Âge des foules* (Paris: Fayard, 1981; pocket edition, Brussels: Ed. Complexe, 1985), and Robert A. Nye, *The Origins of Crowd Psychology: Gustave Le Bon and the Crisis of Mass Democracy in the Third Republic* (London: Sage, 1975).

135. Ibid., p. 195.

136. Ibid., p. 273.

137. Ibid., p. 196.

138. Ibid., p. 95 (italics in original).

139. Ibid., p. 82. See also pp. 94–95, 300, 308, and 312 on Waldeck-Rousseau's plan to "transform the syndicates into politico-criminal associations."

140. Ibid., pp. 96, 114, 119–20, 273, 279.

141. Ibid., p. 120.

142. Ibid., pp. 120, 130–31.

143. Ibid., pp. 315–26. See especially p. 319.

144. Ibid., pp. 246–49.

145. Ibid., p. 269.

146. Ibid., pp. 157–61. 273. See also pp. 279, 283, 314.

147. Ibid., pp. 238–40, 249–53, 263–65, 351–55, 388.

148. Ibid., pp. 434–36.

149. Ibid., pp. 341–43.

150. Ibid., p. 13.

151. Sorel, *Le Procès de Socrate*, p. 41. See also pp. 33–34, 44, 206. On this question, Neil McInnes, "Georges Sorel on the Trial of Socrates," *Politics* 10 (1975): 37–43.

152. Ibid., pp. 90–99, 101, 179, 225.

153. Ibid., pp. 211–16.

154. Ibid., pp. 154–61, 236.

155. Ibid., pp. 183, 237–38; see also, pp. 177–79, 184.

156. Ibid., pp. 237–39, 207; see also p. 209.

157. Ibid., p. 235.

158. Ibid., p. 277; see also pp. 218, 346.

159. G. Sorel, *La Ruine du monde antique. Conception matérialiste de l'Histoire*, 3d ed. (Paris: Marcel Rivière, 1933), with a Foreword by Édouard Berth (1st ed. in 1901), pp. 133–34. See also p. 136.

160. Ibid., p. xiii. Quoted by Édouard Berth.

161. Sorel, *Le Procès de Socrate*, p. 9.

162. Ibid., p. 92.

163. Ibid., pp. 9, 13, 16.

164. Sorel, "Avant-Propos," in *Matériaux*, p. 39. This text was written in 1914 and first published in 1918.

165. Quoted in Jean Prugnot's Foreword to G. Sorel, *Lettres à Paul Delesalle, 1914–1921* (Paris: Grasset, 1947), p. 92. Berth's article was dated 15 September 1922.

166. G. Pirou, *Georges Sorel* (Paris: Marcel Rivière, 1927), p. 15.

167. Sorel, *Le Procès de Socrate*, p. 10.

168. Ibid., pp. 108–109, 172, 239–40, 349.

169. See Sorel, *Réflexions sur la violence*, pp. 13–15, 20–22, 113, 289–92.

170. Ibid., p. 17.

171. Ibid., pp. 19–22.

172. Ibid., pp. 14–17.

173. Ibid., pp. 28–30. On the Sorelian critique of rationalism, see in particular Leszek Kolakowski, "Georges Sorel: Jansenist Marxist," p. 79.

174. Sorel, *Les Illusions du progrès*, p. 6.

175. Ibid., pp. 5–6.

176. Ibid., p. 28.

177. Ibid., pp. 16–48.

178. Ibid., pp. 32–22, 36–38, 45–48.

179. Ibid., p. 35.

180. Ibid., pp. 49–50.

181. Ibid., p. 179. See also pp. 137–71 (italics in original).

182. Ibid., p. 50.

183. Ibid., pp. 54, 74, 80, 87. See also pp. 97–100, 106, 250, 55–88, 181–85.

184. Ibid., pp. 196, 267, 276–86, 335–36.

185. Ibid., p. 335.

186. Ibid., p. 51. About Pascal, cf. pp. 38–48.

187. Ibid., p. 40.

188. Sorel, *Réflexions sur la violence*, pp. 315–16.

189. Ibid., pp. 46–47.

190. Ibid., pp. 206–207.

191. Ibid., p. 130. See also pp. 200 and 434 (italics in original).

192. Ibid., p. 218 (italics in original).

193. "Avant-Propos," in *Matériaux*, pp. 21–25, 35, 39, 44. See n. 3 of p. 21, which gives a good description of Sorel's main criticisms of Hegel.

194. Sorel, *Les Illusions du progrès*, pp. 2, 4.

195. É. Berth, *Les Méfaits des intellectuels*, 2d ed. (Paris: Marcel Rivière, 1926), p. 339.

196. Sorel, "Avant-Propos," in *Matériaux*, pp. 2–4. Sorel quoted Croce: "Socialism found its last refuge in syndicalism. It was in this form that it died" (p. 4 n. 2).

197. Sorel, *Réflexions sur la violence*, p. 249.

198. Sorel, "Avant-Propos," in *Matériaux*, pp. 4, 19.

199. G. Sorel, "Lettre de Georges Sorel à Charles Maurras," 6 July 1909, published in P. Andreu, *Notre Maître M. Sorel* (Paris: Grasset, 1953), pp. 325–26.

200. G. Sorel, "Socialistes antiparlementaires. Un article de M. Georges Sorel," *L'Action française*, 22 August 1909. The original title was "La disfatta di 'mufles.'"

201. "Lettre de M. Georges Sorel," *Revue critique des idées et des livres* 10, no. 155 (25 July 1910): 101.

202. G. Sorel, "Le réveil de l'âme française. *Le Mystère de la Charité de Jeanne d'Arc*," *L'Action française*, 14 April 1910.

203. Sorel, *Réflexions sur la violence*, p. 124.

204. With regard to the "conservative revolution," some interesting comparisons can be drawn between Germany and France. This question, and the studies that have been made of it and that can be consulted, are treated in Z. Sternhell, "Emmanuel Mounier et la contestation de la démocratie libérale dans la France des années trente," *Revue française de Science politique* 34, no. 6 (1984): 1141ff.

205. Letter from Georges Sorel to Pierre Lasserre, *Nation française*, no. 130, 2 April 1958, quoted in P. Andreu, "Lettres de Georges Sorel à Édouard Berth— Première partie: 1904–1908," *Cahiers Georges Sorel*, vol. 3 (1985), p. 93.

206. P. Drieu La Rochelle, *Socialisme fasciste* (Paris: Gallimard, 1934), p. 221.

207. P. Andreu, "Fascisme 1913," *Combat*, no. 2 (February 1936).

208. Drieu La Rochelle, *Socialisme fasciste*, p. 106.

209. P. Andreu, "Le Socialisme de Sorel," *L'Homme nouveau*, no. 17 (June 1935).

210. T. Maulnier, "Le socialisme antidémocratique de Georges Sorel," *La Revue universelle*, no. 21 (1 February 1936): 373 (italics in original).

211. "Ligue d'Action française," *L'Action française*, 1 August 1905, pp. 224–25.

212. *La Révolution dreyfusienne* (Paris: Marcel Rivière, 1909). Sorel saw the Affair as a real political revolution: "The rehabilitation of Captain Dreyfus, twice condemned by court-martial, could have happened only as the result of so great a shake-up of our traditions that we have entered into a new era, which is distinguished by very marked characteristics from former times" (p. 10). See also pp. 24, 31, 32, 36, 45–49, 57, 64.

213. See especially Victor Nguyen's *Aux Origines de l'Action française*. See also two well-known works by Eugen Weber: *Action française* and *The Nationalist Revival in France, 1905–1914* (Berkeley: University of California Press, 1968); and R. Wohl's excellent *The Generation of 1914* (Cambridge, Mass.: Harvard University Press, 1979).

214. *L'Action française*, 15 November 1900, p. 863. For a detailed study of these questions, see Sternhell, *La Droite révolutionnaire*, and P. Mazgaj, *The Action française and Revolutionary Syndicalism* (Chapel Hill: University of North Carolina Press, 1979).

215. Ch. Maurras, *Dictionnaire politique et critique*, vol. 5 (Paris: Fayard, 1931– 1933), p. 213. See also Maurras's "Sur le nom de socialiste," *L'Action française*, no. 34, (15 November 1900): 859–67 (italics in original).

216. J. Bainville, "Antidémocrates d'extrême gauche," *L'Action française*, 15 July 1902, pp. 121–28; J. Rivain, "Les socialistes antidémocrates," *L'Action française*, 1 and 15 March 1905, pp. 412–18, 470–87.

217. Rivain, "Les socialistes antidémocrates," pp. 470, 476.

218. Sorel, *Introduction à l'économie moderne*, p. 174, and ibid., n. 2.

219. Rivain, "Les socialistes antidémocrates," p. 473.

220. G. Valois, "Nationalisme et syndicalisme," *L'Action française*, special number, 31 December 1911, p. 559.

221. J. Rivain, "L'Avenir du syndicalisme," *L'Action française*, 15 September 1908, p. 467.

222. P. Andreu, "Lettres de Georges Sorel à Édouard Berth—Première partie: 1904–1908," p. 94.

223. "L'Indépendance française," a prospectus for *La Cité française* published by its editor, Marcel Rivière, and reproduced as an appendix to Pierre Andreu's *Notre Maître M. Sorel*, p. 329.

224. Ibid., pp. 327–28.

225. "De la nouvelle forme de *L'Indépendance*," *L'Indépendance* 3 (15 June 1912).

226. See, for example, G. Sorel, "L'Abandon de la revanche," *L'Indépendance* 1 (1 April 1911): 75, 84–87; J. de Merlis, "L'Insurrection royaliste de l'an VII dans le Midi," ibid. 4 (15 February 1913): 329–44.

227. See Sorel's letter to Péguy of 31 March 1910 about the duc d'Orléans, Arthur Meyer, and *Le Gaulois*, mentioned by Andreu, "Lettres de Georges Sorel à Édouard Berth," p. 94.

228. "Manifeste de *L'Indépendance*," included as an appendix to Andreu, *Notre Maître M. Sorel*, p. 332.

229. G. Sorel, "Quelques prétentions juives (fin)," *L'Indépendance* 3 (1 June 1912): p. 336.

230. Ch. Maurras, *L'Action française*, 28 March 1911, quoted in Capitan Peter, *Charles Maurras et l'idéologie d'Action française*, p. 75.

231. G. Sorel, "Urbain Gohier," *L'Indépendance*, 2 (September 1911–January 1912): 320.

232. G. Sorel, "Aux temps dreyfusiens," *L'Indépendance* 4 (10 October 1912): 29–56.

233. *L'Indépendance* 3 (1 June 1912): 332.

234. See J. de Labroquère, "Choses de Russie," *L'Indépendance* 1 (March–August 1911): 331–37 and (September 1911): 12–28. One year later, *L'Indépendance* concluded its inquiry by publishing "The Ritual Crime in Kiev." The bottom line was that the "young André Yushinsky, . . . *had his blood drained* by the members of a Jewish sect that uses Christian blood for its religious rites" (vol. 4, 10 October 1912, pp. 107–108).

235. S. Romano, "Georges Sorel et Benedetto Croce," in *Georges Sorel en son temps*, p. 260. This short study by an eminent Italian scholar is of remarkable finesse.

236. See S. Sand, "Sorel, les Juifs et l'antisémitisme," *Cahiers Georges Sorel* 2 (1984): 27–28. This unsophisticated article, apologetic to the point of being laughable, contains some interesting points of information, even if they were already known to careful readers of Sorel.

237. F. de Pressensé, "Chronique du mois," *Le Mouvement socialiste*, no. 230 (April 1911): 288.

238. G. Valois, "Les fausses luttes de classe," a report presented on 28 November 1913 to the sixth congress of L'Action française, in *Histoire et Philosophies sociales*, p. 574 (appendix). One should also consult the well-known work of Henri Massis and Alfred de Tarde, *Les Jeunes Gens d'aujourd'hui* (Paris: Plon, 1913).

239. G. Sorel, "*L'Indépendance* française," in Andreu, *Notre Maître M. Sorel*, p. 331.

240. "Déclaration," *Cahiers du Cercle Proudhon* 1 (January–February 1912): 1.

241. See P. Andreu, *Georges Sorel entre le noir et le rouge* (Paris: Syros, 1982), p. 85.

242. Andreu, "Lettres de Georges Sorel à Édouard Berth," p. 95.

243. *Cahiers du Cercle Proudhon* 3–4 (May–August 1912): 125–33.

244. Ch. Maurras, "A Besançon," *Cahiers du Cercle Proudhon* 1 (January–February 1912): 3–8.

245. See *Cahiers du Cercle Proudhon* 5–6 (September–December 1912): 263–65. This letter was about an article on Proudhon by Daniel Halévy.

246. H. Lagardelle, "La Critique syndicaliste de la démocratie," *Le Mouvement socialiste*, no. 228 (February 1911): p. 81.

247. Letter from Sorel to Berth of 11 September 1914, reproduced as an appendix to Andreu, *Notre Maître M. Sorel*, p. 334.

248. A. O. Olivetti, "Sindacalismo e Nazionalismo," *Pagine libere* 5, no. 4 (15 February 1911). Olivetti meant Boulogne-sur-Seine. (The French word *grincheux*, grouser, was used in the text.)

249. In 1898, when Lagardelle was studying in Berlin, a long correspondence began between the two men which lasted until 1910, the year of their final rupture. Sorel's letters to Lagardelle were published by the latter in *Educazione fascista* 9 (March): 229–43, (April): 320–34, (June): 506–618, (August–September): 760–83, and (November 1933): 956–75. Where the history of ideas is concerned, they are of limited interest, but this correspondence is a mine of useful information for the biographer. One should also consult J. Levey's "The Sorelian Syndicalists: Édouard Berth, Georges Valois, and Hubert Lagardelle," (Ph.D. diss., Columbia University, 1967), pp. 65–67 (microfilm).

250. Berth, *Les Méfaits des intellectuels*, p. 355 (italics in original).

251. G. Sorel, "Préface—Lettre à Édouard Berth," in Berth, *Les Méfaits des intellectuels*, p. xxxvi.

252. Sorel, *Insegnamenti sociali dell'economia contemporanea*, p. 388.

253. Sorel, quoted by Berth in *Les Méfaits des intellectuels*, pp. 19–20. As a reference, Berth gave p. 124 of *Réflexions*, but this text is not in the edition mentioned here. It must have come from another source known to Berth but given wrongly.

254. G. Sorel, letter to E. Berth of 11 September 1914, in Andreu, *Notre Maître M. Sorel*, pp. 333–34.

255. Ibid., p. 333 (italics in original).

256. Sorel, "Préface—Lettre à Édouard Berth," pp. xxxvii–xxxviii.

Chapter Two

1. É. Berth, "Socialisme ou Étatisme," *Le Mouvement socialiste*, no. 111 (January 1903): pp. 1–18; É. Berth, "Catholicisme social et socialisme," *Le Mouvement socialiste*, no. 130 (15 November 1903): 321–50.

2. Andreu, "Lettres de Georges Sorel à Édouard Berth," pp. 79–81.

3. For Édouard Berth's biography, see P. Andreu, "Bibliographie d'Édouard Berth," *Bulletin of the International Institute for Social History* 8 (1953): 196–204, as well as Levey, *The Sorelian Syndicalists*, pp. 33–34, 38–44, 241–50.

4. E. Darville [É. Berth], "La leçon du fascisme," *Clarté*, no. 26 (1922): 43, and É. Berth, "Georges Sorel," ibid., no. 21 (1922): 495–96.

5. These observations were made in no. 3 (October 1931): 107, in connection with a letter signed by P. K. and L. L. that ended a series of extracts from Sorel's letters

274 NOTES TO CHAPTER TWO

to Croce, previously published in Croce's *La Critica*. See *La Critique sociale*, no. 1 (March 1931): 9–15, and no. 2 (July 1931): 56–65. These letters were introduced (p. 9 of no. 1) in a manner that Berth could only regard as disagreeable, no doubt by Souvarine himself.

6. É. Berth, "Sorel . . . pas socialiste!" *La Révolution prolétarienne*, no. 124 (February 1932): 25–57 to 28–60 (this system of pagination was employed at that time by this "leftist" review).

7. See *La Révolution prolétarienne* of 25 December 1935, *Le Populaire* of 17 December 1935, and *Le Nouvel Âge* of 21 December 1935.

8. R. Louzon, "La faillite du dreyfusisme ou le triomphe du parti juif," *Le Mouvement socialiste*, no. 176 (July 1906).

9. É. Berth, "Le cas Valois," *Le Nouvel Âge*, 5 March 1935.

10. As a selection of representative writings by Lagardelle in this period, and in order to gain an idea of the quality of the essays by foreign socialists published in *Le Mouvement socialiste* around 1900, see the following articles: "Vers l'unité," no. 46 (15 November 1900): 577–80; "La leçon de la Conférence Guesde-Jaurès," no. 48 (15 December 1900): 705–707; "Concurrence patriotique," no. 65 (1 September 1901): 257–59; "À propos du Congrès de Tours," no. 81 (1 March 1902): 385–88, in which Lagardelle praised "Kautsky, the celebrated theoretician of German social democracy, whose lucid and youthful spirit commands admiration"; "Les Mots et les Faits," no. 82 (8 March 1902): 433–35; "Illusions tenaces," no. 121 (1 July 1903): 187–90. See also R. Luxemburg, "Une question de tactique," no. 14 (1 August 1899): 132–37; K. Kautsky, "Le Cas Millerand et le Socialisme français," no. 46 (15 November 1900): 592–99; and Lagardelle's reply, "Sur l'article de Kautsky," ibid., 600–606.

11. Levey, *The Sorelian Syndicalists*, p. 65.

12. G. Sorel, "Le syndicalisme révolutionnaire," *Le Mouvement socialiste*, nos. 166–67 (1–15 November 1905): 267.

13. See the note published at the beginning of the issue of 4 January 1902 (no. 73), pp. 1–3.

14. H. Lagardelle, "La Confédération du Travail et le Parti socialiste—Intervention au Congrès socialiste de Nancy," *Le Mouvement socialiste*, no. 189–90 (15 August and 15 September 1907): 97–112, and no. 191 (15 October 1907): 283–87. This text was reprinted in booklet form, including the speeches of Guesde and Vaillant, under the title *Le Parti socialiste et la confédération Générale du Travail* (Paris: Marcel Rivière, 1908).

15. See the records, *5e Congrès national de la S.F.I.O. tenu à Toulouse les 15, 16, 17 et 18 octobre 1908* (Paris: Conseil national, undated), pp. 252–74, 351–55.

16. See the text of all the speeches gathered under the title *Syndicalisme et Socialisme: Discours prononcés au Colloque tenu à Paris le 3 avril 1907* (Paris: Marcel Rivière, 1908).

17. R. Michels, "Le Socialisme allemand après Mannheim," *Le Mouvement socialiste*, no. 182 (January 1907): 7–9, 13–14.

18. P. Orano, "Les Syndicats et le Parti socialiste italien," *Le Mouvement socialiste*, no. 193 (15 December 1907): 462.

19. Lagardelle, "La Confédération du Travail et le Parti socialiste," p. 287.

20. See Chapter 1.

21. See H. Lagardelle, "La Critique syndicaliste de la démocratie," *Le Mouvement socialiste*, no. 228 (February 1911): 81.

22. See Andreu, "Lettres de Georges Sorel à Édouard Berth," p. 81, and Levey, *The Sorelian Syndicalists*, pp. 131–33.

23. Lagardelle, "La Critique syndicaliste de la démocratie," p. 85.

24. H. Lagardelle, "Nouveaux problèmes," *Le Mouvement socialiste*, no. 236 (December 1911): 321–25.

25. É. Berth, "Le Centenaire de Proudhon," *Le Mouvement socialiste*, no. 206 (January 1909): 49–55. The May issue (no. 210) contained a contribution by Orano; the July–August issue (no. 212), contributions by Olivetti, Arturo Labriola, and Orano, and the September and November–December issues (nos. 213 and 215–16), by Labriola again.

26. The January 1910 issue (no. 217) contained a contribution by Labriola; the May–June issue (no. 221), by Panunzio; in the July issue (no. 222), by Leone; the October issue (no. 224), by Masotti; the November issue (no. 225), by Leone and Michels, and the December issue (no. 226), by Panunzio again.

27. Lagardelle, "La Critique syndicaliste de la démocratie," p. 81. See also "Proudhon et les néo-monarchistes," no. 237 (January 1912): 65–69, in which Lagardelle announced the forthcoming *Cahiers du Cercle Proudhon*.

28. See *Le Mouvement socialiste*, nos. 227 (January 1911) and 228 (February 1911), for a study by Michels in two parts, "La Constitution autocratique des Partis"; no. 229 (March 1911), by Panunzio; no. 233 (July–August 1911), by Labriola; and no. 237 (January 1912), by Labriola. There were contributions by Panunzio in nos. 234 (July–August 1912), 244 (September–October 1912), and 253–54 (July-August 1913). See also R. Michels, "Oligarchie et Syndicats (Discussion)," *Le Mouvement socialiste*, nos. 247–48 (January–February 1913): 90–96.

29. J.-B. Sévérac, "Les élections législatives et le parti socialiste," *Le Mouvement socialiste*, nos. 263–64, (May-June 1914): 329.

30. His articles of that period were gathered under the title *Sud-Ouest: Une région française* (Paris: Librairie Valois, 1929). See Sternhell, *Neither Right nor Left*, p. 112.

31. Drieu La Rochelle, *Socialisme fasciste* (Paris: Gallimard, 1934), p. 108.

32. See Le Corbusier's articles: "Une nouvelle ville remplace une ancienne ville," *Plans*, no. 8 (October 1931): 49ff., "Descartes est-il américain," ibid., no. 7 (July 1931), as well as the succeeding issues of *Plans* for 1931. In nos. 1, 2, 5, 7, 8, and 9, Le Corbusier's articles began on p. 49; in no. 6, on p. 65; in no. 3, on p. 33.

33. F.-T. Marinetti, "La nouvelle sensibilité," *Plans*, no. 7 (July 1931): 91. See also P. Latercier, "Éthique de l'automobile," ibid., no. 1 (January 1931): 46ff.

34. H. Lagardelle, "Au-delà de la démocratie. De l'homme abstrait à l'homme réel," *Plans*, no. 3 (March 1931): 24–25.

35. H. Lagardelle, "Au-delà de la démocratie. L'homme réel et le syndicalisme," *Plans*, no. 3 (March 1931): 12, 17. See also H. Lagardelle, "Supercapitalisme," no. 10 (December 1931): 7ff., and "Capitalisme," no. 9 (November 1931): 16ff.; no. 5 (May 1935): 9ff.

36. See Chapter 1.

37. Levey, *The Sorelian Syndicalists*, p. 370.

38. H. Lagardelle, "Retour des barbares," *La France socialiste*, 5 April 1944. See also, as examples, Lagardelle's articles in the following issues of *La France socialiste* from January to June 1944: 31 January, 9 February, 15 and 29 March, 25 and 31 May, and 12 June. See also, on this period, Levey, *The Sorelian Syndicalists*, pp. 331–33.

39. H. Lagardelle, "Le socialisme ouvrier," *Le Mouvement socialiste*, no. 142 (1 November 1904): 1.

40. Lagardelle, "La Confédération du Travail et le Parti socialiste," p. 286.

41. É. Berth, "Le 'Retour à Kant,'" *Le Mouvement socialiste*, no. 134 (15 March 1904): 321.

42. É. Berth, "Notes bibliographiques," *Le Mouvement socialiste*, no. 159 (15 July 1905): 432, and no. 150 (1 March 1905): 255 (italics in original).

43. Berth, "Catholicisme social et socialisme," p. 331, and H. Lagardelle, "Chronique politique et sociale," *Le Mouvement socialiste*, no. 157 (1 April 1905): 497–98.

44. Berth, "Catholicisme social et socialisme," pp. 329–31 (italics in original).

45. G. Sorel, "Enseignements sociaux de l'Économie moderne," *Le Mouvement socialiste*, no. 158 (1 July 1905): 298–99.

46. Berth, *Les Méfaits des intellectuels*): 290–91. (A note of 1913; italics in original.)

47. É. Berth, "Les 'Discours' de Jaurès," *Le Mouvement socialiste*, no. 145 (15 December 1904): 317. Here Berth attacked the social-democratic conception of "a providential state that takes everyone under its lofty protection."

48. Berth, *Les Méfaits des intellectuels*, p. 291 (note of 1913). See the almost identical statement in Berth, "Catholicisme social et socialisme," p. 328.

49. Sorel, "Enseignements sociaux de l'Économie moderne," p. 298.

50. É. Berth, "Politique et Socialisme," *Le Mouvement socialiste*, no. 132 (15 January 1904): 29.

51. See Chapters 3 and 4.

52. Arturo Labriola, "Plus-value et réformisme," *Le Mouvement socialiste*, no. 149 (15 February 1905): 213–14, 218, 223–26, 229 (italics in original).

53. Arturo Labriola, "Syndicalisme et socialisme italien," *Le Mouvement socialiste*, no. 179 (October 1906): 49, 59.

54. Ibid., pp. 49, 51. See p. 52: "The consequence is that social revolution affects not the principle of association and responsibility created by capitalism, but only its autocratic organization."

55. Ibid., p. 50 (italics in original).

56. Ibid., pp. 51, 53, 59.

57. Ibid., p. 52.

58. Berth, *Les Nouveaux aspects du socialisme*, p. 5. Concerning anarchism, see also Berth, *Les Méfaits des intellectuels*, pp. 123–24, 126–28.

59. Ibid., pp. 36, 46–47, 49–50, 63 (italics in original).

60. Ibid., p. 4. On two specific points, anarchism and syndicalism were strongly opposed: on the sacred character of marriage and their view of capitalist civilization. Berth said that whereas the idea of liberty, made by anarchism "into an absolute, destroys the family," syndicalism, following Proudhon, considers the sexual union "an irrevocable, indissoluble union" (p. 50). Sorelian syndicalism—puritanical, Catholic, and fiercely opposed to anticlericalism—was also, in this, out of step with all the other tendencies of socialism. A few years later, this became one of the points in common with nationalism, which was usually tinged in Latin countries with Catholicism. Where capitalism was concerned, Berth was no less categorical: not only did revolutionary syndicalism feel no repulsion for capitalist civilization, but, as we have seen, it had a profound admiration for it (see pp. 37–38).

61. Ibid., p. 36.

62. Berth, *Les Méfaits des intellectuels*, pp. 282–83.

63. Berth, *Les Nouveaux aspects du socialisme*, p. 34.

64. Berth, *Les Méfaits des intellectuels*, p. 286.

65. Berth, *Les Nouveaux aspects du socialisme*): 34–35.

66. Arturo Labriola, "Syndicalisme et réformisme en Italie," *Le Mouvement socialiste*, nos. 168–69 (15 December 1905): 408–409 (italics in original).

67. Berth, *Les Méfaits des intellectuels*, p. 172.

68. See, for example, Berth, *Les Nouveaux aspects du socialisme*, p. 8; "Socialisme ou Étatisme," p. 13; H. Lagardelle, "La France et la paix," *Le Mouvement socialiste*, no. 159 (15 July 1905): 412.

69. Lagardelle, "La France et la paix," p. 414.

70. Berth, "Socialisme ou Étatisme," p. 3.

71. Berth, *Les Nouveaux aspects du socialisme*, p. 4; H. Lagardelle, "Socialisme et le programme minimum," *Le Mouvement socialiste*, no. 87 (12 April 1902): 678–79.

72. Lagardelle, "La France et la paix," pp. 412–14.

73. Lagardelle, "Socialisme ou Étatisme," p. 10.

74. Berth, *Les Nouveaux aspects du socialisme*, pp. 3–6.

75. H. Lagardelle, "Notes bibliographiques," *Le Mouvement socialiste*, no. 179 (October 1906): p. 171.

76. Berth, "Socialisme ou Étatisme," p. 11.

77. Berth, *Les Nouveaux aspects du socialisme*, p. 6.

78. Lagardelle, "*Le Socialisme* ouvrier," p. 6.

79. Lagardelle, "La France et la paix," p. 416.

80. Berth, *Les Méfaits des intellectuels*, pp. 267–87. Berth was quoting *L'Idée générale de la Révolution*, pp. 259, 232 (italics in original).

81. Berth, *Les Nouveaux aspects du socialisme*, pp. 16–17. See also *Les Méfaits des intellectuels*, pp. 264–65.

82. Berth, *Les Méfaits des intellectuels*, pp. 264–67, 211.

83. Lagardelle, "La France et la paix," p. 412.

84. Berth, *Les Nouveaux aspects du socialisme*, p. 31.

85. H. Lagardelle, "Démocratie politique et organisation économique," *Le Mouvement socialiste*, no. 94 (31 May 1902): 1015, and no. 95 (7 June 1902): 1082.

86. Lagardelle, "Démocratie politique et organisation économique," pp. 1015–16.

87. Berth, "Socialisme ou Étatisme," p. 9.

88. Lagardelle, "Démocratie politique et organisation économique," pp. 1015–16. Concerning "workers' democracy" as opposed to "Christian democracy" or "liberal democracy," see Berth, "Catholicisme social et Socialisme," p. 344.

89. Lagardelle, "Démocratie politique et organisation économique," p. 1082.

90. R. Michels, *Political Parties* (London: Jarrold, 1915), p. 407.

91. É. Pouget, *La Confédération Générale du Travail* (Paris: Marcel Rivière, 1909), pp. 35–36.

92. V. Griffuelhes, *L'Action syndicaliste* (Paris: Marcel Rivière, 1908), p. 37.

93. H. Lagardelle, "Le syndicalisme et le socialisme en France," in *Syndicalisme et Socialisme*, pp. 36–37.

94. Pouget, *La Confédération Générale du Travail*, pp. 34–35.

95. Sorel, *La Décomposition du marxisme*, p. 58. See also Pouget, *La Confédération Générale du Travail*, pp. 10, 37–38, as well as Lagardelle, "Avant-Propos" in *Syndicalisme et Socialisme*, p. 5: syndicalism endeavored to destroy "hour by hour, as it appeared, the mendacious objective of a union of classes pursued by democracy."

96. Pouget, *La Confédération Générale du Travail*, p. 34.

97. Berth, "Socialisme ou Étatisme," pp. 12–13 (italics in original).

98. Berth, *Les Méfaits des intellectuels*, pp. 59–60, 64, 232, 258–60. See also Berth, "Socialisme ou Étatisme," p. 1.

99. E. Berth, "Notes bibliographiques," *Le Mouvement socialiste*, no. 179 (October 1906): 183. Concerning Nietzsche, see also "Les 'Considerations inactuelles' de Nietzsche," *Le Mouvement socialiste*, no. 200 (15 July, 1908): 52–63.

100. Berth, *Les Nouveaux aspects du socialisme*, pp. 59–60; É. Berth, "Révolution sociale ou Évolution juridique?" *Le Mouvement socialiste*, no. 143 (15 November 1904): 129; É. Berth, "Revue critique," *Le Mouvement socialiste*, no. 142 (1 November 1904); Berth, "Notes bibliographiques," pp. 180–81; Berth, *Les Méfaits des intellectuels*, p. 126.

101. Berth, *Les Méfaits des intellectuels*, p. 124 (italics in original).

102. Berth, "Catholicisme social et socialisme," p. 348, and "Politique et socialisme," *Le Mouvement socialiste*, no. 132 (15 January 1904): 35.

103. Berth, "Notes bibliographiques," pp. 180–81.

104. Concerning the cult of Proudhon, still associated with Marx, see Berth, *Les Nouveaux aspects du socialisme*, pp. 42–43; "Révolution sociale ou évolution juridique?" p. 25; and "L'Utopie du Professeur Menger," *Le Mouvement socialiste*, no. 136 (15 May, 1904): 36–37.

105. H. Lagardelle, "Démocratie et lutte de classe," *Le Mouvement socialiste*, no. 91, (10 May 1902): 895.

106. H. Lagardelle, "Socialisme ou Démocratie," *Le Mouvement socialiste*, no. 86 (5 April 1902): 631.

107. See C. Willard, *Le Mouvement socialiste en France (1893–1905). Les Guesdistes* (Paris: Éditions Sociales, 1965), p. 525.

108. Lagardelle, "Démocratie et lutte de classe," pp. 1009–12.

109. About the repercussions of the Affair in *Le Mouvement socialiste*, see especially the articles by A. Morizet, "M. Clemenceau ou le dreyfusisme au pouvoir," no. 181 (December 1906), and by R. Louzon, "La Faillite du dreyfusisme ou le triomphe du parti juif," no. 175 (July 1906).

110. H. Lagardelle, "Ministérialisme et Socialisme," *Le Mouvement socialiste*, no. 88 (19 April 1902): 727–29; "Socialisme et programme minimum," p. 781; "Démocratie politique et organisation économique," pp. 1010–12.

111. Lagardelle, "Socialisme et programme minimum," p. 684, and "Socialisme ou Démocratie," pp. 629–30.

112. H. Lagardelle, "Action de parti et action de classe," *Le Mouvement socialiste*, no. 149 (18 July 1905): 284.

113. Lagardelle, "*Le Socialisme* ouvrier," p. 2.

114. É. Berth, "Notes bibliographiques," *Le Mouvement socialiste*, no. 152 (1 April 1905): 494–95; *Les Nouveaux aspects du socialisme*, p. 15.

115. Berth, "Notes bibliographiques," pp. 493–94. See also Arturo Labriola, "L'Erreur tactique du Socialisme," *Le Mouvement socialiste*, no. 157 (15 June 1905): 229; Lagardelle, "*Le Socialisme* ouvrier," pp. 2–4.

116. Berth, *Les Méfaits des intellectuels*, pp. 238–39.

117. Lagardelle, "*Le Socialisme* ouvrier," pp. 2–4 (italics in original); Berth, "Révolution sociale ou Évolution juridique?" p. 133.

118. Berth, *Les Nouveaux aspects du socialisme*, pp. 8, 19–23, 31 (italics in original).

119. Berth, "L'Utopie du Professeur Menger," p. 44.

120. Berth, *Les Méfaits des intellectuels*, pp. 211–12.

121. Arturo Labriola, "Les Partis socialistes (Italie)," *Le Mouvement socialiste*, no. 132 (15 January 1904): 148, and 145. See also 142–149; Labriola, "Plus-value et reformisme," p. 214; Arturo Labriola, "Le Socialisme en Italie," *Le Mouvement socialiste*, no. 136 (15 May 1904): 4–5; and E. Leone, "La Grève générale en Italie et la politique prolétarienne," *Le Mouvement socialiste*, no. 142 (1 November 1904): 9–15.

122. See the manifesto of those resigning published in Leone's *Divenire sociale* and published in French translation in *Le Mouvement socialiste*, no. 157 (15 June 1905): 255–64.

123. Arturo Labriola, "Syndicalistes et Parti socialiste," *Le Mouvement socialiste*, no. 176 (July 1906): 240.

124. O. Dinale, "Controverses sur le Syndicalisme italien," *Le Mouvement socialiste*, nos. 177–78 (August–September 1906): 357, 363–365.

125. Arturo Labriola, "Syndicalistes et Parti socialiste," p. 472.

126. S. Panunzio, "La situation socialiste en Italie," *Le Mouvement socialiste*, nos. 177–78 (August–September 1906): 373.

127. O. Dinale, "Le Parti socialiste et les massacres de classe en Italie," *Le Mouvement socialiste*, nos. 177–78 (August–September 1906): 342–43, and Labriola, "Syndicalistes et Parti socialiste," p. 243 (italics in original).

128. P. Orano, "Les Syndicats et le Parti socialiste en Italie," *Le Mouvement socialiste*, nos. 177–78 (August–September 1906): 472.

129. R. Michels, "Les dangers du Parti socialiste allemand," *Le Mouvement socialiste*, no. 144 (1 December 1904): 201.

130. Ibid., pp. 199–200. See also pp. 193–99.

131. Michels, "Le socialisme allemand après Mannheim," p. 20.

132. R. Michels, "Les syndicats ouvriers," *Le Mouvement socialiste*, no. 158 (1 July 1905): 314–15.

133. Michels, "Les dangers du Parti socialiste allemand," pp. 195–97.

134. See R. Michels's articles in *Le Mouvement socialiste*: "Le prochain Congrès socialiste international," no. 188 (15 July 1907): 43–45; "Les socialistes allemands et la Guerre," no. 171 (5 February 1906): 129–36; "Polémiques sur le socialisme allemand," no. 176 (July 1906): 228–37; and "Le Patriotisme des socialistes allemands et le Congrès d'Essen," no. 194 (15 January 1908): 5–13.

135. R. Michels, "Le socialisme allemand et le Congrès d'Iéna," *Le Mouvement socialiste*, nos. 166–67 (15 November 1905): 305, 307.

136. R. Michels, "La Gréve des Métallurgistes de Berlin," *Le Mouvement socialiste*, no. 170 (15 January 1906): 96–100.

137. Michels, "Le prochain Congrès socialiste international," p. 39. See also Michels's review of E. Belfort Bax, *Essays in Socialism, New and Old* in *Le Mouvement socialiste*, no. 191 (15 October 1907): 349; Michels, "Les Socialistes allemands et la Guerre," p. 139; Michels, "Les dangers du Parti socialiste allemand," pp. 198–99.

138. Michels, "Les dangers du Parti socialiste allemand," pp. 200–201.

139. É. Berth, "Notes bibliographiques," *Le Mouvement socialiste*, no. 174 (15 May 1906): 180–81. See also "Notes bibliographiques," no. 150 (1 March 1905): 253–54.

140. H. Lagardelle, "Le socialisme allemand et les élections," *Le Mouvement socialiste*, no. 183 (February 1907): 196–97.

141. Arturo Labriola, "Le Syndicalisme et le Socialisme en Italie," in *Syndicalisme et Socialisme*, pp. 12–13.

142. H. Lagardelle, "Avant-propos," in *Syndicalisme et Socialisme*, p. 3.

143. H. Lagardelle, "La Confédération du Travail et le Parti socialiste (Intervention au Congres socialiste de Nancy)," *Le Mouvement socialiste*, nos. 189–90 (15 August 1907): 111.

144. Michels, "Les Socialistes allemands et la Guerre," p. 138.

145. H. Lagardelle, "La Confédération du Travail et le Parti socialiste (Intervention au Congres socialiste de Nancy—fin)," *Le Mouvement socialiste*, no. 191 (15 October 1907): 285.

146. Michels, "Les dangers du Parti socialiste allemand," p. 202.

147. E. Berth, "Les 'Discours' de Jaurès," *Le Mouvement socialiste*, no. 144 (1 December 1904). See Berth, "Révolution sociale ou Évolution juridique?" pp. 134–35; "Revue Critique," pp. 100–101; "Politique et Socialisme," *Le Mouvement socialiste*, no. 132 (15 January 1904): 24–25. See also H. Lagardelle, "Chronique politique et sociale," *Le Mouvement socialiste*, no. 152 (1 April 1905): 499; "Action de parti et Action de classe," p. 282; "Notes bibliographiques," *Le Mouvement socialiste*, no. 179 (October 1906); "Démocratie et Lutte de classe," pp. 892–93.

148. Lagardelle, "La France et la Paix," p. 416.

149. Berth, "Revue Critique," p. 104.

150. H. Lagardelle, "Notes bibliographiques," *Le Mouvement socialiste*, no. 179 (October 1906): 173.

151. É. Berth, "Notes bibliographiques," *Le Mouvement socialiste*, no. 179 (October 1906): 175–76.

152. É. Berth, "À propos de la Lutte de classe," *Le Mouvement socialiste*, no. 25 (1 January 1900): 26–27 (italics in original).

153. Berth, "Révolution sociale ou Évolution juridique?" pp. 138–39 (italics in original).

154. Berth, "Notes bibliographiques," p. 179. These notes constitute Berth's reply to Bernstein's attack on Sorel in *Sozialistische Monatschefte* of August 1906. See also, on direct action, *Les Nouveaux aspects du socialisme*, pp. 20–21, 33–34.

155. Berth, *Les Méfaits des intellectuels*, p. 207. See also "Catholicisme social et socialisme," p. 300.

156. Berth, *Les Méfaits des intellectuels*, pp. 201–202, 212–13. See also pp. 271, 293–94 (italics in original).

157. Ibid., Foreword of 1913, p. 12 (italics in original).

158. Berth, *Les Nouveaux aspects du socialisme*, pp. 51–52, 58. See also pp. 28–29, 54, 60, as well as "Revolution sociale ou Évolution juridique?" pp. 126–28.

159. Berth, *Les Méfaits des intellectuels*, p. 238.

160. É. Berth, "Revue critique," *Le Mouvement socialiste*, no. 179 (October 1906): 167.

161. R. Michels, "Revue critique," *Le Mouvement socialiste*, no. 184 (1 March 1907): 280–83 (italics in original).

162. See, for instance, É. Berth, "Politique et socialisme," *Le Mouvement socialiste*, no. 132 (15 January 1904): 33–34; H. Lagardelle, "Le Congrès syndical de Bourges. Le Congrès et le Socialisme ouvrier," *Le Mouvement socialiste*, no. 142 (1 November 1904): 31.

163. Michels, "Revue critique," p. 282, and Berth, "Revue critique," p. 166.

164. Berth, *Les Méfaits des intellectuels* (Foreword of 1913), p. 13. See also p. 12.

165. Ibid., Conclusion of 1913, p. 338 (italics in original).

166. Ibid., Introduction of 1913, p. 105.

167. Ibid., pp. 112–14.

168. Ibid., Foreword of 1913, pp. 14–15.

169. Ibid., Conclusion of 1913, pp. 301–302.

170. Ibid., pp. 346–347.

171. Ibid., pp. 301–302.

172. Ibid., Foreword of 1913, p. 15.

173. Ibid., Note of 1913, p. 292.

174. Ibid., Foreword of 1913, p. 15.

175. Berth, "Revue critique," pp. 166–67. Berth was attacking Michels's study, "Proletariat et bourgeoisie dans le mouvement socialiste italien," *Archiv für Sozialwissenschaft und Sozialpolitik* (Tübingen: J.-C.-B. Mohr, 1906). See Michels's reply in the March 1907 issue (no. 184) of *Le Mouvement socialiste*, "Controverse socialiste," pp. 278–88.

176. Berth, *Les Méfaits des intellectuels*, p. 292 (Note of 1913).

177. Ibid., Introduction of 1913, pp. 84–86.

178. Ibid., Conclusion of 1913, p. 357.

179. Ibid., Note of 1913, p. 292.

180. Ibid., Conclusion of 1913: 299–303.

181. Ibid., pp. 312–13 (italics in original), 350–51.

182. Ibid., Introduction of 1913: 95–100.

183. Ibid., pp. 90–91.

184. Ibid., Note of 1913, p. 275.

185. Ibid., Introduction of 1913, p. 110.

186. Ibid., p. 49.

187. G. Valois, "Notre première année," *Cahiers du Cercle Proudhon*, May–August 1912, p. 157. The *Cahiers* appeared from January 1912 to January 1914 on a two-monthly basis.

188. G. Valois, "Sorel et l'architecture sociale," *Cahiers*, May–August 1912, pp. 111–12. Most of this issue was a tribute to Georges Sorel. See also J. Darville [Édouard Berth], "Satellites de la ploutocratie," *Cahiers*, September–December

1912, p. 209; "Declaration du Cercle," p. 174. The founders of the Cercle were two former revolutionary syndicalists, Berth and Riquier, and six "social" Maurrassians: Valois, Henri Lagrange, Gilbert Maire, René de Marans, Andre Pascalon, and Albert Vincent.

189. G. Maire, "La philosophie de Georges Sorel," *Cahiers*, March–April 1912, pp. 62–74.

190. Berth, *Les Méfaits des intellectuels*, Introduction of 1913, p. 115.

191. "Nos maitres," *L'Action française*, 1 and 15 July 1902, pp. 63–75, 145–52. Among the masters, one should notice the presence of Voltaire on account of his anti-Semitism, that of Fourier on account of his nationalism, and that of Baudelaire on account of his disdain for progress and modernism: 15 January 1901, pp. 147–53; 1 May 1901, pp. 730–32; and 1 September 1902, pp. 394–98.

192. Ch. Maurras, "Besançon," *Cahiers*, January–February 1912, p. 4.

193. P. Galland, "Proudhon et l'ordre," *Cahiers*, January–February 1912, pp. 31–33; H. Lagardelle, "Proudhon et l'ordre européen," *Cahiers*, March–April 1912, p. 97.

194. G. Valois, "L'esprit proudhonien," *Cahiers*, January–February 1912, pp. 34–43.

195. J. Darville, "Proudhon," *Cahiers*, January–February 1912, pp. 10–13.

196. Maire, "La philosophie de Georges Sorel," p. 80.

197. Ibid., p. 62.

198. See, for instance, *Réflexions sur la violence*, pp. 8–9, 41–42, 173, 186–88, and *L'Indépendance*, 1 May 1911, pp. 190–92.

199. Concerning Le Bon, see Sorel's enthusiastic review of *Psychologie de l'éducation* (*L'Indépendance*, 11 April 1911, pp. 109–110), and an article in praise of Le Bon: "Sur la magie moderne," *L'Indépendance*, September 1911, pp. 1–11. Le Bon and Pareto also contributed to *L'Indépendance*: see 1 May 1911, 1 March and 1 May 1912.

200. Darville, "Satellites de la ploutocratie," p. 187, and Valois, *La Monarchie et la Classe ouvrière*, pp. xlvii–xlviii.

201. J. Darville, "La monarchie et la classe ouvrière," *Cahiers*, January–February 1914, p. 29.

202. Ibid., p. 15.

203. Darville, "Satellites de la ploutocratie," p. 209. See the references to Pareto in this article.

204. H. Lagrange, "L'oeuvre de Sorel et le Cercle Proudhon," *Cahiers*, May–August 1912, p. 129, and Valois, "Notre première année," pp. 158–59.

205. Darville, "Satellites de la ploutocratie," pp. 195, 202.

206. Ibid., pp. 195–98, 201–202.

207. Ibid., pp. 202–206 (italics in original). Here one must draw attention to S. F. Finer's important article "Pareto and Pluto-Democracy: The Retreat to Galápagos," *American Political Science Review* 62 (June 1968): 440–50, in which the writer opposes the interpretation of Pareto as a proto-Fascist.

208. Ibid., p. 180 (italics in original).

209. Ibid., p. 210.

210. Berth, *Les Méfaits des intellectuels*, Foreword of 1913, pp. 14, 65–68, 71, 115.

211. Berth, *Les Méfaits des intellectuels*, Introduction of 1913, pp. 52–54 (italics in original).

212. Ibid., Conclusion of 1913, p. 354 n. 1 (italics in original).

213. Ibid., Note of 1913, p. 163 (italics in original).

214. Ibid., Introduction of 1913, p. 97.

215. Ibid., p. 52.

216. Ibid., Conclusion of 1913, p. 347.

217. Ibid., Introduction of 1913, p. 57. See also pp. 97, 162–63, 304–306 (italics in original).

218. Ibid., p. 56.

219. Ibid., pp. 110–11. See also pp. 99–100, 163, Note 1 of 1913.

220. Ibid., Conclusion of 1913, pp. 353–54.

221. Ibid., pp. 345–46.

222. Ibid., p. 352.

Chapter Three

1. On revolutionary syndicalism and socialism in Italy, see R. Michels, *Storia critica del socialismo italiano dagli inizi fino 1911* (Florence: La Voce, 1926); L. Valiani, "Il Partito Socialista Italiano dal 1900 al 1918," *Rivista Storica Italiana*, 75 (1963); and A. Riosa, *Il sindacalismo rivoluzionario in Italia e la lotta politica nel partito socialista dell'età giolittiana* (Bari: De Donato, 1976).

2. On the emergence of revolutionary syndicalism in France, Sorel's role in the creation of its ideology, and the syndrome of Left-Right, Right-Left migration, see H. Dubief, ed., *Le Syndicalisme révolutionnaire* (Paris: A. Colin, 1979); J. Julliard, *Fernand Pelloutier et les origines du syndicalisme d'action directe* (Paris: Seuil, 1971); Z. Sternhell, *La Droite révolutionnaire, 1895–1914*.

3. A. Labriola, *Spiegazioni a me stesso* (Naples: Centro Studi Sociali Dopoguerra, undated), p. 117.

4. The economic development of Italy from the time of its unification to the eve of the First World War is described in L. Cafagna, "The Industrial Revolution in Italy, 1830–1914," in C. M. Cipolla, ed., *The Fontana Economic History of Europe*, vol. 4, pt. 1 (Glasgow: Fontana-Collins, 1975). See also R. A. Webster, *Industrial Imperialism in Italy, 1908–1915* (Berkeley and Los Angeles: University of California Press, 1975); S. Lanaro, *Nazione e lavoro* (Venice: Marsilio, 1979), and *L'Italia nuova. Identità e sviluppo, 1861–1988* (Turin: Einaudi, 1988). For the war period, see L. Salvatorelli and G. Mira, *Storia d'Italia nel periodo fascista*, vol. 1 (Verona: Mondadori, 1972). For a Marxist interpretation of the process of capital accumulation in Italy and on the weaknesses of the Italian economy, see P. Grifone, *Il capitale finanziario in Italia* (Turin: Einaudi, 1971).

5. Roberts exaggerates the antipolitical bias of revolutionary syndicalism. We need only cite Leone. In a reply to an article on the situation of Italian socialism, he wrote: "All economic struggles are political struggles, and thus the economic struggles of syndicalism are also political struggles. The professional syndicalists have all the class functions that the party has arrogated to itself" (E. Leone, "Postilla," *Il divenire sociale*, 16 September 1908, p. 296). These lines throw light on the attitude of the revolutionary syndicalists, who undoubtedly wished to subordinate the political to the economic sphere, but without obscuring the role the former can or ought to play. They derived these conceptions from Marx, whom they accepted and re-

spected at the beginning, even if they wished to adapt or modernize his theories and to find the right way of putting them into practice politically.

Roberts does not give sufficient importance to the "economistic" tendencies of revolutionary syndicalism and its original connection with Marxism, and this is what makes him conclude that the movement was antipolitical. See D. D. Roberts, *The Syndicalist Tradition and Italian Fascism* (Chapel Hill, N.C.: University of North Carolina Press, 1979), chap. 3: "The Origins of the Antipolitical Vision."

6. On political integration and the activities of the revolutionary faction within the PSI, see Riosa, *Il sindacalismo*, chap. 3.

7. For Riosa's excellent analysis on this point, see ibid., pp. 61–83, 135ff.

8. A. Aquarone, *L'Italia giolittiana (1896–1915). Le premesse politiche ed economiche* (Bologna: Il Mulino, 1981), p. 257. It is necessary here to clarify the sequence of events. Following the clashes in Buggerru, the socialist labor circles took the decision to launch a general strike if such incidents recurred.

9. A. Labriola, "Il congresso di Amsterdam," *Avanguardia socialista*, 28 August 1904, p. 1.

10. The Italian delegation to Amsterdam, led by E. Ferri, did not include revolutionary syndicalists. On the polemic conducted by the revolutionary syndicalists in Brescia, Bologna, and Amsterdam, see Riosa, *Il sindacalismo*, pp. 101–31.

11. H. Lagardelle, "Lo sciopero generale e il socialismo," *Avanguardia socialista*, 3 September 1904, p. 1.

12. On this point, see Riosa, *Il sindacalismo*, pp. 145ff.

13. G. Procacci, *La lotta di classe in Italia agli inizi del secolo XX* (Rome: Editori Riuniti, 1970), p. 386.

14. On the revolutionary-syndicalist interpretations of the strike of 1904, see the daily bulletins published in *Avanguardia socialista* from the beginning of the movement, A. Lanzillo, *Le Mouvement ouvrier en Italie* (Paris: Marcel Riviere, [probably 1910]), and A. Labriola, *Storia di dieci anni 1899–1909* (1910; reprint Milan: Feltrinelli, 1975).

15. Lanzillo, *Le Mouvement ouvrier en Italie*, p. 17.

16. See *Avanguardia socialista*, 24 September 1904, p. 1.

17. We are referring here to the events of 18 September 1904 in Milan, where the assembled workers rejected the decision of the political leadership at the Chamber of Labor to stop the strike. Labriola and his colleagues voted to end the strike, but faced with the reaction of the workers, the revolutionary syndicalist leader decided to continue the stoppage. See, "Il quinto comizio. Lo sciopero continua!" *Avanguardia socialista*, 24 September 1904, p. 1.

18. G. B. Furiozzi, *Il sindacalismo rivoluzionario italiano* (Milan: Mursia, 1977), p. 35.

19. See A. Roveri, "Il sindacalismo rivoluzionario in Italia," *Ricerche Storiche*, 1 June 1975, pp. 14–17; and F. M. Snowden, *Violence and Great Estates in the South of Italy: Apulia 1900–1922* (Cambridge, Mass.: Cambridge University Press, 1986), chap. 6.

20. A. Labriola, "Da socialista a reazionario—Lettera aperta a Napoleone Colajanni," *Avanguardia socialista*, 22 April 1905, p. 1.

21. Revolutionary-syndicalist elitism was undoubtedly indebted to the theories of Mosca and Pareto, as claimed by Giovanna Cavallari in her work on Labriola, Leone,

Longobardi, and Italian proto-Marxism, but it also owed much to Sorel's advocacy of a moral renewal. See G. Cavallari, *Classe dirigente e minoranze rivoluzionarie. Il protomarxismo italiano: Arturo Labriola, Enrico Leone, Ernesto Cesare Longobardi* (Pubblicazioni della Facoltà di Giurisprudenza dell'Università di Camerino, Jovene Editore, 1983), pp. 221–26.

22. In May 1907, Alceste De Ambris had already drawn the Parma Chamber of Labor into a successful strike. See T. R. Sykes, "Revolutionary Syndicalism in the Italian Labour Movement: The Agrarian Strikes of 1907–1908 in the Province of Parma," *International Review of Social History* 21 (1976): 186–211.

23. "Lo sciopero generale agrario," *L'internazionale*, 3 May 1908, p. 1.

24. "Lo sciopero generale agrario si estende," *L'internazionale*, 5 May 1908, p. 1; and "La celebrazione d'una data," *L'internazionale*, 21 June 1919, p. 1.

25. Sykes, "Revolutionary Syndicalism," pp. 204–206.

26. Furiozzi, *Il sindacalismo rivoluzionario*, pp. 40–41.

27. This is the argument of Mario Isnenghi in his *Il mito della grande guerra* (Rome and Bari: Laterza, 1973). This book is a brilliant study of the intellectual currents that led up to the view that only war would enable Italy to surmount its internal problems.

28. G. Sorel, "L'antimilitarismo in Francia," *Avanguardia socialista*, 6 January 1906, p. 1.

29. "Impressioni e ricordi," *L'Italia nostra*, 26 October 1918, p. 2.

30. See A. Labriola, "Intorno al herveismo," *Pagine libere*, 1 October 1907.

31. Roberts, *The Syndicalist Tradition*, p. 47. Here Roberts indicates the important role played by the nationalist journal *L'idea nazionale*. See also M. Degl'Innocenti, *Il socialismo italiano e la guerra di Libia* (Rome: Editori Riuniti, 1976), pp. 17, 20–23, in which the writer draws attention to the economic interests supporting the Catholic and nationalist journals and to the demagogic nature of their advocacy of "The New Crusade," "The Holy War," and the march toward the "Promised Land."

32. Degl'Innocenti, *Il socialismo italiano*, p. 45. Benito Mussolini, the head of the revolutionary faction in the PSI, was one of the leaders of the general strike, whose results greatly disappointed him.

33. The disagreements over the Libyan War made De Ambris and Mantica leave the editorial staff of *Pagine libere*, with the result that it stopped appearing. Polemical articles had been published in *L'internazionale* too. Arguments for and against were brought together in the collective work *Pro e contro la guerra di Tripoli. Discussioni nel campo rivoluzionario* (Naples: Società Editrice Partenopea, 1912), which included articles by Labriola, Olivetti, Giulio Barni, De Ambris, Alfredo Polledro, and Libero Tancredi. Leone, who opposed the Libyan campaign, had written in the previous year *Espansionismo e colonie* (Rome: Tipografia Editrice Nazionale, 1911). In 1912, again, Arturo Labriola published *La guerra di Tripoli e l'opinione socialista* (Naples: Morano, 1912), in which he presented arguments in favor of intervention.

34. Furiozzi, *Il sindacalismo rivoluzionario*, pp. 50–55.

35. "Come avvenne l'eccidio di Ancona," *L'internazionale*, 20 June 1914, p. 1. For more details on the general strike of the red week, see "La fiera protesta dei lavoratori romani," p. 5; "Le meravigliose giornate proletarie di Milano," p. 2; and E. Santarelli, *Il socialismo anarchico in Italia* (Milan: Feltrinelli, 1959), p. 164.

36. "Il proletariato è concorde," *L'internazionale*, 8 August 1914, p. 1.

37. A. De Ambris, "I sindacalisti e la guerra," *L'internazionale*, 22 August 1914, p. 1.

38. See R. De Felice, *Mussolini il rivoluzionario* (Turin: Einaudi, 1965), pp. 233–37, 249, 269–78.

39. "I loro ed i nostri," *L'internazionale*, 25 December 1915, p. 3, and "Alceste De Ambris," *L'internazionale*, 6 November 1915, p. 1.

40. Furiozzi, *Il sindacalismo rivoluzionario*, pp. 64–65.

41. S. Nosengo, "Dalmine Docet," *Il sindacato operaio*, 5 March 1920, p. 1.

42. "L'Unione italiana del Lavoro si dichiara disposta ad assumere la gestione delle fabbriche," *L'internazionale*, 4 September 1920, p. 1.

43. "La grande battaglia dei metallurgici," *L'internazionale*, 25 September 1920, p. 1.

44. "Il nuovo testo del decreto," *Avanti!* 21 September 1920, p. 1.

45. G. Giolitti, *Memoirs of My Life* (London and Sydney: Chapman and Dodd, 1923), pp. 439, 441.

46. See "Cronache politiche. L'impresa di Fiume," *Il rinnovamento*, 15 October 1919.

47. R. De Felice, *Sindacalismo rivoluzionario e fiumanesimo nel carteggio De Ambris-D'Annunzio* (Brescia: Morcelliana, 1966), pp. 65–66, and De Felice, *Mussolini il rivoluzionario*, pp. 552–53.

48. A. Labriola, *Riforme e rivoluzione sociale* (Lugano: Società Editrice Avanguardia, 1906), p. 10.

49. A. Labriola, "I limiti del sindacalismo rivoluzionario," *Il divenire sociale*, 1 August 1910, pp. 213–14.

50. Labriola, *Riforme e rivoluzione sociale*, p. 10.

51. Ibid. This conception of the state was the element of continuity behind all the variants of revolutionary syndicalism until the promulgation of the Carta del Carnaro. This view of the state was in total contradiction to the classical approach of fascism, based on the national corporatism of Alfredo Rocco and not on the syndical corporatism of Alceste De Ambris as represented in the Carta del Carnaro.

52. See ibid., p. 214.

53. Ibid., p. 230.

54. Labriola and Leone wrote several articles and participated in several debates on Marxist economic theories. We wish to draw attention to two important works in which they attempted to revise the theory of surplus value. The first, by Labriola, is *La teoria del valore di C. Marx. Studio sul Libro III del Capitale* (Milan and Palermo: Sandron, 1899). This study was prepared with a view to the Tenore Prize at the Pontian Academy, but it did not win an award, apparently on account of the intervention of Benedetto Croce, who preferred the contribution of another candidate. The second, by Leone, is *La revisione del marxismo* (Rome: Biblioteca del Divenire sociale, 1909). This book gathers together articles published in *Il divenire sociale*.

55. On the relationship between Sorel and Italian revolutionary syndicalism, see G. B. Furiozzi, *Sorel e l'Italia* (Florence: D'Anna, 1975).

56. E. Leone, *Il sindacalismo* (Palermo: Sancron, 1910), p. 35.

57. A. Labriola, "Sul momento attuale della scienza economica," *Pagine libere*, 15 February 1907 (actually 1906), p. 13. This article, entirely devoted to the most recent studies in economics, was placed at the beginning of the newest but also the most

important revolutionary syndicalist publication, edited by Labriola and Angelo Oliviero Olivetti.

We must point out and recommend three articles in R. Faucci, ed., *Gli Italiani e Bentham. Dalla "Felicità" pubblica all'economia del benessere* (Milan: Franco Angeli Editore, 1982), which present and analyze the revision of Marx's economic theories undertaken by Labriola and Leone. These articles are V. Gioia, "Enrico Leone fra marxismo ed edonismo," pp. 43–64; E. Santarelli, "Calcolo edonistico e sfruttamento del lavoro nel marxismo 'microeconomico' di Enrico Leone (1898–1916)," pp. 65–90; and S. Perri, "Economia politica o economia pura? Arturo Labriola e la revisione del marxismo," pp. 232–52. On the political revision of Marx, see E. Santarelli, *La revisione del marxismo in Italia* (Milan: Feltrinelli, 1977). If we insist on the importance of Labriola's and Leone's contribution to economic thought in general, it is in order to indicate the cardinal role they played in the ideological transition from socialism to fascism.

58. Labriola, "Sul momento attuale della scienza economica," pp. 8–9, 13.

59. It is worth recalling that Labriola studied and worked with Vilfredo Pareto in Lausanne and was strongly influenced by his economic theories. Pareto himself was one of the most famous disciples of Walras; both are considered precursors of the modern theory of value. Walras developed the analysis of the general equilibrium, whereby the equilibrium between quantities and prices appears to be the result of the play of prices on the market. See R. B. Ekelund, Jr., and R. F. Hebert, *A History of Economic Theory and Method* (Tokyo: McGraw-Hill, 1983), chap. 16.

60. Concerning the hedonist principle in economics, see ibid.

61. E. Leone, "Il materialismo nella storia," *Il divenire sociale*, 16 August 1905, p. 249.

62. Concerning the "society of free producers," see A. Labriola, "I limiti del sindacalismo rivoluzionario," *Il divenire sociale*, 1 August 1910, pp. 212–15, and 16 August 1910, pp. 226–30. Paolo Favilli wrote an excellent article on Labriola and Leone's revision of Marx's economic theory, in which he showed how their attempt to impose a "liberist"–anti-Marxist conception on Marx's model ended by creating something in which the Marxist content had become marginal. Favilli's analysis is subtle and correct. We maintain, however, that many factors, indicated in Favilli's article, demonstrate that this was not deliberate. The two theoreticians of revolutionary syndicalism sought to correct and supplement certain aspects of Marxist economics that seemed to them outdated or that needed to be revised in the light of modern developments in economics. They therefore proposed the synthesis we have described here. In any case, they did not foresee that they would end where they did, and when their disciples began to draw near fascism, they did not give them their approval and even distanced themselves . See P. Favilli, "Economia e politica del sindacalismo rivoluzionario. Due riviste di teoria e socialismo: 'Pagine libere' e 'Divenire sociale,'" *Studi Storici* 1 (1975), and M. Sznajder, "Economic Marginalism and Socialism: Italian Revolutionary Syndicalism and the Revision of Marx," *Praxis International* 11, 1 (April 1991): 114–27.

63. Leone, *La revisione del marxismo*, pp. 42, 50. Leone did not agree with Pareto that it is necessary to take into consideration the influence of noneconomic factors on the economic process. See V. Pareto, "Le mie idee," *Il divenire sociale*, 16 July 1910, p. 195.

64. Leone, *La revisione del marxismo*, p. 67.

65. Ibid., p. 68. In order to reaffirm the connection he perceived between "liberism" and socialism, Leone referred to Walras, who maintained that the "hedonistic maximum" of agricultural production was to be reached only through a collective ownership of land and the organization of production. This was an important example for the purpose of bridging the gap between free-market policies—associated with the idea of individual profits—and socialism.

66. Ibid., p. 70.

67. E. Leone, "Il plusvalore nell'edonismo e nel marxismo," *Il divenire sociale*, 16 July 1907, p. 187.

68. Ibid., pp. 184–85.

69. Ibid., p. 186. In the last part of this article, Leone dealt with one of the principal problems of Marx's economic model, that of transformation. For a more detailed explanation of the revolutionary syndicalists' critique of Marx's theory of value, see Ekelund and Hebert, *A History of Economic Theory*, pp. 238–40.

70. Leone, "Il materialismo nella storia," p. 251.

71. Leone, "Il plusvalore nell'edonismo e nel marxismo," p. 186.

72. Leone, *Il sindacalismo*, pp. 163–64. In March 1904, Labriola was even a member of the antiprotectionist Liberist League founded by Edoardo Giretti, Antonio De Viti De Marco and Luigi Einaudi. See Labriola, *Storia di dieci anni, 1899–1909*, chap. 8; Riosa, *Il sindacalismo rivoluzionario in Italia*, chap. 2.

73. Concerning the problems of the north-south dichotomy and their connection with protectionism, see also Marucco, *Arturo Labriola e il sindacalismo rivoluzionario*, chap. 4: "La questione meridionale," pp. 130–42; and Gregor, *Young Mussolini*, pp. 18–20.

74. Concerning Leone's position on intervention in Libya, see Leone, *Espansionismo e colonie*.

75. Leone, *Il sindacalismo*, p. 103.

76. Ibid., pp. 107–108.

77. A. Lanzillo, "Giorgio Sorel nella storiografia," *Il divenire sociale*, 1 August 1910, p. 220.

78. A. Lanzillo, *La disfatta del socialismo: Critica della guerra e del socialismo*, 2d ed. (Florence: Libreria della Voce, 1918).

79. P. Orano, "Giorgio Sorel," *Pagine libere*, 1 June 1907, pp. 750–56.

80. S. Panunzio, "Socialismo, sindacalismo e sociologia," *Pagine libere*, 15 January 1907, p. 173.

81. Michels, *Storia critica del socialismo*, p. 324.

82. Labriola, *Spiegazioni a me stesso*, p. 124.

83. Leone, *Il sindacalismo*, pp. 226–27.

84. R. Michels, "Kautsky e i rivoluzionari italiani," *Il divenire sociale*, 1 November 1905.

85. Labriola, "Sul momento attuale della scienza economica," p. 17.

86. Pareto, "Le mie idee," p. 194.

87. S. Panunzio, "Autonomia, libertà e reazione," *Il divenire sociale*, 1 March 1910, 1 April 1910, 16 April 1910, and 1 May 1910.

88. On this, see P. Mantica, "L'antropologia delle classe poveri," *Il divenire sociale*, 1 July 1905.

89. Labriola was not elected as a Socialist party candidate in 1904. He was elected

for the first time in 1913, as an independent socialist. In 1920 he became minister of labor in the first Giolitti postwar government.

90. On Sorel and the antecedents of fascism, see Talmon, *The Myth of the Nation and the Vision of Revolution*, p. 458.

91. A. Labriola, "Tirando le somme," *Avanguardia socialista*, 24 September 1904, p. 2.

92. "V giornata—l'ultimo comizio," *Avanguardia socialista*, 24 September 1904, p. 2 (no byline).

93. Labriola, "Tirando le somme," p. 2.

94. Walter Mocchi, the coeditor of *Avanguardia socialista*, wrote: "Well, yes: we have adopted Sorel, but we have also adopted him in order to broaden our ideas" (W. Mocchi, "Dopo lo sciopero generale," *Avanguardia socialista*, 30 September 1904, pp. 1–2).

95. A. Polledro, "La manifestazione proletaria," *Avanguardia socialista*, 7 October 1904, p. 2.

96. "Politica Proletaria," *Il divenire sociale*, 16 January 1909, p. 23 (no byline).

97. P. Mantica, "Mentre a Parma si sciopera," *La cultura socialista*, 15 June 1908, p. 155.

98. P. Orano, "I risultati di un grande sciopero," *La cultura socialista*, 15 June 1908, p. 137.

99. "Le forme della resistenza," *Il divenire sociale*, 16 October 1908, p. 313.

100. Orano, "I risultati," pp. 139–40.

101. Lanzillo, *Le Mouvement ouvrier en Italie*, pp. 34–40.

102. A. Labriola, "Per la teoria dello sciopero," *Pagine libere*, 15 June 1908, pp. 712–13.

103. B. Mussolini, "Un blocco rosso?," *Utopia*, 15–28 February 1914, p. 69.

104. B. Mussolini, "La settimana rossa," *Utopia*, 15–31 July 1914, p. 242.

105. A. De Ambris, "Dopo la bufera," *L'internazionale*, 20 June 1914, p. 1.

106. A. De Ambris, "Ancora in tema di Unità," *L'internazionale*, 1 August 1914, p. 1, and "Dopo la bufera," p. 1.

107. A. O. Olivetti, "Ricominciamo," *Pagine libere*, 10 October 1914, p. 4.

108. C. Morisi, "Orizzonti nuovi," *Battaglie dell'unione italiana del lavoro*, 5 April 1919, p. 1.

109. A. De Ambris, "Bolscevismo e sindicalismo," *L'internazionale*, 26 April 1919, p. 2.

110. "I fatti della settimana," *L'internazionale*, 29 March 1919, p. 1.

Chapter Four

1. We are referring, of course, to a stage in which all economic forces compete freely in an open market. Nevertheless, the social solidarity required by the socialism of the nation originates in the idea of an identity of interests in all sectors engaged in production.

2. See Riosa, *Il sindacalismo*, pp. 360ff.

3. See Isnenghi, *Il mito della grande guerra*, pp. 7–22.

4. C. Lazzari, "Il diritto antimilitarista," *Avanguardia socialista*, 22 September 1906, p. 1.

5. Labriola, "Intorno al herveismo," p. 389.

6. Ibid.

7. Ibid., p. 391.

8. Ibid., p. 396.

9. N. Tranfaglia, "Prefazione," in Labriola, *Storia di dieci anni*, p. xv.

10. P. Orano, "L'antimilitarismo," *Il divenire sociale*, 16 September 1910, p. 3.

11. P. Orano, "L'insipido Adriatico," *Pagine libere*, 1 June 1909, pp. 620–23.

12. G. Prezzolini, *La teoria sindicalista* (Naples: Francesco Perella Editore, 1909), p. 123.

13. Ibid., p. 17.

14. At that period, the name of Sorel was already connected with monarchist-nationalist circles. On Sorel's influence, see Furiozzi, *Sorel e l'Italia*, p. 245. Mario Missiroli was one of the best-known Italian political journalists. At the period referred to, he was very close to revolutionary syndicalism and carried on a continuous correspondence with Sorel. See G. Sorel, *Lettere a un amico in Italia* (Bologna: Capelli, 1963). The economist Alfonso di Pietri Tonelli was one of the revolutionary syndicalist intellectuals who went over to fascism. At that period, he contributed to *Pagine libere*. Massimo Fovel was a nationalist engaged in the syndical struggle.

15. A. Lanzillo, "Gli anarchici e noi," *Il divenire sociale*, 1 May 1910, pp. 104–105. Lanzillo spared no effort in defending Sorel. See "La bancarotta della demagogia," "Giorgio Sorel nella storiografia," "La dissoluzione del regime democratico," "Ancora contro il demagogismo,"—all articles that appeared in *Il divenire sociale*, 16 February 1910, 1 August 1910, 16 August 1910, and 1–16 September 1910.

16. Corradini, *Discorsi politici (1902–1923)*, p. 60.

17. Ibid., p. 57.

18. On these developments and the Biella group, see F. Perfetti, *Il nazionalismo italiano. Dalle origini alla fusione col fascismo* (Bologna: Capelli, 1977), pp. 93ff. Article two of the statutes of the Biella group, the first nationalist formation, stipulated: "The contradiction between the concept of class struggle and that of class collaboration between the productive classes . . . is the foundation of a national union with a vocation of imperial conquest." See Perfetti, *Il nazionalismo italiano*, p. 101. This declaration appeared for the first time in *Il tricolore* on 16 July 1909.

19. M. Viana, "Lotta di classe e solidarietà nazionale," *Il tricolore*, 16 September 1901, in Perfetti, *Il nazionalismo italiano*, p. 100.

20. Corradini, *Discorsi*, p. 62.

21. Ibid., p. 69.

22. E. Corradini, "Nazionalismo e sindacalismo," *La lupa*, 16 October 1910, p. 2.

23. E. Corradini, "Le nazioni proletarie e il nazionalismo" and "Proletariato, emigrazione, Tripoli," in *Discorsi*, pp. 103–18, 119–34.

24. Corradini, "Nazionalismo e sindacalismo," p. 2.

25. For a detailed description and analysis of the discussion in the book among a revolutionary syndicalist, a liberal, and a nationalist, see Isnenghi, *Il mito della grande guerra*, pp. 10–15.

26. A. Labriola, "I due nazionalismi," *La lupa*, 16 October 1910, p. 1.

27. Ibid.

28. Ibid.

29. Postilla, in Corradini, "Nazionalismo e sindacalismo," p. 2.

30. "Presentazione," *Pagine libere*, 15 December 1906, p. 4.

31. A. Labriola, "La prima impresa collettiva della nuova Italia," in *Pro e contro la guerra di Tripoli*, p. 49.

32. A. O. Olivetti, "Sindacalismo e nazionalismo," in *Pro e contro la guerra di Tripoli*, p. 15. This article was first published in *Pagine libere*, 15 February, 1911.

33. Ibid., pp. 16–17.

34. Ibid., p. 18.

35. See E. Corradini, "Utilità nazionalista delle organizzazione operaie," *Il tricolore*, 1 August 1909; and also M. Viana, "La lotta di classe e solidarietà nazionale," *Il tricolore*, 16 September 1909. These two articles were included in Perfetti, *Il nazionalismo italiano*, pp. 96–100.

36. See E. Lazzari, "L'Italia errante," *Avanguardia socialista*, 9 June 1906.

37. E. Corradini, "Relazione presentata al primo congresso nazionalista a Firenze il 3 dicembre 1910," *Discorsi*, pp. 90–102.

38. A. O. Olivetti, "L'altra campana," in *Pro e contro la guerra di Tripoli*, p. 111.

39. Labriola, "La prima impresa," in *Pro e contro la guerra di Tripoli*, p. 54.

40. Ibid., p. 50.

41. P. Orano, "Verso Tripoli," *La lupa*, 10 September 1911, p. 1. The syndicalists did not hide their apprehension that some countries—Argentina, for instance—might be closed to Italian immigration. At that period, *L'internazionale* reported the existence of a student league in Buenos Aires that strongly opposed the immigration of Italians.

42. Olivetti, "L'altra campana," p. 115.

43. L. Tancredi, "Una conquista rivoluzionaria," in *Pro e contro la guerra di Tripoli*, p. 222.

44. L. Tancredi, "Libero Tancredi spiega," *L'internazionale*, 11 November 1911, p. 1.

45. Tancredi, "Una conquista," p. 223.

46. In this connection, see Furiozzi, *Il sindacalismo rivoluzionario italiano*, p. 47, and Degl'Innocenti, *Il socialismo italiano e la guerra di Libia*, pp. 114–15.

47. On Leone's position, see his book *Espansionismo e colonie* and also G. De Falco, "L'espansionismo e le colonie in un libro di Enrico Leone," *L'internazionale*, 9 March 1912, p. 3, and, by the same author, "L'adesione di Enrico Leone," *L'internazionale*, 2 April 1912, p. 1.

48. P. Mantica, "Cos'è che vale l'impresa di Tripoli," *L'internazionale*, 7 October 1911, p. 3.

49. T. Masotti, "L'ora che volge," *L'internazionale*, 30 September 1911, p. 1.

50. G. Barni, "Tripoli e il sindacalismo," in *Pro e contro la guerra di Tripoli*, pp. 163ff.

51. A. De Ambris, "Il Congresso generale. Una lettera di Alceste De Ambris," *L'internazionale*, 4 November 1911, p. 1.

52. A. De Ambris, "Stabiliamo la responsabilità," *L'internazionale*, 25 November 1911, p. 1.

53. P. Mantica, "Gli intellettuali sindacalisti e la politica espansionista," *L'internazionale*, 28 October 1911, p. 1.

54. Labriola, "Gli intellettuali," p. 2.

55. P. Mantica, "Una spiegazione necessaria," *L'internazionale*, 4 November 1911, p. 3.

56. A. O. Olivetti, "Una dichiarazione di Olivetti," *L'internazionale*, 30 December 1911, p. 2.

57. Labriola, "Gli intellettuali," p. 1.

58. "A. De Ambris e P. Mantica si ritirano da *Pagine libere*. See *L'internazionale*, 25 November 1911, p. 1. On the discontinuation of *Pagine libere*, see Roberts, *The Syndicalist Tradition*, p. 104.

59. De Falco, "L'espansionismo e le colonie," p. 3.

60. In his work *The Syndicalist Tradition*, Roberts claimed that only Labriola, Olivetti, and Orano favored intervention in Libya. Furiozzi was concerned in his *Il sindacalismo rivoluzionario*, with describing the profound crisis that the movement experienced at the time of the intervention. Degl'Innocenti, for his part, argued in *Il socialismo italiano e la guerra di Libia* that the Libyan controversy was a polemic between intellectuals and labor leaders, with the former rejoining the nationalists in the cultural sphere of Sorelianism (although they still to a large degree remained positivists and were worried about the evolution of capitalism) and the latter fighting a daily battle for the respect of workers' rights and for strengthening the syndicates. Degl'Innocenti claimed that the aristocratic attitude of the intellectuals enabled them to see themselves, in accordance with the concept of interchangeable elites, as the potential champions of the ruling elite of the moment. It should be pointed out that people like Labriola, although they could be classed as intellectuals, were actively involved in political and syndical life, while others like De Ambris and Mantica were lacking in neither intellectual qualities nor capacities. For ourselves, we believe that the importance of the Libyan episode lay in its role in the evolution of ideologies, inasmuch as it permitted the concepts of war and nation to be regarded as revolutionary.

61. Following the disagreements caused by the Libyan War and the problems due to the refusal of the CGL, in May 1912, to accept the support of the Chambers of Labor of Milan and Cento (controlled by the revolutionary syndicalists), De Ambris decided, at the congress of Modena on the 23–25 November 1912, to found an independent syndical union, the USI, or Unione Sindacale Italiana. For more details, see Furiozzi, *Il sindacalismo rivoluzionario*, pp. 51–54.

62. "Proletari in piedi: Abbasso la guerra!" *L'internazionale*, 1 August 1914, p. 1 (no byline).

63. Ibid.

64. "Mentre tuona il cannone," *L'internazionale*, 1 August 1914, p. 1 (no byline).

65. It should be remembered that at the beginning of 1914 Borghi had succeeded in getting the USI to pass a resolution against the war. On the antiwar positions within the USI, see A. Caciaghi, "Atto di sincerità," *L'internazionale*, 29 August 1914, p. 1, and "Il proletariato è concorde," *L'internazionale*, 8 August 1914, p. 1 (no byline).

66. E. Leone, "La società delle genti e la guerra," *Utopia*, 15 August–1 September 1914, pp. 318–71.

67. F. Andreucci, and T. Detti, *Il Movimento operaio italiano. Dizionario Biografico. 1853–1943*, vol. 3 (Rome: Editore Riuniti, 1977), p. 91. Leone was probably

one of the last revolutionary syndicalists to abandon the liberist, nonmythical ap-proach to the general revolutionary strike.

68. T. Masotti, "Per la libertà dell'Europa," *L'internazionale*, 8 August 1914, p. 1.

69. P. Mantica, "Guerra e speranze," *L'internazionale*, 15 August 1914, p. 3.

70. The call was made from the podium of the USI congress in Milan on 18 August 1914. On the first interventionist steps of the revolutionary syndicalist leader, see De Felice, *Mussolini il rivoluzionario*, pp. 235–36, and Furiozzi, *Il sindacalismo rivoluzionario*, p. 60.

71. A. De Ambris, "I sindacalisti e la guerra," *L'internazionale*, 22 August 1914, p. 2.

72. S. Panunzio, "Il socialismo e la guerra," *Utopia*, 15 August–1 September 1914, p. 324 (italics in original).

73. S. Panunzio, "Guerra e socialismo," *Avanti!* 12 September 1914, p. 2 (italics in original).

74. The two other problems to be solved were (1) the dichotomy between an industrial mass society with strong democratic tendencies and the existence of a traditional monarchy in the same country, and (2) the secret workings of international diplomacy. See A. Labriola, *La conflagrazione europea e il socialismo* (Rome: Atheneum, 1915), pp. 193–97. At the time this book appeared, Labriola had been an independent socialist deputy for two years.

75. Labriola, *La conflagrazione europea*, p. 186. Here he enumerated the psycho-logical factors that in time of war worked in favor of nationalism.

76. A. De Ambris, "Bancarotta!" *L'internazionale*, 5 September 1914, p. 1.

77. Panunzio, "Guerra e socialismo," p. 2.

78. It should be pointed out here that the interventionist wing of the USI, led by De Ambris and Corridoni and benefiting especially from the support of the activists of Parma and Milan, left the union because of the neutralist position it had adopted. These factions, regrouped around *L'internazionale*, were among the founding ele-ments of the UIL (Unione Italiana del Lavoro).

79. This manifesto of the Fascio was dated 5 October 1914; *Pagine libere* renewed publication on the ten that month.

80. "Ai Lavoratori d'Italia," *Pagine libere*, 10 October 1914. The manifesto of this new group—Fascio Rivoluzionario d'Azione Internazionalista—bore the signatures of Deccio Bacchi, Michele Bianchi, Ugo Clerici, Filippo Corridoni, Amilcare De Ambris, Attilio Deffenu, Aurelio Galassi, A. O. Olivetti, Decio Papa, Cesare Rossi, Silvio Rossi, Sincero Rugarli, and Libero Tancredi.

81. A. O. Olivetti, "Europa 1914," *Pagine libere*, 10 October 1914, p. 11.

82. A. O. Olivetti, "Il vaso di Pandora," *Pagine libere*, 10 October 1914, p. 3. See also A. Labriola, *La conflagrazione europea*, p. 192, where, having analyzed the dif-ferent stages of capitalism in different countries, he concluded: "There are as many socialisms as there are countries."

83. A. Lanzillo, "Il fallimento del socialismo," *Pagine libere*, 15 November 1914, p. 3.

84. A. O. Olivetti, "Ricominciamo," *Pagine libere*, 10 October 1914, p. 2.

85. A. O. Olivetti, "Menzogne," *Pagine libere*, 10 January 1915, p. 4.

86. Ibid., p. 5.

87. See the articles that Olivetti published in *Pagine libere* at the end of June 1914

and at the beginning of 1915: "Parole chiare," "Menzogne," "Il vaso di Pandora," and so on.

88. See "I loro ed i nostri," *L'internazionale*, 25 December 1915, p. 3.

89. This explains why initially the revolutionary syndicalists were favorably disposed to the Russian Revolution, although they later rejected Bolshevik ideas and actions. For favorable opinions, see A. De Ambris, "Gli eccessi della Rivoluzione," *L'internazionale*, 31 March 1917, p. 1, and, by the same author, "Profezia russa," *L'internazionale*, 7 April 1917. For anti-Communist views, see A. De Ambris, "Bolscevismo e sindacalismo," *L'internazionale*, 26 April 1919, p. 2; A. O. Olivetti, "Esame di coscienza," *L'internazionale*, 1 May 1920, p. 1, and "Terno secco," *Pagine libere*, 25 April 1920.

90. This slogan was used as a motto by the official daily newspaper of the UIL, *Italia Nostra*, which in 1919 changed its name to *Battaglie dell'Unione Italiana del Lavoro*.

91. See M. Ledeen, *The First Duce* (Baltimore and London: Johns Hopkins University Press, 1977), chap. 9; De Felice, *Sindacalismo rivoluzionario e fiumanesimo*, pp. 90–91; and *La Carta del Carnaro nei testi di Alceste De Ambris e di Gabriele D'Annunzio* (Bologna: Il Mulino, 1973); M. Sznajder, "The Carta del Carnaro and Modernization," *Tel Aviver Jahrbuch für deutsche Geschichte* 19 (1989); Furiozzi, *Il sindacalismo rivoluzionario*, pp. 74–75; and finally Roberts, *The Syndicalist Tradition*, pp. 179–81.

92. *Il rinnovamento* was a monthly journal, edited by Alceste De Ambris, which appeared between March 1918 and October 1919. It was the organ of the new national corporatist trend and expressed productionist ideas. *Pagine libere* reappeared for the fourth time in February 1920; it came out monthly and was published in Milan under the editorship of Angelo Oliviero Olivetti.

93. A. De Ambris, "Programma d'azione," *Pagine libere*, 5 November 1914, p. 3.

94. Lanzillo, "Il fallimento del socialismo," p. 3.

95. S. Panunzio, "Il lato teorico e il lato pratico del socialismo," *Utopia*, 15–31 May 1914, p. 201.

96. Lanzillo, *La disfatta del socialismo*, p. 13.

97. Ibid., p. 28.

98. Ibid., pp. 33–34 (italics in original).

99. Ibid., p. 96.

100. Ibid., pp. 123–24.

101. Ibid., p. 169.

102. Here Lanzillo combined elements that became features of the Fascist ideology: the union of the people and a progress toward a transcendent ideal, embodied in the supreme negation of materialism—death.

103. The influence of Pareto's theory of elites on Lanzillo in particular and on revolutionary syndicalists in general is obvious. Their perception of syndicates as the germ of the future society of "free producers" enabled them to apply the theory of elites to the syndicates. They predicted that in the immediate future syndicates would be run by revolutionary proletarian elites until the time came when these groups would become the social elite, capable of responding with violence to the oppressive use of power by the regime. This new elite would then replace the bourgeoisie and lead society in the process of moral and economic regeneration.

104. Emilio Gentile claims that Mussolini certainly read Lanzillo's book, which appeared for the first time in January 1918 and was republished only a few months later. See Gentile, *Le origini dell'ideologia fascista*, p. 76.

105. See Lanzillo, *La disfatta del socialismo*, p. 13.

106. N. Fiore, "Dalla guerra al socialismo nazionale," *L'internazionale*, 9 February 1909, p. 1. In this article, the writer mentions Labriola as being in favor of some state intervention in the economy in order to facilitate the transition from a war economy to a peacetime economy and in order to defend the interests of the nation against private interests. At this period, Labriola was no longer one of the main syndicalist leaders, but he was still regarded as one of the intelligentsia of the movement.

107. A. De Ambris, "La terra ai contadini," *L'internazionale*, 1 May 1917, p. 1.

108. M., "La terra ai contadini," *L'internazionale*, 24 November 1917, p. 1 (M. is Benito Musssolini).

109. The question was discussed in the Italian parliament. See "Un progetto di legge in favore dei contadini," *L'internazionale*, 1 December 1917.

110. Oliviero Zuccarini claimed that there was no proof that any economic system was more viable than the capitalist system. See O. Zuccarini, "La Revolution future, la propriété de l'État," *Pagine libere*, 15 March 1920, p. 61.

111. This form of self-management was proposed by the UIL as a solution to the crisis of September 1920, at the time of the occupations of factories. See "Il Consiglio Nazionale delle Unione Italiana del Lavoro esamina l'agitazione dei metallurgici," *L'internazionale*, 8 September 1920, p. 1.

112. A. De Ambris, "I sovraprofitti e la guerra," *Il rinnovamento*, year 1, vol. 1 (1918): 228.

113. A. De Ambris, "I rimedi eroici," *Il rinnovamento* 2, no. 4 (1 May 1919): 200.

114. A. De Ambris, "Le classi dirigenti al bivio. O autoespropriazione parziale o bolscevismo," *Battaglie dell'Unione Italiana del Lavoro*, 1 May 1919, pp. 1–2.

115. A. De Ambris, "I limiti dell'espropriazione necessaria," *Il rinnovamento*, 31 May 1919, p. 226. This was the last of three articles in which A. De Ambris presented his plan for the socioeconomic reconstruction of Italy after the war. The other two were "La tempesta che viene," *Il rinnovamento*, 15 April 1919, and "I rimedi eroici" (see n. 113).

116. "Partial agricultural expropriation" meant the transfer of unexploited lands to organized agricultural workers. This is how the slogan The Land to the Peasants was to be understood. The first beneficiaries of this redistribution were to be the families of those who had died in battle, followed by war veterans who had served in the trenches. Compensation to expropriated landowners was to take into account the price of land before the war. This compensation could take the form of government bonds.

117. De Ambris spoke of a compromise of a political sort, whereby the workers and the representatives of the state would cooperate in councils of management "in order to supervise and, if necessary, stimulate the functioning of industry" (De Ambris, "I limiti dell'espropriazione necessaria," p. 229).

118. It should be pointed out that at that time the Milanese Fasci were regarded as belonging to the Left, which explains the proximity of people like De Ambris, Panunzio, and Mussolini. On this, and on the relationship between *Il rinnovamento* and the fascists, see R. De Felice, *Mussolini il rivoluzionario*, pp. 515–19.

119. In fact, what the Fascists called partial expropriation was what De Ambris called necessary expropriation. De Felice points to the fact that *Il popolo d'Italia* published De Ambris's program on 10 June 1919, and De Ambris published a pamphlet containing his program as adopted by the Fascists. See A. De Ambris, *I postulati dei Fasci di Combattimento. L'espropriazione parziale* (Bergamo: N.p. , 1919).

120. "La costituzione dell'Unione Italiana del Lavoro," *L'internazionale*, 29 June 1918, p. 1.

121. A. O. Olivetti, "Le armi al popolo," *Pagine libere*, 15 December 1914.

122. A. De Ambris, "La terra ai contadini," *L'internazionale*, 24 December 1921, p. 21. This was in connection with a discussion between syndicalists and Fascists in which De Ambris expressed surprise that the Fascists had so radically changed their opinion on the agrarian question when in 1919 their positions had resembled those of revolutionary syndicalism.

123. A. De Ambris, "Sempre più che mai sindacalisti," *Il rinnovamento*, 15 July 1919, pp. 297–98.

124. "Scioperi . . . bolscevichi," *L'internazionale*, 19 April 1919, p. 1. (The French word *troupe* is used in the text.)

125. "'Cronache politiche,' I comandamenti dell'ora: Prima agire," *Il rinnovamento*, 15 October 1919, pp. 583–84.

126. On the proposed solution for overcoming the contradiction between state bureacracy and the class interests of the syndicate, see A. Ciattini, "L'evoluzione economica," *Battaglie dell'Unione Italiana del Lavoro*, 5 April 1919. In this article, the writer spoke of national property, which he distinguished from state property or syndical property.

127. S. Panunzio, "Un programma d'azione," *Il rinnovamento*, 15 March 1919, p. 89.

128. S. Panunzio, "Progettismo," *Il rinnovamento*, 31 December 1918, p. 488.

129. S. Panunzio, "La rappresentanza di classe," *Il rinnovamento*, 15 August 1919, pp. 398–99.

130. Panunzio had already envisaged this form of representation toward the end of the first decade of the century. See S. Panunzio, *La persistenza del diritto (Discutendo di Sindacalismo e di Anarchismo)* (Pescara: Casa Editrice Abruzzese, 1909), p. 240.

131. See A. Lanzillo, "Contro l'elezionismo democratico," *Il popolo d'Italia*, 21 May 1919, and "Rappresentanza integrale," *Il popolo d'Italia*, 23 May 1919. These articles are referred to a great deal in Panunzio, "La rappresentanza di classe," p. 406.

132. A. Lanzillo, "Sulla via del sindacalismo," *L'internazionale*, 24 April 1920, p. 1.

133. Ledeen, *The First Duce*, p. 171.

134. On De Ambris and the Carta del Carnaro, see De Felice, *Sindacalismo rivoluzionario e fiumanesimo*, and *La Carta del Carnaro nei testi*.

135. On the new political style D'Annunzio introduced, in which the flamboyant combined with the mystical, see G. L. Mosse, "The Poet and the Exercise of Political Power," in *Yearbook of Comparative and General Literature*, no. 22 (1973).

136. On this, see De Felice, *Sindacalismo rivoluzionario e fiumanesimo*, pp. 63–64.

137. Ibid., pp. 65–66, and De Felice, *Mussolini il rivoluzionario*, pp. 552–53.

138. On the position of national syndicalism with regard to Fiume, see "L'Unione Italiana del Lavoro, la questione di Fiume," *L'internazionale*, 8 May 1919, p. 1; "Fiume," *L'internazionale*, 2 April 1919, p. 1; and "Cronache Politiche. L'impresa di Fiume," *Il rinnovamento*, 15 October 1919, pp. 575–76.

139. Quotation from a letter written by De Ambris to D'Annunzio, dated 13 May 1920; see De Felice, *Sindacalismo rivoluzionario e fiumanesimo*, pp. 183–84. This letter enables us to understand the modus operandi that existed between De Ambris and D'Annunzio. This having been said—and despite what he wrote—it seems that De Ambris's ideological contribution to the Carta del Carnaro was fundamental, especially with regard to the corporatist structure it describes. It should be added that the Commandante was essentially in agreement with De Ambris's national-syndicalist model.

140. This letter was dated 18 September 1920. See ibid., p. 209.

141. A comparison of the two versions of the text—De Ambris's and D'Annunzio's—and the light thrown on the subject by De Felice in the introduction to his work confirm this point beyond any doubt. See De Felice, *La Carta del Carnaro nei testi.*

142. Ibid., p. 45.

143. The Carta del Carnaro envisaged two chambers for purposes of legislation and the election of the government. One was to be elected by all citizens aged twenty or more, and the other was to be elected only by members of corporations—that is, the producers. Since only the latter could participate in both elections, it followed that they were the only ones to enjoy full political rights.

144. Fascism undoubtedly took its first corporatist model from national syndicalism, but it is necessary to distinguish De Ambris's model—democratic, controlled from below, and allowing a place for autonomy—from Alfredo Rocco's, which was authoritarian, controlled from above, and allowed no place for autonomy.

145. We are speaking here of the incidents that took place in Bologna on 21 November 1920 and in Ferrara on 20 December 1920. During these days, the Fascist groups used violence against their socialist enemies, even shooting and killing them.

146. See De Felice, *Sindacalismo rivoluzionario e fiumanesimo*, pp. 246–47.

147. A. O. Olivetti, "Rinnovare!" *Pagine libere*, July 1921.

148. A. De Ambris, "Il nostro nazionalismo," *L'internazionale*, 15 October 1921, p. 1.

149. E. Rossoni, "Fascismo e movimento sindacale," *L'internazionale*, 14 May 1921, p. 4.

150. A. De Ambris, "Rispondendo all'Ordine Nuovo," *L'internazionale*, 20 August 1926.

151. See the opinions of Cesare Rossi (a former revolutionary syndicalist who had become national secretary of the Fascist movement), of Benito Mussolini, and of other Fascist leaders as quoted in "Il fascismo giudicato dai capi fascisti," *L'internazionale*, 19 September 1921, p. 2. Mussolini is quoted as saying: "Fascism is synonymous with terror for the workers. A group of businessmen and politicians has identified fascism with its own interests." The fact that statements of this kind were reported by the editors of *L'internazionale* reveals their doubts and hopes concerning fascism and some of its leaders.

152. A. O. Olivetti, "Nel labirinto," *Pagine libere*, May–June 1922, p. 163.

153. A. De Ambris, "Il fascismo al bivio," published in *La riscossa dei legionari fiumani*, 12 February 1922. This article is given in its entirety in De Felice, *Sindacalismo rivoluzionario e fiumanesimo*, pp. 331–42.

154. E. Ferrari, "Trincerismo, comunismo e fascismo," *Pagine libere*, July 1922.

155. Concerning Labriola, see Marucco, *Arturo Labriola e il sindacalismo rivoluzionario*, chap. 14 and Conclusion.

156. For Leone's biography, see A. Andreassi, "Leone, Enrico," in Andreucci and Detti, *Il movimento operaio*, vol. 3, pp. 89–92.

157. On Mussolini's attitude to D'Annunzio and the Fiume enterprise, see De Felice, *Mussolini il rivoluzionario*, chap. 13.

158. When exiled in France, De Ambris wrote a book presenting his theories on corporatism. The work appeared only after his death. See A. De Ambris, *Dopo un ventennio. Il Corporativismo* (Bordeaux: Augusto Mione Editore, 1935).

159. For more information on the careers of these people, see Roberts, *The Syndicalist Tradition*, pp. 14–15.

160. *Dizionario Enciclopedico Italiano*, vol. 2 (Rome: Istituto della Enciclopedia Italiana, 1970), p. 266.

161. Roberts, *The Syndicalist Tradition*, pp. 13–14.

162. Some contemporaries of Italian fascism stressed Panunzio's influence in the formulation of the Fascist theory of corporatism. See H. Mathews, *The Fruits of Fascism* (New York: Harcourt Brace, 1943), pp. 151–53; M. Prelot, *L'Empire fasciste: Les origines, les tendances et les institutions de la dictature et du corporatisme italiens* (Paris: Librairie du Receuil Sirey, 1936), pp. 72–83; and L. Rosenstock-Franck, *L'Economie corporative fasciste en doctrine et en fait: Ses origines historiques et son evolution* (Paris: Librairie Universitaire de J. Gamber, 1934), p. 10.

163. *Dizionario Enciclopedico Italiano*, vol. 8, p. 593.

164. Ibid., vol. 6, p. 688.

165. See G. M. Bravo, "Michels, Robert," in Andreucci and Detti, *Il movimento operaio*, vol. 3, pp. 451–60.

166. A. O. Olivetti, "Il Manifesto dei Sindacalisti," *Pagine libere* 4–5 (1921): 159, 158.

167. For an account of Leone's revision of Marx's economic theories, we warmly recommend a reading of Willy Gianinazzi's "Enrico Leone, socialiste, revisioniste et syndicaliste revolutionnaire italien au tournant du siecle (1894–1907)" (Ph.D. diss., Université de Paris 8, Vincennes, 1984).

Chapter Five

1. On Mussolini as a socialist leader of national importance, see P. Melograni, "The Cult of the Duce in Mussolini's Italy," *Journal of Contemporary History* 11 (1976): 225. At that period, even Gramsci called him "our leader"; see D. Settembrini, "Mussolini and the Legacy of Revolutionary Socialism," *Journal of Contemporary History* 11 (1976): 251. On the opinion of the younger generation on the eve of the war that Mussolini was the top leader of the Socialist party, see G. Gozzini, "La Federazione Giovanile Socialista tra Bordiga e Mussolini (1912–1914)," *Storia Contemporanea* (February 1980): 103–104; A. Bordiga, and A. Tasca, *I primi dieci anni*

del PCI, pp. 87–88, in R. De Felice, "Presentazione," *Utopia* (Milan: Feltrinelli, un-dated), p. xi n. 11. On Mussolini's place within the Socialist party, see the less objective account of D. Grandi, *Il mio paese. Ricordi autobiografici*, a cura di R. De Felice (Bologna: Il Mulino,1985), p. 65.

2. B. Mussolini, *Opera Omnia*, ed. Edoardo and Duilio Susmel, vol. 1 (Florence: La Fenice, 1972), pp. 9–10, 30, 46–47. (*Opera Omnia* will henceforth be referred to as *O.O.*)

3. Ibid., p. 36. See also, De Felice, *Mussolini il rivoluzionario*, p. 33.

4. Ibid., pp. 59–60.

5. B. Mussolini, "La crisi risolutiva," *Avanguardia socialista*, 3 September 1904, *O.O.*, vol. 1, pp. 70–71.

6. B. Mussolini, "Intorno alla notte del 4 Agosto," in *Avanguardia socialista*, 30 July 1904, and "Per Ferdinando Lassalle (nel 40 anniversario della sua morte)," *Avanguardia socialista*, 20 August 1904, *O.O.*, vol. 1, pp. 61–68.

7. B. Mussolini, "L'individuel et le social," *Avanguardia socialista*, 14 October 1904, *O.O.*, vol. 1, p. 74.

8. B. Mussolini, "La morta gora (confessioni d'un deputato)," *Avanguardia socialista*, 11 March 1905, *O.O.*, vol. 1, pp. 94–97.

9. B. Mussolini, "Intermezzo polemico," *La lima*, 25 April 1908, *O.O.*, vol. 1, p. 128.

10. B. Mussolini, "L'attuale momento politico (considerazioni inattuali)," *La lima*, 18 April 1905, *O.O.*, vol. 1, p. 128.

11. Vero Eretico [Mussolini], "Socialismo e socialisti," *La lima*, 30 May 1908, *O.O.*, vol. 1, p. 142.

12. On the various influences on Mussolini, see E. Santarelli, "Socialismo rivoluzionario e 'Mussolinismo' alla vigilia del primo conflitto europeo," *Rivista Storica del Socialismo*, nos. 13–14 (May–December 1961). On Mussolini's very special conception of Marxism and its connection with the ideas of Sorel, Nietzsche, revolutionary syndicalism, anarchism, and so on, see J. S. Woolf, "Mussolini as Revolutionary," *Journal of Contemporary History* 1, no. 2 (1966): 190. On Sorel's ideological influence on Mussolini, see S. Romano, "Sorel e Mussolini," *Storia Contemporanea* 15, no. 1 (1984). On Luxemburg's influence on Mussolini, see D. Settembrini, "Mussolini and the Legacy," pp. 250–51. On the revision of Marxism in Italy, see Santarelli, *La revisione del marxismo in Italia*. This question is now the subject of a vigorous debate.

13. Some people claim that Mussolini was never a socialist, or was never a true socialist. Such an assertion means disregarding a priori both Mussolini's writings and his career as an activist. It is quite obvious that around 1910 this young revolutionary did not know that he would one day be a Fascist. There is no reason to deny the historical value of his ideas or positions of those days. One example of this controversy is a criticism by Vivarelli of the great work of R. De Felice. Vivarelli reproached this work for taking Mussolini's declarations and writings seriously, which was not, he said, the best way of discovering the secret of Mussolini's success. See R. Vivarelli, "Benito Mussolini dal socialismo al fascismo," in *Il fallimento del liberalismo. Studi sulle origini del fascismo* (Bologna: Il Mulino, 1981), pp. 108–109, which first appeared in *Rivista Storica Italiana* 79 (1967). Vivarelli also cast doubt on the Marxist content of Mussolini's socialism; N. Tranfaglia, "Dalla neutralità italiana alle origini

del fascismo: Tendenze attuale della storiografia," in *Dallo stato liberale al regime fascista. Problemi e ricerche* (Milan: Feltrinelli, 1981), p. 87. At the opposite extreme, A. J. Gregor claimed that fascism was a version of classical Marxism, which is hardly more reasonable. See Gregor, *Young Mussolini*, p. xi.

14. B. Mussolini, "La Crisi," *L'avvenire del lavoratore*, 11 February 1909, *O.O.*, vol. 2, p. 7.

15. B. Mussolini, "Nazionalismo," *La lima*, 17 December 1910. This article appeared without a byline in *La lotta di classe*, 10 December 1910, *O.O.*, vol. 3, pp. 280–81.

16. This is a statement from a speech made by Mussolini in Milan on 17 November 1912 against the intervention of the European powers in the Balkans. B. Mussolini, "Contro la Guerra," *Avanti!* 18 November 1912, *O.O.*, vol. 4, p. 234.

17. B. Mussolini, "Sport di coronati," *Il proletario*, 29 June 1903, *O.O.*, vol. 1, p. 32.

18. This passage, which appeared without a byline, is ascribed to Mussolini: "La Guerra?" *La lotta di classe*, 30 September 1911, *O.O.*, vol. 4, p. 74.

19. B. Mussolini, "Il proletariato ha un interesse alle conservazioni delle patrie attuali?" *L'avvenire del lavatore*, 1 July 1909, *O.O.*, vol. 2, p. 170.

20. Gregor claims that Mussolini's attitude to the Libyan question was motivated by tactical considerations and was intended to strengthen his position in the Socialist party. Gregor, *Young Mussolini*, p. 128.

21. De Felice, *Mussolini il rivoluzionario*, p. 110. See also Degl'Innocenti, *Il socialismo italiano e la guerra di Libia*.

22. B. Mussolini, "Lo sciopero generale e la violenza," *Il popolo*, 25 June 1909, *O.O.*, vol. 2, p. 167.

23. B. Mussolini, "Socialismo e socialisti," *La lima*, 30 May 1908, *O.O.*, vol. 1, p. 143.

24. B. Mussolini, "Per finire," *La lima*, 6 June 1908, *O.O.*, vol. 1, p. 147.

25. B Mussolini, "Lo sciopero generale e la violenza," *Il popolo*, 25 June 1909, *O.O.*, vol. 2, pp. 163–68.

26. B. Mussolini, "La teoria sindacalista," *Il popolo*, 25 May 1909, *O.O.*, vol. 2, p. 124.

27. Ibid., p. 127.

28. See the following articles by Mussolini: "Fra libri e riviste," *Il popolo*, 4 September 1909, *O.O.*, vol. 2, pp. 248–49; "Andrea Costa in un libro di Paolo Orano," *La lotta di classe*, 21 October 1910, *O.O.*, vol. 3, p. 97; "Il socialismo degli avvocati," *La lotta di classe*, 25 June 1910, *O.O.*, vol. 3, p. 122; "Ministerialismo," *La lotta di classe*, 21 May 1910, *O.O.*, vol. 3, p. 95; "Dopo il Congresso di Milano," *La lotta di classe*, 29 October 1910, *O.O.*, vol. 3, p. 253; "L'attuale momento politico e partiti politici in Italia," *O.O.*, vol. 3, p. 284.

29. B. Mussolini, "Varsavia e il 'Pus' Triestino," *Il popolo d'Italia*, 22 August 1920, *O.O.*, vol. 16, p. 155.

30. Mussolini, "La teoria sindacalista," pp. 127–28.

31. See, for instance, B. Mussolini, "La poesia di Klopstock dal 1789 al 1795," *Pagine libere*, 1 November 1908, and "La filosofia della forza (Postille alla conferenza dell'on Treves)," *Il pensiero romagnolo*, 29 November 1908, 6 December 1908, and 13 December 1908, *O.O.*, vol. 1, pp. 174–84.

32. B. Mussolini, "Giovanni Giolitti," *Il popolo*, 12 October 1909, *O.O.*, vol. 2, p. 259, and "Vecchiaia," *La lotta di classe*, 2 July 1910, *O.O.*, vol. 3, p. 130.

33. B. Mussolini, "L'ultima capriola," *La lotta di classe*, 26 November 1910, *O.O.*, vol. 3, p. 272.

34. B. Mussolini, "Da Guicciardini a . . . Sorel," *Avanti!* 18 July 1912, *O.O.*, vol. 4, p. 171. (The French word *poseur* is used in the text.)

35. B. Mussolini, "Fine stagione," *La lotta di classe*, 17 December 1910, *O.O.*, vol. 3, p. 289. (The French phrase *Ancien Régime* is used in the text.)

36. Ibid.

37. See the polemic against Paolo Orano, editor of *La lima*, in B. Mussolini, "Nel mondo dei Rabagas," *La folla*, 18 August 1912, *O.O.*, vol. 4, p. 191.

38. A. De Ambris, "Noi e il Partito Socialista. In guardia contro l'illusione," *L'internazionale*, 27 July 1912, p. 1.

39. On the Mussolini—De Ambris controversy, see B. Mussolini, "La canditatura De Ambris," *Avanti!* 13 April 1913, *O.O.*, vol. 5, p. 153; A. De Ambris, "I nostri casi personali. La storia di una fuga—Dedicato a Benito Mussolini ed a tutti gli eroi della sua forza," *L'internazionale*, 18 April 1913, p. 1; B. Mussolini, "Personalia," *Avanti!* 19 April 1913, *O.O.*, vol. 5, p. 153; and A. De Ambris, "Punto e basta," *L'internazionale*, 3 May 1913.

40. B. Mussolini, "L'atteggiamento del sindacalismo verso le elezioni," *Avanti!* 25 October 1913, *O.O.*, vol. 5, p. 355.

41. B. Mussolini, "Lo sciopero generale di protesta contro l'impresa di Tripoli. Constatazioni," *La lotta di classe*, 30 September 1911, *O.O.*, vol. 4, p. 61.

42. B. Mussolini, "Il Congresso di Modena," *Avanti!* 24 November 1912, *O.O.*, vol. 4, p. 237. The Modena congress took place from 23 to 25 November.

43. Mussolini, "Lo sciopero generale di protesta contro l'impresa di Tripoli. Constatazioni," p. 61.

44. B. Mussolini, "Replica a Graziadei," *Il giornale d'Italia*, 6 July 1914, *O.O.*, vol. 6, p. 244.

45. B. Mussolini, "Metallurgici proclamano lo sciopero generale," *Avanti!* 19 May 1913, *O.O.*, vol. 5, pp. 160–61.

46. B. Mussolini, "Lo sciopero generale," *Avanti!* 8 June 1913, *O.O.*, vol. 5, p. 170, and "Sciopero conservatore," *Avanti!* 15 August 1913, *O.O.*, vol. 5, p. 258.

47. B. Mussolini, "Dopo lo sciopero alle 'Miani e Silvestri.' Una lettera dell'Unione Sindacale," *Avanti!* 26 February 1914, *O.O.*, vol. 6, pp. 103–108.

48. B. Mussolini, "La settimana rossa," *Utopia*, 15–31 July 1914, p. 242.

49. B. Mussolini, "Hervé promette," *Avanti!* 26 September 1914, *O.O.*, vol. 6, p. 370, and "Intermezzo polemico," *Avanti!* 8 October 1914, *O.O.*, vol. 6, pp. 381–85; "Fra la paglia e il bronzo," *La patria. Il resto del carlino*, 13 October 1914, *O.O.*, vol. 6, p. 390.

50. See *Avanti!* 18 October 1914, *O.O.*, vol. 6, pp. 393–403.

51. "Ai lavoratori d'Italia," *Pagine libere*, 10 October 1914, p. 37.

52. De Felice, *Mussolini il rivoluzionario*, p. 272.

53. See the stirring tribute that Mussolini paid to the memory of the syndicalist leader: "Celebrazione della Pace," *Il popolo d'Italia*, 13 November 1918, *O.O.*, vol. 11, pp. 480–81.

54. Mussolini, "Contro la Guerra," pp. 232, 234–35.

55. "Dinnanzi al fatto compiuto," *Avanti!* 9 December 1912, *O.O.*, vol. 5, p. 12. Unsigned article ascribed to Mussolini.

56. "Dopo il fatto compiuto," *Avanti!* 10 December 1912, *O.O.*, vol. 5, p. 14.

57. "Dinnanzi al fatto compiuto," p. 12.

58. The review *Utopia* declared itself to be the "Rivista Quindicinale del Socialismo Rivoluzionario Italiano."

59. B. Mussolini, "Al largo," *Utopia*, 22 November 1913, pp. 1–2.

60. B. Mussolini, "Ai giovani," *Utopia*, 10 December 1913, p. 28.

61. B. Mussolini, "L'impresa disperata," *Utopia*, 15 January 1914, pp. 1–5.

62. Ibid., pp. 1–2.

63. See the letter from Mussolini to Prezzolini of March 25 1914, quoted by R. De Felice in his presentation of *Utopia*, p. ix.

64. Mussolini, "L'impresa disperata," pp. 3–5.

65. S. Panunzio, "Il lato teorico e il lato pratico del socialismo," *Utopia*, 15–31 May 1914, pp. 200–205.

66. L. Salvatorelli, *Nazionalfascismo* (1923; reprint, Turin: Einaudi, 1977), p. 170.

67. B. Mussolini, "Sulla breccia," *Avanti!* 9 January 1914, *O.O.*, vol. 6, pp. 35–40. E. Lazzeri, "Italiani e Slavi a Trieste," *Utopia*, 30 January 1914, pp. 241–52.

68. "Per la concordia ma contro i blocchi," *La patria. Il resto del carlino*, 26 April 1914, *O.O.*, vol. 6, p. 152. See the editorial observations added as a footnote at the bottom of the page.

69. Mussolini, "La settimana rossa," pp. 241–52.

70. Ibid., p. 250.

71. On the connection between Mussolini's ideological crisis and his change from absolute neutralism to interventionism, see A. Balabanoff, *Ricordi di una socialista* (Rome: De Luigi, 1946), pp. 63–68; J. A. Thayer, *Italy and the Great War: Politics and Culture, 1870–1915* (Madison: University of Wisconsin Press, 1964), p. 266; and De Felice, *Mussolini il rivoluzionario*, p. 287.

Many people claim that Italy's entry into the war was the beginning of the Fascist revolution. Among these there are Fascists, of course, but also quite a number of scholars! Although the interventionist minority was indeed the spearhead of the Fascist movement, not all interventionists became Fascists. On this subject, see B. Mussolini, "23 Marzo," *Il popolo d'Italia*, 18 March 1919, *O.O.*, vol. 12, p. 310; Salvatorelli, *Nazionalfascismo*, p. 27; R. Cantalupo, *La classe dirigente* (Milan: Alpes, 1926), pp. 25–27; A. Tasca, *Nascita e avvento del fascismo* (Bari: Laterza, 1974), p. 12; A. Lyttelton, *The Seizure of Power* (London: Weidenfeld and Nicolson, 1973), p. 3; Tranfaglia, *Dallo stato liberale*, p. 53.

72. L'homme qui cherche, "Note di guerra," *Utopia*, 15 August–1 September 1914, p. 306.

73. R. De Felice thinks that Mussolini's decision to support the interventionist position was influenced by the concept of "revolution by means of war." See De Felice, *Mussolini il rivoluzionario*, pp. 288–361. This interpretation may be explained by De Felice's opinion that in 1914 Mussolini still belonged to the revolutionary Left. De Felice goes even farther and claims that until the battle of Caporetto Mussolini remained a "dormant [*dormiente*] socialist, but a socialist nevertheless." On this question, see Tranfaglia, *Dallo stato liberale*, pp. 80–88; Vivarelli, "Benito Mussolini dal socialismo," pp. 77–97; and Isnenghi, *Il mito della grande guerra*.

74. Libero Tancredi [Massimo Rocca], "Il direttore del'*Avanti!* smascherato. Un uomo di paglia," Lettera aperta a Benito Mussolini, *La patria. Il resto del carlino*, 7 October 1914, *O.O.*, vol. 6, pp. 501–503; and T. Masotti, "Da Mussolini al direttore dell'*Avanti!*" *L'internazionale*, 10 October 1914. See also the telegram that Giuseppe Giulietti, the secretary of the sailors' syndicate, who played an important role in the Fiume affair, sent to Mussolini: *Il popolo d'Italia*, 15 November 1914, in *O.O.*, vol. 7, p. 10.

75. B. Mussolini, "Intermezzo polemico," *Avanti!* 8 October 1914, *O.O.*, vol. 6, p. 383.

76. B. Mussolini, "Un accordo anglo-franco-russo per la discussione delle condizioni di pace," *Avanti!* 7 September 1914, *O.O.*, vol. 6, p. 360.

77. B. Mussolini, "Dalla neutralità assoluta alla neutralità attiva ed operante: Nazioni e internazionale," *Avanti!* 18 October 1914, *O.O.*, vol. 6, pp. 400–401; "La situazione internazionale e l'atteggiamento del partito," *Avanti!* 11 November 1914, *O.O.*, vol. 6, p. 427.

78. Mussolini, "La situazione internazionale e l'atteggiamento del partito," p. 428.

79. Interview given by Mussolini to the journal *La patria. Il resto del carlino*, which appeared in the journal on 11 November 1914, *O.O.*, vol. 6, p. 431.

80. See Vivarelli, "Benito Mussolini dal socialismo," pp. 97–105.

81. See the following articles by Mussolini: "Ciò che rimane e ciò che verrà," *Il popolo d'Italia*, 13 November 1920, *O.O.*, vol. 16, p. 5; "Mezzi e fini," *Il popolo d'Italia*, 16 November 1920, *O.O.*, vol. 16, pp. 14–15. See also De Felice, *Sindacalismo rivoluzionario e fiumanesimo*, p. 311.

82. See De Felice, *Mussolini il Rivoluzionario*, p. 344.

83. B. Mussolini, "La necessità dell'intervento," *Il popolo d'Italia*, 6 December 1914, *O.O.*, vol. 7, p. 66; "Per la libertà dei popoli per l'avvenire d'Italia," *Il popolo d'Italia*, 17 December 1914, *O.O.*, vol. 7, p. 80; "Il dovere dell'Italia," *Il lavoro di Genova*, 30 December 1914, *O.O.*, vol. 7, p. 107.

84. B. Mussolini, "È nostra!" *Il popolo d'Italia*, 18 March 1915, *O.O.*, vol. 7, pp. 264–67.

85. B. Mussolini, "Audacia," *Il popolo d'Italia*, 15 November 1914, *O.O.*, vol. 7, pp. 5–6.

86. B. Mussolini, "Il 'pericolo inaudito,'" *Il popolo d'Italia*, 29 May 1915, *O.O.*, vol. 8, p. 6; "Kamarad," *Il popolo d'Italia*, 10 June 1915, *O.O.*, vol. 8, pp. 11–15.

87. B. Mussolini, "Marx e . . . Hindenburg," *Il popolo d'Italia*, 28 August 1915, *O.O.*, vol. 8, pp. 184–85.

88. B. Mussolini, "Popolo e Borghesia," *Il popolo d'Italia*, 12 July 1915, *O.O.*, vol. 8, pp. 71–73.

89. In support of this assertion, one may cite a number of facts: (1) Mussolini's admiration for Blanqui, whom he regarded as the model of a patriotic revolutionary ("È nostra!" pp. 264–67). (2) At the same period as he founded *Il popolo d'Italia*, which first appeared on 15 November 1914, he set up a political movement (on 11 December 1914), the Fasci d'azione rivoluzionaria, which was a fusion of two other movements: the Fasci autonomi d'azione rivoluzionaria (which he had created) and the Fasci d'azione rivoluzionaria internazionalista. This movement was represented as a revolutionary one, at the service of revolutionary objectives. (3) In an article that appeared in December 1917, Mussolini spoke explicitly of a seizure of power by the

new elite, comparing it to that of the French bourgeoisie on the eve of the French Revolution (B. Mussolini, "Trincerocrazia," *Il popolo d'Italia*, 15 December 1917, *O.O.*, vol. 10, p. 140).

90. De Felice, *Mussolini il rivoluzionario*, p. 392.

91. It appears that Mussolini did not know much about Russian socialism and did not give it much attention, unlike French and German socialism. The reason for this was probably his ignorance of the Russian language. See Y. de Begnac, *Palazzo Venezia. Storia di un regime* (Rome: La Rocca, 1951), p. 360. It is probable that Mussolini's decision to support Kerensky rather than Lenin was due to the fact that the former had continued to fight despite the February revolution, while the latter, when the Bolshevik revolution succeeded in October, took his country out of the war. See B. Mussolini, "Bandiere rosse," *Il popolo d'Italia*, 5 July 1917, *O.O.*, vol. 9, pp. 26–28; "Avanti il Mikado!" *Il popolo d'Italia*, 11 November 1917, *O.O.*, vol. 10, p. 41; "La pace dell'infamia," *Il popolo d'Italia*, 4 December 1917, *O.O.*, vol. 10, p. 111; "La maniera dolce," *Il popolo d'Italia*, 7 December 1917, *O.O.*, vol. 10, p. 122; "Il patto della schiavitù," *Il popolo d'Italia*, 19 December 1917, *O.O.*, vol. 10, pp. 149–50; "La social-democrazia: I complici di Ludendorff," *Il popolo d'Italia*, 14 March 1919, *O.O.*, vol. 10, p. 385; "L'hanno voluto!" *Il popolo d'Italia*, 21 March 1918, *O.O.*, vol. 10, p. 395.

92. Mussolini, "Marx e . . . Hindenburg," p. 185, "Da Sturmer a Lenine," *Il popolo d'Italia*, 25 July 1917, *O.O.*, vol. 9, p. 74. Later, in an attempt to justify Fascist violence against the socialists (in Bologna), Mussolini claimed that the Socialist party was merely a division of the Russian army stationed on Italian soil and that the Fascists were really only waging war against a foreign army (B. Mussolini, "L'eccidio di Palazzo d'Accursio," *Il popolo d'Italia*, 23 November 1920, *O.O.*, vol. 16, p. 25).

93. B. Mussolini, "Al bivio," *Il popolo d'Italia*, 30 January 1915, *O.O.*, vol. 7, p. 158.

94. B. Mussolini, "Il tacco sul verme," *Il popolo d'Italia*, 2 September 1915, *O.O.*, vol. 8, p. 194; "Lettera aperta a Vandervelde," *Il popolo d'Italia*, 20 July 1915, *O.O.*, vol. 8, pp. 92–96.

95. In his criticism of De Felice's work, Tranfaglia points out that it was not only the defeat of Caporetto that drove Mussolini to the Right, as De Felice claims, but also Lenin's seizure of power. See Tranfaglia, *Dallo stato liberale*, p. 88. On this point also, Vivarelli agrees with Tranfaglia rather than with De Felice. See R. Vivarelli, *Il dopoguerra in Italia e l'avvento del fascismo, 1918–1922* (Naples: Istituto Italiano per gli studi Storici, 1967), p. 231.

96. Mussolini, "L'impresa disperata," p. 3. See also B. Mussolini, "Divagazioni pel centenario," *Il popolo d'Italia*, 7 May 1918, *O.O.*, vol. 11, p. 46; "Novità," *Il popolo d'Italia*, 1 August 1918, *O.O.*, vol. 11, p. 243.

97. B. Mussolini, "Grecia e Greci," *Il popolo d'Italia*, 16 August 1915, *O.O.*, vol. 3, p. 170; "L'ora dei popoli," *Il popolo d'Italia*, 16 August 1917, *O.O.*, vol. 9, p. 117; "L'adunata di Roma," *Il popolo d'Italia*, 7 April 1918, *O.O.*, vol. 10, pp. 434–35.

98. B. Mussolini, "Patria e terra," *Il popolo d'Italia*, 16 November 1917, *O.O.*, vol. 10, pp. 55–57.

99. P. Orano, *Il fascismo: Vigilia sindacalista dello stato corporativo* (Rome: Pinciana, 1939), vol. 1, pp. 12, 304–310.

100. B. Mussolini, "Variazioni su vecchio motivo. Il fucile e la vanga," *Il popolo d'Italia*, 1 May 1918, *O.O.*, vol. 11, p. 35.

101. B. Mussolini, "Orientamenti e problemi," *Il popolo d'Italia*, 18 August 1918, *O.O.*, vol. 11, pp. 282–84; "Il sindacalismo nazionale per rinascere!" *Il popolo d'Italia*, 17 November 1918, *O.O.*, vol. 12, pp. 11–14.

102. B. Mussolini, "Andante incontro al lavoro che tornera dalle trincee," *Il popolo d'Italia*, 9 November 1918, *O.O.*, vol. 11, pp. 469–72; "La nostra costituente," *Il popolo d'Italia*, 14 November 1918, *O.O.*, vol. 12, pp. 3–4.

103. De Felice, *Mussolini il rivoluzionario*, p. 465.

104. Mussolini, "L'impresa disperata," p. 3.

105. B. Mussolini, "Per intenderci. In tema di 'Costituente,'" *Il popolo d'Italia*, 7 December 1918, *O.O.*, vol. 12, p. 53. On the national syndicalist ideology as a third way, see Gentile, *Le origini dell'ideologia fascista*, pp. 76–90.

106. B. Mussolini, "Viva Kerensky!" *Il popolo d'Italia*, 26 July 1917, *O.O.*, vol. 9, pp. 77–78.

107. B. Mussolini, "La tenda," *Il popolo d'Italia*, 11 October 1917, *O.O.*, vol. 9, p. 251.

108. B. Mussolini, "Fra il secreto e il pubblico," *Il popolo d'Italia*, 14 December 1917, *O.O.*, vol. 10, p. 139.

109. B. Mussolini, "Pace tedesca, mai! Nelle trincee non si vuole la pace tedesca. Una lettera di B. Mussolini," *Il popolo d'Italia*, 27 December 1916, *O.O.*, vol. 8, p. 272; "Trincerocrazia," pp. 140–42.

110. Mussolini, "Trincerocrazia," pp. 141–42.

111. B. Mussolini, "Dopo quattro anni," *Il popolo d'Italia*, 12 May 1918, *O.O.*, vol. 11, pp. 54–55.

112. B. Mussolini, "Il trattato di pace e le classi lavoratrici," *Il popolo d'Italia*, 19 November 1918, *O.O.*, vol. 12, p. 16.

113. Mussolini, "Per intenderci," p. 53.

114. B. Mussolini, "La 'pentapoli' italiana," *Il popolo d'Italia*, 22 November 1918, *O.O.*, vol. 12, p. 22.

115. B. Mussolini, "I Maddaleni," *Il popolo d'Italia*, 5 March 1919, *O.O.*, vol. 12, p. 268. See also "Pro Fiume e Dalmazia," *Il popolo d'Italia*, 15 January 1919, *O.O.*, vol. 12, pp. 144–45.

116. R. De Felice points out that *Il popolo d'Italia* was the only journal to give a long report on the strike at Dalmine, precisely because of the fidelity of the strikers to productionist principles. See De Felice, *Mussolini il rivoluzionario*, p. 503.

117. Ibid., p. 506.

118. "Atto di nascita del fascismo," *Il popolo d'Italia*, 24 March 1919, *O.O.*, vol. 12, p. 327.

119. B. Mussolini, "Per l'espropriazione del capitale," *Il popolo d'Italia*, 10 June 1919, *O.O.*, vol. 13, p. 177.

120. See the following writings by Mussolini: "Il discorso di Dalmine," *Il popolo d'Italia*, 21 March 1919, *O.O.*, vol 12, p. 344; "Per l'espropriazione del capitale"; "Via di Versaglia," *Il popolo d'Italia*, 3 June 1919, *O.O.*, vol. 13, pp. 171–73; and "Atto di nascita del fascismo," in which the Fascists explicitly recognized the similarities between their original program of March 1919 and that of the UIL. The Fascists de-

manded not only the application of Alceste De Ambris's program of partial expropriation, but also an eight-hour working day, a minimum wage, and all the other social reforms in the program of the UIL. The article "The Nation in Arms" was clearly inspired by an article by Olivetti, who in 1914 already asked for arms to be distributed to the people ("Le armi al popolo," *Pagine libere*, 15 December 1914). The full text of the Fascist program of June 1919 can be found in De Felice, *Mussolini il rivoluzionario*, pp. 742–43.

121. B. Mussolini, "Patria e fazione," *Il popolo d'Italia*, 16 June 1920, *O.O.*, p. 40.

122. Lyttelton, *The Seizure of Power*, pp. 46–47. See also, on this period, the already-mentioned works by Renzo De Felice and A. J. Gregor. In French, there is a synthesizing work by P. Milza, *Les fascismes*, and S. Romano's excellent book, *Histoire de l'Italie du Risorgimento à nos jours* (Paris: Éd. du Seuil, 1977). With regard to fascism, Romano's conclusion is very different from mine. "Fascism in government," he wrote, "especially in the first stage, was neither an ideology nor a political program. It was at most an intuition" (p. 181).

123. Lyttelton, in *The Seizure of Power*, p. 67, quotes A. Lanzillo.

124. Ibid., pp. 72–75.

125. Ibid., p. 81.

126. Ibid., p. 243.

127. B. Mussolini, "Chi possiede, paghi!" *Il popolo d'Italia*, 6 July 1919, *O.O.*, vol. 13, p. 224.

128. P. Birnbaum, *La Sociologie de l'État* (Paris: Fayard, 1982), p. 84.

129. B. Mussolini, "Dilemma: Collaborare o perire," *Il popolo d'Italia*, 1 April 1920, *O.O.*, vol. 14, p. 390.

130. B. Mussolini, "Il fascismo nel 1921," *Il popolo d'Italia*, 7 January 1921, *O.O.*, vol. 16, pp. 101–102.

131. B. Mussolini, "Il primo discorso alla camera dei deputati," *Atti del parlamento Italiano*. Camera dei deputati. Sessione 1921. Prima della 26 legislatura. Discussioni, vol. 1 (Rome: Tipografia della Camera dei deputati, 1921), pp. 89–98, *O.O.*, vol. 16, pp. 101–102.

132. B. Mussolini, "Il programma fascista," *O.O.*, vol. 17, pp. 216–23; D. Grandi, quoted in R. De Felice, *Autobiografia del fascismo* (Bergamo: Minerva Italica, 1978), p. 138, and "Programma e statuti del Partito Nazionale Fascista," *O.O.*, vol. 17, pp. 334–40.

133. B. Mussolini, "Primo: Vivere!" *Il popolo d'Italia*, 18 November 1921, *O.O.*, vol. 17, p. 252.

134. B. Mussolini, "Per la vera pacificazione," *Atti*, vol. 3, 1–22 November 1921, *O.O.*, vol. 17, p. 295. On the myth of nation and its role in the Fascist ideology, see B. Mussolini, "Nel solco delle grandi filosofie. Relativismo e fascismo," *Il popolo d'Italia*, 22 November 1921, *O.O.*, vol. 17, p. 269; M. Rocca, *Il primo fascismo* (Rome: G. Volpe, 1964), pp. 50–51; C. Rossi, "La critica alla critica del fascismo," *Gerarchia*, 25 April 1922, p. 190.

135. "Programma e statuti del partito," pp. 334–50.

136. See, for instance, Mussolini's important article "Stato, anti-Stato e Fascismo," *Gerarchia*, 25 June 1922, pp. 295–300.

137. "Il manifesto della nuova direzione del P.N.F.," *O.O.*, vol. 17, pp. 271–72. The influences that went into the making of the Fascist ideology did not originate only with those who, at that exact moment, joined the Fascist movement. Thus, Giovanni Gentile and Alfredo Rocco can be regarded as people who influenced that ideology but joined the party later. See Gentile, *Le origini del l'ideologia fascista*, pp. 349–53, and 377–85; and F. Gaeta, *Il nazionalismo italiano* (Bari: Laterza, 1981), p. 249.

138. G. Lumbroso, "Lo Stato contro lo Stato," *Gerarchia*, 25 July 1922, pp. 378–81.

139. B. Mussolini, "Ai fascisti romani," *Il popolo d'Italia*, 3 August 1922, *O.O.*, vol. 18, pp. 330–31. See also Mussolini's interview in the Neapolitan journal *Il mattino*, in ibid., p. 349. Mussolini reiterated the ideas expressed in *Il mattino* in a speech in Milan at a meeting bringing together the leadership of the PNF, the Central Committee of the Fasci, the Fascist parliamentary group, and the Confederation of Corporations. Mussolini ended the meeting by stating the points on which everyone agreed:

1. Fascism must be the State.
2. Fascism must be the State, not in order to defend its own interests or that of its followers, but in order to preserve those of the State.
3. In order to become the State, fascism has two possibilities: the legal path of elections, or the extralegal one of revolt. (15 August 1922)

See B. Mussolini, "La situazione politica," *Il popolo d'Italia*, 15 August 1922, *O.O.*, vol. 18, pp. 351–52

140. B. Mussolini, "L'azione e la dottrina fascista dinnanzi alle necessità storiche della nazione," *Il popolo d'Italia*, 21 September 1922, *O.O.*, vol. 18, pp. 411–21, and "Dal malinconico tramonto liberale all'aurora fascista della nuova Italia," *Il popolo d'Italia*, 5–6 October 1922, *O.O.*, vol. 18, pp. 434–39.

141. C. Pellizi, "Idealismo e Fascismo," *Gerarchia*, 25 October 1922, p. 571. On Pellizi, the philosopher who attempted to combine liberal idealism and fascism, see Gentile, *Le origini dell'ideologia fascista*, pp. 335–40; Gherardo Casini, "Classici, romantici e scettici del pensiero fascista," *La rivoluzione fascista*, 18 May 1924, appendix, pp. 449–50.

142. P. Ungari, *Alfredo Rocco e l'ideologia giuridica del fascismo* (Brescia: Morcelliana, 1974).

143. A. Rocco, *Scritti e discorsi politici*, vol. 1 (Milan: Giuffrè, 1938), pp. 60–61. Concerning Rocco's ideas on democracy and individualism, see Gentile, *Il mito dello Stato nuovo*, pp. 173–74. On the concept of the national state in Gentile and Rocco, see Gaeta, *Il nazionalismo italiano*, pp. 43–44.

144. A. Rocco, "Mussolini Uomo di Stato," in *Scritti e discorsi*, vol. 3, p. 1145. Some people saw the suppression of representative democracy and the parliamentary system by fascism as an expression of direct government by the people, or, in other words, of popular sovereignty. See G. L. Mosse, ed., *International Fascism: New Thoughts and New Approaches* (London: Sage Publications, 1979), p. 2.

G. Bottai has accused Mussolini of distorting fascism. According to him, the trouble was not the principles of fascism or Fascist methods, but rather Mussolini's use of these principles and methods. See G. Bottai, *Vent'anni e un giorno* (Milan: Garzanti, 1977), pp. 54, 55–62.

It is difficult to accept De Felice's idea that fascism put into practice the principles of the French Revolution. See R. De Felice, *Intervista sul fascismo, a cura di M. A. Ledeen* (Bari: Laterza, 1975), pp. 100–106. De Felice believed that fascism was the type of regime that Talmon described as a "totalitarian democracy" and that he placed on the Left (see J. L. Talmon, *The Origins of Totalitarian Democracy* [London: Secker and Warburg, 1952]). However, the interpretation that De Felice gives to Talmon's concept is really in disagreement with Talmon himself. Thus, while De Felice differentiates between German national-socialism and Italian fascism, including the latter among the "totalitarian democracies" (that is, the totalitarianisms of the Left), Talmon, for his part, places Nazism and fascism in the same category: the radical Right. See Talmon, *The Myth of the Nation and the Vision of Revolution*. We should note, incidentally, that where the application of the principles of the French Revolution is concerned, Talmon has a very different conception from that of Renzo De Felice.

145. Volt [Fani Ciotti], "Il concetto sociologico dello stato," *Gerarchia*, 25 August 1922, pp. 422–28; see also Volt, "Vilfredo Pareto e il fascismo," *Gerarchia*, 25 October 1922, p. 600; and, in the same issue, Lumbroso, "La genesi ed i fini del fascismo," p. 590.

146. C. Pellizzi, *Problemi e realtà del fascismo* (Florence: Vallecchi, 1924), p. 21 (italics in original).

Epilogue

1. Sorel, "Pour Lénine," *Réflexions sur la violence*, p. 454.

2. Sorel, *Lettere a un amico d'Italia*, pp. 306–307, letter to Missirolli of 16 April 1921. The continuation is no less interesting: "It seems to me likely that soon the government will find them too powerful and will persecute them. The bourgeoisie will not be able to accept the competition of forces of this kind; it will find it much easier to get along with the friends of Turati than with the *Fascists*."

3. N. Blumenkranz, "Une poétique de l'héroïsme. L'esthétique de Marinetti," *Présence de Marinetti*, p. 49.

4. Ibid., p. 50.

5. Lista, "Marinetti et les anarcho-syndicalistes," p. 69.

6. Ibid., p. 72.

7. Quoted in ibid., p. 76.

8. Ibid.

9. Ibid., p. 77.

10. Ibid.

11. Ibid., pp. 78, 82. Marinetti reprinted the text of his lecture in *Democrazia futurista*, a work published in 1919.

12. G. Lista, *Marinetti et le futurisme. Études, documents, iconographie*, collected and presented by Giovanni Lista (Lausanne: L'Âge d'Homme, 1977), p. 25.

13. J.-C. Marcadé, "Marinetti et Malévitch," *Présence de Marinetti*, pp. 250–51.

14. Joll, *Intellectuals in Politics*, pp. 150–75.

15. L. Veza, "Marinetti et le vorticisme," *Présence de Marinetti*, p. 277.

16. On Pound see H. Carpenter, *The Life of Ezra Pound* (Boston: Houghton Mifflin, 1988).

17. W. Lewis, *Hitler* (London: Chatto and Windus, 1931).

18. F. Jameson, *Fables of Aggression: Wyndham Lewis, the Modernist as Fascist* (Berkeley: University of California Press, 1979), pp. 6–14.

19. Ibid., pp. 179–85.

20. Veza, "Marinetti et le vorticisme," p. 279.

21. Ibid., pp. 278–79.

22. G.-G. Lemaire, "Prolégomènes au vorticisme: Flux et reflux du futurisme en Angleterre," *Wyndham Lewis et le vorticisme. Cahiers pour un temps* (Paris: Centre Georges Pompidou, Pandora Editions, 1982), p. 11.

23. Veza, "Marinetti et le vorticisme," p. 279.

24. Lemaire, "Prolégomènes au vorticisme," pp. 14–15. The collective work *Wyndham Lewis et le vorticisme* contains a number of major texts of the English writer-painter, especially the "Manifesto" of the movement, signed by the sculptor Gaudier-Brzeska and by Ezra Pound among others (pp. 24–27). In "Vive le Vortex," Lewis settled his accounts with Marinetti: "L'automobilisme [Marinettisme] nous ennuie" (p. 20). See also "Notre Vortex" (pp. 29–31), "La vie est la chose importante" (pp. 33–35), and "Le Mélodrame de la Modernité" (pp. 57–60). There is also some information in A. Hamilton, *L'Illusion fasciste* (Paris: Gallimard, 1973), pp. 301–304, a work that although useful in its time is now out of date. George L. Mosse's "Fascism and the Intellectuals," in S. J. Woolf, *The Nature of Fascism* (London: Weidenfeld and Nicolson, 1968), pp. 205–25, is still of great interest.

25. W. Lewis, *Time and Western Man* (New York: Harcourt, 1928), p. 207.

26. See Preface and Introduction of T. E. Hulme, *Speculations, Essays on Humanism and the Philosophy of Art*, ed. H. Read (1924; reprint, London: Routledge and Kegan Paul, 1954), pp. viii, x.

27. A. R. Jones, *The Life and Opinions of T. E. Hulme* (London: Victor Golancz, 1960), p. 15.

28. T. E. Hulme, *Further Speculations*, ed. Sam Hunes (Minneapolis: University of Minnesota Press, 1955), pp. viii–xiv.

29. T. S. Eliot in *The Criterion*, vol. 2, 7 April 1924, pp. 231–32, quoted in Jones, *The Life and Opinions of T. E. Hulme*, p. 14.

30. Hulme, *Speculations*, pp. 58, 47.

31. Ibid., pp. 60–62.

32. Ibid., pp. 55–57. See also p. 31.

33. Ibid., pp. 68–71. See also p. 256.

34. Ibid., pp. 114–20. See also pp. 255–56.

35. J. R. Harrison, *The Reactionaries. Yeats, Lewis, Pound, Eliot, Lawrence: A Study of the Anti-democratic Intelligentsia* (New York: Schocken Books, 1967), pp. 30–33.

36. See especially *Speculations*, pp. 173–214. On pp. 143–69 is an essay on Bergson's theory of art. See also "Notes on Bergson," in Hulme, *Further Speculations*, pp. 28–63.

37. Hulme, *Speculations*, p. 250 (italics in original).

38. W. Lewis, *The Art of Being Ruled* (London: Chatto and Windus, 1926), p. 128. See also pp. 407–409 on Sorel and Berth.

39. T. S. Eliot, quoted in Jones, *The Life and Opinions of T. E. Hulme*, p. 14.

40. Hulme, *Speculations*, pp. 251–52, 254.

41. Ibid., pp. 257–58.

42. Ibid., pp. 254, 258–60.

43. G. Hervé, *La Guerre sociale*, 17–23 January, 14 February 1912. See also Maurice Rottstein's Ph.D. dissertation, "The Public Life of Gustave Hervé" (New York University, 1956), pp. 100ff.

44. Hervé *La Guerre sociale*, 1–16 July 1912.

45. G. Hervé, "En sortant de la Conciergerie," *La Guerre sociale*, 24-30 July 1912.

46. G. Hervé, "La conquête de l'Armée" and "Un drame passionel," *La Guerre sociale*, 2–8 October 1912.

47. See Hervé's editorials in *La Victoire* of 7, 8, 9, 10, 11, and 12 July 1919, and those of Alexandre Zévaès in the issues of 13, 16, 17, and 20 August 1919.

48. G. Hervé, "Zévaès et le Parti socialiste national," *La Victoire*, 4 August 1919; A. Zévaès, "Le Parti socialiste national," 17 August 1919. See also the pamphlet *Le Parti socialiste national. Doctrine et but* (Paris: Éditions du Comité de Propagande française républicaine et réformiste, 1919).

49. G. Hervé, "Les fascistes" and "La Leçon du fascisme," *La Victoire*, 28 October, 1st November 1922, "Dictature! Dictature!" 19 February, "L'Épreuve du fascisme," 22 June 1924, and "Une République avec un chef!" 15 November 1924, "Éloge du fascisme," 27 December 1924. See also the pamphlets *La République autoritaire* (Paris: Librairie de *La Victoire*, 1925), and *C'est Pétain qu'il nous faut* (Paris: Éditions de *La Victoire*, 1936). *La Victoire* at that time described itself as a "national-socialist daily, organ of the authoritarian Republic and the Pétain Front."

50. Included in G. Hervé, "Le P.S.N. et l'adhésion d'Allemane," *La Victoire*, 2 August 1919. See also G. Hervé, "Vive le Parti socialiste national!" *La Victoire*, 5 August 1919. Despite its importance and significance, this fact is overlooked by Allemane's biographers. One finds it neither in Jean Maitron's *Dictionnaire du Mouvement ouvrier*, vol. 10, pp. 130–34, nor in the recent Ph.D. dissertation by Sian Reynolds, "La Vie de Jean Allemane (1843–1935)," (Université de Paris 8, 1981), pp. 359–71. In these two biographies one learns only that, having become a dissident on the eve of the war, Allemane approved of the Union Sacrée and was sympathetic toward the young Communist party.

51. B. Mussolini to H. De Man, in "Lettres d'Henri De Man," *Écrits de Paris*, no. 184 (July–August 1960): 79–80. This letter is dated 21 July 1930.

52. Letter of H. De Man to Mussolini, dated 23 August 1930, in *Écrits de Paris*, p. 81.

53. H. De Man, *La Leçon de la guerre* (Brussels: Librairie du Peuple, 1920), p. 9.

54. H. De Man, *Au-delà du marxisme* (Paris: Editions du Seuil, 1974), p. 35.

55. H. De Man, *Après Coup* (Brussels: Editions de la Toison d'Or, 1941), p. 191.

56. De Man, *Au-delà du marxisme*, pp. 327–31, 350.

57. H. De Man, *L'Idée socialiste, suivi du Plan de Travail*, translated from the German by H. Corbin and A. Kopevnikov (Paris: Grasset, 1935), p. 435.

58. See Sternhell, *Neither Right nor Left*, chap. 4.

59. De Man, *Au-delà du marxisme*, pp. 68, 145–46, 192.

60. H. De Man, "Discours au Congrès de Noël du P.O.B.," *Chantiers cooperatifs*, 21 March 1934.

61. H. De Man, *Corporatisme et socialisme* (Paris and Brussels: Labor, 1935), pp. 4–35.

62. H. De Man, "Planisme et réformisme," *La Vie socialiste*, 22 December 1934. On De Man's conception of the state, see *Au-delà du marxisme*, pp. 120–21, 180–85.

63. De Man, *Après Coup*, p. 302.

64. The war has brought about the overthrow of the parliamentary regimes and the capitalist plutocracy in the so-called democracies. For the laboring classes and for socialism, this collapse of a decrepit world, far from being a disaster, has been a deliverance. Despite all the setbacks, sufferings, and disillusionments we have experienced, the way is clear for two causes that embody the aspirations of the people: European peace and social justice. Peace did not arise through the voluntary agreement of sovereign states and rival imperialisms, but could arise out of a Europe united by arms, in which economic frontiers have been erased. Social justice could not arise from a regime claiming to be democratic but that in reality was dominated by the power of money and the professional politicians, a regime grown increasingly incapable of any bold initiative, of any serious reform. It could arise out of a regime in which the authority of the state is strong enough to undermine the privileges of the propertied classes and replace unemployment by the obligation of all to work. . . .

You should therefore continue to pursue our economic activities but regard the political role of the Parti Ouvrier Belge as terminated. This role was a fruitful and glorious one, but a different mission now awaits you. Prepare yourselves to enter the cadres of a movement of national resurrection that will embrace all the living forces of the nation, of its youth, of its veterans, within a single party—that of the Belgian people, united by its fidelity to the King and by its desire to realize the Sovereignty of Labor.

65. G. Roditi, "Du néo-marxisme au néo-socialisme," *L'Homme nouveau*, no. 14 (1 March 1935). The editor of the neosocialist journal *L'Homme nouveau*, which appeared from January 1934 to April 1937, Roditi was one of the organizers of the Franco-Italian Symposium on Corporatism held in Rome from 19 to 23 May 1935. The French were represented in particular by Emmanuel Mounier, Robert Aron, Paul Marion, and Jean de Fabrègues, and the Italians by G. Bottai, governor of Rome; E. Rossoni, minister of Agriculture; L. Razzo, minister of corporations; A. Marpicati, director of the Fascist Institute of Culture; and many heads of corporations and Fascist academies. Most addresses at this symposium, extremely revealing of the thinking of part of French intellectual youth, have been published by Michela Nacci and Albertina Vittoria: "Convegno Italo-Francese di Studi Corporativi, Roma 1935," *Dimensioni* 11, nos. 40–41, (September–December 1986): 30–118 (italics in original). This study is prefaced by an excellent article by Michela Nacci: "Intellettuali Francesi e Corporativismo fascista," pp. 6–29.

66. G. Roditi, "Mort ou naissance du néo-socialisme," *L'Homme nouveau*, 1 September 1935 (special issue).

67. See Sternhell, *Neither Right nor Left*, chap. 5.

68. This is what happened to Michel Brélaz, who published an eight-hundred-page book, *Henri De Man: Une autre idée du socialisme* (Geneva: Éditions des Antipodes, 1985). Compared with Peter Dodge's *Beyond Marxism: The Faith and Works of Hendrik De Man* (The Hague: Martinus Nijhoff, 1966), and *A Documentary Study*

of Hendrik De Man, Socialist Critic of Marxism (Princeton: Princeton University Press, 1979), Brélaz's book, despite its biographical details and size, is not of great significance.

69. L. Blum, *L'Oeuvre de Léon Blum*, vol. 3, t. 2 (Paris: Albin Michel, 1954), pp. 543–46, 548, 550, 580–81. See the address of Léon Blum at the Paris Congress, *La Vie socialiste*, 20 July 1933, p. 53, and L. Blum, "Le problème du pouvoir," *Le Populaire*, 13 July 1933. See also "Le pouvoir total" and "La mesure du pouvoir," *Le Populaire*, 14 and 15 July 1933, and the pamphlet by Jean Lebas that coined the term "néo-socialisme" and that presented the official point of view of French socialism: *Le socialisme, but et moyen, suivi de la réfutation d'un néo-socialisme* (Lille: Imprimerie ouvrière, 1931); J. Zyromski, "Au sujet des 'Perspectives socialistes de Marcel Déat,'" *L'Étudiant socialiste*, no. 6 (March 1931): 1–4; J.-B. Sévérac, "Quelques réflexions sur les *Perspectives socialistes* de Marcel Déat," *La Bataille socialiste*, no. 41 (January 1931).

70. The most extraordinary example, of course, is Ernst Nolte. The writer of a classic work referred to earlier, this conscientious historian, some of whose works command respect—even if one cannot agree with all his conclusions—has become in this case, because of the perversity of this approach, what can only be described as a polemicist, some of whose assertions can hardly be taken seriously. See his contributions to the major collective work *Devant l'Histoire. Les documents de la controverse sur la singularité de l'extermination des juifs par le régime nazi* (Paris: Éditions du Cerf, 1988), pp. 188–89.

71. E. Husserl, *La Crise de l'humanité européene et la philosophie* (Paris: Républications Paulet, 1976).

72. Z. Sternhell, "Modernity and Its Enemies: From the Revolt against the Enlightenment to the Undermining of Democracy," in Z. Sternhell, ed., *The Intellectual Revolt against Liberal Democracy* (Jerusalem: Israeli Academy of Sciences and Humanities, forthcoming).

73. B. Mussolini, "La Dottrina del fascismo," *O.O.*, vol. 34, p. 118.

74. José Antonio Primo de Rivera, *Selected Writings* (London: Jonathan Cape, 1972), p. 49.

75. P. Drieu La Rochelle, *Notes pour comprendre le siècle* (Paris: Gallimard, 1941), p. 171. See also Kaplan, *Reproductions of Banality*, pp. 92ff.

76. See Sternhell, *Neither Right nor Left*, pp. 298–303.

77. In 1933 Freud sent the Duce one of his works with the inscription "From an old man who greets in the Ruler the Hero of Culture." Quoted in E. Jones, *Sigmund Freud: Life and Works*, vol. 3, *The Last Phase, 1919–1939* (London: Hogarth Press, 1957), pp. 192–93. See also Bracher, *The Age of Ideologies*, pp. 97ff. The father of one of his patients, a friend of Mussolini, insisted that Freud send one of his books to the Duce.

78. B. Croce, *Scritti e discorsi politici (1943–1947)*, vol. 1 (Bari: Laterza, 1963), pp. 28–29.

79. Sternhell, "Modernity and Its Enemies." Heidegger's quotation is in J. Habermas, *Profils philosophiques et politiques*, trans. François Dastur, Jean-René Ladmiral, and Marc B. de Laurray (Paris: Gallimard, 1974), p. 91. See F. Stern, *Dreams and Illusions* (New York: A. Knopf, 1987), pp. 156–57, 161–65.

80. Habermas, *Profils philosophiques*, p. 90.

81. The problems French fascism posed, especially where the temptation of fascism for French intellectuals is concerned, have in recent years been the subject of a vigorous debate. Even if this appears to be an inexcusable lack of modesty on my part, I must admit that I feel there is nothing to be changed in my exposition of the subject in *Neither Right nor Left*. This exposition has now received extra support from the most recent book by Pierre Birnbaum—*Un mythe politique: La "République juive"* (Paris: Fayard, 1988)—which demonstrates the importance of anti-Semitism in twentieth-century French history. Just as fascism was not confined to Italy, so anti-Semitism was not limited to Germany. France played an all-important role in the rise of these ideologies which destroyed the old order of things. Two major articles consider the questions raised by the reviews of *Neither Right nor Left* and the debates and controversies surrounding the book. These are Antonio Costa-Pinto's essay "Fascist Ideology Revisited: Zeev Sternhell and His Critics," *European History Quarterly* 16 (1986), and Robert Wohl's "French Fascism Both Right and Left: Reflections on the Sternhell Controversy," *The Journal of Modern History* 63 (March 1991). Where the French intellectual milieu is concerned, the nature of the controversy is clearly described in the most recent work devoted to French fascism: Pierre Milza, *Fascisme français. Passé et Présent* (Paris: Flammarion, 1987). Integrity is the great quality of this work, which has no other aim than to give an exact account of a debate that has been in progress for several years. Pierre Milza states the problems honestly, without misrepresenting the spirit of the works he is dealing with, and this is already an achievement in a debate that does not always possess this serene character. In his book, Milza records the failure of a whole generation of French historians, to which he belongs, correctly described as a "nebula, mainly grouped around René Rémond, which especially includes the contemporary historians of the Université de Paris X-Nanterre and the Institut d'Études Politiques." He states that for this group, which speaks on behalf of "French academic history-writing," French fascism has never been anything but marginal (p. 8). In other words, for a quarter of a century these historians have been incapable of going beyond the teachings of the incomparable master who René Rémond remains. Pierre Milza recognizes that for twenty-five years, despite a number of works to their credit, he and his colleagues have made no attempt to do better or even to do otherwise than the consensus of the Institut d'Études Politiques has allowed them.

82. Husserl, *La Crise de l'humanité européenne*, p. 31.

Bibliography

1. Primary Sources

Newspapers and Periodicals

L'Action française
Avanguardia socialista
Avanti!
L'avvenire del lavoratore
Battaglie dell'Unione Italiana del Lavoro
Cahiers du Cercle Proudhon
Clarté
Combat
Courrier de L'Est
La Critique sociale
La cultura socialista
Le Devenir social
Il divenire sociale
Educazione fascista
L'Ère nouvelle
La folla
La France socialiste
Gerarchia
Il giornale d'Italia
La Guerre sociale
Histoire et Philosophies sociales
L'Homme nouveau
L'idea nazionale
L'Indépendance
L'internazionale
L'Italia Nostra
Journal des économistes
Il lavoro di Genova
La lima
La lotta di classe
La lupa
Il mattino
Le Mouvement socialiste
Nation française
Le Nouvel Âge
Pagine libere
La Patria—Il resto del Carlino
Il pensiero romagnolo

Plans
Il popolo
Il popolo d'Italia
Le Populaire
Il proletario
La Révolution prolétarienne
Revue critique des idées et des livres
Revue de métaphysique et de morale
Revue philosophique de la France et de l'Étranger
Revue politique et parlementaire
La Revue socialiste
La Revue universelle
Il rinnovamento
La riscossa dei legionari fiumani
Rivista Storica Italiana
Il sindacato operario
Il tricolore
Utopia
La Victoire
La Vie socialiste

Books

Adler, M. *Démocratie et conseils ouvriers*, traduction, présentation et notes d'Yvon Bourdet. Paris: Maspero, 1967.
Balabanoff, A. *Ricordi di una socialista*. Rome: De Luigi, 1946.
Bauer, O. *La Marche au socialisme*. Paris: Librairie du Parti Socialiste et de L'Humanité, 1919.
Berth, E. *Les Méfaits des intellectuels*. 2d ed. Paris: Rivière, 1926.
———. *Les Nouveaux Aspects du socialisme*. Paris: Rivière, 1908.
Blum, L. *L'œuvre de Léon Blum*. Vol. 3. Paris: Albin Michel, 1954.
Böhm-Bawerk, E. von. *Karl Marx and the Close of his System*. New York: A. M. Kelly, 1949.
———. *Théorie positive du Capital*. Paris: Giard, 1929.
Bottai, G. *Vent'anni e un giorno*. Milan: Garzanti, 1977.
Bourdet, Y., ed. *Otto Bauer et la Révolution*. Textes choisis et présentés par Y. Bourdet. Paris: Études et Documentation Internationales, 1968.
Cantalupo, R. *La classe dirigente*. Milan: Alpes, 1926.
Colajanni, N. *Le Socialisme*. Paris: 1900.
Corradini, E. *Discorsi politici (1902–1923)*. Florence: Vallecchi, 1923.
Croce, B. *Matérialisme historique et économie marxiste, Essais critiques*. Paris: V. Giard et E. Brière, 1901.
———. *Scritti e discorsi politici (1943–1947)*. 2 vols. Bari: Laterza, 1969.
De Ambris, A. *Dopo un ventennio. Il corporativismo*. Bordeaux: Augusto Mione Editore, 1935.
De Man, H. *Après Coup*. Brussels: Éd. de la Toison d'Or, 1941.
———. *Au-delà du marxisme*. Paris: Éd. du Seuil, 1974.

———. *Corporatisme et socialisme*. Paris and Brussels: Labor, 1935.

———. *L'Idée socialiste*, suivi du *Plan de Travail*. Paris: Grasset, 1935.

———. *La Leçon de la guerre*. Brussels: Librairie du Peuple, 1920.

Drieu La Rochelle, P. *Notes pour comprendre le siècle*. Paris: Gallimards, 1941.

———. *Socialisme Fasciste*. Paris: Gallimard, 1934.

Engels, F., P. Lafargue, and L. Lafargue. *Correspondance*. Paris: Éditions Sociales, 1956.

Giolitti, G. *Memories of My Life*. London and Sydney: Chapman and Dodd, 1923.

Grandi, D. *Il mio paese. Ricordi autobiografici*, a cura di R. De Felice. Bologna: Il Mulino, 1985.

Griffuelhes, V. *L'Action syndicaliste*. Paris: Rivière, 1908.

Hilferding, R. *Böhm-Bawerk's Criticism of Marx*. New York: Augustus M. Kelly, 1949.

———. *Le Capital financier. Étude sur le développement récent du capitalisme*. Paris: Éditions de Minuit, 1970. English trans.: *Finance Capital: A Study of the Latest Phase of Capitalist Development*. Ed. with an introduction by Tom Bottomore, from translations by Morris Watnick and Sam Gordon. London: Routledge and Kegan Paul, 1981. Translation of *Das Finanz Kapital*.

Hulme, T. E. *Further Speculations*. Edited by S. Hynes. Minneapolis: University of Minnesota Press, 1955.

———. *Speculations. Essays on Humanism and the Philosophy of Art*. Edited by H. Read. London: Routledge and Kegan Paul, 1954.

Kautsky, K. *Le Chemin du pouvoir*. Paris: Anthropos, 1960.

Labriola, Antonio. *Essais sur la conception matérialiste de l'Histoire*. Paris: V. Giard et E. Brière, 1897.

———. *Socialism and Philosophy*. Translated by E. Untermann. St. Louis: Telos Press, 1980.

———. *Socialisme et philosophie (Lettres à Georges Sorel)*. Paris: V. Giard et E. Brière, 1899.

Labriola, Arturo. *La conflagrazione europea e il socialismo*. Rome: Atheneum, 1915.

———. *Karl Marx, L'Économiste, Le Socialiste*. Translated by E. Berth. Paris: Rivière, 1910.

———. *La guerra di Tripoli e l'opinione socialista*. Naples: Morano, 1912.

———. *Riforme e rivoluzione sociale*. Lugano: Società Editrice Avanguardia, 1906.

———. *Spiegazioni a me stesso*. Naples: Centro Studi Sociali, n.d.

———. *Storia di dieci anni*. 1910. Reprint. Milan: Feltrinelli, 1975.

———. *La teoria del valore di C. Marx, Studio sul III libro del Capitale*. Milan and Palermo: Sandron, 1899.

Lagardelle, H. *Le Parti socialiste et la Confédération Générale du Travail*. Paris: Rivière, 1908.

Lanzillo, A. *La disfatta del socialismo: Critica della guerra e del socialismo*. Florence: Libreria della Voce, 1919.

———. *Le Mouvement ouvrier en Italie*. Paris: Rivière, n.d. [1910].

Laurat, L. *L'Accumulation du Capital d'après Rosa Luxemburg, suivi d'un aperçu sur la discussion du problème depuis la mort de Rosa Luxemburg*. Paris: Rivière, 1930.

Le Bon. *Psychologie de l'éducation*. Paris: Flammarion, 1917.

Leone, E. *Espansionismo e colonie*. Rome: Tipografia Editrice Nazionale, 1911.

———. *La revisione del marxismo*. Rome: Biblioteca del Divenire Sociale, 1909.

———. *Il sindacalismo*. Palermo: Sandron, 1910.

Lewis, W. *The Art of Being Ruled*. London: Chatto and Windus, 1926.

———. *Hitler*. London: Chatto and Windus, 1931.

Luxemburg, R. *L'Accumulation du Capital*. Paris: Maspero, 1967.

Marinetti, F. T. *Enquête internationale sur le vers libre et Manifeste du Futurisme*. Milan: Éditions del "Poesia," 1909.

Marx, K. *Le Capital*. Selections edited by P. Lafargue. Paris: Guillaumin, 1897.

Massis, H., and A. de Tarde. *Les Jeunes Gens d'aujourd'hui*. Paris: Plon, 1913.

Mathews, M. *The Fruit of Fascism*. New York: Harcourt Brace, 1943.

Maurras, Ch. *L'Action française et le Vatican*. Paris: E. Flammarion, 1927.

———. *Dictionnaire politique et critique*. Paris: Fayard, 1931–1933.

Merlino, F. S. *Formes et essence du socialisme*. Paris: V. Giard et E. Brière, 1898.

———. *Pro e contro il socialismo. Esposizione critica dei principi e dei sistemi socialisti*. Milan: Treves, 1897.

Michels, R. *Political Parties*. London: Jarrold, 1915.

———. *Storia critica del socialismo italiano dagli inizi fino 1911*. Florence: La Voce, 1926.

Mussolini, B. "La Doctrine du Fascisme," in *Édition définitive des oeuvres et discours de Benito Mussolini*. Paris: Flammarion, 1935.

———. *Opera Omnia*. Edited by Edoardo and Duilio Susmel. Florence: La Fenice, 1972.

Nenni, P. *Storia di quattro anni: 1919–1922*. Milan: Sugarco Edizioni, 1976.

Orano, R. *Il fascismo*. Vol. 1: *Vigilia sindacalista dello stato corporativo*. Rome: Pinciana, 1939.

Panunzio, S. *La persistenza del diritto (Discutendo di Sindacalismo e di Anarchismo)*. Pescara: Casa Editrice Abruzzese, 1909.

Pareto, V. *Les Systèmes socialistes*. Vol. 2. Paris: Giard, 1926.

Péguy, Ch. *Notre jeunesse*. Paris: Cahiers de la quinzaine, 1910.

———. *Œuvres complètes, 1873–1914*. Paris: Gallimard, 1928.

Pellizi, C. *Problemi e realtà del fascismo*. Florence: Vallecchi, 1929.

Pouget, E. *La Confédération générale du Travail*. Paris: Rivière, 1909.

Prélot, M. *L'Empire fasciste: Les origines, les tendances et les institutions de la dictature et du corporatisme italiens*. Paris: Librairie du Recueil Sirey, 1936.

Prezzolini, G. *La teoria sindacalista*. Naples: Francesco Perella Editore, 1909.

Pro e contro la guerra di Tripoli, Discussioni nel campo rivoluzionnario. Naples: Società Editrice Partenopea, 1912.

Rocca, M. *Il primo fascismo*. Rome: G. Volpe, 1964.

Rocco, A. *Scritti e discorsi politici*. Milan: Giuffré, 1938.

Rosentock, F. L. *L'Économie corporative fasciste en doctrine et en fait: Ses origines historiques et son évolution*. Paris: Librairie Universitaire de J. Gamber, 1934.

Salvotarelli, L. *Nazionalfascismo*. 1923. Reprint. Turin: Einaudi, 1977.

S.F.I.O. *Actes du 5e Congrès national de la S.F.I.O., à Toulouse, le 15, 16, 17, et 18 octobre 1908*. Paris: Conseil national, n.d.

Sorel, G. *D'Aristote à Marx (L'Ancienne et la Nouvelle Métaphysique)*. Paris: Marcel Rivière, 1935.

———. *La Décomposition du marxisme*. An anthology edited by Th. Paquot. Paris: PUF, 1982.

———. *La Décomposition du marxisme*. Paris: Marcel Rivière, 1908.

———. *Les Illusions du progrès*. Paris: Marcel Rivière, 1947.

———. *Insegnamenti sociali dell'economia contemporanea—Degenerazione capitalista e degenerazione socialista*. Milan: Sandron, 1907.

———. *Introduction à l'économie moderne*. 2d ed. Paris: Marcel Rivière, 1922.

———. *Lettere a un amico d'Italia*. Bologna: Capelli, 1963.

———. *Lettres à Paul Delesalle, 1914–1921*. Paris: Grasset, 1947.

———. *Le Procès de Socrate, Examen critique des thèses socratiques*. Paris: Alcan, 1889.

———. *Réflexions sur la violence*. 11th ed. Paris: Marcel Rivière, 1950.

———. *La Révolution dreyfusienne*. Paris: Marcel Rivière, 1921.

———. *La Ruine du Monde antique, Conception matérialiste de l'Histoire*. 3d ed. Paris: Marcel Rivière, 1933.

———. *Le Système historique de Renan*. Paris: G. Jacques, 1905–1906.

Syndicalisme et Socialisme: Discours prononcés au Colloque tenu à Paris le 3 avril 1907. Paris: Marcel Rivière, 1908.

Valois, G. *La Monarchie et la Classe ouvrière*. Paris: Nouvelle Librairie nationale, 1924.

Secondary Sources

Books

Adamson, W. L. *Hegemony and Revolution. Antonio Gramsci's Political and Cultural Theory*. Berkeley and Los Angeles: University of California Press, 1980.

Andreu, P. *Georges Sorel entre le noir et le rouge*. Paris: Syros, 1982. New edition of P. Andreu. *Notre Maître M. Sorel*. Paris: Grasset, 1953.

Andreucci, F., and T. Detti. *Il movimento operario italiano. Dizionario Biografico 1853–1943*. Rome: Editori Riuniti, 1977.

Angel, P. *Eduard Bernstein et l'évolution du socialisme allemand*. Paris: M. Didier, 1961.

Aquarone, A. *L'Italia giolittiana (1896–1915). Le premesse politiche ed economiche*. Bologna: Il Mulino, 1981.

Asselain, Jean-Ch. *Histoire économique de la France du XVIIIe siècle à nos jours. De l'Ancien Régime à la première Guerre mondiale*. Paris: Éd. du Seuil, 1984.

Atti del parlamento Italiano, Sessione 1921, Prima della 26 legislatura. Discussioni. Vol. 1. Rome: Tipografia della Camera dei deputati, 1921.

Begnac, Y. de. *Palazzo Venezia. Storia di un regime*. Rome: La Rocca, 1951.

Birnbaum, P. *Un mythe politique: La "République juive."* Paris: Fayard, 1988.

———. *La Sociologie de l'État*. Paris: Fayard, 1982.

Bottomore, T., and P. Goude, eds. *Austro-Marxism*. Texts translated and edited by T. Bottomore and P. Goude. Oxford: Oxford University Press, 1978.

Bracher, K. D. *The Age of Ideologies. A History of Political Thought in the Twentieth Century*. New York: St. Martin's Press, 1984.

Brélaz, M. *Henri De Man. Une autre idée du socialisme*. Geneva: Éd. des Antipodes, 1985.

Capitan Peter, C. *Charles Maurras et l'Idéologie d'Action française.* Paris: Éd. du Seuil, 1972.

Cavallari, G. *Classe dirigente e minoranze rivoluzionarie, Il protomarxismo italiano: Arturo Labriola, Enrico Leone, Ernesto Cesare Longobardi.* N.p.: Jovene Editore, 1983.

Charzat, M. *Georges Sorel et la Révolution au XXe siècle.* Paris: Hachette, 1977.

Cirillo, R. *The Economics of V. Pareto.* London: Frank Cass, 1979.

Curtis, M. *Three against the Third Republic, Sorel, Barrès, and Maurras.* Princeton: Princeton University Press, 1959.

De Felice, R. *Autobiografia del fascismo.* Bergamo: Minerva Italica, 1978.

―――. *La Carta del Carnaro nei testi di Alceste de Ambris e di Gabriele D'Annunzio.* Bologna: Il Mulino, 1973.

―――. *Comprendre le Fascisme.* Paris: Seghers, 1975.

―――. *Intervista sul fascismo,* a cura di M. A. Ledeen. Bari: Laterza, 1975.

―――. *Mussolini il rivoluzionario.* Turin: Einaudi, 1965.

―――. *Sindacalismo rivoluzionario e fiumanesimo nel carteggio De Ambris—D'Annunzio.* Brescia: Morcelliana, 1966.

Degl'Innocenti, M. *Il socialismo italiano e la guerra di Libia.* Rome: Editori Riuniti, 1976.

Dictionnaire biographique du mouvement ouvrier international. Paris: Éditions Ouvrières, 1971.

Dizionario Enciclopedico Italiano. Rome: Instituto della Enciclopedia, 1970.

Dobb, M. H. *Political Economy and Capitalism, Some Essays in Economic Tradition.* London: Routledge, 1940.

Dodge, P. *Beyond Marxism: The Faith and Works of Hendrik De Man.* The Hague: Martinus Nijhoff, 1966.

―――. *A Documentary Study of Hendrik De Man, Socialist Critic of Marxism.* Princeton: Princeton University Press, 1979.

Dubief, H., ed. *Le Syndicalisme Révolutionnaire.* Paris: A. Colin, 1979.

Ekelund, R. B., Jr., and R. F. Hébert. *A History of Economic Theory and Method.* Tokyo: McGraw-Hill, 1983.

Fauci, R. ed. *Gli Italiani e Bentham, Dalla "Felicità" pubblica all'economia del benessere.* Milan: Franco Angeli Editore, 1982.

Furiozzi, G. B. *Il sindacalismo rivoluzionario italiano.* Milan: Mursia, 1977.

―――. *Sorel e l'Italia.* Messina and Florence: D'Anna, 1975.

Gaeta, F. *Il nazionalismo italiano.* Bari: Laterza, 1981.

Gay, P. *The Dilemma of Democratic Socialism: Eduard Bernstein's Challenge to Marx.* New York: Colliers Books, 1962.

Gentile, E. *Il mito dello Stato Nuovo dall'Antigiolittismo al Fascismo.* Bari: Laterza, 1982.

―――. *Le origini dell'ideologia fascista.* Bari: Laterza, 1975.

Gianinazzi, W. "Enrico Leone, socialiste, révisioniste et syndicaliste révolutionnaire italien au tournant du siècle (1894–1907)." Ph.D. diss., University of Paris 5, 1984.

Gregor, A. J. *The Ideology of Fascism: The Rationale of Totalitarianism.* New York: Free Press, 1969.

―――. *Italian Fascism and Developmental Dictatorship.* Princeton: Princeton University Press, 1979.

————. *Roberto Michels e l'ideologia del fascismo*. Rome: Giovanni Volpe, 1979.

————. *Young Mussolini and the Intellectual Origins of Fascism*. Berkeley and Los Angeles: University of California Press, 1979.

Griffin, R. *The Nature of Fascism*. London: Pinter, 1991.

Grifone, P. *Il capitale finanziario in Italia*. Turin: Einaudi, 1971.

Hamilton, A. *L'Illusion fasciste*. Paris: Gallimard, 1973.

Harrison, J. R. *The Reactionaries. Yeats, Lewis, Pound, Eliot, Lawrence: A Study of the Anti-Democratic Intelligentsia*. New York: Shocken Books, 1967.

Horowitz, I. L. *Radicalism and the Revolt against Reason—The Social Theories of Georges Sorel*. London: Routledge and Kegan Paul, 1961.

Humphrey, R. *Georges Sorel, Prophet without Honor. A Study in Anti-Intellectualism*. Cambridge, Mass.: Harvard University Press, 1951.

Isnenghi, M. *Il mito della grande guerra*. Rome and Bari: Laterza, 1973.

Jameson, F. *Fables of Aggression. Wyndham Lewis, the Modernist as a Fascist*. Berkeley and Los Angeles: University of California Press, 1979.

Joll, J. *Intellectuals in Politics, Three Biographical Essays*. London: Weidenfeld and Nicolson, 1960.

Jones, A. R. *The Life and Opinions of T. E. Hulme*. London: Victor Golancz, 1960.

Jones, E. *Sigmund Freud. Life and Works. The Last Phase, 1919–1939*. London: Hogarth Press, 1957.

Julliard, J. *Fernand Pelloutier et les origines du Syndicalisme d'action directe*. Paris: Éd. du Seuil, 1971.

————. ed., *Georges Sorel en son temps*. Paris: Éd. du Seuil, 1985.

Kaplan, A. Y. *Reproductions of Banality, Fascism, Literature and French Intellectual Life*. Minneapolis: University of Minnesota Press, 1986.

Lanaro, S. *L'Italia nuova. Identità e sviluppo 1861–1988*. Turin: Einaudi, 1988.

————. *Nazione e lavoro*. Venice: Marsilio, 1978.

Leeden, M. *The First Duce*. Baltimore and London: Johns Hopkins University Press, 1977.

Levey, J. "The Sorelian Syndicalists: Édouard Berth, Georges Valois and Hubert Lagardelle." Ph.D. diss., Columbia University, 1967.

Lichtheim, G. *Marxism, An Historical and Critical Study*. London: Routledge and Kegan Paul, 1974.

Lista, G. *Marinetti et le futurisme*. Études, documents, iconographie réunis et présentés par Giovanni Lista. Lausanne: L'Âge d'Homme, 1977.

Lyttelton, A. *The Seizure of Power*. London: Weidenfeld and Nicolson, 1973. Rev. ed. 1987.

Marcadé, J.-C., ed. *Présence de F. T. Marinetti. Actes du Colloque International tenu à l'Unesco*. Lausanne: L'Âge d'Homme, 1982.

Marucco, D. *Arturo Labriola e il sindacalismo rivoluzionario italiano*. Turin: Einaudi, 1970.

Mayeur, J. M. *La Vie politique sous la Troisième République, 1870–1940*. Paris: Éd. du Seuil, 1984.

Meinecke, F. *The German Catastrophe, Reflections and Recollections*. Boston: Beacon Press, 1967.

Meisel, J. H. *The Genesis of Georges Sorel*. Ann Arbor: George-Wahn, 1951.

Milza, P. *Fascisme français, Passé et Présent*. Paris: Flammarion, 1987.

Milza, P. *Les Fascismes*. Paris: Imprimerie Nationale, 1985.

Moscovici, S. *L'Âge des Foules*. Paris: Fayard, 1981; Brussels: Ed. Complexe, 1985 (paperback ed.).

Mosse, G. L. *Masses and Man. Nationalist and Fascist Perceptions of Reality*. New York: Howard Fertig, 1980.

———, ed. *International Fascism: New Thoughts and New Approaches*. London: Sage Publications, 1979.

Nettel, P. *La Vie et l'oeuvre de Rosa Luxemburg*. 2 vols. Paris: Maspero, 1972.

Nguyen, V. *Aux origines de l'Action française. Intelligence et politique à l'aube du XXe siècle*. Paris: Fayard, 1991.

Nolte, E. *Le Fascisme dans son époque*. 3 vols. Paris: Julliard, 1970.

Nye R. A. *The Origins of Crowd Psychology. Gustave Le Bon and the Crisis of Mass Democracy in the Third Republic*. London: Sage, 1975.

Payne, S. G. *Fascism: A Comparative Approach toward a Definition*. Madison: University of Wisconsin Press, 1980.

Perfetti, F. *Il nazionalismo italiano dalle origini alla fusione col Fascismo*. Bologna: Capelli, 1977.

Piccone, P. *Italian Marxism*. Berkeley and Los Angeles: University of California Press, 1983.

Procacci, G. *La lotta di classe in Italia agli inizi del secolo XX*. Rome: Editori Riuniti, 1970.

Rebérioux, M. *La République radicale, 1898–1914*. Paris: Éd. du Seuil, 1975.

Rees, Ph. *Fascism and Pre-Fascism in Europe, 1890–1945: A Bibliography of the Extreme Right*. Totowa, N.J.: Barnes and Noble Books, 1984.

Reynolds, S. "La Vie de Jean Allemane (1843–1935)." Ph.D. diss., University of Paris 8, 1981.

Riosa, A. *Il sindacalismo rivoluzionario in Italia e la lotta politica nel partito socialista dell'età giolittiana*. Bari: De Donato, 1976.

Ritter, G. *The German Problem: Basic Questions of German Political Life, Past and Present*. Columbus: Ohio State University Press, 1965.

———. *The Historical Foundations of the Rise of National Socialism in the Third Reich*. London: Weidenfeld and Nicolson, 1955.

Roberts, D. D. *The Syndicalist Tradition and Italian Fascism*. Chapel Hill, N.C.: University of North Carolina Press, 1979.

Roth, Jack J. *The Cult of Violence: Sorel and the Sorelians*. Berkeley and Los Angeles: University of California Press, 1980.

Salvatorelli, L., and G. Mira. *Storia dell'Italia nel periodo fascista*. Vol. 1. Verona: Mondadori, 1972.

Santarelli, E. *La revisione del Marxismo in Italia*. Milan: Feltrinelli, 1977.

———. *Il socialismo anarchico in Italia*. Milan: Feltrinelli, 1959.

Schorske, C. *German Social Democracy 1905–1917. The Development of the Great Schism*. Cambridge, Mass.: Harvard University Press, 1955.

Snowden, F. M. *Violence and Great Estates in the South of Italy, Apulia 1900–1922*. Cambridge: Cambridge University Press, 1986.

Stanley, J. L. *The Sociology of Virtue: The Political and Social Theories of Georges Sorel*. Berkeley and Los Angeles: University of California Press, 1981.

Sternhell, Z. *La Droite révolutionnaire: Les Origines françaises du Fascisme*. Paris: Éd. du Seuil, 1978 (pocket ed. *Points-Histoire*, 1984).

————. *Maurice Barrès et le nationalisme français*. Paris: A. Colin, 1972; Brussels: Ed. Complexe, 1985 (paperback ed.).

————. *Ni droite, Ni gauche. L'idéologie fasciste en France*. Paris: Éd. du Seuil, 1983; Brussels: Éd. Complexe, 1987 (paperback ed.). English trans.: *Neither Right nor Left: Fascist Ideology in France*. Trans. David Maisel. Berkeley and Los Angeles: University of California Press, 1986. Paperback ed., Princeton University Press, 1995.

Talmon, J. L. *The Myth of the Nation and the Vision of Revolution: The Origins of Ideological Polarization in the Twentieth Century*. London: Weidenfeld and Nicolson, 1981.

————. *The Origins of Totalitarian Democracy*. London: Secker and Warburg, 1952.

Tasca, A. *Nascita e avvento del fascismo*. Bari: Laterza, 1974.

————. *I primi dieci anni del PCI*. Bari: Laterza, 1971.

Thayer, J. A. *Italy and the Great War: Politics and Culture, 1870–1915*. Madison: University of Wisconsin Press, 1964.

Totalitarian Democracy and After, International Colloquium in memory of Jacob L. Talmon. Jerusalem: Magnes Press, 1984.

Ungari, P. *Alfredo Rocco e l'ideologia giuridica del fascismo*. Brescia: Morcelliana, 1974.

Vernon, R. *Commitment and Change: Georges Sorel and the Idea of Revolution, Essay and Translation*. Toronto: University of Toronto Press, 1978.

Vivarelli, R. *Il dopoguerra in Italia e l'avvento del fascismo, 1918–1922*. Naples: Istituto Italiano per gli Studi Storici, 1967.

Weber, E. *L'Action française*. Paris: Stock, 1962. Rev. ed. Paris: Fayard, 1985.

————. *The Nationalist Revival in France, 1905–1914*. Berkeley and Los Angeles: University of California Press, 1968.

Webster, R. A. *Industrial Imperialism in Italy 1908–1915*. Berkeley and Los Angeles: University of California Press, 1975.

Willard, C. *Le Mouvement socialiste en France (1893–1905): Les guesdistes*. Paris: Éditions Sociales, 1965.

Wohl, R. *The Generation of 1914*. Cambridge, Mass.: Harvard University Press, 1979.

Zunino, P. G. *L'ideologia del fascismo. Miti, credenze e valori nella stabilizzazione del regime*. Bologna: Il Mulino, 1985.

Articles

Andreu, P. "Bibliographie d'Édouard Berth." *Bulletin of the International Institute for Social History* (1953).

————. "Lettres de G. Sorel à Édouard Berth—Première partie: 1904–1908." *Cahiers Georges Sorel* 3 (1985).

————. "La préparation morale à l'absolu marxiste." In *Georges Sorel en son Temps*. Paris: Éd. du Seuil, 1985.

————. "Le socialisme de Sorel." *L'Homme nouveau*, no. 17 (June 1935).

Bracher, K. D. "The Role of Hitler: Perspectives of Interpretation." In W. Laqueur, ed. *Fascism: A Reader's Guide. Analyses, Interpretations, Bibliography*. Berkeley and Los Angeles: University of California Press, 1976.

Bergman, P. "L'Esthétique de la vitesse. Origines et premières manifestations." In *Présence de F. T. Marinetti*. Lausanne: L'Âge d'Homme, 1982.

Bourdet, Y. "Introduction à R. Hilferding." *Le Capital financier—Étude sur le développement récent du capitalisme*. Paris: Éditions de Minuit, 1970.

Cafagna, L. "The Industrial Revolution in Italy 1830–1914." In C. M. Cipolla, ed. *The Fontana Economic History of Europe*. Vol. 4. Glasgow: Fontana, Collins, 1975.

Cammet, J. M. "Communist Theories of Fascism (1920–1935)." In *Science and Society* 31 (Winter 1967).

Carpenter, J. "This Is Ole Ezra Speaking. Ezra Pound's Wartime Broadcast from Rome." *Encounter* (June 1988).

Charzat, M. "Georges Sorel et le fascisme. Éléments d'explication d'un légende tenace." *Cahiers Georges Sorel* 1 (1988).

Costa-Pinto, A. "Fascist Ideology Revisited: Zeev Sternhell and His Critics." *European History Quarterly* 16 (1986).

Favilli, P. "Economia e politica del sindacalismo rivoluzionario. Due riviste di teoria e socialismo: 'Pagine Libere' e 'Divenire sociale.'" *Studi Storici* 1, no. 1 (1975).

Finer, S. F. "Pareto and Pluto-Democracy: The Retreat to Galapagos." *American Political Science Review* 62, no. 2 (June 1968).

Gozzini, G. "La Federazione Giovanile Socialista tra Bordiga e Mussolini (1912–1914)." *Storia Contemporanea* (February 1980).

Julliard, J. "Sorel, Rousseau et la Révolution Française." *Cahiers Georges Sorel* 3 (1988).

Kahn, P. "Mythe et réalité sociale chez Sorel." *Cahiers internationaux de Sociologie* 11 (1951).

Kolakowski, L. "Georges Sorel: Jansenist Marxist." *Dissent* 22 (1975).

Lemaire, G.-G. "Prolégomènes au vorticisme: Flux et reflux du futurisme en Angleterre." In *Wyndham Lewis et le vorticisme, Cahiers pour un temps*. Paris: Centre Georges Pompidou—Pandora Éditions, 1982.

Lindenberg, D. "Le débat marxiste au tournant du siècle." In P. Ory, ed. *Nouvelle Histoire des idées politiques*. Paris: Hachette, 1987.

Linz, J. J. "Some Notes toward a Comparative Study of Fascism in Sociological Historical Perspective." In W. Laqueur, ed. *Fascism: A Reader's Guide. Analyses, Interpretations, Bibliography*. Berkeley and Los Angeles: University of California Press, 1976.

Lista, G. "Marinetti et les anarcho-syndicalistes." *Présence de Marinetti*. Lausanne: L'Âge d'Homme, 1982.

McInnes, N. "Georges Sorel on the Trial of Socrates." *Politics* 10 (1975).

Melograni, P. "The Cult of the Duce in Mussolini's Italy." *Journal of Contemporary History* 11 (1976).

Mosse, G. L. "Fascism and the Intellectuals." In S. J. Wolf, ed. *The Nature of Fascism*. London: Weidenfeld and Nicolson, 1968.

Nacci, M. "Intellettuali francesi e corporativismo fascista." *Dimensioni*, nos. 40–41 (September 1986).

Nijhof, P. "Entre violence et vertu: La reconstruction de G. Sorel." *Cahiers Georges Sorel* 1 (1983).

Nolte, E. "La réalité à l'envers." In *Devant l'Histoire. Les documents de la controverse sur la singularité de l'extermination des Juifs par le régime nazi*. Paris: Éd. du Cerf, 1988.

Romano, S. "Georges Sorel et Benedetto Croce." In *Georges Sorel en son temps*. Paris: Éd. du Seuil, 1985.

――――. "Sorel et le système des relations internationales à la fin de la Première Guerre mondiale." *Cahiers Georges Sorel* 3 (1988).

――――. "Sorel e Mussolini." *Storia Contemporanea* 15, no. 1 (1984).

Rouanet, S. P. "Irrationalism and Myth in G. Sorel." *Review of Politics* 26 (1964).

Roveri, A. "Il sindacalismo rivoluzionario in Italia." *Richerche Storiche*, 1 June 1975.

Rubel, M. "Georges Sorel et l'achèvement de l'œuvre de Karl Marx." *Cahiers Georges Sorel* 1 (1983).

Sand, Sh. "Sorel, les Juifs et l'antisémitisme." *Cahiers Georges Sorel* 2 (1984).

Santarelli, E. "Socialismo rivoluzionario e 'Mussolinismo' alla vigila del primo conflitto europeo." *Rivista Storica del Socialismo*, nos. 13–14 (May–December 1961).

Settembrini, D. "Mussolini and the Legacy of Revolutionary Socialism." *Journal of Contemporary History* 11 (1976).

Sternhell, Z. "Emmanuel Mounier et la contestation de la démocratie libérale dans la France des années trente." *Revue française de Science politique* 34, no. 6 (1984).

――――. "Fascist Ideology." In W. Laqueur, ed., *Fascism: A Reader's Guide. Analyses, Interpretations, Bibliography*. Berkeley and Los Angeles: University of California Press, 1976.

Sykes, T. R. "Revolutionary Syndicalism in the Italian Labor Movement. The Agrarian Strikes of 1907–1908 in the Province of Parma." *International Review of Social History* 21 (1976).

Sznajder, M. "The 'Carta del Carnaro' and Modernization." *Tel Aviver Jahrbuch für deutsche Geschichte* 18 (1989).

――――. "Economic Marginalism and Socialism. Italian Revolutionary Syndicalism and the Revision of Marx." *Praxis International* 11, no. 1 (April 1991).

Tager, M. "Myth and Politics in the Works of Sorel and Barthes." *Journal of the History of Ideas*, October–December 1986.

Tranfaglia, N. "Dalla neutralità italiana alle origini del fascismo: tendenze attuali della storiografia." In *Dallo stato liberale al regime fascista. Problemi e richerche*. Milan: Feltrinelli, 1981.

Valiani, L. "Il Partito Socialista Italiano dal 1900 al 1918." *Rivista Storica Italiana* 80 (1963).

Veza, L. "Marinetti et le vorticisme." In *Présence de F. T. Marinetti*. Lausanne: L'Âge d'Homme, 1982.

Vivarelli, R. "Benito Mussolini dal socialismo al fascismo." In *Il fallimento del liberalismo. Studi sulle origini del fascismo*. Bologna: Il Mulino, 1981.

Wohl, R. "French Fascism. Both Right and Left: Reflections on the Sternhell Controversy." *Journal of Modern History* 63 (March 1991).

Woolf, J. S. "Mussolini as Revolutionary." *Journal of Contemporary History* 1, no. 2 (1966).

Index

Académie française, 255

Action française, 9, 37, 38, 78–86, 89, 92, 109, 123–125, 128, 163, 201, 241, 242, 253; on affinities with revolutionary syndicalism, 109; and corporatism, 253; and Sorel, 78–81; and the synthesis of Nationalism and Socialism, 82–86, 89, 92, 123–125

Action républicaine socialiste, 244

Adler, Friedrich, 17

Adler, Max, 17, 18, 19, 22, 37, 49, 249

Adler, Victor, 17

Agathon (pseudonym of Massis, Henri and de Tarde Alfred), 121

Allemane, Jean, 41, 245

Amiens, congress of, 95, 96

Ammon, Otto, 9

Andreu, Pierre, 81, 87, 92

Anti-Fascist and Vigilance Committee. *See* Comité antifasciste et de Vigilance

Antijuif L', 85

Anti-Semitism, 4, 5, 37, 84–86, 124, 127

Anti-Socialist laws (Germany), 14, 26

Anytus, 37, 71

Aristotle, 93

Associazione nazionale d'avanguardia, 236

Associazione Nazionalista Italiana, 11, 32, 197, 230, 236. *See also* Corradini

Austria-Hungary, 16, 139, 161, 165, 169, 207, 218

Avanguardia socialista, 32, 33, 131–134, 141, 173, 174, 192, 196, 209, 234

Avanti!, 132, 134, 195, 198, 205–208, 214, 222

Avvenire del lavoratore, L', 196

Axelrod, Pavel Borissovith, 17

Bainville, Jacques, 82

Bakounine, Mikhail Alexandrovitch, 97, 154, 179

Barbé, Henri, 94

Barni, Giulio, 169

Barrès, Maurice, 37, 79, 80, 90, 243, 257; member of the editorial staff of *L'Indépendance*, 84; and Nationalism of *La Terre et les Morts* (The Land and the Dead), 9–11; and "natural socialism," 11

Bauer, Otto, 17–19, 21

Bebel, August, 15, 113

Belgian Workers' Party. *See* Parti Ouvrier Belge (POB)

Benjamin, Walter, 235

Bergery, Gaston, 94

Bergson, Henri, 24, 37, 38, 48, 56, 61–63, 73, 75, 86, 104, 110, 125, 179, 199, 200, 233, 239, 240, 241; and anti-Cartesianism, 24, 63; and "élan vital," 233; influence on Berth, 110; influence on futurism, 233, 239; influence on revolutionary syndicalism, 179; influence on Sorel, 48, 56, 61–63, 125; and Mussolini, 199, 200; translated by Hulme, 240

Bernstein, Eduard, 14, 16, 17, 22, 33, 40, 42, 43, 47, 48, 50, 57, 58, 68, 80, 92, 94, 99, 110, 113, 131, 145, 146, 151; and the "crisis" of socialism, 146; influence on Italian socialism, 131; and *Le Mouvement Socialiste*, 92; and revision of Marxism, 14, 16, 17, 50, 99, 151; and Sorel, 40, 43, 47, 48, 58, 68, 80

Berth, Édouard, 39, 70, 77, 83, 84, 86–90, 92–97, 99–101, 103–107, 109–111, 115–122, 124–129, 134, 151, 152, 154; and anarchism, 103–104; on the Catholic revival, 121–122; and the Cercle Proudhon, 86–88, 122–127; on democracy, 110; *Dialogues socialistes*, 93; in favor of liberal economics, 105; and heroic values, 117–118; influence by Nietzsche, 126; *Mefaits des intellectuels, Les*, 89, 106, 129; and revision of Marxism, 99–101; on Sorel, 70, 77, 93; on State, 105–106, 128–129; and Valois, 83, 94

Bianchi, Michele, 89, 109, 112, 135, 142, 143, 153, 191, 200, 202, 205, 222, 245; conception of syndicalism, 135; dismissed from *Avanti!*, 112; Fascist leader, 191; founder of the Fascist movement, 142, 143; founder of the Revolutionary Fascio for Internationalist Action, 205; syndicalist leader, 109, 153, 200

Bismarck, Otto Eduard Leopold, 14, 84, 216; and anti-social laws, 26

Blanqui, Louis-Auguste, 216; Blanquism, 48

Blast, 237

Blum, Léon, 33, 229, 249

Blumenkranz, Noémi, 233

UNIVERSITY OF WOLVERHAMPTON
LEARNING RESOURCES